£30 ebay

M

Coaching

Other books published by Kogan Page with the Association for Coaching

Diversity in Coaching: Working with gender, culture, race and age, Second edition, edited by Jonathan Passmore (ISBN 978 0 7494 6662 6)

Excellence in Coaching: The industry guide, Second edition, edited by Jonathan Passmore (ISBN 978 0 7494 5667 2)

Leadership Coaching: Working with leaders to develop elite performance, edited by Jonathan Passmore (ISBN 978 0 7494 5532 3)

Psychometrics in Coaching: Using psychological and psychometric tools for development, Second edition, edited by Jonathan Passmore (ISBN 978 0 7494 6664 0)

Supervision in Coaching: Supervision, ethics and continuous professional development, edited by Jonathan Passmore (ISBN 978 0 7494 5533 0)

Mastery in Coaching

A complete psychological toolkit for advanced coaching

Edited by
Jonathan Passmore

ASSOCIATION FOR COACHING

KoganPage

LONDON PHILADELPHIA NEW DELHI

First published in Great Britain and the United States in 2014 by Kogan Page Limited

2nd Floor, 45 Gee Street	1518 Walnut Street, Suite 1100	4737/23 Ansari Road
London EC1V 3RS	Philadelphia PA 19102	Daryaganj
United Kingdom	USA	New Delhi 110002
www.koganpage.com		India

© Association for Coaching, 2014

The right of the Association for Coaching to be identified as the author of this work has been asserted by them in accordance with the Copyright, Designs and Patents Act 1988.

ISBN   978 0 7494 7179 8
E-ISBN 978 0 7494 7180 4

British Library Cataloguing-in-Publication Data

A CIP record for this book is available from the British Library.

Library of Congress Cataloging-in-Publication Data

CIP data is available.

Library of Congress Control Number: 2014025418

Typeset by Graphicraft Limited, Hong Kong
Print production managed by Jellyfish
Printed and bound by CPI Group (UK) Ltd, Croydon, CR0 4YY

This book is dedicated to Florence Passmore.

CONTENTS

08   Mindful coaching   191

Liz Hall

09   Compassionate mind coaching   225

Tim Anstiss and Paul Gilbert

ABOUT THE CONTRIBUTORS

The editor

Professor Jonathan Passmore is a full professor at the University of Evora, Portugal and the MD for a psychology consulting company. He is a chartered and registered psychologist and holds five degrees and three professional qualifications. Jonathan is the author and editor of over 50 academic papers and 20 books including the popular Association for Coaching series *In Coaching* and *Top Business Psychology Models*, which have been translated into a number of languages. He has presented at conferences all over the world and his company's clients include IKEA, HSBC, BP and Burberry. He was awarded the Association of Coaching Global Impact Award in 2010 and the British Psychological Society SGCP Research Award in 2012. He can be contacted at **jonathancpassmore@yahoo.co.uk**.

The contributors

Julie Allan is a chartered and registered psychologist, a Fellow of the Royal Society for Arts and Manufacture and an experienced coach and praxis supervisor. She has written widely on topics including narratives, gestalt coaching, ethics, supervision and wisdom. She is undertaking a doctorate into metacognition in adult learning.

Dr Tim Anstiss is a medical doctor and part-time academic helping clinicians and teams get better at health coaching in long-term conditions. He runs wellbeing, confidence and resilience workshops for staff, and is currently developing some e-health solutions. He has published a number of articles and book chapters on behaviour change and coaching and is a popular speaker and trainer. Tim is a former international athlete and contender on ITV's Gladiators.

Ulla Charlotte Beck holds an MA in political science and psychology. She has been training himself in organizational psychology, psychoanalytic group therapy, education, and administration and management over the past decade and is the author of *Psychodynamic Coaching: Focus and depth* and has contributed to *Psychodynamic Organizational Psychology – the more work below the surface – Volume II*. She is a member of the following professional societies: GAS, OPUS, ISPSO and NAPSO.

Professor Richard Blonna is a Professor of Public Health at William Paterson University (NJ, US) and an AC Coach in Private Practice. He is the Co-Chair of the Act-Based Coaching SIG of the ACBS and the author of *Maximize Your Coaching Effectiveness with Acceptance and Commitment Therapy*. He is a Board-Certified Coach (BCC), Counsellor (NCC) and Health Education Specialist (CHES) and has over 30 years' experience as an educator, coach, trainer, author and consultant.

Professor Paul Brown is a specialist in applied neuroscience in organizations and in the development of individual executive and leadership talent. He has co-authored three professional books, including *Neuropsychology for Coaches: Understanding the basics* (2012), as well as many academic and management papers and articles, and teaches at a number of universities.

Denyse Busby-Earle is an accredited NLP practitioner, she holds an MBA and is an Imperial College Biochemistry graduate. She has 25 years' director level experience having worked in the private, public and charitable sector and is a licensed practitioner of a range of psychometric and motivation tools.

Dr David Drake is Executive Director of the Center for Narrative Coaching & Leadership in San Francisco and the founder of Narrative Design Labs. He is Associate Editor for *Coaching: An international journal of theory, research and practice*, author of 40 publications, editor of *The Philosophy and Practice of Coaching* (2008, Jossey-Bass), and author of *A Narrative Perspective* on *Organizational Culture and Coaching* (forthcoming, Routledge).

Professor Paul Gilbert OBE is Professor of Clinical Psychology at the University of Derby and Consultant Clinical Psychologist at the Derbyshire Health Care Foundation Trust. He has researched evolutionary approaches to psychopathology for over 35 years with a special focus on shame and the treatment of shame-based difficulties – for which compassion focused therapy was developed. In 2003 he was president of the BABCP and a member of the first NICE depression guidelines for depression. He has written/edited 20 books and over 150 papers. In 2006 he established the Compassionate Mind Foundation charity with the mission statement: *To promote wellbeing through the scientific understanding and application of compassion* (**www. compassionatemind.co.uk**). He was awarded an OBE in March 2011.

Liz Hall is an award-winning journalist and the editor of *Coaching at Work*, a Senior Practitioner coach and the author of *Mindful Coaching*. Liz has been meditating on and off for 30 years and has studied with mindfulness teachers including Thich Nhat Hanh. Liz won the Association for Coaching's Award for Impacting (Leadership/External Focus) in 2011.

Dr Lindsay G Oades is Director of the Australian Institute of Business Wellbeing and is internally recognized for his work in mental health recovery, measurement of psychological recovery and the development of the Collaborative Recovery Model. He has formal training and experience across Clinical, Health, Coaching and Positive Psychology. He has published over 60 refereed journal publications and book chapters.

Professor Reinhard Stelter is Full Professor of Sport and Coaching Psychology at the University of Copenhagen and visiting professor at the Copenhagen Business School (Master of Public Governance). He holds a PhD in psychology and is an accredited coaching psychologist (ISCP). He is an Honorary Vice-President of ISCP and member of the Scientific Advisory Board of the Institute of Coaching at Harvard. He has also published widely in journal articles, book chapters and books.

Helen Whitten is an Accredited Coach with the Association for Coaching and a Fellow of the International Stress Management Association. She founded *Positiveworks* in 1993 and is a specialist in personal and professional effectiveness applying cognitive behavioural approaches to coach individuals and teams. She has written five books.

Dr Alison Whybrow is a Chartered and Registered Psychologist whose practice encompasses working with individual leaders, teams and organizational systems. Alison sits on the editorial board of three peer reviewed coaching publications, and has written previously on gestalt coaching and values in action. She is described by colleagues as 'insatiably curious'.

FOREWORD

Masterful coaching is a thing of beauty, a rich tapestry of art, experience and deep knowledge. But what makes for a masterful coach? What separates the very good from the great coach who can walk clients through transformative odysseys?

At Harvard Business School, leadership is taught from the 'know – do – be' model. As you'll see here, masterful leadership tracks perfectly to masterful coaching. While this book is entitled *Mastery in Coaching: A complete psychological toolkit for advanced coaching*, in fact, it offers far more than a toolkit. It will help you along your coaching journey by offering a wide array of research and perspectives. At the Institute of Coaching at Harvard Medical School we see that the greatest challenge facing coaches today is to bridge good theory and research to best practices.

The Association for Coaching and Jonathan Passmore achieve this difficult challenge with ease and grace. This work will walk you across that bridge. Along the way you will find more than a pathway from knowing to doing. As you absorb the information presented here, the theory, its application and case examples will help you pull knowledge and wisdom from your mind to your heart and gut. It can also shift you further. My hope is that you take what is offered here even deeper. Like coaching, it can shift your mindset and change who you are as a coach – that is, your coaching identity and way of being. In turn, this creates a positive spiral: the more you know, and expand your repertoire of doing and 'being' skills, the more you can serve your clients. The more you serve the clients, the more you learn and grow yourself.

Carol Kauffman PhD ABPP
Assistant Professor, Harvard Medical School
Founder & Executive Director, Institute of Coaching

Mastery in coaching

JONATHAN PASSMORE

Introduction

The rise of coaching seems unstoppable. Over the past two decades coaching has continued to grow in popularity, application and understanding. There now may be as many as 100,000 coaches practising globally, with a growing number of this group having received some formal training. The application of coaching has spread from sports and business to health, wellbeing, driving, education and beyond, as managers, policy makers and educators recognize the contribution coaching can make to learning, personal development and performance. Further, coaching research since 2000 has exploded. While it was difficult in 2001 to support the assertion that 'coaching works', the evidence from a substantial and growing number of randomized control trials and, more recently, meta analysis papers is providing the scientific evidence to demonstrate coaching's contribution in these areas. It is now possible to say that coaching is a positive tool in personal change and development.

The Association for Coaching (AC), along with other professional bodies such as the International Coaching Federation (ICF) and European Mentoring and Coaching Council (EMCC), have played a significant role in the development and professionalization of coaching. In this sense coaching over the past decade has moved from a search for excellence to an understanding of what mastery looks like.

Mastery in Coaching (the Association for Coaching's sixth book) is aimed at the advanced practitioner, meaning coaches who have hundreds of hours of experience. They are likely to have also completed post-graduate coach training and are now looking for their next step in their continued professional development (CPD).

This book offers advanced practitioners chapters by leading names in selected areas of practice. Each chapter provides an evidence-based platform, before offering insights into tools and techniques of practice, combined with a short case study to explore how experienced coaches apply their ideas.

Most advanced practitioners are familiar with more than one coaching model. Most will integrate two or three models into their practice. They often select the model to apply based on the client, the issue and their judgement of what will best help their client to move forward. They have read the key books relevant to the models they use, they are likely to have reviewed the research about their model and are skilled in the application of the tools and techniques of the approach.

However, we hope that even the most experienced practitioner will find new and useful insights from the wide range of chapters on offer in *Mastery in Coaching*. By offering an in-depth review of the model, supported by research and how such approaches can be applied, we hope advanced practitioners will be able to add to their knowledge. Further we are confident that almost all practitioners will find one or more models that they are less familiar with and thus can add to their knowledge, and repertoire of skills. In short we hope this title is CPD for advanced coaching practitioners on their journey of continual pursuit of coaching mastery.

What is mastery in coaching?

The selection of the term 'mastery' reflects the view that coaching is a skill. While scientific knowledge underpins the skill, coaching is foremost about the application of the skill, in the same way that a chef or surgeon needs to understand the science of food or the science of the human body, as well as being able to master the use of their tools. However, what makes a master chef or consultant surgeon is the application of their knowledge to a specific plate of food or specific patient undergoing a specific procedure.

Coaching's leading professional bodies have helped in this process through their development of competency frameworks to define and clarify what competence in coaching should look like. The reason why input measures remain the focus for accreditation is because they are easier to collect and assess than seeking to differentiate between levels of competence in coaches through assessing output measures. However, in my view output measures of performance must be the direction we continue to travel in, as assessed through peer review, in the same way consultant surgeons and master chefs are assessed by their peers. The use of diaries, transcripts and examinations are the way forward, along with more high quality research. To achieve this we need to work harder at understanding the key ingredients of coaching, and what makes the difference between good outcomes and outstanding outcomes.

A number of models of competence have been offered by various writers, as well as by professional bodies such as the Association for Coaching. The AC's Executive Coaching Framework is summarized in Table 1.1, with a full copy of the competencies contained in Table 1.2. This is a scheme that was updated in 2012, to align more with the ways organizations select coaches.

Since 2005 a number of organizations have considered and developed competency frameworks for coaches. David Lane's work for the British

FIGURE 1.1   Being, doing and relating

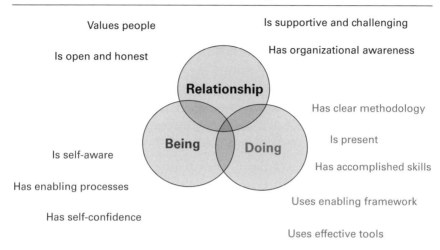

Psychological Society Special Interest Group in Coaching led to the development of a comprehensive model for coaching psychologists.

Other professional bodies, such as the International Coaching Federation, have also produced frameworks for practitioners. These have subsequently been incorporated into the assessment frameworks for membership grades, along with a requirement to complete a specified number of hours.

One of the simplest is Ben Renshaw and Graham Alexander's 'Being, doing and knowing' model described in *Supercoaching* (Renshaw and Alexander, 2005). The model sets out the modes which the coach must master and while based on experience rather than primary research, the model combines both insight and simplicity.

While competencies have emerged over the past five years we need to do more work to refine these, making them more behaviourally based, so it's possible to observe the behaviour during an assessed coaching session, as well as to underpin each aspect with evidence. This is difficult and the field of counselling is still struggling to fully achieve this after 50 years of attempts of codifying intervention methods.

Despite some challenges we now have methods for assessing levels of competence and thus mastery and an evidence base which supports our knowledge of whether coaching works, what coaching can positive impact upon and how it works.

As increasing numbers of coaches qualify through various commercial and academic institutions the new challenge is supporting these individuals to continue their personal development journey on to mastery.

TABLE 1.1   Association for Coaching Framework

Coach competencies for general coaches	1. Meeting ethical, legal and professional guidelines
	2. Establishing the coaching agreement and outcomes
	3. Establishing a trust-based relationship with the client
	4. Managing self and maintaining coaching presence
	5. Communicating effectively
	6. Raising awareness and insight
	7. Designing strategies and actions
	8. Maintaining forward momentum and evaluation
	9. Undertaking continuous coach development
Additional competencies for executive coaches	10. Working within the organizational context
	11. Understanding leadership issues
	12. Working in partnership with the organization

TABLE 1.2   Association for Coaching Competencies

AC COMPETENCY FRAMEWORK
Revised June 2012

Coaching competencies for all coaches

1. Meeting ethical, legal and professional guidelines
2. Establishing the coaching agreement and outcomes
3. Establishing a trust-based relationship with the client
4. Managing self and maintaining coaching presence
5. Communicating effectively
6. Raising awareness and insight
7. Designing strategies and actions
8. Maintaining forward momentum and evaluation
9. Undertaking continuous coach development

Additional competencies for executive coaches

10. Working within the organizational context
11. Understanding leadership issues
12. Working in partnership with the organization

TABLE 1.2   *continued*

COACH COMPETENCIES AND INDICATORS – ALL COACHES

1. Meeting ethical, legal and professional guidelines

Indicators of competence:

- Follows the AC's professional standards and codes of conduct, including the AC's Code of Ethics and Good Practice and Statement of Shared Professional Values
- Acts ethically and with the highest integrity
- Promotes the coaching profession in a positive light to all stakeholders
- Complies with the prevailing laws of the country in which the coaching takes place and/or client organization is operating, whichever is the most applicable and stringent
- Clearly communicates how coaching is different from other helping professions
- Is aware of professional boundaries and refers on to another professional as appropriate

2. Establishing the coaching agreement and outcomes

Indicators of competence:

- Clearly explains the coaching process and own coaching approach, models and techniques
- Helps the client establish coaching goals and outcomes and agrees an approach to working with the client that will achieve them
- Agrees a formal coaching agreement with client and all stakeholders, including clear and measurable outcomes, plus confidentiality, logistics of coaching sessions (duration, frequency, location), purpose, contingencies, monitoring and reporting on progress, and commercial arrangements
- Establishes clear roles, responsibilities and boundaries between the different stakeholders, including coach and client

3. Establishing a trust-based relationship with the client

Indicators of competence:

- Treats people equally and fairly, with respect and dignity
- Is optimistic for and encourages self-belief in the client
- Establishes a high level of rapport to build an open dialogue with the client
- Accepts the client 'as is' and believes in the client's potential and capability
- Acts openly and honestly, including tackling difficult conversations with the client, using self and personal reactions to offer client feedback, avoiding colluding with the client on issues that block progress
- Maintains agreed levels of confidentiality

TABLE 1.2 *continued*

4. Managing self and maintaining coaching presence
Indicators of competence:
- Pays close attention to the client, staying fully present and engaged
- Remains focused on the agreed client agenda and outcomes
- Acts flexibly whilst staying aligned to own coaching approach
- Stays aligned to personal values whilst respecting the values of the client
- Works to ensure interventions get the best outcome for the client

5. Communicating effectively
Indicators of competence:
- Demonstrates effective listening and clarifying skills and differentiates between what is said and what's left unsaid
- Uses straightforward, easy-to-understand language that moves the client towards the agreed outcomes
- Adapts communication style to reflect the client's needs and outcomes
- Provides relevant information and feedback to serve the client's learning and goals
- Communicates clearly, confidently and credibly with the client

6. Raising awareness and insight
Indicators of competence:
- Asks questions to challenge client's assumptions, elicit new insights, raise self-awareness and gain learning
- Helps broaden a client's perception of an issue and challenges to stimulate new possibilities
- Supports the client to generate options to achieve agreed outcomes
- Provides observational feedback where relevant, leaving client free to choose to act upon it or not
- Uses 'self' as a resource for the development of the client's self-awareness and learning by offering 'here and now' feedback

7. Designing strategies and actions
Indicators of competence:
- Supports the client to build strategies to meet their outcomes
- Inspires the client to identify and implement self-directed learning opportunities
- Leaves accountability with the client while following through on own actions and commitments
- Encourages the client to seek support from others to help achieve the client outcomes
- Provides support while the client tries out new ways of working/behaviours

TABLE 1.2 *continued*

8. Maintaining forward momentum and evaluation

Indicators of competence:

- Maintains an outcome-focused approach
- Asks powerful questions that move the client forwards towards the agreed outcome
- Checks and acknowledges client progress and achievements
- Explores what is working, what is getting in the way and challenges lack of progress
- Discourages dependency on the coach and develops the client's ability to self-coach
- Checks the client's motivation to apply learning from the coaching
- Measures effectiveness of coaching

9. Undertaking continuous coach development

Indicators of competence:

- Regularly requests client feedback
- Actively reflects on coaching practice and outcomes
- Acts on own critical reflections and client feedback to improve coaching practice
- Participates in regular coaching supervision to reflect on, and improve, practice
- Participates in continuous professional development (CPD) activities

ADDITIONAL COMPETENCIES AND INDICATORS – EXECUTIVE COACHES

10. Working within the organizational context

Indicators of competence:

- Understands the organizational context in which the client operates (eg is aware of the long term vision, mission, values, strategic objectives, market/competitive pressures, etc)
- Understands the client's role, position and authority within the organizational system
- Is aware of key stakeholders (internal and external) within the organizational system
- Aligns coaching goals to support organizational aims and objectives
- Understands the relationship between the coach, client and internal sponsor(s) of coaching
- Is aware of, and works with the organization's values, policies and practices, including human resource and people policies and practices
- Takes a systemic approach to coaching the client, encompassing the complexities of multiple stakeholders, different perspectives and conflicting priorities

TABLE 1.2 *continued*

11. Understanding leadership issues

Indicators of competence:

- Recognizes the challenges faced by leaders working in organizations
- Identifies ways of, and opportunities for, developing leadership behaviours and attributes through coaching
- Demonstrates knowledge and experience of working with organizational leaders
- Uses language appropriate for, and recognized by, the client and organization
- Constructively challenges the leader to raise his/her standards in areas key to the organization
- Understands the leader's sphere of influence

12. Working in partnership with the organization

Indicators of competence:

- Develops relevant networks and strategic partnerships in the organization
- Designs an effective coaching contract, commercial agreement and working alliance with the client, line manager and coaching sponsor(s) within organizational parameters and policies for coaching
- Actively involves key stakeholders in the set-up, monitoring and evaluation of the coaching, whilst maintaining agreed levels of confidentiality
- Communicates the progress of the coaching with key stakeholders openly and honestly, whilst maintaining agreed levels of confidentiality
- Identifies ways of adding value to the client at the individual, team and organizational level

SOURCE: www.associationforcoaching.com

Evidence-based practice

In 2001, as the coaching revolution got fully underway, the rush to coaching led to what I considered to be inflated claims. These claims were often based on personal experience and ad hoc case studies. Some claimed coaching would enable personal transformation, almost like a light switch. Just ask a question and their client saw the light and was transformed. Too often I hear practitioners lay claim to the 'magic of coaching'. Others suggested that coaching is the solution to all organizational and personal problems: a 'silver bullet'.

While at the time I shared the sense that clients have both enjoyed and benefited from the time we had together in coaching conversations, I felt, as a psychologist, that I lacked the evidence to respond to the question, 'so does it work?' with an answer that would satisfy a critical mind with compelling research evidence. However, I was certain that coaching was no magic – and I was no magician.

Partly in trying to respond to this challenge, I undertook doctoral research into coaching in an attempt to better understand the behaviours that contributed to positive outcomes. Like studies before and since, the general conclusion was that outcomes were influenced by the ability of the coach to build and maintain a relationship with their client, along with wider competence in adapting to and working with a wide range of individuals, issues and frameworks responding in the moment flexibly and empathically towards their client.

Not surprisingly these finding echoed earlier work in counselling that has shown the centrality of the client–therapist relationship and specifically the contribution of empathy as the single biggest factor in building and maintaining the relationship (see Table 1.3).

Since 2000 the number of randomized controlled trial (RCT) studies has increased. Between 2001 and 2010 we saw a growing number of RCT studies

TABLE 1.3　Sample of early Between-Subject Design studies

Study	Intervention overview	Type of study	Findings
Miller (1990)	33 employees. Some received coaching by their managers over four weeks.	Quasi-experimental field study: (a) coaching group; (b) control group.	No sig. differences pre-post for interpersonal communication skill.
Grant (2002)	62 trainee accountants received group coaching over one semester.	Randomized controlled study: (a) cognitive coaching only; (b) behavioural coaching only; (c) combined – Cognitive and behavioural coaching; (d) control groups for each condition.	Combined cognitive and behavioural coaching most effective in increasing grade point average, study skills, self-regulation, and mental health. GPA gains maintained in 12 month follow-up.

TABLE 1.4   Sample of RCT studies 2001–2014

Study	Intervention overview	Type of study	Findings
Evers, Brouwers & Tomic (2006)	60 managers of the federal government.	Quasi-experimental field study: (a) coaching group; (b) control group.	Coaching increased outcome expectancies and self-efficacy.
Green, Grant & Rynsaardt (2007)	56 female high school students took part in SF-CB life coaching program for 10 individual coaching sessions over two school terms.	Randomized controlled study: (a) coaching group; (b) waitlist control group.	Coaching increased cognitive hardiness, mental health and hope.

that have demonstrated the positive effects of coaching on clients' wellbeing, learning and skills development.

The research has also shown, as did previous work on behavioural change, that change is hard work and occurs slowly over time. The work achieved by clients, supported and facilitated by their coaches, is not magic, but human. It reveals the power of humans to learn, adapt and change when encouraged, supported and challenged to do so (see Table 1.4).

In addition to the 40-plus RCT papers published to date, there is the emergence of a number of meta-analysis published studies. It has been argued that RCT is the gold standard in evidence-based practice. This is because, unlike a case study, qualitative research that is open to personal bias and contamination factors, a well conducted RCT enables a true comparison between one intervention and another (or a control group). It is for this reason that RCTs are the standard method for assessing drugs prior to licensing.

More recently, however, statistical techniques have allowed meta-studies to supersede the RCT as the ultimate research methodology for demonstrating impact (measured by effect size). The meta-analysis involves combining results from different RCT studies, with the aim of identifying patterns among study results. In its simplest form, the meta-analysis is done to identify the average effect size from these previous studies, such as those listed in Table 1.3. This average is then weighted relative to the sample sizes within the individual studies, to reduce the impact of small-scale studies on the overall results. By combining results, the method removes variables such as differences in individual population groups, researchers or individual coaches. In this sense the meta-analysis results provide a more accurate view as to the effect or impact of a particular method.

TABLE 1.5   Effect size explained

Effect size (often described as g)	Effect
0.3	Small
0.31–0.5	Moderate
Over 0.5	Large

(based on Cohen, 1988)

The first published meta-analysis identified 12 papers that it reduced to four studies for inclusion in the analysis (De Meuse *et al*, 2009). The four studies included contained wide variations, but the authors noted that 'executive coaching generally leads to a moderate to large amount of improvement in the coachee's skills and/or performance rating' (de Meuse *et al*, 2009, p 120). The coachees estimated the effect size on their skill/performance to be 1.27, while managers were considerably more cautious with an effect size estimated at 0.5. To put this in perspective, an effect size of 0.3 would be considered small, while 0.31–0.5 is considered moderate and over 0.5 is considered a strong effect (see Table 1.5). The authors, however, rightly noted that extreme caution should be used in generalizing their results, given the small number of studies.

The second published study (Theeboom *et al*, 2013) included 107 studies. These were ultimately reduced to 18 studies used in the actual analysis. The study focused on the effect of coaching in five categories: performance/skills, wellbeing, coping, work attitudes and goal-directed self-regulation (see Table 1.6). The results indicate that coaching interventions had a significant positive effects on all outcome categories: performance and skills ($g = 0.60$, 95% CI, 0.04–0.60, $p = 0.036$), wellbeing ($g = 0.46$, 95% CI, 0.28–0.62, $p < 0.001$), coping ($g = 0.43$, 95% CI, 0.25–0.61, $p < 0.001$), work attitudes ($g = 0.54$, 95% CI, 0.34–0.73, $p < 0.001$), and goal-directed self-regulation ($g = 0.74$, 95% CI, 0.42–1.06, $p < 0.001$). In reviewing these results the authors concluded that coaching was 'an effective intervention in organizations'.

A third meta-analysis study (Jones *et al*, 2014) considered the value of executive coaching across different styles of intervention. Three were included: face-to-face ($d = 0.27$), internal ($d = 0.19$) and external coaching ($d = 0.69$). These results too reveal positive impact, as measured by effect size, from each of these styles of intervention. Jones *et al* (2014) also urged caution due to the relatively small sample of studies they reviewed – which was limited to 24 studies.

These three meta-analysis papers need to be considered in the light of previous organizational research reviewing the efficacy of other interventions

TABLE 1.6 Weighted effect sizes of coaching interventions for studies by number of coaching sessions

Measures	Effect size (fewer than five interventions)	Effect size (five or more interventions)
Coping	0.54	0.35
Goal-directed self-regulation	1.02	0.52
Performance/skills	0.11	0.26
Attitudes	0.35	0.67
Wellbeing	0.46	0.47

Adapted from Theeboom *et al*, 2013

that have shown ranging effect size from 0.60 to 0.63 for training effectiveness (Arthur *et al*, 2003), 0.24 for managerial training effectiveness (Powell and Yalcin, 2010) and 0.5 to 0.15 for appraisal/multi-source feedback (Smither, London and Reilly, 2005).

As can be noted, the evidence from the initial coaching studies confirms that coaching is as powerful an intervention as training and feedback, which are commonly used by managers to help performance improvement. Further, the results from the three studies suggest a moderate effect of coaching overall.

This evidence means that master practitioners can now respond with confidence to questions about efficacy by drawing on research to inform clients about the power of coaching, as one tool to support learning, behavioural change and performance improvement.

These meta-studies, when combined with the growing literature on coaching using RCT methodologies, provides conclusive evidence that coaching does work. With this knowledge in place practitioners can now support their claims with scientific evidence. The power of coaching is not magic, it is science.

Conclusion

The journey of building mastery is a continuous one. The most dangerous position is to claim that we are a master coach now and can thus stop learning. Master coaches are always seeking new approaches, fresh insights and leading edge research to help them reflect, refine and finesse their approach. They are hungry for new knowledge with which to experiment. For the master coach, mastery is a journey that can enhance their service to their clients, but is also one of pleasure and enjoyment as they learn, develop and grow.

References

Arthur, W, Bennett, W, Edens, P S and Bell, S T (2003) Effectiveness of training in organizations: a meta-analysis of design and evaluation features, *Journal of Applied Psychology*, **88** (2), pp 234–35

Cohen, J (1988) *Statistical power analysis for the behavioural sciences*, Lawrence Erlbaum, Hillsdale, NJ

De Meuse, K, Dai, G and Lee, R (2009) Evaluating the effectiveness of executive coaching: beyond ROI, *Coaching: An International Journal of Theory, Research and Practice*, **2** (2), pp 117–34

Deviney, D E (1994) The effects of coaching using multiple rater feedback to change supervisor behavior, *Dissertation Abstracts International Section A*, **55**, p 114

Duijts, S F A P, Kant, I P, van den Brandt, P A P and Swaen, G M H P (2008) Effectiveness of a preventive coaching intervention for employees at risk for sickness absence due to psychosocial health complaints: results of a randomized controlled trial, *Journal of Occupational and Environmental Medicine*, **50** (7), pp 765–76

Evers, W J, Brouwers, A and Tomic, W (2006) A quasi-experimental study on management coaching effectiveness, *Consulting Psychology Journal: Practice and research*, **58**, pp 174–82

Franklin, J and Franklin, A (2012) The long term independent assessed benefits of coaching, *International Coaching Psychology Review*, **7** (1), pp 33–38

Gattellari, M, Donnelly, N, Taylor, N, Meerkin, M, Hirst, G and Ward, J (2005) Does 'peer coaching' increase GP capacity to promote informed decision making about PSA screening? A cluster randomised trial, *Family Practice*, **22** (3), pp 253–65

Grant, A M (2002) Towards a psychology of coaching: the impact of coaching on metacognition, mental health and goal attainment, *Dissertation Abstracts International Section A: Humanities and Social Sciences*, **63** (12), pp 6094 (June)

Grant, A M (2012) Making positive change: a randomized study comparing solution-focused vs. problem focused coaching questions, *Journal of Systemic Therapies*, **31** (2), pp 21–35

Grant, A M, Frith, L and Burton, G (2009) Executive coaching enhances goal attainment, resilience and workplace well-being: a randomised controlled study, *Journal of Positive Psychology*, **4** (5), pp 396–407

Grant, A M, Passmore, J, Cavanagh, M and Parker, H (2010) The state of play in coaching, *International Review of Industrial and Organizational Psychology*, **25**, pp 125–68

Green, L S, Grant, A M and Rynsaardt, J (2007) Evidence-based life coaching for senior high school students: building hardiness and hope, *International Coaching Psychology Review*, **2** (1), pp 24–32

Green, L, Oades, L and Grant, A (2006) Cognitive-behavioral, solution-focused life coaching: enhancing goal striving, well-being, and hope, *The Journal of Positive Psychology*, **1** (3), pp 142–49

Gyllensten, K and Palmer, S (2005) Can coaching reduce workplace stress: a quasi-experimental study, *International Journal of Evidence Based Coaching and Mentoring*, **3** (2), pp 75–85

Jones, R J, Woods, S A and Guillaume, Y (2014) *A meta-analysis of the effectiveness of executive coaching at improving work-based performance and moderators of coaching effectiveness.* Paper presented to the British Psychological Society Division of Occupational Psychology Conference in January 2014

Miller, D J (1990) The effect of managerial coaching on transfer of training, *Dissertation Abstracts International Section B*, **50** (2435)

Miller, W R, Yahne, C E, Moyers, T B, Martinez, J and Pirritano, M (2004) A randomized trial of methods to help clinicians learn motivational interviewing, *Journal of Consulting and Clinical Psychology*, **72** (6), pp 1050–62

Passmore, J and Rehman, H (2012) Coaching as a learning methodology – a mixed methods study in driver development – a Randomised Controlled Trial and thematic analysis, *International Coaching Psychology Review*, **7** (2), pp 166–84

Passmore, J and Velez, M J (2012) Coaching fleet drivers – a randomized controlled trial (RCT) of 'short coaching' interventions to improve driver safety in fleet drivers, *The Coaching Psychologist*, **8** (1), pp 20–26

Powell, K S and Yalcin, S (2010) Managerial training effectiveness: a meta-analysis 1952–2002, *Personnel Review*, **39** (2), pp 227–41

Renshaw, B and Alexander, G (2005) *Supercoaching*, Random House, London

Smither, J W, London, M and Reilly, R R (2005) Does performance improve following multisource feedback? A theoretical model, meta-analysis, and a review of empirical findings, *Personnel Psychology*, **54**, pp 33–66, 3–9760

Spence, G B, Cavanagh, M J and Grant, A M (2008) The integration of mindfulness training and health coaching: an exploratory study, *Coaching: An international journal of theory, research and practice*, **1** (2), pp 145–63

Spence, G B and Grant, A (2007) Professional and peer life coaching and the enhancement of goal striving and well-being: an exploratory study, *The Journal of Positive Psychology*, **2**, pp 185–94

Sue-Chan, C and Latham, G P (2004) The relative effectiveness of expert, peer and self coaches, *Applied Psychology*, **53** (2), pp 260–78

Taylor, L M (1997) The relation between resilience, coaching, coping skills training, and perceived stress during a career-threatening milestone [Empirical, PhD, WS] DAI-B 58/05, p 2738, November 1997

Theeboom, T, Beersma, B and van Vianen, A E M (2013) Does coaching work? A meta-analysis on the effects of coaching on individual level outcomes in an organizational context, *Journal of Positive Psychology*, **8** (6), pp 174–96

Positive psychology coaching

02

LINDSAY G OADES AND JONATHAN PASSMORE

Introduction

Positive psychology has been referred to as the science at the heart of coaching (Kauffman *et al*, 2010). Positive psychology coaching (PPC) is a term increasingly used to signify coaching methods and approaches, alongside similar approaches including evidence-based coaching (Grant and Cavanagh, 2007) and strengths coaching (Govindji and Linley, 2007). While these approaches overlap, this chapter will describe PPC as having some unique characteristics that warrant it being referred to as a separate endeavour (Linley, 2005). This chapter commences with an introduction to positive psychology and its central tenets, models and practices, and key definitions of wellbeing needed to understand the context and purpose of PPC. We then move on to define and outline what exactly is meant by PPC. Our definition for PPC is *coaching approaches that seek to improve short-term wellbeing (ie hedonic wellbeing) and sustainable wellbeing (ie eudaimonic wellbeing) using evidence-based approaches from positive psychology and the science of wellbeing and enable the person to do this in an ongoing manner after coaching has completed.* Short-term (hedonic) wellbeing is viewed as analogous to cash flow – something great to have, but short term and easily gone if there is not a longer-term supply. Sustainable (eudaimonic) wellbeing is viewed as analogous to an asset – it can be built or lost, and also impacts upon cash flow. These analogies may also be useful to coachee clients when collaboratively discussing aspects of wellbeing.

In addition to the definitions of wellbeing, four key positive psychological theories are summarized, namely strengths theory (Proctor *et al*, 2011), broaden-and-build theory (Fredrickson, 2009), self-determination theory (Spence and Oades, 2011) and wellbeing theory (Seligman, 2011). Relevant evidence within applied positive psychology is described and the early emerging evidence for PPC is then summarized.

Within the distinction of the two types of wellbeing, 10 aims for PPC coaching are outlined to match the definition of PPC provided. More detailed descriptions of coaching models and processes that will assist in meeting these aims are then described. Five prototypical PPC processes are summarized as: 1) opportunity based; 2) positive lens; 3) approach motivation based; 4) growth expectation; and 5) collaborative working alliance.

Positive psychological case conceptualization and assessment are discussed before providing examples of four frequently used PPC techniques: active constructive responding, three good things, gratitude exercises and random acts of kindness.

The techniques and processes are combined and illustrated in a case study. The chapter concludes by outlining when PPC is most suitable, and when it may not be the optimal choice. For those interested in exploring more about PPC, resources and professional development for a positive psychology coach are included at the end of the chapter.

Theory and evidence underpinning positive psychology coaching

In considering the theory and evidence underpinning PPC it is useful to start with the conceptualization of wellbeing, followed by models that assist in predicting and measuring what constitutes or leads to wellbeing. This is followed by some brief examination of evidence for interventions that have sought to increase wellbeing, particularly subjective wellbeing. Finally, the nascent evidence for PPC is discussed.

Starting with wellbeing, short-term or hedonic wellbeing, often measured through subjective wellbeing, is one type of wellbeing. This is derived from the Bentham philosophy of utility, related to *maximizing pleasure and minimizing pain*, which is what the hedonist does, hence the term *hedonic* wellbeing. This is the type of wellbeing most closely related to the lay notion of happiness. Sustainable wellbeing or eudaimonic wellbeing, literally *eu* (wellbeing – or good) and *daimonia* (demon or spirit) – and virtuous action, often measured by flourishing or psychological wellbeing, is the complementary type of wellbeing. This is derived from Aristotlean philosophy and is related *to reaching one's true potential or having a life well lived*, and has an explicit ethical component. As mentioned for explanatory purposes, the analogy of 'cash flow' is used to describe hedonic wellbeing (ie more positive emotions than negative emotions, analogous to more income than expense). The analogy of an 'asset' is used to describe eudaimonic wellbeing, as assets can be built or eroded but usually in a manner slower than the changes of cash flow. Moreover, having more assets makes cash flow easier to gain. Hence, rather than an either/or approach to which type of wellbeing, in coaching it may be explained as a dynamic and dual process. In the next section we will shift from a philosophical understanding of wellbeing to a psychological understanding. Four influential positive psychological theories are summarized before we consider relevant evidence of positive psychological interventions in general, and PPC in particular.

Strengths theory

Strengths theory (ST) is perhaps better considered a family of theories, or a unifying proposition as opposed to a single theory. The central proposition is that people will perform, feel and function better if they are using their strengths. For this reason, strengths researchers and practitioners have developed strengths assessment tools, to assist people to gain knowledge of their strengths, and then use their strengths and spot strengths in others. It is useful for coaches to understand and sometimes explore with coachees two different conceptualizations of personal strengths. The first is character strengths, which constitute a person's values put into action. These have been developed largely by Peterson and Seligman (2004). Character strengths cluster as virtues, and represent things that are good in an ethical sense, based on virtue ethics. The assessment tool Values in Action (VIA – see *Psychometrics in Coaching* for a fuller discussion of the tool within coaching), often referred to as the 'signature strengths survey', is very well known internationally. Performance strengths are different to character strengths in that they relate to something a person feels good at, and something they are energized by doing. The Realise2 instrument developed by Linley and colleagues is an example of an assessment tool used to measure performance strengths. Linley and colleagues have developed strengths coaching, which is more specific than PPC as it focuses mainly on strengths – but it may be considered part of the PPC family. This approach includes the relationship between strengths knowledge, strengths use and spotting strengths in others.

Broaden-and-build theory

Broaden-and-build theory (BBT) was primarily developed to seek answers to the question 'what is the function of positive emotion?' (Fredrickson, 1998, 2001). The broaden-and-build theory proposes that experiences of positive emotions *broaden* people's momentary thought-action repertoires – that is, the menu of choices of thinking and acting is broader when a person is experiencing positive emotions. In turn, the theory holds that this serves to *build* enduring personal resources including physical, intellectual, social and psychological resources. In Fredrickson's (2009) popular book *Positivity*, she describes the optimal ratio of three positive emotions to one negative emotion. This is a useful heuristic for discussions of the role of positive emotions in PPC. Positive emotions are central to PPC and, as illustrated in Table 2.1, form the starting point for discussions underpinning subjective wellbeing.

Self-determination theory

Self-determination theory (SDT), sometimes referred to as meta-theory, is a set of theories which examine the effects of different types of motivation (Deci and Ryan, 2000). The sub-theories are basic needs theory, cognitive evaluation theory, organismic integration theory, causality orientations theory, relationships motivation theory and goal contents theory. SDT is a needs theory that posits three universal psychological needs: a) autonomy; b) relatedness; and c) competence. Hence, people need to make their own choices, connect with others and feel competent as they exercise and grow their capacities. The theory proposes that if these three needs are met, a person will have increased autonomous motivation. Autonomous motivation leads to greater perseverance as tasks that have originally been from an external origin, eg a boss or a parent, become more internalized. And although such motivation is still extrinsic, the person starts to self-regulate rather than feeling as though they are being externally regulated.

For a person new to PPC, the language of SDT can seem inaccessible at first, however the theory is comprehensive and can be a useful background to a deeper understanding of wellbeing.

Wellbeing theory

Wellbeing theory (WT) (Seligman, 2011) is similar to aspects of SDT (Deci and Ryan, 2000). Wellbeing theory, sometimes referred to simply as PERMA theory (the acronym making up the five components), posits that there are five domains of life that both constitute and may be instruments towards wellbeing, and they each have a unique contribution. The five components are Positive Emotions, Engagement, (Positive) Relationships, Meaning and Accomplishment. The reader is encouraged to explore how PERMA is dispersed across the objectives outlined in Table 2.1. PERMA is an evolution of Seligman's previous work on authentic happiness, which included positive emotions, engagement and meaning (relationships and accomplishment have been added to the theory).

These are broad theories of positive psychology and wellbeing that are not interventions and hence not coaching based. In seeking to understand the evidence base informing PPC it is useful to first gain an awareness of a range of interventions that have sought to improve wellbeing more generally, whether delivered in a coaching format or not. Many of these are described in Lyubomirsky (2007) and include expressing gratitude, cultivating optimism, avoiding overthinking and social comparison, nurturing social relationships, increasing flow experiences and committing to your goals.

The emerging evidence of coaching psychology in general, and positive psychology in particular, is now discussed. Linley (2006) asserts that coaching researchers should utilize five key questions to conduct and, we suggest, understand coaching research. While coach practitioners may not conduct research, it is useful for their practice to be good consumers of research, and these five questions are helpful in that regard:

1 Who? Who is participating in the investigation, and for whom is the investigation designed?

2 What? Which approach yields the best results, and what are the commonalities among different approaches?

3 Where? What different locations of coaching sessions can influence the methodology?

4 When? Should we give priority to longitudinal designs with pre- and post-test measures when possible to understand the process of coaching?

5 Why? 'Why' is the fundamental question with which every researcher should begin his or her study.

Given that PPC has much in common with evidence-based coaching skills more broadly, question 2 above is very poignant. As mentioned in the previous definition provided, the explicit focus on wellbeing is a key identifying characteristic; hence most outcome studies on PPC will likely measure wellbeing, in hedonic or eudaimonic forms or both. We recommend also that further research is needed on the relationship aspects of coaching and the coaching process, such as those issues summarized in Table 2.3 and which are discussed in more detail in Chapter 1.

Hence, there is an increasing wellbeing evidence base that relates to the two types of wellbeing and coaching aims listed in Table 2.1 below.

TABLE 2.1   Positive psychology coaching aims by the two complementary types of wellbeing

Short-term wellbeing (hedonic wellbeing) 'the cash flow'	Sustainable wellbeing (eudaimonic wellbeing) 'the asset'
1 Modulate ratio of positive to negative emotions	1 Increase sense of meaning and purpose
2 Ensure basic life needs are satisfied	2 Live authentically in line with strengths and values
3 Foster positive relationships	3 Increase sense of autonomy including seeking autonomy-supportive environments
4 Know and use strengths to gain mastery and feel energized	4 Live in line with 'true self' and strive to achieve perceived potential
5 Increase experiences of flow	5 Build resilience resources, eg optimism, functional social support, mindfulness skills, willpower

Spence and Grant (2013) recently conducted a brief review of the coaching related evidence for practitioners. These authors provide a cautionary note stating that while some of the evidence has been generated through the use of robust scientific methods, there remains a pressing need for research. They identify two key areas: 1) the specific impact of coaching across different domains, eg workplace and executive coaching, life coaching, health coaching and coaching in educational settings; and 2) what psychological processes coaching activates to generate these effects.

In 2006 Green, Oades and Grant conducted a randomized controlled test (pre-post design) on group-based life coaching and demonstrated increases in goal striving, wellbeing and hope, including some gains being maintained at 30 weeks. In a randomized controlled trial, Grant, Curtayne and Burton (2009) examined the effectiveness of executive coaching demonstrating a reduction in stress and depression, and an improvement in goal attainment and resilience.

Given the limited number of randomized controlled trials in coaching it is prudent to say that much of coaching psychology in general, and PPC, is evidence informed rather than fully evidence based. There is increasing evidence for wellbeing interventions and increasing scientific publications reporting coaching and coaching research. For this reason, we carefully define PPC and its various aims in terms of the two types of wellbeing. While we do not present a research protocol nor manualization here, such a framework may provide the parameters for that endeavour.

The aims and processes of positive psychology coaching

PPC coaching aims, as illustrated in Table 2.1, are based on the definition provided for PPC involving short-term and sustainable wellbeing.

Modulate ratio of positive to negative emotions

Broaden-and-build theory (Fredrickson, 2009), as mentioned, has led to evidence that shows there is an optimal ratio of 3:1 positive to negative emotions for people functioning well. While the academic and research debates will continue, this provides a useful heuristic for discussion in coaching sessions, enabling the coach to underscore the role of emotions in general, and the newly recognized importance of positive emotions. Coaching sessions may include an educational component here, assisting people to understand the respective roles of positive and negative emotions. Positive emotions enable people to broaden their menu of thoughts and actions, and being associated with approach motivation, helps us move towards something we want. Conversely, negative emotions deliberately constrict our menu of thoughts and actions, and being associated with avoidance motivation, move us away from something we do not want or often need for survival. The task of the PPC coach is to enable the coachee to understand the role and importance of emotion, and then apply its relevance to their own life, in their own context. Discussion of emotion, in general, and positive emotions in particular may be foreign to certain contexts and cultures. The skill of the coach is to adapt the language while still assisting the coachee to move to a greater understanding of the application of the emerging science of positive emotion. For example, in working with some older men, emotions may be referred to as physical activity of the brain, rather than feelings etc.

Diener's Scale for Positive and Negative Experience (SPANE) is a short quantitative scale that can be used to assess positive and negative emotions (details of the survey are included in the resources section at the end of the chapter). A coach may choose to discuss the questions one by one or use it as a scale and discuss the results. This will be guided by the coach's judgement and coachee willingness.

Ensure basic life needs are satisfied

Many people are familiar with Maslow's hierarchy of needs, but less familiar with self-determination theory and the idea of universal basic psychological needs. Stated simply, basic needs satisfaction leads to short-term wellbeing. While some people may look down upon simple pleasures and need satisfaction, it remains an important component of overall wellbeing, as cash flow is to business. However, since Maslow's earlier needs theory, self-determination theory has highlighted the three universal psychological needs of autonomy, relatedness and competence. Spence and Oades (2011) provide descriptions of 'how to coach with self-determination theory in mind'. Hence, in addition to considering a person's strengths and values, their basic psychological needs should also be prominent in the discussion. In the case of Susan (see page 30), her core relationships with her husband and children remained central to her decision making during the case conceptualization, but so did the autonomy she sought in her work, and the need to feel competent in what she was doing. A coach working with this in mind needs to also look at the affordances the environments provide, ie how do the job or the house enable Susan to have good relationships, have choices and feel competent?

Lyubomirksy's (2007) *The How of Happiness* is recommended reading to assist coachees in thinking about working to their happiness more actively, and taking responsibility for it. This will help coachees to understand the many things they can do to improve their wellbeing.

Foster satisfying relationships

The importance of relationships remains a key component of wellbeing, somewhat ubiquitous to a happy life. There are many ways a person can seek to improve their relationships and many techniques that could be highlighted. Active constructive responding will be illustrated below as one technique to improve relationships.

Know and use strengths to gain mastery and feel energized

As mentioned, strengths theory is a central theory underpinning PPC. The case of Susan (see page 30) involves the use of the Realise2 outputs. A useful distinction in the strengths literature is between strengths knowledge, strengths use and strengths spotting (Govindji and Linley, 2007). Strengths knowledge is gained by completing personal strengths assessments such as the Realise2. There are multiple benefits to using strengths including improved wellbeing, feeling energized and performing better. Strengths coaching is a type of coaching that seeks to enable people to increase their use of their strengths (Linley, 2006). It is also useful in coaching to link strengths to goals; that is, once coaches have identified their strengths, the question becomes 'how can you use these strengths to achieve the goal you have set?' As is evident in the case study below, Susan's personal strength of reconfiguration was employed to assist with her significant life transition.

Increase experiences of flow

Flow has been described as an optimal experience (Csikszentmihalyi, 1990; Csikszentmihalyi and LeFevre, 1989). This experience requires multiple conditions to be met, in which a person becomes fully absorbed in an activity that matches their skill level, and provides immediate feedback for a goal directed activity. Flow is an enjoyable state, and involves intrinsic motivation. Importantly, people who experience more flow tend to have higher levels of wellbeing and are performing a goal directed activity at the same time! The PPC objective here is that people should seek to plan and increase their opportunities for such experiences. For example, how can they craft their job so they can use their strengths on appropriately challenging activities in which they become absorbed? In the case example of Susan, she began to experience flow as she returned to her creative art projects, building a sculpture. In Susan's case, she sought to change employment status altogether. However, some people can stay with the same employer and job, but craft the job so it contains more flow-affording opportunities.

Bakker's (2008) Work Related Flow Inventory (WOLF) can be adapted and discussed in coaching as a way of measuring people's flow states at work. A conversation seeking examples around its three factors – absorption, work enjoyment and intrinsic motivation – is a useful way to have more rigorous conversations around flow. A key risk during coaching or teaching people about flow is that they believe anything that involves absorption is therefore flow, and they overlook the goal directed component of flow, requiring feedback and matching the challenge to one's skill level.

Increase sense of meaning and purpose

As mentioned, to move to thinking about sustainable wellbeing, in addition to shorter-term wellbeing supported by positive emotions, it is important to consider meaning and purpose. As mentioned previously, wellbeing theory includes meaning, ie the M of PERMA, in which meaning may be summarized as doing something that is greater than for oneself. Discussion of meaning often leads psychologists to quote Jung or Frankl; however, the modern day corporate world is full of people searching for meaning in life, and meaningful work (Steger, Dik and Duffy, 2014). Steger, Dik and Shim (2014) provide a case vignette, which is a useful way to assess and discuss meaningful work with individual coaches. Steger's Work and Meaning Inventory (WAMI) is a useful positive psychological assessment that can be used as part of the coaching process.

Prototypical characteristics of the process of positive psychology coaching

Experienced coaches manage the process of coaching as much as the tangible techniques used. Table 2.2 illustrates characteristics of the coaching process that should be evident if observing an actual coaching session. PPC experienced practitioners often use a variety of styles from the checklist (Table 2.2) and reflect on these after each coaching session. The collaborative working alliance is not unique of course to PPC, but the ways the goals

TABLE 2.2 Prototypical characteristics of the process of PPC

Prototypical characteristic	Description
Opportunity-based	The coaching process will seek to find and use personal and environmental opportunities rather than a problem-solving or reparative focus.
Positive lens	The coachee and their environments will be examined through a positive lens, not denying the negative but looking to draw out personal strengths and environmental resources.
Approach motivation-based	Approach motivation is moving towards something that you want, as opposed to moving away from something you don't want. The coaching process is likely to involve goals, and PPC process will usually elicit or discuss more approach goals than avoidance goals.

TABLE 2.2   *continued*

Prototypical characteristic	Description
Growth expectation	The core assumption underpinning psychological change in PPC is that people will seek to grow and develop and that they can with the right environment. Their capacities can change, and a coach needs to engender a growth mindset. This is supported by a positive case conceptualization.
Collaborative working alliance	Similar to other types of coaching, a collaborative working alliance is optimal in PPC. However, for this to occur, there needs to be agreement on goals, which in this case should be (a) approach goals, (b) goals with high levels of subjective ownership, (c) goals supported by personal strengths use and (d) goals consistent with personal values.
	The collaborative working alliance is also supported by (a) collaborative discussion and choice of positive psychological assessment and (b) collaborative development of the positive case conceptualization.

are constructed (eg approach goals and subjective ownership) has a heightened importance for PPC, with the overarching aim of not just increasing the two types of wellbeing, but enabling the coachee to learn how to do it themselves in an ongoing way after the cessation of the coaching proper.

Positive case conceptualization

Positive case conceptualization is similar to Biswas-Diener's (2010) notion of a positive diagnosis, and the idea of a solution-focused case conceptualization (Green, Oades and Grant, 2006). As illustrated in Figure 2.1, this is a version of how the coach and coachee make sense of the relationships between key aspects of the person's psychological and social world, using key concepts within positive psychology, such as strengths, positive emotions and meaning. The aim here is not to diagnose, find deficits or causes to problems, but rather to reconfigure possibilities and look for opportunities. A key guiding question is 'if things are functioning really well, and people in the system are feeling good, what does it look like?' Hence, while the coaching may be triggered by a problem, difficulty or transition, the conceptualization itself seeks to identify what things functioning well look like, using the language of positive psychology and the science of wellbeing applied to the context.

Biswas-Diener (2010) describes three core areas of PPC as: a) a positive focus; b) benefits of positive emotion; and c) the science of strengths. While this is appropriate, the conceptualization expands the approach to include a greater emphasis on the sustainable wellbeing (eudaimonic wellbeing) components, which emphasizes the importance of meaning in life, a sense of purpose and striving towards one's perceived full potential. The important distinction of short-term and sustainable wellbeing are illustrated in Table 2.1. Table 2.1 bridges the philosophy behind the two types of wellbeing with overarching aims that may be employed as part of PPC. Numerous cells from the table corresponding to important tools and techniques of PPC are now discussed directly or illustrated in the case study to follow.

Positive psychological assessment

With the increased scientific development of positive psychology, and the science of wellbeing, there is an increasing number of brief, easy to use and valid positive psychological assessment tools that can form part of the PPC process. An exhaustive review of these tools is beyond the scope of this chapter, so an indicative sample has been chosen. The following assessments are illustrated within the case study: performance strengths assessment; positive and negative emotions; and life satisfaction.

The brief 'Satisfaction with Life' scale is available online (**http://internal. psychology.illinois.edu/~ediener/SWLS.html**) and can be used as part of an early PPC coaching assessment as can the 'Basic Needs Satisfaction' scale. Both are brief, and if followed by appropriate discussion will enable the person to consider wellbeing in a way deeper than positive emotions.

The 'Values into Action' (VIA) instrument is one of a number of instruments for reviewing strengths. What is most powerful is that it has been completed for thousands of users over the past decade, partly because access is free. VIA provides the user with a strengths-based report that is e-mailed to them, highlighting the individual's personal strengths. The use of VIA in respect of coaching conversations and how the tool can be best used by the coach has been discussed in detail by Kauffman and colleagues (Kauffman, Silberman and Sharpley, 2008).

A second example of a strengths psychometric is the Realise2 questionnaire, which was developed in the United Kingdom and is published by CAPP (The Centre of Applied Positive Psychology). We describe how the instrument is used in the case study below.

Practice: tools and techniques

In this section we will review the practical tools and techniques that coaches use in their practice. This includes positive case conceptualization, positive psychological assessment and a small selection of short techniques, active constructive responding, three good things, gratitude and random acts of kindness.

Active constructive responding

Active constructive responding (ACR) (Gable *et al*, 2004; Gable, Gonzaga and Strachman, 2006; Magyar-Moe, 2009) is a simple and understandable technique that can assist people to improve their close relationships, by enabling people to respond more actively and constructively when things go right for their loved ones or colleagues.

Table 2.3 illustrates how the case study character, Susan, could respond to her husband when he gains his promotion. During coaching Susan expressed that she was supportive of her husband's new role, but did not believe she may have expressed her support verbally to her husband in a way in which he understood that support. Active and constructive responses will help Susan to leave her husband feeling more positive and that his efforts are recognized and appreciated.

Three good things

Three good things, like ACR, is a technique that can be used both in coaching conversation and more generally in one-to-one conversation where the

TABLE 2.3   Active constructive responding: when husband gets promoted

John returns home to tell Susan he has been promoted. He is very proud and excited about the opportunities it will bring.	Constructive	Destructive
Active	'I'm so pleased for you John, because you have worked so hard, and you deserve this... well done... I'm so proud.'	'Right, so this means you will be spending more time away from the home, and the kids won't see you.'
Passive	'That's good John. Can you help get the groceries in from the car?'	'Oh okay, whatever, things are busy. Can you help get the groceries in from the car?'

coach or manager (or leader of the conversation) wishes to encourage a more positive response from their coachee (team member).

The technique starts with the use of a question – 'what are the best three things about working here' (or similar). Some individuals are able to respond by listing the three aspects, which opens up a conversation about these aspects; with the coachee encouraged to provide an example, to talk about a recent experience or to explain why these are the top three items. Other individuals find it hard to either start with a positive statement, or find it hard to complete the description with three positives without moving into downsides. If the coachee mentions a negative aspect, the coach intervenes: 'we can look at some of the downsides later, but what have you enjoyed most?' The intervention brings the focus back to the positive.

The coach is encouraging the coachee to focus on the positive aspects of an issue, day or relationship, rather than being drawn to the negative. It has been suggested that repeated use of the technique (for example, daily practice over several months or even better a year or more) will strengthen the neural pathways that look for the positive aspects or issues which the individual encounters, as a result the negative (downsides) focus and thinking is reduced.

One of us has used the technique extensively with his children, as part of a coaching conversation at the end of the day. To our surprise children respond positively to coaching as a learning aid, which helps with understanding reasons for doing or not doing things, such as running in the road or standing on a chair. Table 2.4 shows two real exchanges with a three-year-old

TABLE 2.4   Three good things – example

Typical coaching questions	Three good things questions
Dad: *'So Florence, how was your day?'*	Dad: *'Florence what were the best three things you did today?'*
Florence: *'It was ok'*	Florence: *'Going to Valerie's house'*
Dad: *'What did you do?'*	Dad: *'What else?'*
Florence: *'I played dollies at school'*	Florence: *'Getting a present from Valerie – baby'*
Dad: *'What else?'*	Dad: *'What did you like about the baby?'*
Florence: *'I played with Tabatha'*	Florence: *'Cuddling baby... playing with baby'*
	Dad: *'What else did you enjoy?'*
	Florence: *'Pasta and ice cream tea... chocolate ice cream'* (Florence starts feeding pretend food to her new baby doll).

(Florence) used on two consecutive days. The first uses standard open questions to encourage reflection on the day. The second places a positive focus on the reflection, with the specific aim of encouraging the child to talk about their positive experiences, and in doing so think about these experiences. What was interesting is the positive experience led to Florence acting out her own positive experience with her doll, as she thought and described the experience.

The power of the technique is in repeated use. With adults the coachee can take the intervention away as a homework task. The coachee can, for example, be encouraged to undertake the exercise at the end of the day, with the coachee capturing their three best parts of the day on a note pad – and dwell on these memories as they go to sleep. From personal experience, using this technique often means coachees describe going to sleep smiling!

Gratitude

Gratitude is a concept that has diminished in Western society, almost in parallel with the increasing wealth that most members of Western societies enjoy. Wealth, possessions and health have, for many, become expected norms, rather than personal 'blessings' that are appreciated. As expectations have changed, so gratitude has diminished. Gratitude has, for many, been replaced by disappointment, anger and resentment when these expected 'blessings' do not appear (or they disappear).

This view contrasts with many religious traditions. Jews may start the day with Modeh Ani, a short Hebrew blessing in which God is thanked for life. The Christian tradition too shows gratitude to God for blessings from food, with a short prayer of Grace, to give thanks for life, family and the many blessings that life bestows.

Writers have suggested that gratitude serves a social function in helping to build and maintain relationships between family members and the wider kinship group. More importantly, gratitude encourages individuals to focus their attention on the positive aspects of their life, in contrast with dwelling on negative issues and events.

Research (McCullough *et al*, 2002 and 2003) too has linked gratitude with more proactive behaviours towards others, as well as to hope and life satisfaction.

By applying these insights through simple exercises for coachees, we have found similar positive effects. For Christians and others with religious beliefs the exercise can be set around finding a time each day to reflect on the good things in the coachee's life and to say a short two-minute prayer expressing gratitude to God for these blessings. For coachees without a faith, a reflective exercise can be set where the client is asked to spend a similar short period reflecting on the things that they most appreciate during their day.

The technique can be adapted to manage conflict situations, where the coachee is asked to reflect on the individual they are in conflict with or where a relationship is less strong and for the coachee to identify one (or even better two or three) characteristics of the person who they admire and which they appreciate in the other person.

The techniques set as activities outside of coaching are useful as they can form part of a regular routine that the person can develop and that can be used to help individuals manage workplace stress, challenging times or situations and as a way of helping build positivity.

A word of caution, however. If the exercise is overdone, this can become boring and repetitive, so it is better undertaken as a weekly task, rather than a daily task. Again, for Christians and those with a faith, this can fit well with a Sunday (or weekly attendance) at church, synagogue or mosque. It is also more likely to be completed and repeated if the activity is meditative rather than written down in the form of a letter or notes.

These practical experiences of what works is supported by research on intervention frequency and method conducted by Seligman and colleagues (Seligman *et al*, 2005). Seligman found individuals who did the task every day became bored while those asked to write their gratitude down felt anxious about the letter becoming public.

Random acts of kindness

Random acts of kindness (RAK) are selfless acts performed by a person wishing to either help or cheer up another person. Anne Herbert, a journalist, claims to have invented the phrase in a call to others to 'Practice random kindness and senseless acts of beauty'. However, the idea pre-dates positive psychology and again has its roots in religion. Jesus preached the idea of showing kindness not just to friends, but to those we don't like and our enemies. Judaism too places a focus on kindness to others: 'the world is built on kindness'.

However, our experience is that in an individualistic world, where time is money, these elements are forgotten. In using the technique, we might encourage the coachee to slow their pace, and to both savour each experience and to show appreciation to those they encounter. The nature of RAK is that they cannot be prescribed, but are a response to a situation; one example was the viral video a few years ago of an on-duty US police officer who went into a store to buy socks and shoes for a homeless man he had met on the street and who was barefoot. We have listed a few ideas in Table 2.5, but the aim is for the coachee to respond to situations and to report back in the following coaching session on their experiences of applying random acts of kindness in their life.

TABLE 2.5   Ideas for random acts of kindness

1 Compliment one thing that you like on/about three people you meet during the day.
2 Write a hand-written card to a teacher, boss or colleague to thank them for something they have done.
3 Say good morning to the person next to you in the lift.
4 Pick up some litter and put it in the bin on your way to work.
5 Place an uplifting note in library books or on a colleague's computer screen.
6 Put an inspiring sign in your office window during the rush hour.
7 Leave a really generous tip, for excellent service.
8 Send flowers to a friend or a parent.
9 Thank the person at the checkout till for their great customer service.
10 Use people's names (read their name badge) when talking to the staff in the canteen and ask about their day.

CASE STUDY

Susan is a 44-year-old, married mother of two, living in London. Her children are aged 11 and eight and she is back in full-time employment after having been in part-time employment for several years when the children were younger. Susan works as an Executive Assistant in a financial services company, which has recently merged and restructured. Her mother lives fairly close, and continues to provide much support with the children. Susan's husband of 15 years also works full time, at an IT firm. Susan describes her life as extremely busy, and while her children are healthy she feels they do not appreciate her. Susan describes her marriage as stable, and her husband as a bit self-absorbed and boring at times, and emphasizes that unlike her friends she is 'still married'. Susan sought coaching when the opportunity for coaching was made available at work. She stated on her coaching referral that she was looking to improve her professional skills. Early on in the coaching sessions the key reasons regarding needs for greater work–life balance and more meaning in her work became very prominent. Susan also expressed feeling exhausted at times, and frustrated by 'the bollocks at work during the restructure'.

Susan undertook several assessments that were discussed within the first two of the six face-to-face sessions that took place over a four-month period. Susan completed the Scale of Positive and Negative Experiences at each session, and also the Satisfaction with Life Scale. These were discussed and explained each time as a way to assist Susan to make sense of subjective wellbeing or happiness. Susan was quite interested and after further discussion was lent a copy of the book *Positivity*, which she read on the train in and out of London each day. Susan also completed the Realise2 personal strengths assessment and was debriefed about what it meant by Jane – with multiple examples elicited from Susan's day-to-day life.

Susan's Realise2 strengths profile was as follows:

- Realized Strengths: Relationship Deepener, Planful, Listener, Gratitude, Persistence, Unconditionality.
- Learned Behaviours: Adherence, Time Optimizer, Resolver, Detail.
- Weaknesses: Centred.
- Unrealized Strengths: Creativity, Innovation, Reconfiguration, Change Agent, Authenticity, Self Awareness.

Susan completed a positive psychological case conceptualization. This involved sitting with one of us (her coach) and drawing onto a smart board (electronic whiteboard which keeps a copy) a series of interacting parts of her preferred psychological and social system. This is illustrated in Figure 2.1.

The overall sequence of content and homework covered in the coaching sessions with Susan is summarized in Table 2.6.

FIGURE 2.1   Diagrammatic representation of positive case conceptualization developed during coaching

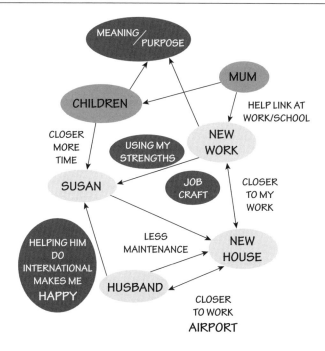

TABLE 2.6   Session topics and homework for Susan's positive psychology coaching

Session	Topic	Homework
1	Introduction to coaching and clarification of the scope of coaching. Discussion of key objectives to gain from the coaching series and socialization to PPC approach.	Complete Realise2, Satisfaction with Life Scale, and Positive and Negative Affect Scale.
2	Debrief on Realise2 and relate to Susan's current and desired situation. Discussion and exploration of the role of positive and negative emotion in Susan's life.	Commence and continue to read *Positivity*. Complete the online tools of **www.positivityratio.com/index.php**
3	Check in on Susan's progress with *Positivity* and the online exercises. Positive Case Conceptualization and discussion (see Figure 2.1).	Discuss new job and relocation with husband. Find examples of actual possible new jobs that would lead to greater strengths use.
4	Discussion of homework outcomes. Revisiting Positive Case Conceptualization in relation to husband, mother, children and relate to work–life balance, strengths and positive relationships.	Complete reflected best possible self exercise with feedback from children and husband and close friend.
5	Discuss best possible self, and how it relates to strengths, values, emotions and the case conceptualization. Update on things already done to generate change, regarding moving house and moving jobs.	Design with husband a 'strengths date holiday' in Europe.
6	Review strengths date. Consolidate and summarize commitments, and forward plan how transition will be monitored and supported.	

When Susan commenced coaching, her mental set was that it might be more like advice giving and listening. However, once she was socialized to the collaborative and opportunity focused approach, an immediate shift occurred. Given Susan's time pressures, the coaching provided a fairly unique and safe context in which she could explore ideas without necessarily having to act on them immediately. The following is a transcript of the conversation:

Coach: So let's think about your job, your husband's job, the kids, your mum, and the work you do... if all of these people were relating to each other better, if people were using their strengths more often, and you were being the best you could be... what would that look like? Don't assume anything for a moment...

Susan: [laugh]... as though I could just change it around...

Coach: Yes, keeping the people, dare to have a think... you can draw it, speak it, whatever works.

Susan: To be honest I don't think I would stay working where I am... I now see how it's de-energizing me...

Coach: Okay, tell me more...

Susan: Well it's not only the recent restructure, it's what I do... it's not really me... I was an administrator and I've just kept moving up... and then I got Executive Assistant... the strengths stuff showed that I'm not really in the right place... and the emotions stuff showed that I'm enjoying my kids and my art more than I am my work.

Coach: I see, you have really been exploring things...

Susan: And it's silly really, as my husband John is very supportive for me to change... and bless him, since he has the new role, more travel but more pay... so financially we could absorb me making a change.

Coach: Okay, is there a barrier to overcome?

Susan: [pause] Yes I think it's the kids, and mum who is getting older...

Coach: Okay, looking at the whiteboard again, so we can see all these things at once... where do mum and the kids fit in here?

Susan committed to major change during the process of the positive psychology coaching sessions. The Realise2 strengths profiling, combined with extended discussion about meaning and positive emotions, provided a language for her to narrate her change. While she was generally motivated and diligent as a coachee, the positive case conceptualization enabled her to transcend the current situation to explore possibilities previously not seen.

Susan committed to several major changes by the end of Session 6, and had declared and discussed these wishes with her husband, children, mother and even employer.

1 Susan committed to changing jobs within six months to find something, possibly lower paying, in the first instance, which was more in line with her creative strengths and desire for visual art.

2 Susan committed to supporting her husband to travel, but joining him on occasions while her mum stayed with the children. This enabled her to increase positive relationships and positive emotion.

3 Susan committed with her husband to pursue moving to a new house within 12 months, closer to (a) her new workplace, when that arises, and (b) closer to the airport as her husband was now travelling more and (c) keeping the kids within same school.

4 Susan committed to continuing to receive help from her mother, but more in terms of getting kids to and from school (as opposed to home caring) and more in terms of looking after them while she and John went for short weekends at locations attached to John's travel. At the end of coaching, Susan had already discussed this with her mother several times.

5 Susan committed to reminding herself of her values and that the kids were getting older, when she felt guilty for not being around enough for the children. Susan had commenced using a visual summary of her strengths and values.

6 Susan had recommenced her visual art, consistent with unrealized strengths of *Creativity, Innovation, Reconfiguration, Change Agent* and *Authenticity* and was working on a sculpture to symbolize the transition through which she was going. Her children were involved in a similar process.

Susan's significant change process provided examples of several key components of PPC: a growth and possibility focus, more approach rather than avoidance goals, a collaborative relationship (as per Table 2.2), the use of positive psychological assessments and a positive case conceptualization (see Figure 2.1). Positive psychological concepts and evidence used in the coaching included the Realise2 to assist with understanding and using strengths, a strengths date (or vacation/holiday), discussion of meaning and positive emotion, job crafting to increase experience of flow at work, and a *reflected best self portrait*, adapted from work to home life (Roberts *et al*, 2005). Importantly, however, these were all nested within Susan's key relationships, and situated geographically in Susan's world and that of her important family members.

When might positive psychology coaching be most suitable?

As in the psychotherapy research, the question should no longer be 'Does PPC coaching work?' Rather, a better question is 'For whom is PPC most beneficial, and when?'

Similar to most growth and future-based coaching approaches, a key cautionary note is for a person with a mental illness, be it depression or anxiety or other. This depends on both the skill set of the coach and also the degree of distress and psychopathology of the coachee. Some authors argue that coaching and clinical populations should be kept separate, while others apply coaching methodologies with those with serious mental illness. Hence, it may not be an either/or but rather a realization that for a person to be able to employ growth and approach motivation approaches, they need to have a certain level of stability, psychological assets and not be overwhelmed by negative affect and distress when they embark upon growth-based approaches. A depressed person, for example, may be experiencing significant hopelessness and guilt. This will make it difficult for the person to project into the future as they experience foreshortened timeframes. In turn this makes goal setting more difficult. Also, such a person may be at risk of setting unrealistic goals, almost as a way of appeasing personal guilt associated with the depressive process. For a highly anxious and/or obsessive client, certain parts of the goal striving and commitment process may exacerbate anxiety symptoms. For this reason, major caution is necessary before proceeding.

With that caveat in mind, there are other coachee factors that are likely to predict successful coachee outcomes for PPC. Firstly, underpinning PPC is applied positive psychology, which has humanistic and positive assumptions about human nature. There is a belief that a person is fundamentally good, will try to grow when given the environmental opportunity, and that they will seek meaning. These assumptions are not consistent with some world views, particularly those that are authoritarian, extremely nature focused (ie biologically based) or those that simply do not believe in the agency of a person to influence their destiny.

Conclusion

PPC, while having some commonalities with other coaching approaches, has a specific emphasis on building wellbeing, using the growing theory and evidence base from positive psychology and the science of wellbeing. The working definition for PPC used here is *coaching approaches that seek to improve short-term wellbeing (ie hedonic wellbeing) and sustainable wellbeing (ie eudaimonic wellbeing) using evidence-based approaches from positive psychology and the science of wellbeing* – with the aim of the coachee being able to do this in an ongoing manner after coaching has ended. Five aims to improve short-term wellbeing were described before five aims to improve sustainable wellbeing. With each of these aims, a technique/tool was discussed, in addition to a relevant positive psychological assessment to underpin the PPC decision making. The case study illustrated these techniques and processes in action, including the important positive psychological assessment. The role of short-term and sustainable wellbeing were balanced throughout the coaching intervention. Prototypical characteristics of the PPC coaching process were summarized to encourage coaches to examine and identify coaching processes as well as coaching techniques. Resources and professional development are now discussed.

Developing yourself as a positive psychology coach

Developing your skills

Coaches wishing to learn more about and develop their skills in PPC may wish to explore the following practitioner texts:

- Biswas-Diener, R (2010) *Practicing Positive Psychology Coaching: Assessment, activities and strategies for success*, Wiley, New York
- Driver, M (2011) *Coaching Positively: Lessons for coaches from positive psychology*, Open University Press, Maidenhead

A further useful way of developing positive psychology skills is through being a coach using a positive psychology approach. This 'parallel process' of skill development enables a greater understanding and skill development (Crowe *et al*, 2011).

Deepening your understanding

The components of Table 2.2 may be used as a reflective checklist for a coach after each coaching session to ensure they are adhering to a PPC process and not defaulting to a more problem-based stance. The positive case conceptualization is central to this.

Web resources

The following is a brief list of URLs that positive psychology coach practitioners will likely find useful for their own professional development or to give to clients:

- **www.authentichappiness.com**. This is the University of Pennsylvania website, which includes a range of psychology assessments that can be completed online with feedback for coaches and coachees alike including Values into Action (VIA) questionnaire and the Positive and Negative Affect Scale (PANAS).

- **www.positivityratio.com/index.php**. This is the accompanying website for Barbara Fredrickson's book, *Positivity*, providing an online quiz and useful introductions to the role of positive emotions in accessible language.

- **www.selfdeterminationtheory.org**. This website describes self-determination theory and provides a range of measurement tools also. See Spence and Oades (2011) for coaching using self-determination theory.

- **http://internal.psychology.illinois.edu/~ediener/SPANE.html**. This site is Ed Deiner's site, and it provides access to important measures of wellbeing. The Satisfaction With Life Scale, the Scale for Positive and Negative Emotions (SPANE) and the Flourishing Questionnaire. These questionnaires are brief and can form the basis of discussion and assessment in coaching, or be used as a repeated measure.

- **www.centreforconfidence.co.uk/**. This comprehensive site includes a section on positive psychology resources, with multiple brief audio resources to help people understand key concepts of positive psychology. It could be used for inquisitive coachees.

- **www.randomactsofkindness.org**. This website provides resources on how people can deliver random acts of kindness to others and shares stories of acts undertaken.

References

Bakker, A B (2008) The work-related flow inventory: construction and initial validation of the WOLF, *Journal of Vocational Behaviour*, **72** (3), pp 400–14

Biswas-Diener, R (2010) *Practicing Positive Psychology Coaching: Assessment, activities, and strategies for success*, Wiley, Hoboken, NJ

Biswas-Diener, R and Dean, B (2007) *Positive Psychology Coaching: Putting the science of happiness to work for your clients*, John Wiley & Sons, Inc, Hoboken, NJ

Boniwell, I (2012) *Positive Psychology in a Nutshell: The science of happiness*, Open University Press, Maidenhead

Crowe, T P, Oades, L G, Deane, F P, Ciarrochi, J and Williams, V C (2011) Parallel processes in clinical supervision: implications for coaching mental health practitioners, *International Journal of Evidence Based Coaching and Mentoring*, **9** (2), pp 56–66

Csikszentmihalyi, M (1990) *Flow: The psychology of optimal experience*, Harper and Row, New York

Csikszentmihalyi, M and LeFevre, J (1989) Optimal experience in work and leisure, *Journal of Personality and Social Psychology*, **56** (5) pp 815–22 de Carvalho, J R, Neeskens, B *et al* (2012) Practicing and validating positive psychology coaching: empowering strengths, positive emotions, hope and well-being, *International Journal of Psychology*, **47**, p 626

Deci, E L and Ryan, R M (2000) The 'what' and 'why' of goal pursuits: human needs and the self-determination of behaviour, *Psychological Inquiry*, **11** (4), pp 227–68

Diener, E (2013) Satisfaction with Life Scale, http://internal.psychology.illinois.edu/~ediener/SWLS.html

Diener, E (2013) Scale of Positive and Negative Experiences, http://internal.psychology.illinois.edu/~ediener/SPANE.html

Emmons, R and McCullough, M E (2003) Counting blessings versus burdens: an experimental investigation into gratitude and subjective well-being in daily life, *Journal of Personality & Social Psychology*, **84**, pp 377–89

Fredrickson, B L (1998) What good are positive emotions? *Review of General Psychology*, **2**, pp 300–19

Fredrickson, B L (2001) The role of positive emotions in positive psychology: the broaden-and-build theory of positive emotions, *American Psychologist*, **56**, pp 218–26

Fredrickson, B L (2009) *Positivity: Groundbreaking research reveals how to release the hidden strength of positive emotions, overcome negativity and thrive*, Random House, New York

Gable, S L, Gonzaga, G C and Strachman, A (2006) Will you be there for me when things go right? Supportive responses to positive event disclosures, *Journal of Personality and Social Psychology*, **91**, pp 904–17

Gable, S L, Reis, H T, Impett, E A and Asher, E R (2004) What do you do when things go right? The intrapersonal and interpersonal benefits of sharing positive events, *Journal of Personality and Social Psychology*, **87**, pp 228–45

Govindji, R and Linley, P A (2007) Strengths use, self-concordance and well-being: implications for strengths coaching and coaching psychologists, *International Coaching Psychology Review*, **2** (2), pp 143–53

Grant, A M and Cavanagh, M J (2007) Evidence-based coaching: flourishing or languishing? *Australian Psychologist*, **42** (4), pp 239–54

Grant, A M and Cavanagh, M J (2011) Coaching and positive psychology, in K M Sheldo, T B, Kashdan and M F Steger (Eds), *Designing Positive Psychology: Taking Stock and Moving Forward*, 293–309, Oxford University Press, New York

Grant, A M, Curtayne, L and Burton, G (2009) Executive coaching enhances goal attainment, resilience and workplace well-being: a randomised controlled study, *Journal of Positive Psychology*, **4** (5), 396–407

Green, L S, Oades, L G and Grant, A M (2006) Cognitive-behavioural, solution-focused life coaching: enhancing goal striving, well-being and hope, *Journal of Positive Psychology*, **1** (3), pp 142–49

Kauffman, C (2010) Positive psychology: the science at the heart of coaching, in *Evidence Based Coaching Handbook: Putting best practices to work for your clients*, eds D R Stober and A M Grant, John Wiley & Sons, Inc, Hoboken, pp 193–225

Kauffman, C, Boniwell, I *et al* (2010) The positive psychology approach to coaching, in *The Complete Handbook of Coaching*, eds E Cox, T Bachkirova and D Clutterbuck, Sage, Los Angeles, pp 158–71

Kauffman, C, Silberman, J and Sharpley, D (2008) Coaching for strengths using VIA, in J Passmore (ed), *Psychometrics in coaching*, Kogan Page, London, pp 239–53

Linley, A, Willars, J L and Biswas-Diener, R (2010) *The Strengths Book: Be confident, be successful, and enjoy better relationships by realising the best of you*, Capp Press, London

Linley, P A (2005) Positive psychology and coaching psychology: perspectives on integration, *The Coaching Psychologist*, **1** (1), pp 13–14

Linley, P A (2006) Strengths coaching: a potential-guided approach to coaching psychology, *International Coaching Psychology Review*, **1** (1), pp 37–46

Linley, P A (2011) The strengths of the strengthspotter: individual characteristics associated with the identification of strengths in others, *International Coaching Psychology Review*, **6** (1), pp 6–15

Lyubomirsky, S (2007) *The How of Happiness: A practical approach to getting the life you want*, Piatkus, London

Magyar-Moe, J L (2009) Positive psychological interventions, *Therapist's Guide to Positive Psychological Interventions*, Academic Press, San Diego, pp 73–176

McCullough, M E, Emmons, R and Tsang, J (2002) The grateful disposition: A conceptual and empirical topography, *Journal of Personality & Social Psychology*, **82**, pp 112–27

Peterson, C and Seligman, M E P (2004) *Character Strengths and Virtues: A handbook and classification*, Oxford University Press, Oxford

Proctor, C, Maltby, J *et al* (2011) Strengths used as a predictor of well-being and health-related quality of life, *Journal of Happiness Studies*, **12** (1), pp 153–69

Roberts, L M, Dutton, J E, Spreitzer, G M, Heaphy, E D and Quinn, R E (2005) Composing the reflected best-self portrait: building pathways for becoming extraordinary in work organizations, *Academy of Management Review*, **30** (4), pp 712–36

Ryan, R M and Deci, E L (2000) On happiness and human potentials: a review of research on hedonic and eudaimonic well-being, *Annual Review of Psychology*, **52**, pp 141–66

Salanova, M, Bakker A B and Llorens, S (2006) Flow at work: evidence for an upward spiral of personal and organizational resources, *Journal of Happiness Studies*, **7**, pp 1–22

Seligman, M E P (2002) *Authentic Happiness: Using the new positive psychology to realize your potential for lasting fulfilment*, Free Press, New York

Seligman, M (2007) Coaching and positive psychology, *Australian Psychologist*, **42** (4), pp 266–67

Seligman, M (2011) *Flourish*, Simon & Schuster, New York

Seligman, M, Steen, T, Park, N and Peterson, C (2005) Positive psychology progress: empirical validation of interventions, *American Psychologist*, **60**, pp 410–21

Spence, G B and Grant, A M (2013) Coaching and well-being: a brief review of existing evidence, relevant theory and implications for practitioners, in *Oxford*

Handbook of Happiness, eds S David, I Boniwell and A Ayers, 1009–25, Oxford University Press, London

Spence, G B and Oades, L G (2011) Coaching with self-determination theory in mind: using theory to advance evidence-based coaching practice, *International Journal of Evidence Based Coaching and Mentoring*, **9** (2), 37–55

Steger, M F, Dik, B J and Duffy, R D (2014) Measuring Meaningful Work: The Work and Meaning Inventory (WAMI), *Journal of Career Assessment*

Steger, M F, Dik, B J and Shim, Y (2014) Assessing meaning and satisfaction at work, in *The Oxford Handbook of Positive Psychology Assessment*, ed S J Lopez, (2nd Edn), Oxford University Press, Oxford

Waterman, A S (1993) Two conceptions of happiness: Contrasts of personal expressiveness (eudaemonia) and hedonic enjoyment, *Journal of Personality and Social Psychology*, **64**, pp 678–91

Psychodynamic coaching

03

ULLA CHARLOTTE BECK

Introduction

The aim of psychodynamic coaching is to create change with a purpose (Beck, 2012). That means change that is realistic and permanent. The person being coached – the client – through acknowledgement and insight into his or her own history, personal patterns, inner structure, and into the present context and its dynamics, is enabled to combine past, present and wishes for the future with realistic, feasible actions.

Psychodynamic coaching will typically be aimed at individuals, but it may also help a group who want to understand and change some aspect of their life. The wish for change is quite central. The factors they wish to change may be external, such as relations with others, situations at work or their situation in life, either specifically or more broadly. The wish for change may also be directed towards internal factors such as self-esteem, self-awareness and handling emotions, understanding particular situations or understanding oneself. Both may be included – with the interaction between inner and outer factors. The focal point can vary enormously, from something very precise – a future decision – to something more diffuse – an inner state – unrest and stress. Every individual and every group exists within a system, and most often in several systems at the same time. The dynamics of these systems affect the individual or group, and will be represented in coaching by the unconscious, which is something psychodynamic coaching, through its theoretical foundation, keeps in focus throughout the coaching process.

Psychodynamic coaching starts out from the position that the present situation in life is always bound up with what has gone before. What is going on now is not happening by chance, but is connected with something that happened earlier. The underlying patterns that originate in infancy, childhood and youth have an important bearing on the way situations will be managed later in life. Without awareness of these patterns, they will very probably be repeated again and again. The original patterns are co-designers of the basal ways in which we perceive our surroundings, ourselves, and ourselves in relation to our surroundings. That is why a large part of coaching is concerned with history. Our histories consist of remembered and repressed parts. The history that can be told is inevitably the remembered part – but at the same time the repressed part is told in what could be called the 'subtitling' (Gullestad and Killingmo, 2007; Lemma, 2003). It is necessary in psychodynamic coaching to interpret the 'subtitling' in order to bring about lasting changes.

Psychodynamic coaching is built on the diversified complex of psycho-analytical theory, which in turn is founded on Freud's thoroughly described and evidence-based concept of 'the unconscious' (Freud, 1915, 1921, 1923, 1933). Since the 1920s, psychoanalytical theory and practice have developed in countless areas. This means that there is a highly abundant theoretical basis for coaching. As this kind of thinking has spread to other areas besides individual psychology, the term 'psychodynamic' has gained acceptance rather than psychoanalytical. Psychodynamic refers to the unconscious psychological dynamics and not specifically to the concept of psychoanalytical practice, which can easily be confused with the therapeutic practice of psychoanalysis.

'The unconscious' is a specific term in the theory of the profession, but it is also a familiar everyday expression. When our own actions or the actions of other people are not immediately understandable, for example disproportionate outbursts of anger, or an appointment is forgotten that we really knew we had made, when something is suddenly impossible, or we accidentally say something different from what we meant – a Freudian slip – we often explain it away as something unconscious. Thus even though psychoanalysis and the associated psychodynamic professional associations and environments have had their ups and downs, the expression has spread widely as an immediate and highly valued explanation in popular psychology.

We have in many ways adopted the idea that the mind also consists of forces beyond the control of the conscious will. The situation is quite different in scientific and professional connections. In certain periods the psycho-dynamic approach has been widely accepted in both psychiatry and psychology, accompanied by waves of applicants seeking psychodynamically-based professional training. At other times there was not only stagnation, but even decline. According to Eisold (2009) psychoanalysts and psychoanalytically oriented psychologists have contributed to the decline themselves, by secluding themselves in narrowly exclusive professional associations, and making it very demanding and difficult to qualify to join them, rejecting ideas that psychodynamic functions could be considered far away from 'the couch'. In short, they excluded rather than included others. Naturally, this becomes 'suffocating' and chokes the further development and spread of psycho-dynamic theory and practice. Combining psychodynamic understanding with coaching is precisely an attempt to open up and include. Psychodynamic coaching demonstrates that the psychodynamic approach can certainly be transferred to other methods and surroundings without losing in value.

Postmodern life, with its rapid shifts, overwhelming amounts of information, fierce competition in all areas and enormous demands for performance, has created an epidemic of stress and stress-related conditions. To cope with all this it is increasingly necessary to find room for reflection. There must be a space where it is possible to find out who you are and what you want, where you can try to understand relationships and interactions with others. There must be space to examine challenges and opportunities and to develop a human robustness. We need somewhere to understand the connections between our past and our present, and think about the future, where we can take a break and gather the energy to act – or not to act – in our own lives. We need freedom to take advantage of the opportunities.

Bringing psychodynamic theory and coaching practice together represents a new way of thinking, which in many ways matches the need for a space to reflect, which can create something more than a merely superficial sensation of being in control.

The purpose of this chapter is to give an insight into what psychodynamic coaching is. The chapter seeks to give a broad outline of the theoretical foundations, to describe different methods, and also to illustrate through a case study how psychodynamic coaching can be put into practice in real life.

The theoretical foundations

Psychodynamic coaching draws on the whole of the extensive complex of theory that comprises theories of personality, development, couples and close relations, groups and organizations. Both the older classical theories and the newest theories of mentalization are significant for practical coaching.

Psychodynamic personality and developmental psychology

The point of departure for psychodynamic theory is Freud's concept of 'the unconscious'. The unconscious can be defined as: 'unintended transformations of motive (changes, distortions, redirections of instinctual impulses, wishes or intentions) which can be analysed psychologically' (Olsen, 2002: 5).

Thus the fact that we have 'an unconscious' in us means that we do things, think thoughts and have feelings that in reality arise from different motives from the ones we are aware and convinced of. This is essentially a very provocative assertion – even now, more than a century after Freud formulated it. Freud explained his personality model with the threefold division into Id, Ego and Superego, how the unconscious is formed as the result of repressions. The proposition of the unconscious is provocative and at the same time not surprising – few will claim they have never experienced coming to understand themselves better with hindsight. Or the ability to see others who act *as if* – but where we, because we are not them – and thus we experience it all from the outside and not from the inside – can see that it is really all about something different. However, this proposition of the unconscious takes from us the supposition that we are in control, perhaps triggering considerable anxiety – and it may even be or feel like a threat to our psychological existence – our identity.

Theories have been developed further by other clinically oriented researchers, about how our personalities are formed and what role early childhood plays. The theories were developed though an interplay of criticism of existing models, new discoveries and surprise arising from clinical practice with patients, new thinking, and the collection and systematization of new empirical research. Not everyone agrees on everything. The complex of psychodynamic theory is diversified and inspiring. In the field of personality psychology, the following deserve particular mention.

Melanie Klein (1975) formulated the object relation theory, which gives insight into the relationship of a baby with its mother, and the importance of this relationship later in life. Especially important in psychodynamic coaching are the concepts of *positions*, which are specific and characteristic psychological stages in the child's development, and contribute to the formation of the general ways in which the adult functions psychologically. In particular there are implications for relations with figures in authority. The *splitting mechanism, projections* and *projective identification* are also central concepts with great analytical value in coaching. They make it possible to a greater degree to investigate what belongs to the client and what belongs to the system and the relationships in which the client finds him or herself.

Margaret Mahler (Mahler, Pine and Bergman, 1975) was concerned with how the child becomes itself – and with what she called the *psychological birth*. She studied the relationship between the baby and its mother through three years, and hereby defined the psychological development tasks that the child goes through. The way the child passes through these phases determine how the child will individualize. The process of individualization is critical for the adult's ability to be alone with himself/herself, and to be together with others, while at the same time holding on to him or herself. These concepts are of great value in understanding the client's self image, self-confidence and ability to handle ambivalence, and to be an authority for himself.

Winnicott (1960, 1971, 1990, 2010) contributed with vital central terms that help us to grasp the development of the self, interactions with others and especially the parents and close family – and their importance in the development of *the true self* in contrast with the *false self*. The understanding of the significance of the surroundings – the environment and the atmosphere for our development and social behaviour – can also be ascribed to Winnicott. The concepts of the *holding environment, potential space* and the *transitional object* make possible a deep and differentiated understanding of the meaning of the interactions of the people around the client – and thus of the organization too. This is very valuable when applied to the understanding of the consequences for the client of changes in the organization or changes in the closest relationships. What are the possibilities and limitations that they hold?

Erikson (1977) was concerned with our 'ego development': How do I become me? And how do I develop myself? According to Freud's structural personality model it is the task of the ego to solve the conflict between the id and the superego, or in other words between the instinctual impulses and moral or social control and will. A strong (but not rigid) ego that can find a balance is a great help in a turbulent late-modern working life. The development of the ego forms the basis for identity. In the postmodern world the identity is under many forms of pressure. Erikson's model is of interest in coaching, because it differentiates our understanding and expands our view of opportunities for personal development. Additionally, with his epigenetic model, Erikson draws attention to the fact that development does not end with childhood, but that we develop continually all through life. We build, so to speak, on earlier stages of development, which also means there are chances to repair and correct the way in which the earlier 'steps' were managed. This is a less determinative model than the earlier models for development, and it provides inspiration for the 'way forward' in coaching.

John Bowlby (1988) is accredited with the theory of attachment and the concept of 'inner working models' derived from it. Bowlby was concerned especially with the significance of the mother-and-child relationship, but also with the other family relationships and how the mother and child interact with them. This led him away from the theory of instincts, and over to more biologically founded behaviour studies. Bowlby identified what he called paths of development, which are the formative element in personality structure. To begin with the child has many mutually separated paths, but as time passes, the paths are differentiated more and more, and the number of open paths is reduced. Bowlby believed that the number of possibilities is determined by heredity, while the choice of paths is determined by the environment. The distinctive feature of good attachments is that the individual can form bonds with others (and to systems, groups and organizations), and can also detach from them again. In postmodern life our ability to form bonds and detach them again is constantly brought into play. The changing family and organizational structures that have become possible through cultural liberation and globalization define the infinite numbers of choices open to us. The way we conduct ourselves emotionally through all these choices – whether voluntary or involuntary – is associated with our inner working model for relationships and our attachment patterns. To what extent do we seek security? How do we balance between conflict and continuity?

Heinz Kohut (1990) is associated with the modern psychology of the self, and through him it became an independent theoretical school of thought. Kohut was concerned with various degrees of narcissistic disturbance. Until then, the self had been understood as the ego in action. Kohut defines the self as an overall designation for the whole of the psychological structure –

the personality, and affirms that they are both formed through early relationships. Children are born with narcissistic needs that must be satisfied by others. These are not just any others, but specific others, normally the parents. For the child, the mother is what Kohut calls a self-object. A self-object is an object that the child imagines to be part of itself, or as an extension of itself. All humans have self-objects throughout life, and their function is to stabilize the emotional life and psychological makeup. In connection with coaching and personal development, it is often relevant to look out for the role played by the narcissistic needs. When we see ourselves mirrored in others – what do we see? Is it frustrating? Is it satisfying? Is it a barrier to development? Like Kernberg (1978, 1984, 1994) one can assert that it is a necessity for a leader to possess a realistic self image that enables him or her to be an authority, leading with self-assurance without being authoritarian, and a leader must not be so self-effacing that in the decisions are actually taken by others. The problems associated with authority are often a theme when coaching leaders. Together with Kernberg and Obholzer (Obholzer, 1994), Kohut made it conceptually possible to work on the understanding of authority seriously and with the necessary differentiation in a period when authority has to be borne by the person rather than the formal role.

Daniel Stern (Stern, 1985, 2004; Fonagy, Shore and Stern, 2007) opened up completely new insights through his work on the relationship between mother and child. He demonstrated that the child perceives and experiences far more, and in far more subtle ways than was previously known – or assumed. Stern demonstrated the existence of *mirror neurons*, which make it possible to sense and feel what another person senses and feels. He operates with the concept of the *core self*, which is formed at the age of two to six months. He emphasizes the quality of the mother's presence – she must not simply be there, but must also be attentive and sensitive to the child and the child's inner state. This is called the capacity for *affective harmonization*, ie the ability to understand the child's emotional state as a basis for adapting to it in an accommodating way, which influences and if necessary calms the child. It is expressed verbally, non-verbally and in expressions of mood. The understanding between mother and child is internalized, leaving neural traces, and thus forming the prerequisites that will enable the child to understand other people's states of mind and share feelings with them later in life. In other words these are the prerequisites for empathy and *intersubjectivity*. It is central in connection with coaching leaders to be able to identify and reflect over the client's capacity for empathy, since this is an essential prerequisite for being able to form relationships, and for leaders to be able to create a following. The ability to tune in effectively is a necessary quality in the coach. If no capacity for empathy is unfolded, it is practically impossible to facilitate development together with and for someone else. Stern develops the attachment theory and the theory of inner working models further with his description of *RIG – representations of interactions in generalized form*.

Fonagy, Gergely, Elliot and Target (Fonagy *et al*, 2007; Fonagy and Target, 1996) form the group behind the research that led to the theory of mentalization. Mentalization is the ability to see oneself from the outside and see others from inside at one and the same moment. The concept of mentalization and the therapeutic practice that followed, extending the development of the theory, is the result of a fusion of neural science and a broad understanding of attachment theory. The technical possibilities that have opened up with three-dimensional scanning and measurements of cerebral activity have made it possible to investigate something of what happens in the brain, generated by relationships and social activity. To put it very simply, one could say that evidence has been found that heredity, interacting with earlier relationships and experiences, has a decisive influence on how the personality develops, and that its foundations are neurobiological. It has also been shown how therapy based on mentalization can increase and stabilize the ability to mentalize. This capacity for mentalization – even when under pressure of different kinds – is an essential prerequisite for being able to enter into relationships and maintain them. It is therefore interesting from a coaching perspective. A client who wants to develop, achieve specific goals or become better at dealing with particular situations needs to develop the ability to think and feel in different ways from the ways he or she immediately thinks or feels – but like the others in the relationships he enters into. Breakdowns in mentalization occur when the inner pressure – psychological or physiological – becomes too great. It can manifest itself as: 1) *psychic equivalence*, which means believing the world is as it is experienced. Mental representations are not separated from the external reality. Frightening thoughts are perceived as reality, and investigating alternatives can be experienced as futile; 2) the *teleological mode*, in which mental states are expressed in actions. Instead of reflecting and understanding what lies behind a pattern of actions, a new action or routine is started; 3) the *pretend mode*, in which the inner world is disconnected from the outer world. Feelings are disconnected by pseudomentalization, intellectualization and unconnected explanations; 4) *mind blindness*, when other people's feelings and intentions are neglected. This can lead to abuse or betrayal of others. It is a great help to the psychodynamic coach to be able to identify these states as a precondition for working on them with the client. The theory of mentalization does not provide proof of the existence of the unconscious, but of the central importance of early relationships in the personality through the neural responses – and thereby for the possibilities and limitations of adult life.

One thing all the theories mentioned have in common is the importance attached to childhood. It is precisely there that the basal structures are formed, and the seeds of relational capacity are sown. All life exists in relationships, and it is crucial that we can understand the dynamics behind them when we are coaching.

The concept of the unconscious has moved from being understood as something that belonged and was resident solely in the individual – in body and mind – to the understanding that it is not bound to time and place, but is more a matter of relationships and reflection. The unconscious is to be found *inside* the individual and *between* people in relationships as couples, and in groups, both large and small, and in organizations and in society as a whole. We discover the unconscious in the moments when it is revealed and becomes visible to the inner eye, and thus to consciousness. It is in this transformation from unconscious to conscious that liberation takes place, and the possibilities appear. Examining and uncovering the importance of the unconscious in particular relationships and situations does not necessarily require therapy for indefinite periods. It does require separation and distance, and assumes attention and insight (Stern, 2004; Eisold, 2009).

Psychodynamic group psychology

The complex of psychodynamic theory also comprises theories about groups and theories of what happens in groups. The group is an independent unit that requires its own concepts. Different theories focus on different parts of the group.

Foulkes (1984/1964) sees the group primarily as a healing and constructive phenomenon. The fundamental idea is that humans are social – the individual has been formed as the result of development in the community. We are psychologically born in the social relationships that surround us – in the groups we are members of. We can therefore only be understood in the social networks we take part in. As a consequence of this fundamental idea, people's problems, difficulties and psychological dysfunction must also be understood as having arisen in social networks. The groups that have formed a person have become internalized, and are present inside that person – as a foreground or background – at any time. Foulkes compared the individual person with a node in a neural network. There will be spoken and unspoken communications, conscious and unconscious communication, emotional and thought-based communication, and hypothetical communications between conceptions and fantasies. They go on at the same time and in one group. The communications extend beyond the single individual. In order to grasp this, Foulkes created the concept of the *matrix*. The matrix is a superordinate for the total of states in the group. It consists of the *basic matrix* and the *dynamic matrix*. The basic matrix refers to what the members of the group have in common. The dynamic matrix consists of the specific, ie where the members are different from each other: their history and thus their personalities and their current situations. One of the central concepts that Foulkes builds up in order to grasp what happens in the 'group as a whole' is *reflection*, which is an overall designation for the projections, identifications and anti-identifications that go on between the members. *Condensation* is connected to the way that in group's feelings can be released because members stimulate each other to do so. *Resonance* means that there is a sympathetic response in the group. When one person says something, there will be different responses from different members depending on who they are. A special type of resonance is *polarization*, ie when something arouses opposing feelings in the group.

Bion (1961) sees the group as a place where primitive and destructive processes occur. Bion (Bion, 1961; Armstrong, 2005) believed that people tend to act in groups, and that this tendency originates from our childhood in the family. This group tendency is not an instinct, but one of the conditions of human life. Thus the people who react independently of their group membership are also a group. Bion formed two central concepts that describe a group. The *basic assumption state* describes the state the members get into when the individuals regress because of a threat into a primitive defence position, where individuality disappears and the sense of reality is weakened. This state is the opposite of when the group is in the *working group state*, when it is orientated towards reality and working to achieve its task. Bion localized and described the three general basic assumption states, each of which has its joint fantasy. He called one of the basic assumption states the *dependency group*, in which groups unconsciously imagine that if they blindly and uncritically follow their leader and the group ideas and policies, and keep the rules and regulations, they will stay together and nothing will happen. Another basic assumption state – *the fight or flight group* – is characterized by the fantasy that there is a common enemy, and 'if this enemy can be knocked out or we can flee from it, then we can stay together'. The third basic assumption state is the *pairing group*, in which the members (often a pair – two persons) share an idealistic fantasy that something truly fantastic is about to happen for the group – they are waiting for the 'Messiah'. A common feature of the basic assumption groups is the risk that they are self-perpetuating. It could be called the group's repetitive compulsion.

Rogers (1971, 1992) was the originator of new thinking and movements in group psychology. He retained the idea of the unconscious, and of the vital importance of childhood in later life. He was concerned with the formation of the self, and how it influences the possibilities of living a satisfactory life as an adult. In his opinion a realistic perception of oneself and the situations a person brings himself into is the best guarantee for a satisfactory life. Rogers formed the concepts of the real self and the ideal self. He is a central figure in the group of psychologists who form new training units: *encounter groups*, *sensitivity groups* and *T-groups*. These are three group forms that focus on creating learning and acknowledgement of how humans relate to each other. It is characteristic for the groups that they work with structured tasks that must be carried out, and instead of focusing on the result, the process was analysed and learning was extracted.

Psychodynamic organizational psychology: the system theory

In psychodynamic coaching the individual is always seen as part of a system. We bear the systems with us. We contain the reminiscences from our original systems, primarily the family, but also from school and youth groups. We also bring our present systems with us. If a leader in an organization comes to work on relationships with colleagues, the system is included in the coaching, in the sense that the leader represents part of the organization. She may have become the carrier of the system's dilemmas – and until she acknowledges it, she cannot free herself. The complex of psychodynamic theory also includes a theory for the dynamics of systems. This theory emerged in a fruitful process between thinking, reflection, empirical work in organizations and at conferences on group relationships.

Von Bertalanffy (1968), who formulated the open system theory, sets out from the understanding of the living systems in biology – in the cell. The central elements are the nucleus and the membrane and an understanding of how development is generated by transporting material through the membrane. Miller and Rice (1975) stated that the same principles apply to social systems. The nucleus is the *primary task*, and the membrane is the *boundary* with the surroundings. A healthy social system that is functioning smoothly – a family or organization – must have a clear primary task and a boundary that permits the exchange of input and output with the surroundings. An impermeable boundary will bring life to a standstill, and if the boundary is too open, the result will be difficulty in knowing what is part of the system and what belongs on the outside. With these concepts it is possible to identify the problems of a system. The objective of the system is to survive and develop, and this requires 'sufficient permeability' in the boundary, which it is the leadership's task to create. Contact with the outside world is necessary. Since it is a system consisting of people, the forces and dynamics that people and relationships bring with them and are subject to will also prevail in the system. This adds a psychodynamic perspective to the open system theory. The rational processes in the system are the conscious processes directed at performing the primary task. The irrational processes are unconscious processes that give rise to activities that are not directed towards the primary task, but towards the unconscious motives. The optimal state for a system is when the irrational processes support the rational ones. A system will often consist of several subsystems – and the interaction between these is described in *inter-group psychology*, which has its roots in social psychology. In inter-group psychology all the members of the group are understood as the single individuals they are, but at the same time each is a representative of the whole group. Alderfer (1987) has described how the dynamics between groups form a complexity between the dynamics in the system as a whole, with the dynamics of the individual group, the individual members' personalities and the individual group members' internal relationships. This is an important perspective to be aware of in psychodynamic coaching: what inter-group dynamics are active in the system the client comes from? Is the client the carrier of unconscious motives other than his/her own?

Practice in psychodynamic coaching

The aim of psychodynamic coaching is to create development and learning for the client or the group that has asked to be coached. Within the wish for development and learning there is often a concealed wish for greater freedom. Freedom to work out what one wants, and freedom to let go of goals that are unrealistic and feel comfortable about it. Freedom to stand still and reflect. Freedom from pressure and frustration. Freedom to unfold and feel one's full potential. Freedom to catch sight of and pursue goals that are realistic. Freedom to work in the interests of one's own life. Freedom to take life simply as it comes. Freedom is not taken to mean independence. Nor is it an expectation of escaping from all misfortunes. What is meant by freedom is release from the restraining bands of the unconscious – and freedom from repeating patterns that do not lead to satisfaction. The way to freedom is not easy. The Norwegian author Karl Ove Knausgaard expresses it this way: 'Freedom is destruction plus movement' (Knausgaard, 2008: 220). This captures very well the psychodynamic idea of the interconnection between the fundamental energies that drive us: libido and aggression. Life swings like a pendulum between building up and breaking down. It is elementary: the corn must wither and die to allow a new one to shoot up. Some projects must be abandoned in order to allow others to bear fruit. When you accept one lover, you are at the same time saying no to some others. To make room for freedom it is necessary to let go of something – perhaps other people's expectations, or perhaps one's own ambitions, conceptions of what one can or cannot do, and conceptions and fantasies about other people – what others do, believe and think. Not infrequently, what one has to let go of is the idea of one's own limitations. That is not at all easy. It is often accompanied by anxiety or sorrow, and perhaps ambivalence and perplexity. To do so may be almost impossible, and this is when it becomes obvious that work with coaching is not all a bed of roses. Development is demanding and difficult – but also encouraging and stimulating. It requires cooperation between the coach and client, which can bear and last. In order to set up a relationship that can survive through this, the roles in the task of coaching must be clear.

Practice: tools and techniques

A course of psychodynamic coaching consists of four parts:

1 The first contact.
2 The first coaching session: the goal and framework.
3 The course of coaching – investigation, hypotheses and acknowledgements.
4 Conclusion, evaluation and leave-taking.

The first contact

When the client or client group first makes contact there is – almost always – a lot of information about what the unconscious problem behind the presenting problem is all about. An analysis of the character of the enquiry and the immediate feelings and thoughts the enquiry produces in the coach will often reveal some of the hidden material. This is data from which the coach can form hypotheses. So the coach's work begins right from the first contact. It requires knowledge and training to analyse the material from transference and counter transferences that are presented at the first contact. The awareness of this can easily evaporate – the first contact is often a short telephone call or an e-mail. It is advantageous to establish a fixed working method of registering, so that it becomes a routine. It is important to underline that random sensations and free imagination are no use. As in any other research process, hypotheses and assertions must be documented and justified or proved on a balance of probability. Although a great deal may already be told at the first contact about the material that will manifest itself later, in many cases the discovery may not be clear until the end, when the work is evaluated. Working proactively with this 'discovery' has proved to help sharpen focus during the coaching process.

The first coaching session: objectives and framework

The first coaching session is the first physical meeting between the coach and the client or client group. Two factors are particularly central at this point: the vital precondition for the relational work – the psychological contract and the conclusion of definite agreements on the goal, the cost and the framework. What do they want to change? How do they want things to be at the end of the process? What idea do they have about why precisely that change is desirable? How many sessions should be planned, and how often should the sessions be held? It is important that the client or client group should share the responsibility for these things. It places a useful pressure on the work and sharpens focus – also when working on the resistance that arises along the way. The framework for what is to be done must be clarified at this first session.

The course of coaching: investigation, hypotheses and acknowledgements

What is the client's personal history – or the group's history? Just like individuals, a group has a story with a 'conception', 'birth' and 'growing up'. Work can be done on the story in writing, or through verbal accounts, or drawing can be included as a medium for the narrative. It is a very special task to write one's personal history. It can feel overwhelming, but as a rule it is also exciting. The client often makes contact with episodes that have led a quiet existence in their memories for a long time. The client can be asked a few helpful questions to support the work and bring out relevant data. In particular, *writing* one's story is a special process. It is tempting to delete, revise or embroider the story. As a rule the coach does not know about all that, but it will be present in the client's consciousness. The story supplies data for the coach, who works on it consciously and at different levels: transference and counter transference, here-and-now in what is told; which basal experiences does the client or group have with relationships and with themselves? What are the client's or client group's fundamental values? What is the client's general habitus? This means a fundamental disposition in relation to keeping down anxiety and establishing a 'good enough space' inside and in relation to others (Winnicot, 2010). Which central developmental problems, attachment patterns and valencies are 'in play'? (Olsen, 2002; Klein, 1975, Mahler, 1975; Bowlby, 1988).

The present: the current situation

What is the client's or client group's current context? Which pressures and demands are present, and which are absent in the situation? Which inner pictures – specifically and emotionally – does the client or group have of the surrounding world – the system – that the wish for change is directed towards? How and when do the unsatisfactory situations and states of affairs show themselves? When are they absent? It is important that the investigation of the relevant contexts is thorough and detailed. The catalyst 'clou' is often to be found in the details. It can be a special facial expression when the client talks about a special relation or feeling, a repeated confusion of names, an incorrect use of words, an autonomic response such as a small coughing or breathing. A 'clou' could be the repeated detail that did not make sense in the first place, but after a while – realized in a different way – make sense and a new understanding of what is hidden in the unconscious. It may be helpful to return to the same starting point many times to bring out new elucidations and new data. It is predominantly in the perspective of the present that the system (organization or family) comes into focus. Most of us are connected to several kinds of system, and our understanding of ourselves, of others and of situations is determined by these systems. Therefore the system perspective is crucial to include. It may be important in connection with the acknowledgement of pressures and needs that come from outside, and it is central in connection with the later investigation of realistic possibilities for action.

The future: the expectation of what is to come and what is desired

Some groups and clients have wishes that are unrealistic, and there may be many reasons why they are unrealistic. It is necessary to work on the client's wishes for the future in relation to what has become common knowledge about the client's or client group's options – potentials and limitations. What can be achieved in most cases is the liberation that comes from being able to recognize oneself, and getting to know one's patterns, valences and tendencies in such a way that the person is able to make allowances for them, self-adjust and choose to do something different. It means fewer impulse-generated actions and disappointments. It is the ability to feel, register and choose between several possible, realistic actions in the present. With the future, the task of coaching quite logically is of a hypothetical nature, but it is not purely hypothetical. It is also work with rational data, like a kind of scanning or sounding out of a field, from which information is collected and prognoses can be calculated.

The weighting of the three elements – history, present and future – must be decided in the specific course of coaching, but the decision is not for the coach to make alone. The client or client group and the coach reflect continually over the work in a mental metaposition, and from there it is relevant to discuss whether they should go back to their earlier work, stay where they are, or make a change and drive the process forward. The relationship between the coach and the client or client group is characterized by cooperation and fellowship, but each has an individual role and primary task.

Primary task and role for the coach and client or client group

The primary tasks are defined in the first session, when the goal and framework are agreed upon.

The client's primary task is to open up and speak honestly. The client has to try to open himself/herself to the feelings, thoughts and associations that arise during the process and report them to the coach, and the client must make an effort to come into contact with himself or herself and the roles that appear as coaching progresses, since they provide information about transference factors. The coach's primary task is to take charge of the framework, become involved in the work and put forward possible hypotheses, and let the client know what relevant ideas and possible explanations emerge in the coach's mind. The coach must contribute by obtaining data through questions, structure and assignments etc. The coach's hypotheses and interpretations will be based on a blend of knowledge, experience, data from the client or client group's narratives, continual observations and data from the coach's 'inner world', ie the coach's own associations and counter transferences. If and when there are disturbances in connection with carrying out the primary tasks, these must be brought up as far as possible in reflections on the process, since these will also constitute data that can contribute to the work of development.

The coach works according to his/her knowledge and training, the situation and the current goal. The coach must also support the constructive forces in the relationship. This means drawing attention to the fact if and when unrealistic wishes and ideas creep in. It is possible that it may not seem constructive to the client at the time, to have problems raised about hopes for the future, but it is most constructive in the long term. It is in the relationship that the work is carried out. Heart, mind and memory open up in a secure and honest relationship. To play the coach's part, it is necessary to be 'personally committed through the role'. This means being present emotionally, with attention focused, registering with freely floating attention both to the client and to oneself, and striving to maintain the greatest possible freedom of relationship, while working in a neutral location and not reacting normatively. The coach's engagement consists of open, but timed sharing of data that is relevant to the goal as counter transference, interpretations, hypotheses, observations and associations.

Conclusions, evaluation and leave-taking

Continual evaluations of the process are made with reference to the initially defined goal, and then rounded off with an overall evaluation and summing up of the contributions of both parties and their joint efforts. Rounding off in this way makes it possible to take leave of each other, comment on one's own contribution and make any necessary adjustments, and to explain what was particularly important along the way. It is not only the end of a piece of work. It is also a relationship, where those involved have had feelings about the roles they have taken. It is a human relationship where people have been important to each other. A considered and conscious conclusion makes it possible to come out of the roles again and put into words whatever may be emotionally important. The 'added bonus' of learning that comes from rounding off carefully is that the client gains experience of the pleasure and satisfaction associated with leaving a relationship in a considered manner.

CASE STUDY

The first contact: Tom contacted me on the phone, and asked for an appointment. I asked him to outline for me briefly why he had decided to call. Tom said he was a police officer, and enjoyed his work, but that he and his earlier colleagues had been split up and really moved around a lot in the last couple of years. Departments had been merged, and work allocated differently, and teams were split up. He felt he had been dis-treated. He wanted to find out why it had hit him so hard – he felt dismal and unable to make decisions. He did not think the same thing was happening to his colleagues, so he felt alone with his feelings.

We made an appointment. When the call was over, I mulled over this expression 'dis-treated'. I did not think the word existed. You can be ill-treated and you can be or have been treated, understood to mean cured. I made a note of this consideration.

The first coaching session: When Tom came for the first coaching session, it struck me how big he was. He was almost six foot six, muscular and squarely built. When I stood beside him to welcome him in, I either had to take a step back or tip my head further back than normal to make eye contact. Quite lucky for a policeman, I thought. Later, I discovered that in spite of his size, his face had the expression of a boy.

Tom told me that for the first years of his life he had lived alone with his mother and younger brother. When Tom visited his mother's parents, his granddad would often remark: 'It's a good thing your mum has you, so you can look after everything and be the man in the house.' Later on, Tom had a stepfather. The stepfather had unpredictable moods, and was sometimes violent. He hit Tom's mother, Tom himself and his younger brother. So Tom had many memories of hiding and running away from home. He was frightened and had a guilty conscience about not taking care of things. Tom's story was full of these memories. When Tom was in the tenth form at a continuation school, he decided to become a policeman. His own thought about his choice was that then he could help to prevent that kind of domestic violence and ill treatment of innocent people. A kind of compensation or restitution for the 'sins' of the past. Tom felt himself to be fragile. His thoughts were constantly circling round his work in a negative way. He had lost the satisfaction he felt about his work, and it seemed meaningless. He wanted to understand why he felt like that. Tom's goal was to regain his pride in his work and his job satisfaction, and to restore his belief that working for 'what is right' does make a difference.

The present – the current situation: Tom's previous place of work was merged with another a few months earlier. The team he was part of was disbanded, and they were now scattered in other teams. Tom was assigned to a team with a leader he found uncongenial. He described the leader as one who 'looked upwards' in the system – interested in his own career, and not concerned about the team or job satisfaction. Tom could feel as he talked about it how angry he was with this leader. But he also made excuses for him all the time: 'We are policemen after all, with the same interests – we are a community, and he is good at his job and has to take care of himself.' Every time the anger surfaces Tom inhibited it and denied it. In Tom's idealized version, the police were a big family who showed solidarity and wanted the best for each other. The more we worked on the present situation and the present emotional state, the clearer it became that Tom felt he had been let down, and he was unhappy with the thought that the team leader did not take care of him, and his vision was an illusion. Tom had felt like leaving. He could work in the local authority in the SSP (School – Social services – Police) scheme. As he understood it, then he could help children and young people even more. But then he felt guilty every time he started to write applications – and tore them up. Tom could see the dilemma: it was painful to see that the world was not what he wanted it to be, but his 'solution' of getting out gave him a guilty conscience. There was nowhere he could find what he really wanted deep down – someone to take care of him and create security so he could be free. Someone who would give him permission to follow his own wishes and allow him to have the feelings that he really had when all was said and done. If he stayed, he felt anxious and insecure, but if he left, he would feel guilty and deserve to be 'punished'. The team leader becomes the object of Tom's projections – by pursuing his own interests – in Tom's opinion ruthlessly and illegitimately. And not even the police would take care of him. This was a serious loss for Tom. His experience of the team leader's behaviour and motives were mixed with the feelings Tom originally had about his stepfather. The fact that Tom's experience was 'coloured' by this situation of transference did not alter the fact that the team leader is really not playing his leadership role adequately, and showed no sense of caring. Tom's understanding of his choice of a career (wanting to look after and defend others) served as a refined defence for the real reason: his longing for someone to take care of him, and to know and feel that he was good enough – to liberate him.

The future – the expectation of what is to come and what is desired: Tom had to let go of his idealized notion of the police. He had to let go of the longing for a symbolic father who could supply the needs and things he had missed as a child. He had to grieve over that loss. He had to become his own father.

Tom wanted to be part of a team where the members cared for each other, respected each other on equal terms, and found solutions by working together. This was a realistic wish, that could bring him back to his team, and which he could work on from there. Tom decided to stand for election to the workplace committee, because, as he said: 'Then it is my duty to do it too.' Naturally, Tom was most concerned about himself and his own need for change. In the coaching process we also worked on the part concerned with the system. Because of his valences, Tom was receptive to the silent needs of the system for someone who could absorb and act on the feelings of anger, resentment and powerlessness that had been at play in the process of organizational change. If Tom had not come for coaching, he would very probably have left the police with all the feelings that could not be contained and worked through, both his own and those that were projected into him. It would have helped the system for a short time. However, because they were projections, the source of them would still be in the system, and they would emerge again and again, looking for a new place to attach themselves. Tom stayed on, and found a way to reject the projections from inside the limits of the system, and direct the work with feelings into the workplace committee. This also became the way in which Tom was able to maintain his own task of differentiating what was his and what came from the system. It gave him the freedom to make other choices and thereby have experiences that stimulated other, positive feelings, such as being able to cope with a process of change in spite of loss.

Leave taking: Where Tom is concerned, we can return to the word 'dis-treated'. He said he had been ill-treated, but he could not bear the feeling in the truth of it. He felt that his stepfather had 'a sick mind' and needed treatment, but he was afraid of the consequences if he said it to anyone. He therefore – unconsciously – took 'the evil' on himself. 'I thought it was my fault that everything went wrong, because I ran away, so I was terrified that 'they' would discover it and think I was the one who needed treatment.'

When does psychodynamic coaching work best?

Psychodynamic coaching is suitable when the client/client group itself has a feeling that the current problem is connected to the past. When the problem has proven to be complex and impossible to solve and when there are many systems, roles and emotions involved. Psychodynamic coaching is not therapy, in the sense that it is more basic to the way in which you are in the world. Even though it has the same theoretical point of departure as psychoanalysis and psychoanalytical psychotherapy. It differs from therapy with regard to the question of time and roles in the process. Psychodynamic coaching operates with a shorter timeframe and a coach who intervenes actively. The rule of abstinence, which is known from psychoanalysis, recurs in a highly modified form, in the requirement of freedom from relationships. There must be no relationship between the client and the coach, apart from precisely this relationship of client and coach because it disturbs the freedom to interpret. The coach must not react on impulse or normatively in relation to the client. In psychodynamic coaching the coach makes a directly active contribution, openly drawing in counter transferences, interpretations and hypotheses as data on what is going on within the client, and what is going on in the relationship between the client and the coach. It therefore requires that the client can endure that the coach is not an 'ally' or cannot respond normatively – but is focused on the 'case' – and this therefore can cause frustration in the relationship. This is possible on the precondition that the coach is reflective and self-reflective, with a general stability with regard to impulses and emotions. It is therefore a requirement that the coach must be trained in a way that includes analysing her own history and unconscious patterns through therapy and/or analysis. The client is involved in the work of interpretation, in the course of working on the problem and working through to the goal. The client must therefore be prepared to cooperate and accept not getting answers served through conclusive models or concepts. Traditionally, psychoanalysis and psychoanalytical psychotherapy work exclusively through words and verbal expressions, since speech is regarded as the primary medium for consciousness and the formation of symbols. In psychodynamic coaching, clients can be given 'homework', asked to do drawings or write poems, or more structured tasks can be included, and more didactic steps can be taken, that resemble instruction or information. Role-play or acting out scenes can also be useful in psychodynamic coaching. Psychodynamic coaching focuses more and directly on the desired goal than on the process itself. If the client is a 'couple at work' the coach does not take sides, but the coach is not neutral in relation to the content, since this must link up with the goal and the underlying assumptions. The point of departure for management by two people may for example be that *if* they are to be in management at all, then they must be there together. A division or 'divorce', where one of them remains and is awarded 'parental rights', speaking symbolically, is not possible. Psychodynamic coaching for groups are often most applicable in connection with working groups. The members of the groups have relationships with each other in their daily lives – like the working couple has – so in the context of work they are dependent on each other. However, a process can include sessions of here-and-now work. In this way data can be registered about the interplay between conscious and unconscious communications in the group, and it becomes possible to see the different dynamics unfolding between the members. It is often an advantage to include both structured and non-structured sessions in connection with working couples and with group coaching, as they provided different types of information. In both cases clients should be prepared to work with reality and that includes very often unpleasant feelings.

The coach's interpretations and hypotheses can be discussed, since both the client/client group and the coach are working on the task of investigation, although they each have their own partial task and focus.

Coaching is started in connection with development in working life, as part of management development programmes or special efforts to help new managers, or managers with special tasks, and for HR employees and consultants. During the last 10 years, coaching has been mentioned more and more frequently in connection with management: the coaching manager or a coaching style of management. It is referred to and used as a tool for management (Beck, 2012). This can be understood as an effect of the desire to underline and make plain the caring side of the management role, and there is nothing wrong in what is intended. Nevertheless, power and authority are involved in management relationships, which can make coaching inappropriate in the practice of management. Managers overstep ethical limits if they coach their employees, if it is understood as playing the role of coach in connection with an employee's personal development and/or problems. Managers have the option of sanctions, which they cannot simply set aside for a time. To ask an employee to open up, in the way that is necessary for personal development to take place, is at the very limits of what is permissible. It may constitute an assault. Coaching can take place under these auspices, for example as an external offer to employees, paid for by the organization, but it is – as mentioned above – crucial that the coach and the employee are not in any other form of relationship, and that the coach has a duty of professional confidentiality. The caring side of management must be played out in the decisions made by the manager and in the way she fulfils her role.

So when coaching does not take place under the auspices of working life, but on the client's own initiative, when and for who is coaching the answer to a need for development? It could be the answer for people who need to work through situations and feelings that have arisen after major changes in life, such as problematic relationships in couples, divorce, a death in the family, problems with children, changed roles in life, long-term or chronic illness, unemployment, or persistent difficulties at work. It could also be the answer for people facing existential problems, who need a private space to work with themselves, and in that way heighten their general robustness, capacity for reflection and quality of life. Psychodynamic coaching is attractive for modern people, precisely because of its target-oriented nature, and because it takes less time than many other serious personal developmental methods.

Is it possible to measure the useful value of psychodynamic coaching? If not, how can we then know when it works best? There are numerous difficulties, just as in evaluating and measuring the useful value of various psychotherapies. It is not easy to establish valid objective measurements. Research into psychotherapy shows that the actual therapeutic school of thought is not crucial, but that the therapist's relation to the method and mastery of it make a difference, and that the relationship between the therapist and the patient is decisive (Hougaard, 2004). No scientific studies have been carried out to measure and compare the effects of coaching methods. Besides, the definitions of coaching as a broad phenomenon are so imprecise that this fact alone raises problems. To establish, define, develop and describe psychodynamic coaching as an applicable method is an attempt to update a method of psychodynamic development that fulfils the post-modern requirement for turbo-development without at the same time losing depth and seriousness. It is open to discussion whether it is worthwhile to attempt such a compromise at all, or whether one ends up falling between two stools, so that the result is neither one thing nor the other. Psychodynamic coaching is, as it is described, a method and a way of thinking that has grown from long traditions of both theory and method. That is precisely one of its strengths: the method is solidly planted in the psychodynamic tradition and evidence. What is new consists of:

- the orientation towards action and a goal: the work is motivated by a specific wish on the part of the client or clients;

- the time perspective: it must take place within a limited length of time and not be a lifetime project; and
- the fact that the coach contributes actively and as an equal.

The developing effect lies in the content of the work that is going on, and that work is only possible because of the commitment, the emotional contact and the relationship between the client and the coach. The roles and the tasks of the coach and client are different, but both work with attentiveness and passion from their respective positions.

The work with psychodynamic coaching is relatively new and scientific studies are needed if we are to say something 'hardcore randomized evidence based' about how and when it works the best. The above description is based on that sort of evidence that many years reflexive – practical and theoretical – work experience can provide.

I have found it necessary to modernize the work of psychodynamic development in this way in a world where personal development is a criterion for survival, and where the market is full of dubious offers of development.

We must not compromise on quality when we are dealing with other people's wishes, and our own, for development.

Conclusion

This chapter describes in short what psychodynamic coaching is. The point of departure is the basic psychodynamic understanding of the individual, groups and systems. The psychodynamic concept helps the coach and the client to work together with the complexity in the interactions between the client's inner world and the outer world he is in contact with – concrete or in the mind. They are working on understanding what kind of dynamics and patterns the client brings with him into his world and perceptions. They are working to find some of the actual repressed material – create consciousness – and investigate what the realistic possibilities are. The coach is using her inner world – feelings, associations and professional skills – to do her part of the work. To get to know more of our hidden patterns and blind spots awakens both our anxiety and our curiosity. There is a reason why the repressed is repressed. The coaching process is hard work and demands the capacity to work both with the told material and with the feelings and associations occurred through the process as data in the uncovering. Psychodynamic coaching creates resistance from the client and it requires empathy and mentalization capability in the coach to work with this. The case shows how a personal pattern and valence can be interwoven with the system dynamics. The coaching process promotes understanding and emotional insight so new realistic possibilities can emerge. That's what psychodynamics is about.

Developing yourself as a psychodynamic coach

Developing your skills

Coaches wishing to learn more about and develop their skills in psychodynamic coaching may wish to explore the following practitioner texts:

- Beck, U (2012) *Psychodynamic Coaching: Focus & depth*, Karnac Press, London
- Sandler, C (2011) *Executive Coaching: A psychodynamic approach*, Open University Press, Maidenhead
- Brunning, H (2007) *Executive Coaching: Systems psychodynamic perspective*, Karnac Press, London

Deepening your understanding

Coaches wishing to recommend psychodynamic based self-help books and workbooks for their clients may wish to consider the following:

- Burgo, J (2012) *Why Do I Do That?: Psychological defense mechanisms and the hidden ways they shape our lives*, New Rise Press, Chapel Hill, MC

References

Alderfer, C P (1987) An intergroup perspective on group dynamics, in J W Lorsch (Ed), *Handbook of Organizational Behavior* (pp 190–222), Prentice Hall, Englewoods Cliffs, NJ

Armstrong, D (2005) *Organization in the Mind: Psychoanalysis, group relations, and organizational consultancy*, The Tavistock Clinic Series, Karnac, London

Beck, U C (2012) *Psychodynamic Coaching: Focus and depth*, Karnac, London

Bion, W R (1961) *Experiences in Groups and other Papers*, Tavistock, London

Bowlby, John (1988) *En sikker base*, Frederiksberg 1994, Det lille forlag

Eisold, K (2009) *What you don't know you know*, Other Press, New York

Erikson, E H (1977) *Barnet og samfundet*, Hans Reitzels, Copenhagen

Fonagy, P (1999) Memory and therapeutic action, *International Journal of Psychoanalysis*, **80**, pp 215–23

Fonagy, P, Gergely, G, Elliot, L J and Target, M (2007) *Affektregulering, mentalisering og selvets udvikling*, Akademisk Forlag København

Fonagy, P, Shore, A N and Stern, D N (2007) *Affektregulering i udvikling og psykoterapi*, Hans Reitzels Forlag København

Fonagy, P and Target, M (1996) Playing with reality I, *International Journey of Psychoanalysis*, **77**, pp 217–33

Fonagy, P and Target, M (1997) Attachment and reflective function: their role in self-organisation, *Development Psychopathology*, 9, pp 679–700

Foulkes, S H (1984/1964) *Therapeutic Group Analysis*, Maresfield Reprints, London

Freud, S (1915) *The Unconscious. S.E.*, *14*, Hogarth, London

Freud, S (1921) *Group Psychology and the Analysis of the Ego. S.E.*, *18*, Hogarth, London

Freud, S (1923) *The Ego and the Id. S.E.*, *19*, Hogarth, London

Freud, S (1933) *New Introductory Lectures on Psycho-Analysis. S.E.*, *22*, Hogarth, London

Gullestad, S and Og Killingmo, B (2007) *Underteksten – Psykoanalytisk Terapi i Praksis*, Kbh, Akademisk Forlag

Hougaard, E (2004) *Psykoterapi og Forskning*, DpF 2. udgave Kbh.

Kernberg, O (1978) Leadership and organizational functioning: organizational regression, *International Journal Group Psychotherapy*, *28*, pp 3–25

Kernberg, O (1984) The couch at sea: the psychoanalysis of organizations, *International Journal Group Psychotherapy*, *34*, pp 5–23

Kernberg, O (1994) Leadership styles and organizational paranoiagenesis, in J Oldham and S Bone (Eds), *Paranoia: New psychoanalytic perspectives*, (pp 61–69), International Universities Press, Madison, Conn

Kernberg, O (1998) *Ideology, Conflict and Leadership in Groups and Organizations*, Yale University Press, New Haven

Klein, M (1975) *Envy and Gratitude and Other Works*, The Free Press, New York

Knausgaard, K O (2008) *Min kamp*, Bd. I, København: Lindhardt og Ringhoff

Kohut, H (1990) *Selvets psykologi*, Hans Reitzel, Copenhagen

Lemma, A (2003) *Introduction to The Practice of Psychoanalytic Psychotherapy*, Wiley, West Sussex, England

Mahler, M S, Pine, F and Bergman, A (1975) *The Psychological Birth of the Human Infant*, Basic Books, New York

Miller, E J and Rice, A K (1975) Selections from systems of organizations, in A D Colman and H Bexton (Eds), *Group Relations Reader 1* (pp 43–68), AK Rice Institute, Washington

Obholzer, A (1994) Authority, power and leadership: contributions from group relations training, in Obholzer, A and Roberts, V (Eds) *The Unconscious at Work*, Routledge, London

Olsen, O A (2002) *Psykodynamisk Leksikon*, Gyldendal, København

Rogers, C (1971) *Om encountergrupper*, Jespersen og Pios, Copenhagen

Rogers, C (1992) *The characteristics of a helping relation*, Harvard Business School (Paper), Boston, MA

Stern, D (1985) *The Interpersonal World of the Infant*, Basic Books, New York

Stern, D (2004) *The Present Moment in Psychotherapy and Everyday life*, WW Norton and Company Inc, New York

Von Bertalanffy, L (1968) *General System Theory. Foundations, Development and Application*, George Braziller, New York

Willi, Jürg (1984) The concept of collusion – a combined systemic psychodynamic approach to marital therapy, *Family Process*, 23

Winnicott, D W (1960) *The Maturational Processes and Facilitating Environment*, The Hogarth Press and the Institute for Psycho-Analysis, London

Winnicott, D W (1971) *Playing and Reality*, Tavistock, London

Winnicott, D W (1990) *Home is Where We Start From*, Penguin Books, London

Winnicott, D W (2010) *The Family and Individual Development*, Routledge Classics, London

Narrative coaching

04

DAVID DRAKE AND REINHARD STELTER

Introduction

While a narrative frame is relatively new in the fields of psychotherapy and coaching, stories have been an essential component of cultures and communities since the dawn of time and are fundamental to the way we make sense and meaning. We use stories to structure our experience as 'events' in space and seek to join them together in a sensible causal timeline in keeping with the fact that our brains use space and time as primary coordinates (see Schank, 1990). In many ways, our identity becomes a reflection of the embodied schemas we adopt over time and the stories we keep individually and collectively telling ourselves that reinforce them. As such, they are at the core of what it means to be human – as reflected in our biology, ontology, epistemology and cosmology – and a natural medium for use in coaching. Narrative coaches are, therefore, keenly interested in what Foucault (1965) called people's 'theory of events', particularly as they wrestle with existential issues and choices in their life and work.

We believe that people can increase their capacity for *intimacy* (making connections) and *agency* (making contributions) (Bakan, 1966; McAdams, 1985) and live more authentic, meaningful and fulfilling lives (Polkinghorne, 1988; Sarbin, 1986) by telling and living their stories in new ways. This is because our stories shape how we see what is happening within and around us and enable us to mentalize (Fonagy, 2001) in terms of what might be happening for others. This evolutionary imperative for individual and collective survival is reflected in the power many coachees experience when they work at deep levels with their stories. Narrative coaches bring a philosophy and a set of practices to help people do the work of reconfiguring their stories and their lives. This chapter provides an overview of the origins of narrative coaching, some of its current practices and a few of its future possibilities. In doing so, it offers the premise that coaching is as much about a philosophical orientation to people and their stories as it is about a technical skill set.

The early foundations of narrative coaching were set out by David Drake (2003, 2004a, 2004b, 2007, 2008a) in the United States, Reinhard Stelter (2007, 2009; Stelter and Law, 2010) in Denmark and Ho Law (Law, 2007; Law, Ireland and Hussain, 2007) in the United Kingdom. As the field of coaching has evolved, so too has our approach to this work – both in our own careers and in comparison to one another as scholar-practitioners. Drake has focused more on developing transformative narrative practices adapted from other disciplines (eg, psychodrama, gestalt, family constellations, mindfulness and trauma recovery) and Stelter has focused more on developing a deeper understanding of the philosophical foundations and collaborative nature of narrative practice. The growth of the field can be seen in the hundreds of coaches around the world who are integrating narrative coaching into their practice and taking it in new directions.

Narrative coaching provides a safe and structured space in which people can hear themselves tell their stories and experiment with new ones – without the need for specialized terminology or normative labels. Instead, it focuses on the actual lived experience and enacted narration in coaching conversations as the currency of change. Coaches play an important role, then, in helping people to re-author their stories about themselves, others and life itself in service of the developmental tasks at hand. In doing so, they recognize that stories do not exist as intact objects in coachees' minds, but rather emerge in a co-creative process between the coachee(s) and the coach (Gergen and Gergen, 2006; Kraus, 2006), serve a variety of functions (Barthes, 1975) within and beyond sessions, and are more social and embodied in nature than is often acknowledged (see Drake, 2014).

As such, narrative coaches pay significant attention to the 'field' between their coachees and themselves (see Drake 2003, 2007) as the container for change and monitor their patterns of formulation (Drake, 2010) as the stories they tell themselves about what is going on and how they decide, communicate and act as a result. Their primary aims are to assist coachees in developing a greater sense of acuity, agency and/or authenticity in terms of their stories; a more mature mindset, more generative possibilities for behaviours; and a more positive impact on their environments. To do so, narrative coaches work with the literal and symbolic material in coachees' stories in real time, to release and/or reconfigure any narratives that no longer serve them; step across the threshold into new ones; and make new choices, take new actions and flourish as a result.

The first part of this chapter focuses on the philosophical foundations and evidence-based approaches that underpin narrative practices such as coaching. In doing so, we look at evidence holistically and from both a theoretical and empirical perspective. The second part looks at some narrative coaching practices, tools and techniques. The third part offers a view on why and when practitioners would find particular value in using a narrative approach. The fourth part focuses on a case involving a client of one of the authors (DD) and offers both a critical analysis and a professional reflection on working narratively. The final part offers concluding remarks about the past, present and future of this work and why narrative coaching is both timeless and timely.

Evidence-based approach to narrative coaching

In her history of the narrative turn in the social sciences, Czarniawska (2004) outlined the three main fields that fed into what became narrative studies and are, therefore, key to understanding narrative coaching: 1) literary theory; 2) humanities; and 3) psychology. This aligns with Drake's (2009a) view that narrative coaching draws on: 1) *narrative structure* to understand the material that is narrated and enable the reconfiguration of stories; 2) *narrative processes* to understand the dynamics in the narrative field and guide people across transitional thresholds; and 3) *narrative psychology* to understand humans as narrators in support of their development and performance. Drake's (Drake, 2012; Drake and Wycherley, 2013) narrative design model integrates these three fields into a unified process of change that can be used in coaching to work with the cognitive, discursive and dispositional aspects of narratives (Gergen and Gergen, 2006).

We would propose that narrative practices are based on the following theoretical pillars: 1) social constructionism and post-structuralism; 2) phenomenology and existentialism; 3) narrative structure and literary analysis; and 4) narrative psychology and social sciences (eg anthropology). Narrative coaching is more deeply tied to a strong philosophical foundation than most other approaches because of its holistic focus on the building blocks of human experience and development at both individual and collective levels. Stelter (see 2009, 2014) has done extensive work on these philosophical foundations for narrative practice as reflected in pillars one and two below, and Drake (see 2007, 2008a, 2014) has done extensive work on the developmental processes in narrative practices as reflected in pillars three and four below. Let us begin with one of the cornerstones of narrative work.

1. Social constructionism

The strengths of social constructionism lie in its epistemology – and the subsequent challenge to the notion of universal truths (see Kvale, 1992) – and its support for the notion of 'authorship' that is central to narrative practice. The introduction of social constructionism in psychology can be found in the early work of Kenneth Gergen (1973) where he emphasized that all knowledge is historically and culturally specific and that the development of a contemporary psychology requires the inclusion and understanding of social, political and economic phenomena. This requires a sociocentric perspective (see Bourdieu, 1993) and a focus on the role of relationships and communities in shaping both psychological and social phenomena. As such, his work offers a challenge to coaches who operate within an atomistic or individualistic set of theories and practices to step into a more contextual and co-constructed frame. More recently, Gergen (2009) developed the notion of 'relational beings' and underscores how our identities, interactions and institutions are co-created and co-acted through dialogue and social interaction.

Post-structuralism

Post-structuralists do not see literary texts as having one single purpose and interpretation. As a result, they conclude that the reader creates meaning and forms a specific perspective through their engagement with a text. They break with the understanding of one right and true view. Instead, they assume that many possibilities and worldviews are possible and that stories may hold multiple possible interpretations and, thus, multiple realities. The notion of a fixed meaning is destabilized in order for new understandings to unfold (Derrida, 1978). According to White (2004), this involves processes of deconstruction that critically examine the taken-for-granted understanding of life and identity in order to 'exoticize the familiar', ie, to break with one's original intimate relationship with certain ways of living and thinking, go on a journey of discovery in one's own life, and eventually form a new plot for selected stories.

2. Phenomenology and existentialism

Phenomenology began with the German philosopher Edmund Husserl (1971/1927) and it represents a theoretical understanding that focuses on the phenomenon itself, eg how things appear to oneself. He speaks of a 'descriptive psychology' where the point of departure for psychological examinations is people's perception and experience of a phenomenon (Ihde, 1977) and how they attribute meaning to the world in which they are a part. As such, phenomenology may be considered a true experiential science and a method for exploring oneself and others. This can be seen in their development of *epoché*, an empirical method that allows for an open approach to the phenomenon through bracketing one's immediate judgement and interpretation of a situation.

Phenomenology looks to the present-moment and embodied experiences with the aim of enabling the individual to focus on *specific situations* that he or she is involved in. This situation-specific perspective helps establish a *context* that both the coach and coachee can refer to even as the focus is on the coachee's lifeworld in sessions. 'Lifeworld' is a concept from the tradition of existential phenomenological theory (Husserl, 1931; Merleau-Ponty, 2012) which captures the individual's everyday understanding and reality while fully recognizing that this understanding is largely pre-reflexive and therefore likely to be unarticulated. A narrative coach, therefore, focuses on the situated aspects as presented in stories and helps coachees to dive into their lifeworld through facilitating an in-depth, experiential immersion in and examination of the situation's existential nature and complexity (see Spinelli, 2010) and a verbalization of issues that are often rooted in their habits and action routines. This focus on the phenomena of elemental human emotions, experiences and existential pursuits is served well by a narrative approach since that is what stories are designed to communicate.

3. Narrative structure and literary analysis

The study of narratives from a literary perspective focuses on the structure and analysis of texts in order to deepen our understanding of their significance and purpose. Burke (1969) identified the central elements of a narrative as a Pentad: 'what was done (act), when and where it was done (scene), who did it (agent), how he did it (agency), and why (purpose)'. Bruner (2002) later added the 'coda' as a sixth element to refer to the meaning and implications of stories. With the rise of hermeneutics came a growing interest in the analysis of the context and the interactions of the text and the reader – as reflected in the shift from 'stories-as-objects' to 'stories-in-context' (Boje, 1998). With the rise of social technologies in the 21st century has come a growing interest in the dynamic interactions between readers (and collectively with texts) and the diverse subtexts in play.

Methods such as narrative therapy and narrative coaching, therefore, see stories as situated, emergent and co-constructed 'texts' that have the potential for perpetuating hegemonies or sparking liberation. Therefore, it is critical for coaches to understand narrative structure in order to expertly listen to people's stories and help coachees to reconfigure these elements to create new possibilities. Stories provide powerful openings because they bring to the surface how people construct and navigate their world, the discourse that is available and what else might be possible, the dominant cultural and contextual narratives that affect them, and points of leverage to accelerate their growth. While psychology has emerged as the dominant discourse in coaching, coaches would do well to also understand narrative structure and literary analysis if they want to excel at working with coachees and their stories.

4. Narrative psychology and social sciences

Identity

William James was a seminal figure in bringing a narrative frame to psychology. For example, he (1927/1892) wrote about the distinction between the *I* (the subject) and the *Me* (the object) – a distinction carried forward as the *self-as-knower* and the *self-as known* (Hermans, 2004) and the *author* and the *actor* (Mancuso and Sarbin, 1983). 'This dialectic reflects the ongoing tensions for people in negotiating their narrative identity over time as they move between presenting identities that are socially acceptable and functional (*Me*) and embodying identities that are authentic and consistent with how they see themselves (*I*)' (Drake, 2009a). Scholars such as Carol Gilligan (1982) and Peter McLaren (1993) extended this dialectic by highlighting, respectively, the relational and liminal nature of identity formation. Further work has been done to frame the dialectic as *Me* and *We* – as seen in the *optimal distinctiveness model* of identity (Brewer, 2003; Brewer and Pickett, 1999) in terms of internal and external forces for inclusion versus uniqueness; and the *optimal balance model* of identity (Kreiner *et al*, 2006) in terms of situational identity demands/forces for integration versus individual identity tensions/forces for differentiation.

These extensions of James' original work reflect a broader challenge coachees face to retain a sense of coherence, continuity and contentment in terms of their identity. Their search for identity (or, more truthfully, identities) has become a complex process as reflected in their portfolio, often pastiche lives (Gergen, 1991), and the third spaces (Bhabha, 1990) in which they increasingly operate. Keupp *et al* (1999) have proposed the term 'patchwork identity' to reflect the notion that we construct ourselves and behave in a variety of ways depending on our current context – though even then we are often faced with multiple identity pressures. The individual 'patches' in the quilt describe the multiplicity and variety of possible identities, roles and actions. Even so, when a person's identity patchwork is viewed as a whole, a coherent impression tends to emerge despite the diversity of the individual patches or self-presentations (see Stelter, 2014). This is consistent with the distinction between our overall narrative identity and the core stories from which it is composed and in which we are embedded.

Identity is anchored in two basic orientations people have in interacting with their environment: striving for stability, consistency and continuity as the basis for safety and security; and striving for agility, novelty and discontinuity as the basis for exploration and growth (Drake, 2008a, 2009b). These are inextricably linked in specific action contexts (Stelter, 2014) and are shaped by coachees' narratives and how they interact with them. We consider it crucial to link these two orientations in coaching to foster greater integration between coachees' awareness and wellbeing *and* coachees' action and growth. The coaching dialogue can thus be seen as a process of identity negotiation and integration that enables coaches to extend and sustain their development.

Therefore, we see the coaching dialogue as: a) describing, reflecting on and speaking about the coachee's experiences related to their current situation; b) exploring and reflecting on their self-presentation in related social contexts (Goffman, 1959); c) gaining new insights and more meaningful options as a result; and d) integrating and sustaining the new self-narration over time (see Drake, 2012). By telling stories of their experiences within and beyond coaching sessions, coachees can better connect their subjective realities to the challenges of the social world. Identity development is thus an integrative process balancing individual, experiential aspects on the one hand and relational, interactive aspects on the other. In this process of identity negotiation, coachees are invited to reflect on, experience and test new stories and may temporarily adopt what Ibarra (1999) calls a 'provisional self' as part of their transition.

Play

An underappreciated element in people's growth through coaching is their willingness to 'play' in exploring new possibilities for their narratives and identities (see Drake and Wycherley, 2013). As it turns out, what children experience through play has a lot in common with adults' experience in developing themselves and making transitions. Both require: 1) re-aligning identity and role expectations in order to be successful (Hall, 1971); 2) negotiating between 'identities claimed' and 'identities granted' (Bartel and Dutton, 2001); 3) navigating the threshold between fantasy and reality (Ibarra and Petriglieri, 2010); 4) circumscribing activities within boundaries and limits in time and space (Mainemelis and Ronson, 2006); and 5) integrating body, spirit and mind at a higher level yet in a non-threatening way (Erikson, 1950). Incorporating a safe space for play enables both children and adults to experiment with releasing and rehearsing identities they may need to meet their current or anticipated needs and to try out new and untested behaviours (Drake, 2007, 2008a; Ibarra, 1999, 2005; Kolb and Kolb, 2010). While children are using play to help form their ego structure, adults can use play within coaching to suspend their usual ego structures in order to re-form their identity to meet their evolving needs (see Ibarra and Petriglieri, 2010).

Development

The literature on child development also has relevance in understanding the nature and function of narrative work in coaching adults: 1) Bowlby's (1988) work in attachment theory and its notion of a secure base that provides an infant with both a sense of safety and the confidence to explore; 2) Winnicott's (1965) notion that parents can provide a 'holding environment' for the developing child and the need to address the 'false self' he or she develops to survive; 3) Horney's (1945) notion of 'divided wishes' as a source for neurosis and the three patterns of response that are formed (moving away, against and with); and 4) Piaget's (1962) identification of imitation/accommodation and play/assimilation that reflect the tensions we face between preserving safety/the desire for inclusion and seeking self-expression/the desire for uniqueness and differentiation.

Taken together, we can see in these bodies of work the origins of many of the issues that coachees bring to sessions. At the same time, they offer us insights on how to help coachees have new experiences they can use to reconfigure their often long-held narrative patterns. We would define a narrative pattern as 'a habitual way of framing one's experience that reinforces a set of expectations, actions and rewards'. A key principle in working with these patterns is to focus on one thing at a time, such as a bird circling a tree. For example, coaches can work with a coachee to increase her ability to self-regulate in situations she finds stressful by inviting her to enact a recent related experience, identify the developmental threshold that is involved for her, and step across by embodying a new story/action in real time. Narrative coaches can also (appropriately) use practices based in this work to help clients access preverbal patterns in order to make deeper shifts in how they think, relate, communicate and/or act. These patterns largely operate at non-conscious and somatic levels, but they can be made conscious and malleable through coaching (see Siegel, 1999; Wallin, 2007). One of the tensions coaches face in doing so is how to intervene in ways that address a coachee's core issues while remaining in integrity with their own capabilities and contractual commitments. Even so, this work is important because – as Vygotsky (1987/1934) noted – what a coachee does in collaboration with the coach today they will likely be able to do more independently and capably tomorrow.

Learning

Echoing the contemporary view of stories, a situated, social and context-dependent view of learning (Lave and Wenger, 1991) has largely replaced more traditional views that were often associated with individual rote acquisition of simple action patterns, cognition processes and/or normative information (see Freire, 1970). As a result, there is an increasing focus in learning on the importance of a 'growth mindset' (Dweck, 2008), intrinsic motivation, meaningful application and social processes. In light of this, Drake (2014) has developed 'narrative design' as a new approach to coaching that integrates mindsets, behaviours and environments in support of agile, yet sustainable, learning and development. Working in this integrative fashion is more effective than traditional approaches based in isolated development goals that are often disconnected and increasingly insufficient for the complex situations we face.

Narrative coaches see learning as a *transformative* process (Mezirow, 2000; Illeris, 2004) in which people can see and interpret their experiences – and their stories about these experiences – in new ways. Mezirow (2000: 14) describes it as:

> the process of becoming critically aware of how and why our presuppositions
> have come to constrain the way we perceive, understand, and feel about
> our world; of reformulating these assumptions to permit a more inclusive,
> discriminating, permeable, and integrative perspective; and of making decisions
> or otherwise acting upon these new understandings.

This reinterpretation generally involves reflection processes to explore the perceptions and assumptions inherent in coachees' stories; experiential processes to generate new understandings and configurations of certain narrative elements, and social processes to provide avenues for new ways of acting and communicating. Narrative coaching uses a whole person approach that accounts for individual, biographical factors as well as collective, cultural factors and works at all levels (eg cognitive, emotional, somatic, spiritual, relational, ecological) to foster more lasting and transformative learning.

Social sciences

Rites of passage

We will focus here on anthropology, and rites of passage in particular, because it places a coachee's development in a contextual frame in support of the mutual evolution of individuals and their environments. Rites of passage provide a theoretical and practical roadmap for working with people's stories as they move through transitions and development – particularly in addressing the liminal aspects that are often marginalized. Campbell's (1973) work on the hero's journey, van Gennep's (1960) work on rites of passage and Turner's (1969) work on using this model in broader cultural life are important resources. As part of a recent research project Drake (Drake and Wycherley, 2013) offered four contributions to this literature that are relevant for narrative practitioners: 1) expanded the traditional rites of passage model from one threshold to four thresholds through the introduction of the narrative design model; 2) positioned thresholds as a useful frame for understanding the dynamics of identity work as coachees negotiate tensions between their personal and social identities; 3) extended the role of play into adult development; and 4) outlined what coachees may need at each threshold in terms of identity work in order to move on to the next stage of their transition and/or development.

Building on the classic rites of passage framework, the narrative design model (Drake, 2012; Drake and Wycherley, 2013) depicts a person's movement between their inner worlds (eg identities, beliefs, attitudes) and their outer worlds (eg states, roles, statuses) and between their past worlds (eg career path, old role(s), organizational culture) and their future worlds (eg career aspirations, succession planning and organizational vision). A unique feature of the model (Figure 4.1) is that it integrates the flow of narrative structure, the flow of development and transitions, and the flow of a narrative coaching session into an integrated process in which change is occurring at multiple levels simultaneously.

The four stages in the model are seen as natural points along a spiral of change and development rather than as a set of process-driven steps to be taken: 1) *Situate*, which focuses on 'what IS true for me?'; 2) *Search*, which focuses on 'what if I told my story like this?'; 3) *Shift*, which focuses on 'what matters most to me now?'; and (4) *Sustain*, which focuses on 'what works better as a result?'. This human-centred approach to coaching moves beyond modernist assumptions, linear development models, extroverted goal orientation and lingering biases toward behaviourism to create a truly post-professional and integrative approach to developing people. It shifts the emphasis from the coach and coaching methodologies to the coaching relationship and the stories that emerge there. In the end, it is about their journey not our jargon.

Thresholds

Each of the four stages in narrative design is separated from the one that follows by a threshold, a doorway that marks a shift in attention in terms of

FIGURE 4.1   Narrative design model

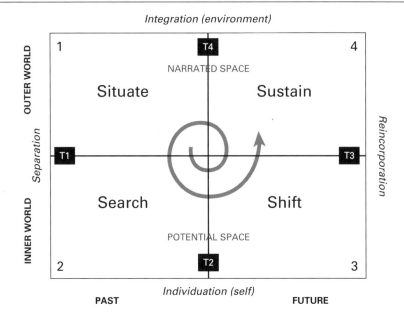

what is happening for the person in transition, eg from an outer loss to an inner journey, from a past orientation to a future imagination. Eliade (1959: 24) described the threshold as 'the limit, the boundary, the frontier that distinguishes and opposes two worlds – and at the same time the paradoxical place where these worlds communicate'. Thresholds are often 'characterised by changes in decisional balance ... between the perceived costs and benefits associated with engaging in a particular behavior' (Moore, 2005: 400). As such, thresholds can be seen as both a doorway and the movement through it, and coaches can be seen as guardians at these gates to support people in their decision making. To move through these passages requires respect for the process and a guide for the journey because the forces at play there offer great potential but are not for the ill-prepared. As such, it is often suggested to focus on one threshold at a time, in keeping with Fredrickson's (2006) 'broaden-and-build' approach.

The notion of thresholds has been picked up in other disciplines related to narrative coaching. Meyer and Land (2003) developed the notion of 'threshold concepts' in learning that are transformative, integrative, irreversible and troublesome and, as a result, provide much the same challenge for our thinking and practice as thresholds in development. In Lewin's (1951) work on field theory, he posited that groups and individuals operate in a 'field' defined by a set of opposing forces between them. He believed that changes in people's behaviour stem from changes in the forces within the field, particularly at the boundaries [thresholds] where they meet. Drake's work in narrative design addresses the same theme in advocating for the integration of our shadows to temper and mature our strengths – a process often forged from the energies at a threshold. Overall, thresholds offer a useful frame for working with coachees' stories in the moment because they represent potential openings for step changes in their development.

Empirical evidence

We share a common understanding of 'evidence' as seen from a relational and applied perspective (see Barkham *et al*, 2010 on practice-based evidence). We view evidence as a dynamic process that informs the decisions made in coaching, emerges from what is generated in the conversation, gleans meaning from the results and feeds back into the conversation and the broader evidentiary base (Drake, 2014). In doing so, we reject the narrow and positivistic discourse on evidence in favour of a broader approach to evidence that is more closely tied to and useful for practice. Consistent with the four elements of the Mastery Window (Drake, 2008b, 2011, 2014), we believe that decisions in coaching should astutely draw on personal reflexivity, valid and relevant research, professional experience, and contextual awareness on behalf of coachees and the environments in which they live and work.

Given the values at the heart of narrative practice – the direct experience of human phenomena, the advocacy for alternate discourses, the recognition of collective and non-conscious forces affecting our narration, and the commitment to a non-reductionist orientation – it is not surprising that most narrative research is descriptive and qualitative in nature. However, scholars such as Abma (1999); Clandinin and Connelly (2000); Gergen and Davis (2005); Lieblich, Tuval-Mashiach and Zilber (1998); Mattingly (1991); Mishler (1995); Ollerenshaw and Creswell (2002); Pals (2006) and Rappaport (1993) have laid down a strong foundation of narrative analysis and research in other disciplines from which coaching could benefit. We would both like to see more opportunities for narrative researchers and narrative practitioners to share their respective bodies of evidence with one another in order to leverage their respective insights and advance their respective practices.

The only randomized controlled study we are aware of was conducted by one of the authors (RS) (Stelter, 2014; Stelter, Nielsen and Wikmann, 2011). The overall goal of this study was to examine the influence of narrative collaborative group coaching in the career development, self-reflection and general wellbeing of young sports talents with the purpose of facilitating the integration of their athletic career, educational requirements and personal lives. The study was based on a randomized, controlled design with 77 subjects, 31 of whom participated in group coaching, while 46 were assigned to the control group. All the participants filled out a validated questionnaire prior to the study, at the midway point, immediately after the final intervention session and five months after the end of the intervention. The findings showed significant improvements among the subjects who participated in group coaching. Figure 4.2 illustrates how the 12-week-long coaching intervention influenced the level of *social recovery*[1]; this positive effect was also present in comparisons between the situation before the intervention and the situation five months after completion of the intervention.

FIGURE 4.2   Positive development in social recovery among the group coaching participants

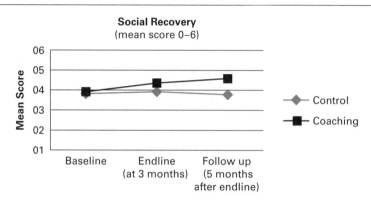

Positive effect of group coaching (measured immediately before the beginning of and immediately after the completion of the intervention). Adjusted for baseline scores, coaching group had 0.381 higher social recovery score after 12 weeks compared to control group. Effect size was medium (r = 0.24, p = 0.038).

Positive long-term effect of group coaching (measured immediately before the beginning of and five months after the completion of the intervention).

Adjusted for baseline scores, coaching group had 0.584 higher social recovery score at follow-up compared to control group. Effect size was moderate (r = 0.275, p = 0.035).

No long-term effect of group coaching (five months after completion).

Adjusted for week 12 scores, coaching group had 0.359 insignificant (p = 0.247) higher social recovery score at follow-up compared to control group. Effect size was low (r = 0.163) and insignificant (p = 0.247).

Practices: tools and techniques

Coachees perceive and experience the world (and their place in it) and act on the basis of the stories they tell and that are told about them. One of the challenges in bringing about and sustaining change is that there is often a reinforcing loop between people's expectations *and* experiences that ensures that their views of themselves and the world remain intact (Siegel, 1999). Swann and Read (1981: 371) remarked: 'Through such processes, people may create – both in their minds and in the actual environment – a social reality that verifies, validates and sustains the very conceptions that initiate and guide these processes.' A key process in narrative coaching is making these loops visible in a non-judgemental fashion so that coachees can act with greater awareness and choice and widen the neural paths associated with a new story. In this sense, as Hewson (1991) notes, the new story is not a turn-off from the habitual old road, but the continuation of a nascent, underutilized road – one on which the person had occasionally been travelling without previously recognizing they were doing so.

At the same time, if coachees are to sustain new behaviours or new results, they must embody an identity and discourse from which to do so and from which the desired actions naturally (in time) arise. If they are to sustain this new identity, they need to regularly enact these new forms of engagement and the stories that go with them. This is true because people generally can only see as far as their stories will take them and they can only act as far as their stories will back them. The aim in narrative coaching, then, is to help coachees loosen their *narrative grip* on the past, present and/or future (Boscolo and Bertrando, 1992) to create the space for new stories about themselves and others. As such, narrative coaches help people change the way they connect their personal stories with the social contexts from which they came and to which they will return so that the seeds of their new stories will flourish.

One of the ways that narrative coaches do this is by providing both an *interpersonal structure*, eg a safe space, and a *narrative structure*, eg Bruner's (1990) notions of landscapes of action and landscapes of consciousness, to help people to fully engage with and explore their stories. Without the former, their stories can easily devolve into detached chronicles and without the latter they can default to their habitual tales. To help with this, narrative coaches make the distinction between *available narratives* and *potential stories* (Drake, 2007) in helping coachees design a new story. Available narratives are drawn from the vocabulary and grammar, the plot lines and historical conventions, and the beliefs and norms of our cultural systems (Freedman and Combs, 1996). As people begin to recognize the limitations inherent in these available narratives, they can create more distance from them, see them more clearly and surface other 'selves' they can draw on to achieve what they are looking for in their lives or work. In addition, as potential stories become more available, other 'sympathetic' and previously neglected aspects of the person's experience can be expressed (White and Epston, 1990) and embodied.

'Re-storying' or 're-authoring' is the process of designing new, more powerful, narratives (Swart, 2013; White and Epston, 1990) through a stronger alignment between a coachee's mindset, behaviour and environment in service of their aspirations. To support this process, narrative coaches stay as much as possible in *storytime* and *storyspace* in sessions, focus on the story as it is being told in the here and now, and keep bringing coachees back to the present moment. This approach is based on the belief that people need new experiences, not more explanations, to create and sustain meaningful change. Gallwey's (2009/1981) work on the inner game and Kramer's (2007) work on relational meditation have influenced Drake's (2012, 2014) experiential approach and align with Stelter's (2014) phenomenological approach. Both equip narrative coaches and their coachees to be present with the story as it is narrated now without judgement and use this awareness to develop and move towards a new story.

Narrative therapy pioneers such as Michael White (White, 1988; White and Epston, 1990) helped lead the way by advocating for the deconstruction of dominant narratives, the externalization of problems, and the valuation of 'unique outcomes' or 'exceptions' (Hewson, 1991) in a person's life as contradictions to internalized dominant narratives. Narrative coaches draw on this work to help people explore alternative territories and possibilities and renegotiate the relationships between their identities and their stories, their internal experiences and their external narratives, and their narrative desires and their narrative patterns. Key to these processes is the observation that a major source of scaffolding for new behaviours can be found in the clients' current stories themselves (Drake, 2003, 2007; Gergen and Gergen, 2006; Hewson, 1991) – both for what is present in them and what is absent.

Narrative coaching is, however, more than just narrative therapy adapted for a coaching context. For example, Drake has demonstrated that narrative coaching is unique in that it offers the possibility to:

- address the personal and collective unconscious using transpersonal means;
- use the rites of passage framework as a systemic approach to transitions and change;
- address attachment issues using archetypes and somatic practices;
- pay more attention to the nuances of and points of leverage in narrative structure;
- attend to issues of power through a lens of emergence more than a lens of justice; and
- use directive energies judiciously in service of a more overt focus on outcomes.

In teaching this work, Drake (2012) draws on seven principles of narrative coaching, including: 1) trust that everything you need is right in front of you; 2) be fully present without judgement to what *is* and trust the process; and 3) inquire based on what you hear and speak only if you can improve on silence. These principles are reflected in two of the key narrative practices that one of us (DD) teaches: radical presence and inside-out listening. One of the tools that Drake (2012) uses to bring these practices to life with coachees is the notion of a 'pivot' as a simple, memorable and binary choice between an old story and a new story that will enable them to nudge their mindset, behaviour and/or environment towards the desired change.

Radical presence

We share Boscolo and Bertrando's (1992) belief that 'the present is the only time frame for action, which means that all problems are problems of the present' (p 121). In order to work this way, coaches need to be quite present at a number of levels: to themselves, the coachee, the conversation, the content, the context and the commitments to other stakeholders. In working with groups of coaching psychologists, Drake has developed the concept of 'radical presence': the proposition that masterful coaches can use their well-tuned presence as a generative, yet invitational, force to get to the crux of the matter and affect change. This is consistent with a phenomenological approach to coaching that focuses on the potential power in the 'field' in sessions and recognizes that embodiment may be more valuable than epiphany.

As such, we teach narrative coaches to work in the moment with the unfolding narration and what *is* rather than prematurely move to what *could be* as is common in many other approaches. This requires coaches to non-judgementally and gracefully hold the stories as they are shared before any invitations are extended to try to change them or the coachee (see Gallwey, 2009/1981). Often this level of presence leads to an evaporation of initial goals that makes room for a deeper level of truth. This offers coachees the opportunity to stand more fully in their experience as the precursor to more meaningful development and change. In this sense, we see narrative coaches in 'maieutic' terms (Kenyon and Randall, 1997; Stein and Stein, 1987) as midwives who help people to birth new stories and facilitate their transformation at key junctures.

Inside-out listening

Central to a narrative approach is the notion of *dialogical space* wherein 'new relationships are established between existing story parts or new elements are introduced' (Hermans, 2004: 175) – as seen in the work of narrative researchers who study how people locate characters in their stories in relation to one another and in relation to themselves (Riessman, 2002) and how they position and reposition these characters within a constantly moving interpersonal field (Anderson, 2004). In his doctoral work, Drake extended this line of thinking by asking himself,

> What if we applied Jung's (see 1970) theory of dreams to the study of narratives? What if the stories we tell in the daytime serve the same function as the dreams we have at night? What if, in both cases, the characters are all parts of ourselves, projected onto familiar forms as a means to work through developmental issues or needs in our identity?
>
> (Drake, 2003)

These are all important questions because people are continually attempting to clarify, claim and convince others of their identity through positioning (Davies and Harré, 1990) themselves in both their internal and external narration. Coaches can help people notice the ways in which they currently position themselves and other characters in their stories and to explore how they might enhance or reconfigure their positional repertoire (Hermans, 2004) in order to increase their options. For example, you often see this in coaching people who have moved up in their organization but still talk about their role in old positional terms. We see narrative coaching as a trialogic process between the narrator, the listener and the story (Drake, 2003) in which the characters, objects and elements that appear in stories are systematically related to the other figures in ways that are important to explore. In this way, stories and lives become mirrors of one another and the role of a coach is to listen for discrepancies between the stories coachees live and the stories they tell.

Drake (2007) developed *The Narrative Diamond* as a framework that narrative coaches can use to listen to their coachees' stories and how they are in positioned in them. The four points in the diamond reflect the four elements in these conversations – the coach, the coachee, the story and the characters (eg person, place, metaphor, phrase, object). Narrative coaches can move between the four points like a master chef in the kitchen in order to facilitate the progression of the conversation and the movement toward the coachee's objectives. In doing so, they can help coachees show up more fully as narrators by witnessing *what is being said* by the narrator, recognizing *what is not being said* by advocating for the whole story, stepping into *what wants to be said* by working with key characters and narrative elements, and building on *what is being said differently* through attending to the shifts in narration already emerging in the conversation. It seldom matters which stories people choose to share first; narrative coaches trust that people will begin at the level at which they are ready and the critical themes will ultimately be forthcoming regardless of where they begin.

In coaching this way, narrative coaches often move between centred and decentred positions relative to their clients, eg facing the client at the start to build sufficient rapport and trust, decentring ourselves by shifting our position to be more at an angle to explore the narrative material with the client, and recentring ourselves when a stronger relational connection is needed (eg due to increased vulnerability) or a new experience seems called for in the moment. In moving back and forth, the coach continues to triangulate between the client, the stories and themselves as each interacts with the other in the field between them. It allows the coach to move between first, second and third positions in neuro-linguistic programming terms yet always keep the stories present and owned by the client. In this process of co-creation, the freedom to centre oneself as a practitioner when appropriate is one of the critical differences between narrative therapy and narrative coaching, and reflects the greater emphasis in coaching on shorter interventions, self-efficacy and outcomes.

This literal and symbolic movement by narrative coaches reflects the nature of inside-out listening in which the coach must be fully immersed (inside) in what is happening in the conversation to be able to listen deeply and, at the same time, be non-attached (outside) the conversation to be able to listen obliquely to what is going on. Kaplan (2002) describes inside-out listening as follows, 'To apprehend [what is going on], we have to move into a different state of being – one which is simultaneously inside and outside, participant and observer, analyst and artist' (xvii). To do this, narrative coaches use what Reik (1998) called the 'third ear' to listen with a non-judgemental presence, an engaged mindfulness and a multilayered attention to what emerges in the conversation. As a general rule in narrative coaching, listening precedes talking and what coaches hear drives what they say – rather than the usual frame in which listening is what we do after we stop talking. A light yet disciplined touch is, therefore, required by coaches to remain full present and fully trust the process as they move inside and outside of coachees' stories.

Listening to people's stories in this way enables coaches to pay close attention to the nuances of what is said and not said – verbally and non-verbally – in sessions, and be more aware of the ways in which their conscious and unconscious formulations are shaping the conversation (Drake, 2010). This approach to listening as the primary driver for narrative coaching is consistent with the phenomenological roots of narrative work and requires a high degree of 'radical presence' as proposed earlier. Working with people's stories and the characters in them is powerful because it gives them access to aspects of themselves that are often hidden yet in motion in their psyche. This is important because development generally occurs for people outside their habitual plot lines and their psyche's defences. Narrative coaches support this process through listening in a way that is active yet non-directive, engaged yet non-attached, circling slowly yet able to pivot quickly.

This can be seen in the way that narrative coaches work with the metaphors, analogies and the like in coachees' stories that often make visible their otherwise invisible identity processes (see case examples in Drake, 2007, 2008a, 2014; Stelter, 2014). A participant in one of his (DD) programmes described coaching as not something we do 'to' or even 'for' people, but 'with' them as co-explorers. A participant in another workshop realized that in order to really work with the coachee's image she had to get off her chair and into the scene as if it was real. When she did this, there was a rapid progression of the process and a breakthrough for the person being coached. Working with metaphors, analogies and the like is quite useful in coaching this way because they:

- provide heuristics and mental models by which we operate every day;
- draw on and combine resources from both the left and right hemispheres;
- bridge the symbolic and the literal, the verbal and nonverbal, the emotive and the logical;
- provide access into the coachee's world, into the spaces in-between their stories; and
- inspire meaning, generate memes and support movement toward transformation (Drake, 2012).

For example, one of us (DD) was asked to coach a key contributor in a manufacturing company to help her address some difficult relational and performance issues. Her initial stories were of anger at her employer and her colleagues. However, through exploring her story more fully she was able to reframe the issue as one in which she felt her professional passions had been compromised as the company had grown significantly. Her willingness to engage in these deeper truths emerged from a conversation about a pet and, with that, what 'home' meant for her. In the end, what she wanted was the chance to leave with dignity and the courage to return to the work she loved. To do so, she needed to shift from what she came to call her 'they don't appreciate or respect me' story to her 'I want to do what I love' story. In the end, she left the organization, moved to a new city and found a new job where she could thrive again. I helped the VP of HR reflect on how much the culture had changed over the years and what they needed to adjust in order to retain their legacy talent.

Suitability

This work is based on a commitment by narrative coaches to: 1) be mindful and compassionate; 2) listen deeply and respectfully; 3) engage courageously and fluidly with stories in the field; and 4) help people pivot in the direction of new ways of being and acting in the world. Narrative coaching seems to works best with coachees who have: 1) a comfort with silence and self-reflection; 2) a willingness to work at emotional, metaphorical, and non-rational levels; 3) an astute awareness of and ability to articulate their experience; and 4) the necessary ego strength to be able to self-disclose through their stories. Obviously, this approach is more challenging if any of these four conditions are not present in the coach and/or coachee.

Narrative coaching has been applied in any number of individual and group settings. It paradoxically feels slow to those who are in it or are observing it, but can often lead to significant breakthroughs more quickly than more traditional methods. Even so, it works best when both parties are willing to work in a collaborative and emergent manner. What we find in teaching this work is the sense of relief people feel to be able to work in a more natural and human way rather than having to remember lots of models, acronyms and steps. As such, the work is quite accessible to most professionals in the workplace even if they only apply the basic principles. More advanced practitioners with backgrounds in areas such as gestalt, family constellations, acceptance and commitment therapy, etc report a sense of fuller integration of what they know in using a narrative approach and the ability to work at deeper levels more simply.

CASE STUDY

Wayne[1] was a man in his early forties who came to coaching with one of us (DD) to sort out some career issues. In particular, he was neither satisfied in his current role nor clear what to do next. He had a vague sense of déjà vu in assessing his current dilemma and was curious how he could forge a new path for himself in his career. He had been seen as a top talent in his early corporate career, but had migrated to smaller firms over time. Along the way, he had developed significant expertise, but continued to struggle with finding suitable and satisfying employment. Early in our sessions together he identified what he saw as the crux of the matter, 'I notice whenever I go into really downward spirals in my career it's been around injustice – in situations where healing and flow were being blocked by power and unfairness.'

We explored that observation in terms of 'Where have you been here before?' and 'What stories are you still carrying?', and co-created experiences in which he could experiment with other ways of being that would attract situations more likely to fulfil his deeper desires around work and self-expression.

One of the key themes that emerged was the similarities between his relational and positional patterns within his family of origin and those he kept repeating with his choices of roles and workplaces. This is consistent with the precepts of *imago theory* (Hendrix, 1988) and *attachment theory* (see Drake, 2009b) which suggest that we tend to repeat our early patterns across our lifetimes – often unconsciously seeking to complete that which was unfulfilled – unless re-authored through processes such as those provided in narrative coaching. James Hollis (2005) described it in terms of what Freud called the 'repetition compulsion', as 'the magnetic summons of an old wound in our lives that has so much energy, such a familiar script, and such a predictable outcome attached to it that we feel obliged to relive it or pass it on to our children' (81).

The key elements in Wayne's coaching journey across four 90-minute sessions are organized using the four stages in the narrative design model (Drake, 2012). The model was used as a guide in the sessions and for interpreting the data from the transcripts. I've included representative text from him, brief descriptions of what was done by the coach, and some reflections on the process.

SITUATE ('what is')

We spent much of the first session reflecting on an initial dream about paddling his boat upstream (to no avail) and gathering stories about his family and career path

1 The name and identifying details have been changed to preserve anonymity.

to surface the core themes and patterns. While strong emotions such as anger and betrayal emerged fairly quickly, we were able to get to the crux of the issues as a result of remaining non-judgemental about the coachee, his stories and the characters in his stories. As the key themes started to emerge we increasingly focused our conversation on related stories so as to develop a deeper understanding of the core narrative patterns and dynamics to address. However, the purpose for doing so was to create experiences (familiar and new) not offer explanations. One of the core themes is reflected in his comment:

> I felt my family [of origin] life was unstable; I wanted to leave, but couldn't; I often felt stuck in the middle. I went on a number of long journeys in search of what I perceived I lost (or on behalf of what I perceived others lost), but I'm not sure where to go, often get blocked or lost along the way, and often feel like an exile.

We explored the key phrases 'being stuck', 'being lost' and 'being an exile' so they came alive for him in a palpable way and could be used in creating subsequent experiences in our sessions. We worked cognitively, emotionally and somatically with these narrative elements so that he had the full sense of those experiences, how he positioned himself in those stories and the impact of doing so. We also explored his continual efforts to return 'home' in the workplaces he chose in an attempt to redeem his unfulfilled quest on behalf of himself and others. He became aware early on about the price he had paid (as well as the payoffs) as a result of staying stuck in this cycle and his strong desire to change this pattern. The latter became his call to adventure in hero's journey terms.

We worked in more depth with a story about being a kid in his front yard and feeling torn between home (his house) and the world (across the street) – and his subsequent sense of wanting to keep a foot in two worlds and holding himself back. As he put it, rather than become the king (a man in his own right) – proclaiming his innate right to be here – he often abdicated his space or overspent his energy. He talked about these issues this way:

> Part of what keeps me stuck is a sense of the binary nature of my life – the sense that I have one foot in this camp and one foot in another – and a lack of faith that I can generate prosperity on my own. There is a sense of being trapped, a fear that if I turn one way I will be 'sucked back into the evil empire' so need to keep it at arm's length, but if I go in the direction of my true values I can't be generative enough.
>
> If I could just find the right place, then my gifts could flourish. So everything is about the drama of finding the right place. And I go black and white over it. This is not the right place any more. Now I've got to leave, but where do I go? It's almost like if I find the right place then I'll know what my gift is or what my work is.

By this point we had assembled a rich palette of narrative images and elements to work with and it was time to move onto the search for new ways to tell his stories. It is important in this stage to get a few ripe stories on the table in a focused fashion, then circle the key themes to understand their dynamics and points of leverage for change. As in the Narrative Diamond, the primary focus is on the narrator and developing a rich field in which the stories can emerge and be reconfigured.

SEARCH ('what if')

As we moved deeper into his issues, I asked Wayne to keep a journal of his dreams as often they can shed light on what is at stake. They can be particularly useful in the search phase in surfacing the Shadow and opening up new possibilities. There is often a quickening of the pace as coachees move through this stage – and new energy that had been locked up in old stories starts to become available. Wayne reported that:

> *Images of leprosy, dissolution, letting go, unlocking doors behind which sits a sense of vitality (and danger) kept appearing in my dreams and stories – signalling to me that something important was happening.*

We created an experiential activity to help him embody his perceived binary choice between: 1) staying in the family pattern (eg in the front yard), thereby losing himself but gaining rewards; or 2) leaving the family pattern (eg crossing the street), thereby gaining himself but losing rewards. The basic structure for the experience was drawn from the images and language in his actual stories, and unfolded based on what he/we noticed as he stepped into the story in the coaching room. The aim was to give him a visceral sense of what it was like for him to live out these stories, how it felt when he made these sensations conscious, how he was narrating these stories by hearing himself talk about them out loud, and what he would like to be and do instead. The latter emerged from within his own experience and the story itself, not by stepping outside the experience to analyse it or offer advice. As was noted earlier, everything – including the new story – was right in front of us and already there.

We spent most of our time in this long session working with the two primary obstacles that kept appearing in his stories and dreams: the 'rock' to which he had been attached and the 'fence/wall' he kept trying to break through. We set up an experience in which he tried to move away from the rock towards a new life – which he discovered symbolized his parents and the stories surrounding them. As he began to release the ties he felt from the rock, he sensed a chasm in front of him – not too dissimilar to the street in front of his house as a boy – that he would need to cross in order to more fully attend to his own family (and life and career). The latent desire to break through the fence/wall was captured in his surge to cross this chasm. In guiding him through the process, I responded to what his body seemed to be signalling, and I moved between centred and decentred positions as well as between facilitator and character roles depending on what the story called for. Through the process, he gained a palpable sense of renewed energy by severing the ties to the rock and breaking free to step across the chasm. Once there, I helped him to solidify his new place so that he had enough of a foundation to begin embodying the new story.

He came to recognize in doing this exercise that the fight for him was not to change or redeem the others – to whom he often felt indentured for rescuing him from the pain of feeling trapped – but to acknowledge them and fight for what is important *to him*. We then could move on to explore what would have to change within himself and in his relationship with others in order to bring these new stories to life. Around this time, Wayne was having some initial conversations with another firm as part of his desire to move to a new job. At the next session, he shared:

> I noticed my old patterns appearing as I went through the interview process for a senior role with [this] firm. I began to connect the dots between that opportunity and my family pattern. I used what we have done in coaching to name the Story I would have entered if I took that position, the peacemaker role I would have ended up playing yet again, and how it would likely end for me. In doing so, I had the courage to turn down the offer.

This stage is about clarifying the deeper purpose for the coaching work and channelling the new insights and energy that have been liberated and begin bringing them to life. This phase often requires patience and perseverance on the part of both the coach and the coachee as it is often tempting to want to skip this work, but doing so often results in outcomes that are more shallow and less sustainable. To leverage the powerful experiences people like Wayne have in doing narrative work, it is helpful to have outlets where they can practice living from their new story. It helps expedite the movement from the past to the future, from searching to shifting.

SHIFT ('what matters')

As he began to name what mattered to him most from doing the work in the previous stage, he shared:

> I was particularly struck by the return of energy, the thrumming, that came into my legs when I did the work with the 'rock'. Somehow the phrase, 'cut off at the knees' came to mind in thinking about my past. I now feel I can claim more of my right to stand on my own two feet, on my terms – and with this claim comes a new sense of energy.

I acknowledged that it felt like it was time for him to honour that 'thrum' in his heart and body and began to explore what that meant for him in making new choices about his work. I reminded him of what the 'rock' had 'said' in the powerful experience he had had in the previous session, 'You have our blessing to go embrace your own children and your life.' We spent a fair bit of time letting that blessing sink him so he really felt it and it was anchored in him. As noted earlier, this accountability and anchoring is important because new behaviours flow more easily from identities (and their stories) that support them.

We developed a profile for what kinds of work environments would bring out the best in him and support his efforts to live out a new story of himself at work. This became a template by which he gauged potential opportunities, particularly in terms of the relationships with key figures on any executive team with whom he would work. He was able to see the imago nature of many of his previous roles and was curious about how to do it differently. In doing this work he was able to move beyond the earlier fantasies about a place for himself based on 'if only...' to say:

> It seems like maybe what I'm being asked right now is to say, maybe it's the opposite of what I thought for a long time: I need to own my gifts and the right place will come to me [rather than the other way around].

As is often the case in narrative work, there was not a significant need for goals at this stage. He was now starting from a new sense of himself, had some key pivots (clear choices between old and new stories he could use in the moment relative to his mindset, behaviour or environment) to make decisions, strong intrinsic motivation to chart a new path and a template to use in making healthier choices about work. He ended this session by saying,

> There is a greater lightness and sense of freedom that is emerging. There were some wonderful moments near the end of our sessions when I felt much more in flow and could take an observer's stance on my own stories rather than being enmeshed in them.

SUSTAIN ('what works')

As we reached the final session, the focus was on consolidating his gains from our work together and identifying next steps for him. He decided to forego the job search for a while but quit his position any way with a plan to do contract work while he sorted out the various aspects of his life that had been built up around the old story, eg like some important conversations with his wife and kids. I referred him to a colleague who specializes in career strategies for creative people like him to get some tactical support in searching for a new job in keeping with his new insights and requirements when he was ready. He checked out at the end by saying,

> I feel such relief in beginning to put down all these burdens I have carried. I feel freer now to pursue a path that is healthier for me. I recognize that these are just the first steps of a longer journey.

Conclusion

As narrative coaching has evolved over the past 10 years, it has become an increasingly powerful method for helping people to: 1) become more aware of their own stories; 2) recognize that these stories are personally and socially constructed; 3) understand how these stories shape their identity and behaviour at both conscious and unconscious levels; and 4) be more authorial in aligning their stories with identities and actions that would enable them to live more fully and authentically. It is both a distinct body of work and a philosophical orientation that can be used by any coach. While it pays homage to narrative therapy (and Michael White in particular) as one of its key sources, narrative coaching has evolved to the point where it has become a distinct field in its own right. It is a fluid yet powerful approach to working with people that draws on a rich tradition that predates coaching, incorporates practices that transcend coaching and offers glimpses into what coaching could become.

David has gone on to create narrative design as a new, integral approach to development, deepened his exploration of the dynamics of this work (most recently through his study of improvisational theatre and somatic practices), and continued to teach advanced professionals and help organizations reshape their development and change initiatives using narrative approaches. Reinhard has gone on to do some fascinating work with narrative practice in groups, deepened his exploration of the philosophy behind this work (most recently through his study of Kierkegaard), and embarked on some interesting research projects as part of his commitment to narrative practice as a third-generation approach to coaching.

Together, we see a bright future for narrative coaching as a powerful and agile resource that practitioners can use to help transform people and organizations and their stories. As colleagues, we share many of the common foundational and philosophical elements even as we have diverged in certain aspects of our practices. However, this reflects part of the eclectic mix and elegant beauty of narrative coaching. While other approaches can sometimes get locked in their 'isms', a narrative approach is both more intrinsically human and more extrinsically adaptive. We look forward to increased scholarship and research to help us better understand when, how and why it works so that we can continue to advance the field and those who do this work.

We see narrative work as increasingly critical in helping people to adapt and flourish as we move into an increasingly complex world. As Salman Rushdie once said, 'Those who do not have power over the story that dominates their lives, the power to retell it, to rethink it, deconstruct it, joke about it, and change it as times change, truly are powerless, because they cannot think new thoughts.' Narrative coaching invites people to individually and collectively step into deeper and more courageous connections with themselves and with others in order to wake up and do the developmental, relational and/or vocational work at hand.

Developing yourself as a narrative coach

Developing your skills

Coaches wishing to learn more about and develop their skills in narrative coaching may wish to explore the following practitioner texts:

- Freedman, J and Combs, G (1996) *Narrative Therapy: The social construction of preferred realities*, WW Norton and Company, New York
- McKee, R (1997) *Story: Substance, structure, style and the principles of screenwriting*, HarperCollins, New York
- Swart, C (2013) *Re-authoring the World: The narrative lens and practices for organisations, communities and individuals*, Knowres Publishing, Bryanston, South Africa

Deepening your understanding

Coaches wishing to recommend narrative based self-help books and workbooks for their clients may wish to consider the following:

- Drake, D B (2012) *An Introduction to Narrative Design*, Center for Narrative Coaching and Leadership, San Francisco
- Kramer, G (2007) *Insight Dialogue: The interpersonal path to freedom*, Shambhala, Boston
- Polkinghorne, D (1988) *Narrative Knowing and the Human Sciences*, SUNY Press, Albany
- Sarbin, T R (Ed) (1986) *Narrative Psychology: The storied nature of human conduct*, Praeger, New York
- Schank, R (1990) *Tell Me a Story: A new look at real and artificial memory*, Charles Scribner's Sons, New York
- Stelter, R (2014) *A Guide to Third Generation Coaching: Narrative-collaborative theory and practice*, Springer, Dordrecht
- White, M (2007) *Maps of Narrative Practice*, Norton, New York

Web resources

Useful websites for both coaches and clients include:

- Center for Narrative Coaching and Leadership/David Drake: **www.narrativecoaching.com**
- Narrative Design Labs/David Drake: **www.narrativedesignlabs.com**
- Coaching psychology program at University of Copenhagen: **www.nexs.ku.dk/coaching**

- Reinhard Stelter: **www.sp-coaching.dk**
- Dulwich Centre and the international narrative therapy library: **www.dulwichcentre.com.au** (see **www.dulwichcentre.com.au/ narrative-coaching-in-france.html**)
- CCS Consulting in San Francisco Bay Area: **http://ccs-consultinginc.com/**
- Centre for Systemic Change in Sydney: **www.systemic-change.com.au/**
- In Dialogue in Denmark: **www.in-dialogue.org**
- Certificate in narrative coaching from Simon Fraser University: **www.sfu.ca/continuing-studies/courses/cpc/narrative-coaching.html**

References

Abma, T A (1999) Powerful stories: the role of stories in sustaining and transforming professional practice within a mental hospital, in R Josselson and A Lieblich (Eds), *Making Meaning of Narratives* (6, pp 169–95), Sage Publications, Thousand Oaks

Anderson, T (2004) 'To tell my story': configuring interpersonal relations within narrative process, in *Handbook of Narrative and Psychotherapy: Practice, theory, and research*, eds L E Angus and J McLeod, (pp 315–29), Sage Publications, Thousand Oaks

Bakan, D (1966) *The duality of human existence: Isolation and communion in Western man*, Beacon, Boston

Barkham, M, Hardy, G E and Mellor-Clark, J (2010) *Developing and Delivering Practice-Based Evidence: A guide for the psychological therapies*, Wiley-Blackwell, Chichester, UK

Bartel, C and Dutton, J E (2001) Ambiguous organizational memberships: constructing organizational identities in interactions with others, in Hogg M A and Terry D J (Eds) *Social Identity Processes in Organizational Contexts*, Psychology Press, Philadelphia, pp 115–30

Barthes, R (1975) *An introduction to the structural analysis of narratives*, New Literary History, 6, pp 237–72

Bhabha, H (1990) The third space: interview with Homi Bhabha, in J Rutherford (Ed), *Identity: Community, culture and difference* (pp 207–21), Lawrence and Wishart, London

Boje, D M (1998) The postmodern turn from stories-as-objects to stories-in-context methods, *Research Methods Forum*, Retrieved 7 January 2006, from www.aom.pace.edu/rmd/1998_forum_postmodern_stories.html

Boscolo, L and Bertrando, P (1992) The reflexive loop of past, present, and future in systemic therapy and consultation, *Family Process*, **31**, pp 119–30

Bourdieu, P (1993) *The Field of Cultural Production*, Polity Press, Cambridge

Bowlby, J (1988) *A Secure Base: Clinical applications of attachment theory*, Routledge, London

Brewer, M B (2003) Optimal distinctiveness, social identity, and the self, in *Handbook of Self and Identity*, eds M R Leary and J P Tangney, (pp 480–91), Guilford Press, New York

Brewer, M B and Pickett, C L (1999) Distinctiveness motives as a source of the social self, in *The Psychology of the Social Self: Applied social research*, eds T R Tyler and R M Kramer, (pp 71–87), Erlbaum, Mahweh, NJ

Bruner, J (1990) *Acts of Meaning*, Harvard University Press, Cambridge

Bruner, J (2002) *Making Stories: Law, literature, life*, Harvard University Press, Cambridge, MA

Burke, K (1969) *A Grammar of Motives*, University of California Press, Berkeley, CA

Campbell, J (1973) *The Hero with a Thousand Faces*, Princeton University Press, Princeton

Clandinin, D J and Connelly, F M (2000) *Narrative Inquiry: Experience and story in qualitative research*, Jossey-Bass Publishers, San Francisco

Czarniawska, B (2004) *Narratives in Social Science Research*, Sage, London

Davies, B and Harré, R (1990) Positioning: The discursive production of selves, *Journal for the Theory of Social Behavior*, **20** (1), pp 43–63

Derrida, J (1978) *Writing and Difference*, University of Chicago, Chicago

Drake, D B (2003) *How stories change: a narrative analysis of liminal experiences and transitions in identity* (dissertation), Fielding Graduate Institute, Santa Barbara

Drake, D B (2004a) Creating third space: the use of narrative liminality in coaching, in *Second ICF Coaching Research Symposium*, eds I Stein, F Campone and L J Page, (pp 50–59), International Coaching Federation, Quebec City, Canada

Drake, D B (2004b) Once upon a time: depression as an expression of untold narratives. Paper presented at Narrative Matters Conference, Fredericton, NB, Canada

Drake, D B (2007) The art of thinking narratively: implications for coaching psychology and practice, *Australian Psychologist*, **42** (4), pp 283–94

Drake, D B (2008a) Thrice upon a time: narrative structure and psychology as a platform for coaching, in *The Philosophy and Practice of Coaching: Insights and issues for a new era*, eds D B Drake, K Gortz and D Brennan, (pp 55–71), John Wiley and Sons, London

Drake, D B (2008b) Finding our way home: coaching's search for identity in a new era, *Coaching: An international journal of theory, research and practice*, **1** (1), pp 15–26

Drake, D B (2009a) Narrative coaching, in *The Sage Handbook of Coaching*, eds E Cox, T Bachkirova and D Clutterbuck, (pp 120–131), Sage, London

Drake, D B (2009b) Using attachment theory in coaching leaders: the search for a coherent narrative, *International Coaching Psychology Review*, **4** (1), pp 49–58

Drake, D B (2010) What story are you in? Four elements of a narrative approach to formulation in coaching, in *Constructing Stories, Telling Tales: A guide to formulation in applied psychology*, eds S Corrie and D Lane, (pp 239–58), Karnac, London

Drake, D B (2011) What do coaches need to know? Using the Mastery Window to assess and develop expertise, *Coaching: An international journal of theory, research and practice*, **4** (2), pp 138–55

Drake, D B (2012) *An Introduction to Narrative Design*, Center for Narrative Coaching and Leadership, San Francisco

Drake, D B (2014) Three windows of development: a post-professional perspective on supervision, *International Coaching Psychology Review*, **9** (1), pp 36–48

Drake, D B and Wycherley, I M (2013) *Thresholds: Navigating identity work and play for managers in transition*, Working Paper

Dweck, C S (2008) *Mindset: The psychology of success*, Ballantine Books, New York

Eliade, M (1959) *The Sacred and Profane: The nature of religion*, Harcourt, New York

Erikson, E H (1950) *Childhood and Society*, WW Norton, New York

Fonagy, P (2001) *Attachment Theory and Psychoanalysis*, Other Press, New York

Foucault, M (1965) *Madness and Reason: A history of insanity in the age of reason*, Random House, New York

Fredrickson, B (2006) The broaden-and-build theory of positive emotions, in *A Life Worth Living: Contributions to positive psychology*, eds M Csikszentmihalyi and I Csikszentmihalyi, Oxford University Press, New York

Freedman, J and Combs, G (1996) *Narrative Therapy: The social construction of preferred realities*, WW Norton and Company, New York

Freire, P (1970) *Pedagogy of the Oppressed*, Seabury Press, New York

Gallwey, T (2009/1981) *The Inner Game of Golf*, Random House, New York

Gergen, K J (1973) Social psychology as history, *Journal of Personality and Social Psychology*, **26** (2), pp 309–20

Gergen, K J (1991) *The Saturated Self: Dilemmas of identity in contemporary life*, Basic Books, New York

Gergen, K J (2009) *Relational Being: Beyond self and community*, Oxford University Press, Oxford

Gergen, M and Davis, S N (2005) Dialogic pedagogy: Developing narrative research perspectives through conversation, in *Up Close and Personal: The teaching and learning of narrative research*, eds R Josselson, A Lieblich and D P McAdams, (pp 239–57), American Psychological Association, Washington DC

Gergen, M M and Gergen, K J (2006) Narratives in action, *Narrative Inquiry*, **16** (1), pp 112–21

Gilligan, C (1982) *In a Different Voice: Psychological theory and women's development*, Harvard Business School Press, Cambridge, MA

Goffman, E (1959) *The Presentation of Self in Everyday Life*, Doubleday, Garden City, NY

Hall, D T (1971) A theoretical model of career subidentity development in organizational settings, *Organizational Behavior and Human Performance*, **6**, pp 50–76

Hermans, H J M (2004) The innovation of self-narratives: a dialogical approach, in *Handbook of Narrative and Psychotherapy: Practice, theory, and research*, eds L E Angus and J McLeod, (pp 175–91), Sage Publications, Thousand Oaks

Hewson, D (1991) From laboratory to therapy room: prediction questions for reconstructing the 'new-old' story, *Dulwich Centre Newsletter*, **3**, pp 5–12

Hollis, J (2005) *Finding Meaning in the Second Half of Life*, Penguin Books, New York

Horney, K (1945) *Our Inner Conflicts: A constructive theory of neurosis*, WW Norton and Company, New York

Husserl, E (1931) *Ideas: General introduction to pure phenomenology*, George Allen and Unwin, London

Husserl, E (1971/1927) 'Phenomenology,' Edmund Husserl's Article for the Encyclopedia Britannica', Translated by R Palmer, *The Journal of the British Society for Phenomenology*, **2**, pp 77–90

Ibarra, H (1999) Provisional selves: experimenting with image and identity in professional adaptation, *Administrative Science Quarterly*, **44** (4), pp 764–91

Ibarra, H (2005) *Identity Transitions: Possible selves, liminality and the dynamics of career change* (Vol 2005/24/OB) INSEAD, Fontainbleau, France

Ibarra, H and Petriglieri, J L (2010) Identity work and play, *Journal of Organizational Change Management*, **23** (1), 10–25

Ihde, D (1977) *Experimental Phenomenology: An introduction*, Putnam's Sons, New York

Illeris, K (2004) Transformative learning in the perspective of a comprehensive learning theory, *Journal of Transformative Education*, **2**, pp 79–89

James, W (1927/1892) *Psychology: Briefer course*, Henry Holt and Company, New York

Josselson, R and Lieblich, A (2005) A framework for narrative research proposals in psychology, in *Up Close and Personal: The teaching and learning of narrative research*, eds R Josselson, A Lieblich and D P McAdams, (pp 259–74) American Psychological Association, Washington, DC

Jung, C G (1970) *Psychological Reflections*, Princeton University Press, Princeton

Kaplan, A (2002) *Development Practitioners and Social Process: Artists of the invisible*, Pluto Press, London

Kenyon, G M and Randall, W L (1997) *Restorying our Lives: Personal growth through autobiographical reflection*, Praeger, Westport, CT

Keupp, H, Ahbe, T, Gmür, W, Höfer, R, Mitzscherlich, B, Kraus, W and Straus, F (1999) *Identitätskonstruktionen: Das Patchwork der Identitäten in der Spätmoderne*, Rowohlt, Reinbek

Kolb, A Y and Kolb, D A (2010) Learning to play, playing to learn: a case study of a ludic learning space, *Journal of Organizational Change Management*, **32** (1), pp 26–50

Kramer, G (2007) *Insight Dialogue: The interpersonal path to freedom*, Shambhala, Boston

Kraus, W (2006) The narrative negotiation of identity and belonging, *Narrative Inquiry*, **16** (1), pp 103–11

Kreiner, G E, Hollensbe, E C and Sheep, M L (2006) Where is the 'me' among the 'we': identity work and the search for the optimal balance, *Academy of Management Journal*, **49** (5), pp 1031–57

Kvale, S (Ed) (1992) *Psychology and Postmodernism*, Sage, London

Lave, J and Wenger, E (1991) *Situated Learning: Legitimate peripheral participation*, Cambridge University Press, Cambridge

Law, H C (2007) Narrative coaching and psychology of learning from multicultural perspectives, in *Handbook of Coaching Psychology*, eds S Palmer and A Whybrow, Routledge, East Sussex

Law, H C, Ireland, S and Hussain, Z (2007) *Psychology of Coaching, Mentoring and Learning*, John Wiley and Sons, Chichester

Lewin, K (1951) *Field Theory in Social Science: Selected papers on group dynamics* (G W Lewin Ed) Harper and Brothers, New York

Lieblich, A, Tuval-Mashiach and Zilber, T (1998) *Narrative Research: Reading, analysis and interpretation* (Vol 47) Sage Publications, Thousand Oaks

Mainemelis, C and Ronson, S (2006) Ideas are born in fields of play: towards a theory of play and creativity in organizational settings, *Research in Organizational Behavior*, 27, pp 69–81

Mancuso, J C and Sarbin, T R (1983) The self-narrative in the enactment of roles, in *Studies in Social Identity*, eds T R Sarbin and K E Scheibe, (pp 233–53), Praeger, Westport

Mattingly, C (1991) Narrative reflections on practical actions: two learning experiments in reflective storytelling, in *The Reflective Turn: Case studies in and on educational practice*, ed D A Schön, (pp 235–57), Teachers College Press, New York

McAdams, D P (1985) *Power, Intimacy, and the Life Story*, The Dorsey Press, Homewood

McKee, R (1997) *Story: Substance, structure, style and the principles of screenwriting*, HarperCollins, New York

McLaren, P (1993) Border disputes: multicultural narrative, identity formation, and critical pedagogy in postmodern America, in *Naming Silenced Lives: Personal narratives and processes of educational change*, eds D McLaughlin and W G Tierney, (pp 201–35), Routledge, New York

Merleau-Ponty, M (2012/1996) *Phenomenology of Perception*, Routledge, London

Meyer, J H F and Land, R (2003) Threshold concepts and troublesome knowledge (1): linkages to ways of thinking and practising, in C Rust (Ed) *Improving Student Learning: Theory and practice: Ten years on*, Oxford: Oxford Centre for Staff and Learning Development, Oxford Brookes University, pp 412–24

Mezirow, J (Ed) (2000) *Learning as Transformation: Critical perspectives on a theory in progress*, Jossey-Bass, San Francisco

Mishler, E G (1995) Models of narrative analysis: a typology, *Journal of Narrative and Life History*, 5 (2), pp 87–123

Moore, M J (2005) The transtheoretical model of the stages of change and the phases of transformative learning, *Journal of Transformative Education*, 3 (4), pp 394–415

Ollerenshaw, J and Creswell, J W (2002) Narrative research: a comparison of two restorying data analysis approaches, *Qualitative Inquiry*, 8 (3), pp 329–47

Pals, J L (2006) Narrative identity processing of difficult life experiences: pathways of personality development and positive self-transformation in adulthood, *Journal of Personality*, 74 (4), pp 1079–09

Piaget, J (1962) *Play, Dreams and Imitation in Childhood* (C Gattegno and F M Hodgson, Trans), WW Norton, New York

Polkinghorne, D P (1988) *Narrative Knowing and the Human Sciences*, SUNY Press, Albany, NY

Rappaport, J (1993) Narrative studies, personal stories, and identity transformation in the mutual help context, *Journal of Applied Behavioral Science*, **29** (2), pp 239–56

Reik, T (1998) *Listening with the Third Ear: The inner experience of a psychoanalyst* (Twelfth edn), Farrar, Strauss and Giroux, New York

Riessman, C K (2002) Analysis of personal narrative, in J F Gubrium and J A Holstein (Eds), *Handbook of Interview Research* (pp 695–710), Sage, Thousand Oaks, CA

Sarbin, T R (Ed) (1986) *Narrative Psychology: The storied nature of human conduct*, Praeger, New York

Schank, R (1990) *Tell Me A Story: A new look at real and artificial memory*, Charles Scribner's Sons, New York

Siegel, D J (1999) *The Developing Mind*, New York: Guilford Press.

Spinelli, E (2010) Existential coaching, in *The Complete Handbook of Coaching*, eds E Cox, T Bachkirova and D Clutterbuck, (pp 94–106), Sage, London

Stein, J O and Stein, M (1987) Psychotherapy, initiation and the midlife transition, in *Betwixt and Between: Patterns of masculine and feminine initiation*, eds L C Mahdi, S Foster and M Little, (pp 287–303), Open Court, La Salle, IL

Stelter, R (2007) Coaching: a process of personal and social meaning making, *International Coaching Psychology Review*, **2** (2), pp 191–201

Stelter, R (2009) Coaching as a reflective space in a society of growing diversity: towards a narrative, postmodern paradigm, *International Coaching Psychology Review*, **4** (2), pp 207–17

Stelter, R (2014) *A Guide to Third Generation Coaching: narrative-collaborative theory and practice*, Springer, Dordrecht

Stelter, R and Law, H (2010) Coaching: narrative-collaborative practice, *International Coaching Psychology Review*, **5** (2), pp 152–64

Stelter, R, Nielsen, G and Wikmann, J (2011) Narrative-collaborative group coaching develops social capital: a randomized control trial and further implications of the social impact of the intervention, *Coaching: Theory, Research and Practice*, **4** (2), pp 123–37

Swann, W B, Jr, and Read, S J (1981) Self-verification processes: how we sustain our self-conceptions, *Journal of Experimental Social Psychology*, **17**, pp 351–72

Swart, C (2013) *Re-authoring the World: The narrative lens and practices for organisations, communities and individuals*, Knowres Publishing, Bryanston, South Africa

Turner, V (1969) *The Ritual Process: Structure and anti-structure*, Aldine Publishing, New York

van Gennep, A (1960) *The Rites of Passage*, Routledge and Kegan Paul, London

Vygotsky, L S (1934/1987) Thinking and speech (N Minick, Trans), in *The Collected Works of L S Vygotsky (Vol 1: Problems of general psychology)*, eds R W Rieber and A S Carton, (pp 39–285), Plenum Press, New York

Wallin, D J (2007) *Attachment in Psychotherapy*, The Guilford Press, New York

White, M (1988) The process of questioning: a therapy of literary merit? In
    M White (Ed), *Collected papers* (pp 37–46), Dulwich Centre Publications,
    Adelaide, South Australia

White, M (2004) Narrative practice and the unpacking of identity conclusions,
    in M White, *Narrative Practice and Exotic Lives: Resurrecting diversity in
    everyday life* (pp 119–48), Dulwich Centre Publications, Adelaide

White, M and Epston, D (1990) *Narrative Means to Therapeutic Ends*, WW
    Norton and Company, New York

Winnicott, D W (1965) *The Maturational Processes and the Facilitating
    Environment*, International Universities Press, New York

Note

1 In order to measure social recovery, a form of social satisfaction, the participants
   were asked,
   'In the course of the past three days,
   ... I have laughed
   ... I have had fun with friends
   ... I have seen close friends
   ... I have enjoyed myself'

Scores of 0–6 corresponding to never, rarely, occasionally, several times, often, very
often, always.

Gestalt approaches

05

ALISON WHYBROW AND JULIE ALLAN

Introduction

Gestalt approaches to coaching have developed from diverse theoretical, philosophical and pragmatic inputs, with equally diverse ideas about what constitutes a gestalt approach. Gaie Houston (2007) notes that when we say 'in Gestalt we do this' she is not suggesting gestalt has taken out patents on any aspect of the truth. And that 'countless thousands of wise people who lived before the word psychology had been invented are all likely to have made some of the very same discoveries that you will make as you explore what we are calling Gestalt' (Houston, 2007). We hope to be true to this perspective in this chapter, and have written with the knowledge that we are curious enquirers into gestalt principles and approaches and what they can bring to coaching practice. Our intention is to be thoughtful, perhaps provocative, to share some insights and observations, offering material and discussion with the purpose of enhancing and stretching your own understanding of, and insight into, gestalt coaching.

What do we mean by gestalt? A gestalt is a shape, pattern, configuration, the structural whole (Clarkson, 1995, 2003), the totality of a person (Mann, 2010), an organization or pattern of data, a foreground that can be described against a background context or field and is something that is whole in itself. The word gestalt means a unified or meaningful whole. Writers in the field point to the difficulty of defining gestalt approaches to therapy or coaching in a few words as it isn't one thing that remains fixed, but a process of discovery and, through exploration, awareness (Mann, 2010; Allan and Whybrow, 2007).

The goal or purpose of the gestalt therapeutic approach is a process of becoming aware: 'for clients to become aware of what they are doing, how they are doing it, and how they can change themselves, and at the same time, to learn to accept and value themselves' (Yontef , 1993). This goal of awareness transfers directly to gestalt coaching (Allan and Whybrow, 2007). According to Perls, Hefferline and Goodman (1954/1991), awareness and acceptance leads to wholeness through integration. As Perls points out 'every bit of integration will strengthen [the client]' (Perls, 1965).

Awareness is achieved through the medium of relationship co-created between the coach and their client.

In this chapter we explore the answers to the three questions below:

● How has gestalt coaching developed?

● What is the evidence base of gestalt coaching and the core theoretical elements?

● What might a gestalt coaching practice include?

We share vignettes as we go, bringing different aspects to life. A wealth of gestalt materials already exists from the therapeutic and organizational consulting world, which a gestalt coaching practitioner might draw from. We won't repeat this here, but rather organize and apply to the coaching context, and perhaps deepen some of the approaches discussed. We explore when, where and with whom gestalt approaches might 'work better', and include a brief case study at the end.

The development of gestalt coaching

The development of gestalt approaches as a way of working with people and groups started with the pioneering work of Max Wertheimer (1880–1943), Wolfgang Köhler (1887–1967) and Kurt Koffka (1886–1941). Their interest in the nature and structure of perceptual experience led to their conclusion that 'people strive to impose order and meaningful wholes on what they see and experience' (Bluckert, 2010: 81). This idea of an 'interpreted world' firmly challenged the belief that there is an independent 'objective reality'.

Fritz Perls (1893–1970), the originator of gestalt therapy, developed his ideas through the 1920s and onwards along with Laura Perls and Paul Goodman. Their influences included psychoanalysis, gestalt psychology, field theory, existential philosophy and humanistic therapy (Bluckert, 2010). Perls had a very rigorous and perhaps uncompromising attitude to how 'authentic' the therapist needed to be in the relationship with their client in order that the client is 'confronting himself' (Perls, 1965). Gestalt coaching might differ from Perls' practice, as indeed might gestalt therapy, yet the intention of a very 'full' experience of the coachee, the coach and the relationship between them in the 'here-and-now', is a central part of a gestalt coaching approach (Allan and Whybrow, 2007).

Gestalt is fundamentally a holistic approach and so it makes sense that, in addition to the two developments described, a third root of gestalt coaching (Bluckert, 2010) is the practice of gestalt thinking with wider systems (eg families, teams and organizations). Examples can be found in the works of Stanley Herman, Michael Korenich (1977) and Edwin Nevis (1987). The work of Nevis and subsequent colleagues continues through the Gestalt

Institute of Cleveland's Center for Organization and Systems Development, which he co-founded.

Gestalt ideas have informed diverse and different approaches to coaching practice. For example, the first theoretical modelling project of neuro-linguistic programming was based on gestalt therapy (Grimley, 2007). So the principles of gestalt are not limited to those who describe themselves as working with a gestalt approach although there is likely to be a greater integration of gestalt in practice among those who do. Resnick's quote below rightly acknowledges that the label is less important than the work being done, that the stance is more fundamental than particular techniques.

> Every Gestalt therapist could stop doing any gestalt technique that had ever been done and go right on doing gestalt therapy. If they couldn't, then they weren't doing Gestalt therapy in the first place. They were fooling around with a bag of tricks and a bunch of gimmicks.
>
> (Resnick, 1984: 19)

It is possible that a coach might be working with an implicit integrated gestalt framework that they do not necessarily 'tag' as gestalt. At the same time, a self-acclaimed gestalt coach may not, in reality, have an integrated or integrating gestalt practice. The boundaries around what gestalt coaching is, and is not, are not clear. Gestalt approaches are creative processes in which the coach and client co-create a system of coaching; one part cannot be fully separated from another either logically or experientially. This co-creation means the experience of gestalt is co-experienced. Gestalt practices are varied; it is a suitably gestalt way of working to adopt what is worth experimenting with in the context of the joint endeavour.

It was challenging to choose a stance for this chapter that could en-compass, not reduce, gestalt's historical development and complexity. We experienced the frustrating limitations of language and the challenges of meaning making at the conceptual edges. We settled more or less on taking a view of gestalt or 'gestaltiness' as an intention to practise according to the principles described by Yontef within a transparent, co-created way of working. This builds directly from Mann's view of gestalt therapy as an integrative approach, practising the three pillars of gestalt defined by Yontef (1999): field theory, phenomenology and dialogue (Mann, 2010). A person working from a gestalt perspective may have been working with this intent for six months or 10 years, yet each encounter with a client is novel. The expertise the gestalt practitioner brings is awareness of herself and skill in using herself and the relationship with her client as the instruments of awareness. This perspective is based on the view that there is always more to learn and greater awareness to be had, and that this may afford a virtuous circle of growth, exploration and enquiry.

There are shifts currently ongoing in the context of organizational work that may bring gestalt coaching more to the fore. There is greater acceptance that individual, and indeed organizational, ability to thrive in an increasingly complex, ambiguous and uncertain context requires working with what is 'fuzzy' and emergent. Gestalt coaching approaches embracing this context, may grow in popularity. And, further, gestalt coaching may have particular resonance as the concept of embodied and integrated leadership moves to a more central focus.

Where goal-focused and gestalt approaches become a little more popular is in the world of coaching supervision (Whybrow, 2013). Here, a significant part of the emphasis is developmental, with a particular intent to enable coach integration through the concept of 'self-as-instrument' (Long, 2011; Rowan and Jacobs, 2002). For more, see the section on coach development towards the end of this chapter (page 121).

The evidence base of gestalt coaching

Looking for the evidence of gestalt practice through a positivist scientific lens does not sit easily with the principles of gestalt. It does not tie in with the concept of praxis through a gestalt lens because it emphasizes absolute scientific verification of experience, rather than accepting the intrinsic validity of the experience. In this section we outline some of the challenges for gestalt research as well as some of the approaches that have been followed and evidence in support of the conceptual underpinnings.

Phenomenology as a gestalt practice is concerned with noticing rather than with interpretation; it is not about explaining which elements are more important than others. In this context, Crocker points out that any theoretical construct has only transitory validity (2005). Separating cause and effect immediately runs into an obstacle as, although gestalt work may attend to what becomes figural, the perceiver(s) are active participants in an inter-relating non-static world. What Drake has called the artistic aspects of gestalt coaching makes it impossible to predict what will emerge and how they might be implemented (Drake, 2009). The coach and coachee are responding to each other in novel ways, working with what is emerging between them, so prediction of a particular outcome becomes redundant. Finally, the researcher or the intent to research is part of the relational field, not separate from it, and the impact of this presence as part of the context is impossible to quantify.

These factors in part (and perhaps wholly) explain why there are no outcome studies of gestalt coaching, and little urgency in the field to validate its efficacy in this way. Rather, a fractal view of the evidence base of gestalt approaches may well be more helpful in determining what patterns might emerge – a fractal being a small part that, nonetheless, contains the whole (Mandelbrot, 1982). If this approach is accepted as a stance for enquiry, then fully understanding a small part leads to insight regarding the whole (Clarkson, 1995) and descriptive, qualitative and case study materials offer a grounded evidence base. A critical look at the two opposing perspectives in the question of 'evidence', namely the Empirically Supported Treatments (EST) perspective and the Common Factors perspective, can be found in Gianluca Castelnuovo and colleagues (2004).

While strictly defined empirical studies are not such a feature of enquiry into gestalt approaches, there is documentation of gestalt coaching impact through case studies, examples from practice and anecdotes as well as heuristic enquiry. Six gestalt coaching articles were published between 2000 and 2008 (Simon, 2009). Additionally, a study by Leahy and Magerman (2009) revealed five core aspects of a gestalt coaching experience. Three reflected classical gestalt concepts: namely, the coach–client relationship (leading to a better relationship with oneself and others), experiencing and experimenting (leading to getting beyond self-judgement) and becoming aware (leading to expanded awareness of self and self-in-environment). The two other aspects of gestalt coaching were more goal focused: a person with a goal; and realizing the person's desired results. These exploratory approaches offer a logical point from which to explore gestalt coaching. As yet, no meta-exploration of the fractals and patterns emerging from these qualitative sources has been conducted.

A further factor regarding an evidence base is the relative lack of popularity of gestalt as a coaching approach among coaching psychologists (Palmer and Whybrow, 2007) and coaches (Grant and le Roux, 2011). A lack of very direct empirical evidence, and the complex, emergent nature of the approach, can make gestalt approaches less easily embraced by traditional goal-oriented organizational cultures where high certainty is desired (Spoth *et al*, 2013). Gestalt coaching would incorporate the need for high certainty as an interesting and likely fruitful context, however an organizational buyer may have less clarity on the value of the existential position. The paradox here is that a gestalt coaching approach is likely to support truly sustainable change: the holistic discovery process enables depth in understanding the dynamics involved and how to see/create new options (Spoth *et al*, 2013).

Spoth and colleagues, perhaps in acknowledgement of the call for rigour in the coaching field, assert that the work to document the potency and efficacy of gestalt coaching as a methodology 'must be done' (Spoth *et al*, 2013: 401). 'If coaching research is in its infancy, then gestalt coaching research has yet to be born' (Spoth *et al*, 2013: 400).

When discussing the research to be done, Spoth and colleagues focus on a need for separately following the impact gestalt principles and practices have. This is what we look to next. We have discussed above the diverse origins of gestalt, fundamentally dealing with holism and existentialism. From these roots emerge a number of core principles, namely:

- the gestalt principle of perceptual organization;
- phenomenology;
- dialogic existentialism; and
- field theory.

Yontef (1980) noted the three principles of phenomenology, dialogic existentialism and field theory as interlinked and, when fully understood, encompassing each other. In this further exploration of the evidence for the principles of gestalt, we discuss the principles in more depth, exploring a little of the impact as well as support for their validity.

Gestalt principles of perceptual organization

How we perceive things is the result of who we are at one moment in time (Allan and Whybrow, 2007). Demonstrated through the work of the early psychologists, Wertheimer, Kohler and Koffka, the gestalt principles of perceptual organization have had a fundamental impact on psychology and gestalt approaches and demonstrate that we make sense (things become figural) in a particular context (ground) that is changing momentarily. Later work identifies more clearly the active process of visual identification and clarifies the interactive nature of cognitive and visual process. We look at what is interesting, 'but what is interesting changes from moment to moment, guided by the observers thought processes and action plans' (Findlay and Gilchrist, 2003, p 6). David Mann notes we are constantly and creatively adjusting throughout our lives in relation to our ever-changing environment (Mann, 2010: 8).

A second principle of perceptual organization concerns our pattern-seeking behaviour. We are predisposed to:

- group similar things together, seeing patterns;
- group things together that are closer to each other;
- see the most obvious and simple configuration, reducing many to few;
- see smooth lines or continuity where there in fact might be discontinuity; and
- see wholes, to make connections without conscious awareness that there was a gap to be filled – integration rather than segregation.

Pinna brings together substantial work on the gestalt principles of perceptual organization and notes there is 'no perception without three forms of organisation imposed: grouping, shape and meaning' (Pinna, 2010: 69).

We reinterpret our world in some way in the light of new experiences and thus our understanding of who we are through our experiences is continually shifting (Allan and Whybrow, 2007). As an example, a client shared a story about her grandfather's passing. For more than 20 years there had been bitterness between two sides of the family about the inheritance of the family estate, which the grandfather had gifted to his youngest daughter. After her grandfather's death, my client realized on speaking to her aunt what the real cost of the inheritance had been: Her aunt had spent the last 25 years of her life as a devoted carer to her father – and in her words, had lost her life from her late twenties through to her early fifties. The bitterness my client felt towards her aunt evaporated immediately and the 25 years of pain and hurt were immediately reconfigured in the light of this new awareness.

This idea of many truths rather than one truth is articulated well from an existential perspective. From this view, people are endlessly remaking or discovering themselves. There is no essence of human nature to be discovered once and for all. There are always new horizons, new problems and new opportunities (Yontef, 1993).

Phenomenology

It follows that if perception and, effectively, reality are subjective, then inviting the client to be curious about what they see, using descriptive methods rather than analytical methods, is of value (Clarkson, 1989). It is this picking at the foreground, naming what's most simple and obvious about the data, experiencing it, illuminating it, being curious, that exposes the phenomenology of the pattern. A phenomenological approach is inherently non-judgemental, requiring practitioners to bracket any judgements or potential judgements they may make and to adopt a stance of curiosity. Non-judgemental noticing might seem to be the most simple task to achieve – but our perceptual filters are strong, and get in the way of seeing what is in plain sight.

Sometimes it's the throwaway comments, the asides, the noise before the 'real issue' that houses these patterns most vividly. Just such a seemingly peripheral example is shared below:

Coach: 'Picking up on our call the other day, you described the solution you had come to for Ben following a conversation with Adam. I am really curious about how you made that decision.'

John: 'Yes, I remember the conversation, what did I do?'

Coach: 'What I noticed is that when Adam shared his view with you, you created a solution for Ben almost immediately, there was no discussion with Ben. In that call, we came to a view that you would not pursue your solution immediately. You've now shared that in fact Ben has already started to shift how he's working – so the solution's not required. Does that pattern of decision making resonate at all?'

John: [*Pause and energized response*] 'I take responsibility – it's my job as a leader to find the solution – and I assume that the data that has been presented is the total data that is available at that time and act on it.'

Coach: 'And yet, you've got your head under the car bonnet.' [*referring to earlier metaphor and bringing the conversation into the present*]

John: 'I'm not even aware that there is more to the whole picture.'

Coach: 'What is it like to step back a bit and look at the whole picture?'

John: 'I'm a leader and leaders take responsibility to find the answer – it's ingrained.'

Coach: 'What is it like to be a responsible leader *and* to step back a bit and look at the whole picture' [*Putting together two ends of a paradox that John has created so they exist together in the present moment.*]

John: 'Ah.'

Bringing the peripheral into focus, illuminated a core assumption for John, and working with that phenomenologically generated a different awareness.

Phenomenology is one of the three defining principles of gestalt therapy (Yontef, 1980). It is a principle that is wholly adopted in gestalt coaching. In the above example we're exploring the action of being a leader from a descriptive perspective in the present moment. While the past and future exist, it is the present moment that houses the most potent information to promote awareness and decide on action. Reaching full awareness from a gestalt perspective includes using all the data available through the five body senses – involving and evoking a full experience of what is happening at any one moment to become aware. Using this approach the coach pays attention to all the data emitting from the client: feelings, movements, postures, energy changes and so on, while accepting that the whole is also more than the sum of the parts. In the example with John, there was more data the coach could have drawn on, for example the energy displayed when the decision process was described. Another client example is below – where a simple noticing of a facial habit allows a deeper awareness and sharing.

> Coach: 'I notice when you finished speaking that the corner of your mouth went down and backwards, what was your mouth saying there?'
>
> Vaishali: 'I'm really not confident about taking that step, I don't like asking for things – for me.'

In gestalt there is a focus on process. Working from a phenomenological perspective the aim is to clarify what's really being felt and experienced now rather than getting caught up in the stories and interpretations that take us to the past or the expected future. Accordingly, Yontef has stated that gestalt has awareness as its only goal and its methodology (Yontef, 1980).

A phenomenological approach allows us to explore the ways we are creatively adjusting in the moment as our internal and external worlds fluctuate (Mann, 2010). This stance is fundamentally positive in that rather than seeing 'resistance', a gestalt coach sees a creative adjustment that is the best solution to the situation in which that person perceives themselves to be at the current time (Heidegger, 1962). Rather than being analytical and judgemental, a gestalt coach would be curious.

A careful, phenomenological approach to building awareness is likely to lead to developmental growth by:

- allowing information we might usually judgementally filter out of conscious awareness actually come into our consciousness through acceptance and non-judgement;

- raising awareness of contradictions between what is said and done in the present moment ('you smile and yet you say you are angry'); and

- enabling a person to own all parts of themselves and their story, thus facilitating change through integration.

The paradoxical theory of change (Beisser, 1970) holds that in order to transition from A to B, it is first necessary to fully engage with A. Clarkson (1995) is among those who have forwarded a gestaltist view that whatever is said fully and completely, the opposite also begins to be true. In other words, once you are fully aware of what 'A' is, you then become aware of the opposite situation and any number of alternatives in between (B1, B2, ... Bx). A gestalt coach helps the coachee very fully raise and explore awareness of the state they are in because with this sharpness or intensity of experience there also comes an ability for the coachee to come unstuck and move forward.

A final source of support for the value of phenomenological awareness comes from the research into mindfulness. Mindfulness is a form of 'in the moment awareness' defined by Jon Kabat-Zinn as: 'the awareness that emerges through paying attention on purpose, in the present moment, and non judgementally to the unfolding of experience moment by moment' (Kabat-Zinn, 2003). Mindfulness practice and phenomenological awareness have a significant overlap. The research into the impact of mindfulness practice is starting to grow. One study shows that even short-term mindfulness practice can lead to increased attention and stress reduction (eg Tang *et al*, 2007). As the development of gestalt therapy drew on zen philosophy (Clarkson, 1989) this connection between mindfulness and gestalt practices is not surprising. For a more detailed insight into mindfulness and coaching see Chapter 8.

Dialogic existentialism

In gestalt approaches, we exist at the point of dialogue with another (Allan and Whybrow, 2007). The medium by which awareness is realized in gestalt coaching is through dialogue at the contact boundary – the boundary of self and other (Nevis, 1987), by which we mean the individual's experience of what is 'me' and 'not me' (Yontef, 1993). In gestalt, a person only exists in relation with others (Buber, 1970). Contact is the experience of interacting with the 'not me' while maintaining a self-identity that is 'me'. This may seem obvious, however, full awareness is often denied as we experience interruptions to the contact that we have with the world in which we live. Our perceptual filters and habits, our past experience and future aspirations all keep us out of contact, interrupt contact, with what is happening here and now. To use an overgeneralized example, the busy executive is perhaps building for the future life that they can enjoy – denying current moments and experiences, denying an awareness of what is happening now and denying the opportunity to adjust accordingly. The bitter colleague might be continuing to act out deeply hurtful patterns that occurred in their past that they do not allow into awareness or think to forgive – reducing their contact with the present context. Interruptions to contact can be very useful strategies for navigating in life; it's sticking with ones that are no longer useful that can lead to suboptimal choices and responses.

Contact in the here and now – true connection between two human beings, as the medium of growth and development, throws the coach/client relationship into central focus. Contact can be achieved when there is full acceptance of self and other. Dialogic existentialism is the second of the three defining principles of gestalt therapy (Yontef, 1980) and of gestalt coaching. Through this lens, the relationship is *the* most important aspect. This is a differentiating and defining aspect of gestalt coaching when compared with many other (but not all) coaching approaches.

If we exist in relationship with others, we experience ourselves in relationship with others, and those formative relationships where we experienced interruptions to full contact continue to be played out until we become 'unstuck'. Honouring this relational stance, gestalt coaches work with the person in an 'I – thou' way (for example, person to person) rather than an 'I – It' frame (or object relation view, for example – 'I'm the coach' – 'you're the client'). The person to person relationship or 'real' relationship of gestalt is a meeting between human beings, both risking themselves, who nourish and are nourished by the encounter (Clarkson, 2003) in the here and now.

What happens in the relationship between coach and client impacts all the other relationships that that client has in his/her system. So, a newly discovered way of being in relationship in the coaching session makes this way of being an option with others outside the coaching relationship.

There is agreement as to the importance of dialogue and relationship. Sylvie Crocker explains that caring, openness, being with the client and respect for the client's perspective all help to create an I-Thou, person-to-person relationship (Crocker, 2005). O'Broin's work isolates the importance of the coach proactively attending to the development of the coaching relationship to create a generative alliance and engagement where goals and roles are mutually created and understood with mutual empathy and respect (O'Broin and Palmer, 2010; Bordin, 1994). Juliann Spoth and colleagues confirm the importance of dialogue, 'being in conversation around the other's story and experience', as vital to gestalt (Spoth *et al*, 2013: 386).

There is limited research on the coaching relationship specifically and even less that isolates the qualities of the relationship among practitioners using an explicitly gestalt coaching approach. However, research that has been done points to the importance of relationship in therapy settings. Assay and Lambert (1999), studying factors that led to therapeutic success, concluded that therapeutic relationship accounts for 30 per cent of the variance in psychotherapy outcomes. The primary differentiating factor was due to the individual client factors outside the therapy itself. There is also agreement as to what good might look like in terms of the quality of relationship forged in gestalt coaching. Beyond the study by Assay and Lambert, however, we are not clear what the impact of the particular dialogic quality of the gestalt practitioner might be.

Field Theory

And, just as when you turn a kaleidoscope, the pattern of data moves and shifts, bearing similarities, but never exactly the same as that which went before – dynamic change is a constant in the gestalt worldview. Each moment is interrelated with others and includes the gestalt coach, the client and all that arrives with them. The gestalt coach is part of the field and cannot be separated from it. We are products of experience and our interpretations of that experience, so awareness also concerns what might have arrived with whom and what is shared and created in the space between.

Lewin is the name most closely associated with field theory in human behaviour. He viewed individuals as comprising interacting subsystems and existing in, possibly as, a dynamic field in which every part is dependent on every other part. This systemic interdependence is very compatible with what has more latterly been referred to as holism. Lewin's view of how 'tensions' existed, producing observable behaviour, was taken up by Perls in gestalt therapy and so gestalt coaching has inherited concepts that include the dynamic interrelatedness of the field (in which something may become temporarily figural) and has also inherited Lewin's approach of attempting to encompass 'the whole' and to represent the field 'correctly as it exists for the individual in question at a particular time' (Lewin, 1946/2008: 338).

While Lewin's own field was sociology and social psychology, the work of physicists some 50 years later seems very compatible and offers an additional perspective. In 1993 David Bohm and Basil Hiley's book *The Undivided Universe* set out to offer an ontological interpretation of quantum theory. Rather more steeped in physics and mathematics than a typical coach or psychologist may be used to, the preface nonetheless contains an interesting assertion for those of a gestalt persuasion: 'Indeed the most radical view to emerge from our deliberations was the concept of wholeness, a notion in which a system formed a totality whose overall behaviour was richer than could be obtained from the sum of its parts' (Bohm, 1993: xi). In other works by Bohm (1980, 1985/1996; Nichol, 1996; Krishnamurti and Bohm, 1999), he has highlighted views that a gestalt practitioner would recognize, including that meaning is co-created, that questions are framed as a result of experiences or acquired beliefs so an objective position isn't possible, and that we may be deluded when we believe we are in charge of our thinking – it's already in charge of us. Fritjof Capra is another physicist who has highlighted the fundamental interconnectedness of living systems (such as human beings) in his works including *The Turning Point* (1988) and *The Web of Life* (1997). In the latter, provocatively stating the promise to overcome 'the Cartesian division between mind and matter', Capra states, 'mind is not a thing but a process – the very process of life' (1997: 168).

In this chapter alone, we have created a field, a foreground, arranged some data and shared an articulation of some of the core elements of gestalt coaching. Others who work from a gestalt perspective may rightfully agree or disagree. Assuming that there is some agreed truth to what has been described, it follows that gestalt approaches to coaching are inevitably difficult to quantify, to boundary and to research from the perspective of an exact science.

Gestalt approaches have been adopted and integrated into a range of methodologies and vice versa over the last 50 years since the work of Smuts and Perls. It would nevertheless be interesting to discover what differences in description and impact might occur when gestalt approaches to coaching are practiced through a declared gestalt lens rather than implicitly as part of a different coaching methodology. Rather than simply looking to understand the differences between gestalt and other approaches, what difference might we expect a gestalt approach to make from a theoretical perspective?

An idea of development and change offered by Perls, Hefferline and Goodman (1954/1991) was that through awareness generated by a gestalt therapeutic approach, integration of the many parts of self could be achieved with positive consequences. Finding a means of exploring the impact of a gestalt approach on individual integration and resourcefulness would constitute a useful enquiry in terms of the development of gestalt coaching.

Practice: tools and techniques

The practices of gestalt coaching emerge and build from the purpose of awareness and the way of achieving that through the medium of relationship. The perspective of the gestalt coach is that the coachee is making the best creative adjustment that they can in each moment. Through greater awareness, a coachee can have greater choice about how to creatively respond as each moment occurs.

In this section, we offer some practices and approaches a gestalt coach might attend to. We present the cycle of experience, a frame that a gestalt coach may use in describing the figure/ground formation and completion, and to conceptualize the contact boundary and explore how contact is made or not. We discuss a number of 'blocks' to contact that might be familiar to a gestalt coach. We also look at three practices a gestalt coach might freely adapt and adopt as a means of supporting the coachee to become aware through different ways of knowing and experiencing.

The cycle of experience

The process of becoming aware, individually or collectively, of what is going on at any moment is known as the gestalt cycle of experience (Nevis, 1987). Through this awareness, individuals then mobilize energy to take action and constructively employ the new awareness. Learning or completion closes the cycle. A complete, uninterrupted experience starts with sensation and ends with withdrawal of attention as the experience moves into the 'ground' or context, and attention moves to a newly emerging sensation or figure.

Applied to an example taken from Allan and Whybrow (2007: 140), this seven stage cycle might start with the client feeling 'not at all comfortable' (sensation) and 'fear, actually. I might fail', with anxiety held in their stomach (awareness), understanding how they might make a really effective connection with a particular person even though they are holding anxiety in their stomach (mobilization), realization that 'he might be quite anxious too' (action), 'excited' about the meeting (final contact), 'warmer towards the situation' (satisfaction) and finally, rest (withdrawal), before the cycle begins again. Allowing the initial sensation to develop into full awareness feeds into new cycles as different options and choices emerge, leading to still greater awareness. It follows that cycles of experience flow into one another, so rather than a discrete cycle, a wave depicting the flow of continuous experience is described (Zinker, 1977: 77) and shown in Figure 5.1 below.

FIGURE 5.1   The cycle of experience

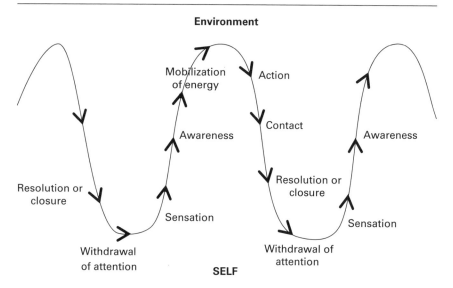

In reality there isn't one wave, but multiple, many aspects competing for attention, many possible figures that can be attended to (see Figure 5.2). Slowing down to the present moment to increase our awareness of moments, to become fully aware of an experience, allows us to see so much more and hold a greater awareness of possible choices at any one time.

The cycle of experience indicates the concept of 'self' as a process of relating an actual point at which the self is distinguished from the not-self (Perls, 1957), and changes from moment to moment as our understanding and awareness of our self changes.

FIGURE 5.2   Multiple possible figures competing for attention

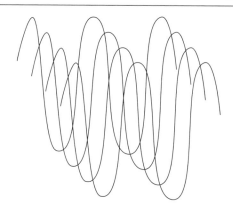

A healthy creative adjustment from a gestalt perspective, a healthy contact, is when a person or group has contact with what is happening now, rather than basing momentary adjustments on a future imagined state or a past experience. Growth is through renewal and revising responses as the context shifts. When a person loses fluidity, and adopts rigid ways of being, with habitual responses that are quickly outdated in relation to what is happening now – they display 'fixed gestalts' or patterns. The rigidity houses a 'disconnection' from the present moment, the 'here and now' experience.

This rigidity or block leads to stuckness from incomplete or confused cycles. An incomplete figure or cycle is described as 'unfinished' and, as humans, we are motivated to complete.

Blocks to awareness

Blocks to awareness are ways of creatively adjusting to reduce the level of contact experienced. These blocks occur at the contact boundary (self/other) and aren't in themselves positive or negative adjustments – rather, they need to be viewed in the context of the current situation. For example, I might sense a hollow feeling in my stomach and interpret this as a hunger. As I'm currently in a meeting for the afternoon and have no means of satisfying my hunger, I choose to deflect the sensation and not allow hunger awareness to fully form. An appropriate response in the short term, but habitually deflecting and turning away from physical and psychological needs or blocking gestalt formation and completion at other points in the cycle may have an unhealthy impact over time.

The blocks to awareness are indicated in Figure 5.3. Each block is labelled alongside a part of the cycle of experience, but the experience of blocks doesn't occur with the neatness suggested (Clarkson, 1989: 50). Taken from Petruska Clarkson, we have included phrases from Gaie Houston (2007: 38), and added a dashed line to indicate the boundary between self/other as self is part of the field and not separate to it.

A gestalt coaching approach would be one of curiosity rather than analysis, with the coach holding this cycle of experience and associated blocks lightly, remembering the map is not the territory. Each block is described in relation to therapy (Clarkson, 1989: 51–57) and coaching (Allan and Whybrow, 2007: 141–42). We have drawn out and illuminated how we might work with three blocks here, namely desensitization, introjection and retroflection.

Desensitization is about turning away from a sensation and not allowing it to come into full awareness, as in the example about hunger above. In situations where we are bombarded with information, imagery, requests; where the boundary between one thing and another is very blurred; and 'life' is fast paced and ambiguous, a level of desensitization is found by many people to be a necessary survival strategy. Yet, if we are too de-sensitized, we lose touch with our self, those around us and situations we are in. We lose things on the edge of awareness, things nearly said, asides; we diminish what

FIGURE 5.3   Cycle of experience showing blocks to awareness

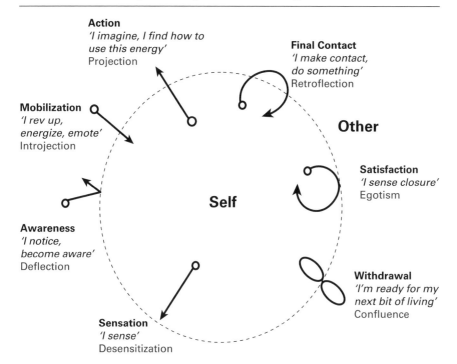

may be highly important because it is not the 'focus' of the dialogue. And, the early clues to this pattern or block are easy to skip past. The client in this example is a leader in a development aid agency.

Coach: 'What have you done to help a child today?'

Client: 'I have no idea. I am pushing paper. And getting on another plane. And not paying attention to my wife and son when I'm at home. My back aches constantly. I'm so preoccupied with the stress I feel about work, that I don't take care of my own health or my own family's needs. I am a health professional. But I write never ending documents and proposals. How have I helped improve a child's health today? I probably haven't.'

Client: 'A colleague said to me "In India, we have a saying: If you were an Indian woman, you'd be pregnant all the time. Because you can't say no."' [As he worked with women and children previously, rather than let this 'aside' disappear, the coach brought this into the present with this client.]

Coach: 'And what is it like to be pregnant all the time because you can't say no?' [The intention of the coach here is to bring the client into fuller contact with what he has just said.]

This example of working with desensitization comes from a colleague, whose careful attention to and application of her clients' language constantly throws light onto fixed, potentially unhealthy patterns (Ellison, unpublished case study).

Introjection is about swallowing whole, without 'chewing over'. Our perceptions and ideas about the world can be simply taken on board from those around us (family, friends, mentors), the culture we live in, the daily habits we unconsciously adopt. Having constantly been told when growing up that 'good mothers stay at home to bring up their children'; or 'you don't show weakness', or 'if you're going to do something, do it as well as you can', we end up with 'an internalised rule book of shoulds, oughts and similar absolutes' (Mann, 2010: 44). It's worth remembering that these, sometimes deeply held, assumptions are not necessarily good or bad but can lead to fixed patterns or ways of how 'I should be in the world' that have never been questioned. In a coaching context, this may show up as a client that is not aware of their own needs, and instead behaves according to a set of beliefs about what a situation demands, perhaps to appear more acceptable. As an example, a client who, keen to be a good mother, wife, wage earner, and never makes time for herself, may have a belief, 'In order to be a good person, others' needs come first'.

People who habitually introject lack a sense of self and are constantly on the lookout for how they should or ought to behave (Mann, 2010).

Introjections can turn up as musts, should haves, shoulds, or other demands that the world, people in it or ourself become somehow different. Very simple and 'light' enquiries open up an introject for further enquiry, for example: reflecting back the demand with a question 'should?', 'must?', 'have to?' Introjects may not be clearly flagged by your client because they are 'usual' for them and often considered advantageous, if noticed. Careful listening is required, for example:

> Client: 'It's really important to be here and accessible for my team.'
>
> Coach: 'I wonder what it is like to be accessible all the time.'

The opportunity to become aware of and chew over what we have previously swallowed whole, enables us to work out what is relevant (and when) and what is no longer relevant. This increases flexibility and responsiveness.

Retroflection is doing to yourself what you would like to do to another, or doing for yourself that which you would like someone/your environment to do for you. Perhaps you're angry or frustrated because you didn't share some feedback with a colleague whom you felt had let you down. You might say and feel 'I'm cross with myself', thus turning the anger you feel towards your colleague inwards towards yourself.

Retroflection can be thought of as keeping the self 'in' or turning inwards and not letting things come out. David Mann describes that 'the contact boundary increases in rigidity' as a person 'protects herself from the environment and in protecting herself, holds her body back from contact with her environment' (2010: 47). Emerging from times when self-expression was not validated, or expression of natural impulses was not allowed (Clarkson, 1989), individuals can learn to suppress their own needs even though they and the context they are in are now different. The self-punishment aspects of retroflection can be associated with guilt and shame.

As with other interruptions to contact, retroflection is not in itself positive or negative. In fact, the turning inwards process of having a conversation with yourself, or self talk, can be a way of positively mobilizing to take action. For example, to encourage yourself to have a difficult conversation with someone who reports to you, or to put yourself forward for that presentation slot at the executive board meeting. Another positive example might be restraining yourself from shouting at a colleague in a meeting; this becomes negative if you never express your anger, hurt or pain.

The second form of retroflection, doing to yourself what you need from the environment, can often be about more intimate needs, such as being cared for, or soothed. This form of retroflection can again be positive in the short term when things are not available in the environment.

Retroflection uses energy and can lead to bodily tension – across the shoulders, held in the jaw; perhaps restriction in physical movement or use of space available (Mann, 2010). It's worth noting 'without the ability to hold back our impulses our society would disintegrate' (Mann, 2010: 48).

Three practices

With an eye on Resnick, we share three practices that might be creatively adapted by a gestalt coach to access what might be seeking to emerge at the edge of awareness, to allow our 'felt sense' to emerge and to enable our whole self to be engaged in creating awareness. The first comes from a significant work, *Focusing*, by the philosopher Eugene Gendlin (2003). Focusing is a means of accessing and working with the knowledge held implicitly within your body. Focusing is not limited to gestalt approaches; it is an approach in its own right. Focusing is useful in a gestalt repertoire to allow what might be at the edge of awareness to come to the fore. We have used Gendlin's instruction set here to illustrate focusing, although, as highlighted by the Focusing Institute, every teacher has a different version or approach. This short exercise is designed to slow down and quieten the mind and body, enabling a different level of listening or focus on what is emerging as figural when all other concerns have been cared for and set aside. This form of exercise attends to what might be at the edge of awareness and the 'felt sense'.

This exercise isn't one used with every client, or used routinely with any client. One example of its use came in Session 1 working with a CEO. The client was late, and described herself prior to the session as rushing around everywhere. As I brought the client to mind in preparation for the session, some slowing, breathing and focusing seemed to be a really important and caring thing to do right at the start. I welcomed my client in and organized refreshments, I then offered a short 'mindfulness' exercise that I would like to do in order to bring us fully present into the coaching space, to which my client agreed. At the end of the exercise, my client stated 'I needed that!' And we continued.

FIGURE 5.4   Focusing (Gendlin, Focusing: Short form, 2012)

1. Clear a space
How are you? What's between you and feeling fine?
Don't answer; let what comes in your body do the answering.
Don't go into anything.
Greet each concern that comes. Put each aside for a while, next to you.
Except for that, are you fine?

2. Felt Sense
Pick one problem to focus on.
Don't go into the problem.
What do you sense in your body when you sense the whole of that problem?
Sense all of that, the sense of the whole thing, the murky discomfort or the
unclear body-sense of it.

3. Get a handle
What is the quality of the felt sense?
What one word, phrase, or image comes out of this felt sense?
What quality-word would fit it best?

4. Resonate
Go back and forth between word (or image) and the felt sense.
Is that right?
If they match, have the sensation of matching several times.
If the felt sense changes, follow it with your attention.
When you get a perfect match, the words (images) being just right for this
feeling, let yourself feel that for a minute.

5. Ask
What is it, about the whole problem, that makes me so _____?
When stuck, ask questions:
What is the worst of this feeling?
What's really so bad about this?
What does it need?
What should happen?
Don't answer; wait for the feeling to stir and give you an answer.
What would it feel like if it was all OK?
Let the body answer.
What is in the way of that?

6. Receive
Welcome what came. Be glad it spoke.
It is only one step on this problem, not the last.
Now that you know where it is, you can leave it and come back to it later.
Protect it from critical voices that interrupt.
Does your body want another round of focusing, or is this a good stopping
place?

The second practice, presencing (Yalom, 1991), is a very simple and powerful practice that can be integrated into any session at any point. This practice brings the speaker's attention to language. Just as we spend our time thinking about future or past events, when we describe things, we use past or future tense rather than the here and now. The practice of presencing simply brings whatever is being shared into the present by asking your client to use the present tense, to speak about the people or things in the story as if they are here and now making them very present.

This practice brings to life hidden aspects, leading to a much greater 'felt awareness' or presence to what is happening as the experience unfolds and insight into what is happening now in relation to the event. Highlighting the dialogical self (ie how I speak about me and others impacts significantly on how I experience myself), this practice also brings the possibility of suspending habitual ways of thinking and 'hanging our assumptions in front of us' (Bohm and Edwards, 1991: 6). The process of presencing, as described by Peter Senge and colleagues, encompasses the idea of 'letting come' as part of Theory U, where future possibilities might come to the fore (Senge *et al*, 2004).

The third practice is selfing. The me and not me described by Gary Yontef describes the process of making contact with the environment – and it's in that place, where we make that contact, that we exist (McLeod, 1993). Self is not a separate, fixed entity, but a vibrant lived process. David Mann (2010) introduces the term 'selfing' as a process or constant creative adjustment to the context we are in. Given this fluidity, the idea of many possible selves can be a useful concept to work with to bring about a shift. There is a point to make though about the selves not being 'fixed' identities but fluid possibilities that might, through phenomenological exploration, enable greater awareness.

Vignette: Working with selfing as a creative process:

Coach: 'I'm wondering whether we might look a bit more at the "you" that is grounded, that is comfortable in your own skin, and think about that you. We can use this chair here.' [coach indicates chair pulled up to the table they are working with].

Client: 'I'm curious about doing that.'

Coach: 'Let's have a go then and see (coach clears the chair of coats and bags). So, let's imagine in this chair sits the you that is grounded, that is comfortable in your own skin, professional, managing. What do you see?'

Client: 'She is sitting differently, she's more upright, shoulders back.'

Coach: 'So you're sitting differently, you're more upright.' [mimics the movement from client to offer stronger contact]

Client: [changes language to 'you'] 'You've got important things to say, interesting, you're creative, you are good to get along with, you're fun, you're taken seriously and have serious things to say.'
[At this point, an obvious choice from a gestalt frame would have been to ask the client to use 'I' rather than 'you'. There are a number of things to work with – the potential paradox, for example, of fun and

serious is among them, so a useful line of enquiry could easily have been – what is it like to be fun and serious?]

Coach: 'Do you feel you've got a clear sense of yourself in that chair? Being grounded and comfortable in your own skin, being taken seriously? Can you see yourself there?'

Client: 'Yes.'

Coach: 'Would you like to take that space to sit in the chair and be that "you"?' [Instead of a suggestion to speak as 'I', the client has been invited to physically inhabit the space they chose to call 'you'. Without hesitation, the client moves quickly to the chair]

Coach: 'What is it like sitting there and being taken seriously?'

Client: 'My posture has changed, I'm sitting up straighter and my shoulders are back, I feel lighter. I've got more energy.'

[Client is now owning this part of themselves through the use of 'I']

Coach: 'Where is that energy?' [indicates body]

Client: 'It's running up the middle of me and out across my shoulders. I feel stronger – energetically.'

Coach: 'What do you see around you?'

[This phase of enquiry, exploring what can be seen, what is noticed, what is happening, who is around, what are they doing is a creative and embedding process. In closing the phase of creative inquiry, it's useful to anchor this resourceful state – to find a way back to it quickly.]

Coach: 'How can you remind yourself of this resourceful place?'

Client: 'I'm not sure, perhaps there's something about this movement.' [opening chest and pushing shoulders back]

Coach: [mirrors the action] 'Does that remind you?'

Client: 'Yes [tries the action a few times], Yes – I'll try it out.'

The idea of 'selfing' fits conceptually with 'becoming' according to Neitzsche and Heraclitus (Cox, 1999). Selfing or becoming reduces the idea of things being fixed or existing in a rigid form, making way for flexibility and fluidity. McNamee and Gergen (1990) highlight the view of self being something that exists/is created only in relationship – 'Personal identity (motive, character, intention, action) is a by-product of negotiations within relationships' (p 20). In their work they offer an invitation, 'Let us here distinguish selves from persons, viewing the former as constructions of relationships and the latter as individual bodies' (p 22).

From Maturana and Varela's work in the 1970s (1973: 198) comes the term autopoiesis (self-producing), also referenced by Capra (1997). This term signifies a view of humans as living systems that constantly and pro-actively create themselves – so they are both the 'product' and the means of production, and there is never a definitively finished article. Further, the individual human is in many ways not individual because there is constant co-evolution or mutual adaptation (with others, with societies etc). Maturana and Varela (1987/1998) explored the implications of the reciprocal relationship between what we think or know and what we do, pointing out that 'Everything said is said by someone' (p 26) and that 'the knower and known are mutually specified' as 'the autonomy of the living being [is] given its full place' (p 253).

CASE STUDY

Words and language limit what can be expressed about any one moment 'and it can take a thousand words to (fail to?) explain that moment of time in which the world came to be differently viewed' (Allan and Whybrow, 2007: 147). A case study splits up a whole into parts. The present moment is preserved rather than transformed. And yet, we offer the following in the knowledge that you will create the meaning required to gain value for yourself.

This case study focuses on a first session, with a follow-up point in session two, drawing out and highlighting the approach that the coach took with explicit reference to gestalt approaches. This first session takes place after an initial discussion of focus has taken place, with practical considerations for the coaching as a whole and appropriate attention to boundaries, although in a gestalt frame, boundaries are also an emergent part of the process.

Bruce is Creative Director in a small media organization. He has recently received feedback as part of a 360° process. The areas he has chosen to focus on include increasing his capability to lead the way for others in the organization and to develop his effectiveness at delivering. By learning about how he might perform more effectively in these aspects of his role he believes he will have reduced anxiety and more time and energy to focus on product development.

Session 1: Starting and co-creating the focus

On starting, the coach welcomes the client and is aware of the client stating how pleased they are to be here, smiling in response, and also of them drawing their bottom lip up as if clamping their mouth shut. This is a momentary action.

Coach: 'What would you like to spend the time on today, what would be useful for you?'

Bruce: [Facing to the right, away from the coach who is positioned in front of him before turning back to the coach] 'In my work as erm Creative Director, I'm often helping people take their ideas or... or dreams and to turn those into some kind of reality, whether it's a film, a campaign or well, lots of possibilities. Often, I first meet them, they're a bit stuck – and the first thing I have to do is unstick them. Right now, I'm feeling a bit stuck myself and would appreciate some help unsticking.'

Coach: 'Hmmm. So unsticking you?'

Bruce: 'Yes, there's things I'm trying to avoid – to hide from, and another view might help me see what they are and to "get in there".'

Coach: 'So, let's keep track of these, it sounds interesting (coach reaches for pen and paper). So, hiding?'

Bruce: 'I think so, I think I'm avoiding some things, and really not quite sure what that is about, yeah.'

Coach: 'And "getting in there."'

Bruce: 'Yes, "just do it"!'

Coach: 'And some unsticking, and another view?'

Bruce: 'Yeah, yes. Seeing where I'm going as well as moving some of the blocks.' [laughs]

Coach: 'I'm noticing the laugh and I'm tempted to ask you to say more...'

Bruce: 'It's just ironic, I sound like one of my clients... for me, what I mean is I want to see the direction I'm heading and use that to help me decide how to tackle what's right in front of me – so I don't put things off, or avoid things which means they turn into big issues – much more challenging than when I first encountered them. There's something here about being a good role model in the business too. I'm a Director, I need to step up a bit I think.'

Coach: 'So there's something also about stepping up and perhaps standing out?'

Bruce: 'That's it – standing out. That's it.'

Coach: 'And standing out would be like...'

Bruce: 'Really being clear about myself as a Director, knowing where I'm headed and knowing I can tackle what comes my way.' [Bruce pushes himself forward in his chair and sits upright]

Coach: 'Hmmm. So by the time we've finished unsticking and finding clarity, not hiding and standing out – have you an idea of when you will know "yes, we've got there"?'

Bruce: 'Hmmm. I will definitely feel calmer, less turmoil [client takes a long breath in and breathes out slowly], yes... less turmoil.'

Coach: 'So more... [coach mirrors the breathing]... and more [pushes herself forward and sits upright]?'

Bruce: 'Yes, that's it [breathes in and out once more and regains the upright posture].'

As the session begins, the coach is noticing as much as she can of Bruce as he talks, including content, physical posture and gesture. Using the client's language, creating a stance of curiosity and enquiry, there is a co-created focus and a shared 'felt sense' of what it might be like when a good outcome for this session is achieved. At this point, the coach suggests a pause to reflect on what has emerged in this early part of the session, to encourage the client to take any notes that they may want before moving on. In moving on, the client is invited to share which aspect of the discussion they have had so far that they most want to move on to explore now. The client chose to work on unsticking and standing out. The client left the session with an idea of himself being at the hub of a wheel, the spokes being aspects to attend to that will keep him unstuck and away from potholes. Between sessions, the coach asked Bruce to notice when he is standing out, and to reflect on the image of being at the hub.

Session 2: Working with a block

Arriving in Session 2 there is attention to how Bruce is arriving, in what 'state', and a question as to the focus now in this session. Bruce chooses to provide a story about what has happened between sessions and in particular noticing that he has come up against a block, where he feels unable to attend to all that he needs to in order to keep him on track.

Coach: *'Blocked?'*

Bruce: *'Yes, a block of some kind, that stops me paying attention to all the aspects that I need to – I just can't hear it. [Bruce starts speaking more quickly at this point.] And I don't notice until I'm heading into a situation where I realize I'm not quite prepared. Even then, I'm not that clear on what I need to be listening to at that moment – it's almost like I need a structured 'check list'. Just when I notice I've not done what I need to, I feel really anxious, a void opens up and I start mentally spinning.'*

Coach: *[Speaking deliberately slowly] 'Spinning and a void? I'm noticing your pace of talking has increased.'*

Bruce: *'It's how I feel inside, everything speeds up.'*

Coach: *'Can I invite you to explore this with me, perhaps we can run the sequence in slow motion somehow?'*

Bruce: *[an audible out breath as he blows air out] 'That sounds good.'*

At this point, the coach invites Bruce to stand up and step into a space in the room where they can explore the void and the spinning. The coach invites Bruce to stand as if on the edge of the void he experiences. Bruce takes up a position that is 'rigid' and still, shoulders pulled back, slightly leaning backwards.

Coach: *'What is happening now?'*

Bruce: *'I notice I'm not prepared – it happened yesterday, I was about to present a solution I've been working on to the MD, and I hadn't factored in a key stakeholder request, or made explicit some of the key financial and operational assumptions I've been working with.'*

Coach: *'Can I invite you to speak as if this is happening now, in the present tense?'*

Bruce: *'So... I am giving the presentation and outlining the solution, and as I am speaking I am adding in the bits of information that are missing and as I talk, I make a good guess as to what the stakeholders' needs are. I know I am sounding muddled.'*

Coach: *'There is a lot going on.'*

Bruce: *'There is!' [Speaks this firmly and clearly]*

Coach: *'What happens just before you notice the void?'*

Bruce: *'I've been so focused on the detailed content.'*

Coach: *'What happens in your body as you start to notice the void?'*

Bruce: *'I freeze, like a bunny in headlights. There's an inner "oh no" and a tightening in my chest that quickly moves to my stomach...' [looks at coach]*

Coach: *[keeps deliberately quiet with slightly raised eyebrows]*

Bruce: *'... and my stomach lurches' [client stops talking and holds stomach]*

Coach: *[mimics the coachee's stance] 'Let's take a step back.'*

Bruce steps back and Coach follows – mirroring the gesture.

Bruce: *'That's much better. I can see now what I have missed before.'*

Coach: *'What's happened to the feeling?'*

Bruce: *'I feel excited.'*

Coach: *'And what has happened in your body?'*

Bruce: *'The energy has flown up and into my mind.' [Gestures with both hands an upwards flow] 'I feel switched on and focused.'*

The session continues, Bruce notices that his being 'hooked' by content, is rather limiting his awareness of what's required in many situations. The gesture of stepping back is adopted and experimented with to free up his thinking.

When might a gestalt approach be most suitable?

The purpose of working from a gestalt frame is awareness, but there are other ways to awareness rather than a gestalt approach. Another way of framing this question is to see a gestalt approach as co-creating a coaching space that: a) suits the figural and b) might be useful in terms of the zone of proximal development, as part of c) enabling greater awareness. Of course, c) reciprocally serves the other two. Used in isolation from a gestalt stance (ie reduced to tools and techniques,) gestalt practices could lead to an overwhelm for a client suddenly faced with a lot of sensations and data that they (or the coach) have little skills or experience to process. This could lead to some panic and withdrawal of contact, which under the circumstances may form a very healthy choice by the coachee. However, keeping people inside a circle of 'tried and tested' again (and again), where nothing is ventured, is not likely to lead to new perspectives and choices. But the coaching space must be skilfully created. Two examples are used to illustrate working from where the client is.

A client, Georgia, whose internal landscape and embodied landscape was regarded by her as a mystery and something to be feared. However, any question concerning noticing feelings and emotions led to either tears or a blank – and not a lot of repertoire in between. This shifted through the coaching work; finding ways to talk about emotions in the coaching space led to great sharing of feelings in the work space, enhancing relationships. Standing in another's shoes was an exercise that generated insight and movement including compassion for the other.

A client, Frank, for whom thinking about his thinking seemed an impossible task and something outside his capability to articulate. Bringing awareness directly into the room to experience and 'play with' in the moment, through gestalt techniques of empty chair, future walk and making things playfully 'real', developed his awareness.

Allan and Whybrow note that 'those who are inclined to regard themselves holistically as the "equipment for the job" and have an interest in using their own presence as a catalyst for change' may find gestalt coaching most appropriate (2007: 146). Those in senior roles and leadership positions who have a systemic, interrelational, viewpoint may value a gestalt approach as this is a feature of the lens. Those who would prefer a more structured, tools based approach, perhaps seeming more logical/rational in its focus, may not choose a gestalt approach.

Conclusion

Gestalt coaching is a stance, a way of being in relationship with yourself and those with whom you work. In this chapter, we hope to have expanded your insight and knowledge about gestalt coaching, and also added greater flavour of what it is like to work with a gestalt orientation and the potential benefits for coaching clients.

Developing yourself as a gestalt coach

Developing your skills

Working as a gestalt coach is complex and demanding. You are offering yourself as the instrument of change. While individuals can start to include a gestalt stance and principles in their practice with relatively little input, there is ongoing and significant work to be done to develop capability to practice using gestalt principles in their full sense.

Mee-Yan Cheung-Judge (2001) describes the self work as:

- owning your 'instrumentality' by devoting time and energy to knowing yourself; and

- dedicating time to the maintenance of your self understanding and capability by developing lifelong learning habits, working through issues of power and control, building emotional and intuitive self-awareness and committing to self-care.

Rowan and Jacobs (2002) elaborate on this concept of self as instrument in relation to therapy, distinguishing between an instrumental, an authentic and a transpersonal 'self' that a therapist may inhabit for their work, noting the centrality of the relationship with the client in all (Clarkson, 1995). They point to the requirement for self development that enables the therapist to engage in the relationship in ways that enable beneficial outcomes. Their 'authentic' self is, arguably, the one that shares most in common with gestalt approaches, with an I-Thou emphasis (Buber, 1970), Person-to-Person or I-You relationship as described by Clarkson (1995).

The medium of development for a gestalt coach reflects the medium of awareness in the gestalt approach – through relationship. The skills to acquire 'focus on awareness and action, rather than on the questions' (Nevis, 1987: 89). Nevis describes in detail the skills of awareness that includes the ability to stay in the present and focus on the ongoing process, with sensitivity to sensory, physical functioning of self and others, through:

- frequent tuning into your emotions and those of others;
- separating data from interpretation and emphasizing non-judgemental observations;
- putting things succinctly, clearly and directly;
- awareness of your intentions, of what you want to do or say, together with the ability to be clear in letting others know what you want of and from them;
- seeing where the client is at any time, and respecting that in working with the system;
- facing and accepting emotional situations with a minimum of personal defensiveness;
- making good contact with others;
- presenting self as a highly attractive yet non-charismatic presence;
- capacity to be both tough and supportive during the same work session;
- helping the client system draw meaning or understanding from its experience with you;
- appreciation of the significant contextual issues involved in system intervention; and
- awareness of the aesthetic, transcendent, and creative aspects of working.

These ideas about the work required to develop as a gestalt practitioner and coach follow from using the Cycle of Experience and apply to you and to your clients, as you step forward. There is a sense of becoming rather than having arrived, and the starting point is an intent and orientation. You have already started the process by virtue of being a coach and being human.

An example of the self development, awareness and skill of the gestalt practitioner came in conversation with a colleague describing a client case they had taken to supervision. The colleague, a coach, was feeling anger and frustration while with a client whose purpose for coaching included interpersonal skill development. The coach was aware that this anger and frustration was different to what was 'normal' for her. Following supervision, she was able to use her capability to enable this dynamic to emerge in a session, rather than try to suppress and contain the dynamic. In doing so, both coach and client had the opportunity to become curious about the dynamic and to fruitfully explore it. This enabled the client to become more aware of their interpersonal patterns and to hold this awareness moving forward.

Deepening your understanding

A great resource for developing your insight into gestalt is *The Now Red Book of Gestalt* (Gaie Houston, 2007). There are multiple examples of exercises and approaches you might use to develop your awareness of you-in-process that are particularly powerful and informative to explore with a practice group.

Web resources

Without providing an exhaustive list, you might find the following links and resources useful as a starter for further exploration:

- For individual and organizational development the Gestalt Institute of Cleveland (**www.gestaltcleveland.org/index.php**) and the Gestalt International Study Centre (**www.gisc.org/**) might prove valuable sources of resources and programmes. The difference is articulated in Spoth *et al* (2013).

- The Focusing Institute offers a number of resources to support you to make explicit what might be held implicitly (**www.focusing.org/**).

References

Allan, J and Whybrow, A (2007) Gestalt coaching, in *Handbook of Coaching Psychology: A guide for practitioners*, eds S Palmer and A Whybrow, (pp 133–59), Routledge, London and New York

Assay, T P and Lambert, M J (1999) The empirical case for the common factors in therapy: qualitative findings, in *The Heart and Soul of Change: What works in therapy*, eds M A Hubble, B L Duncan and S D Miller, (pp 33–56), American Psychological Association, Washington, DC

Bachkirova, T (2011) *Developmental Coaching: Working with the Self*, Open University Press, Maidenhead

Baron, L and Morin, L (2009) The coach-coachee relationship in executive coaching: a field study, *Human Resource Development Quarterly*, 20, pp 85–106

Beisser, A (1970) The paradoxical theory of change, in Fagan and Shepard, *Gestalt Therapy Now*, pp 77–80, Harper, New York [It is also available here: https://gestalttherapy.org/_publications/paradoxical_theoryofchange.pdf]

Bluckert, P (2010) The gestalt approach to coaching, in *The Complete Handbook of Coaching*, ed T B Elaine Cox, (pp 80–93), Sage, London

Bohm, D (1980) *Wholeness and the Implicate Order*, Routledge, London

Bohm, D (1985/1996) *Unfolding Meaning: A weekend of dialogue with David Bohm* (D Factor, Ed), Routledge, London

Bohm, D (1993) *The Undivided Universe*, Routledge, London

Bohm, D and Edwards, M (1991) *Changing Consciousness: Exploring the hidden source of the social, political and environmental crisis facing the world*, Harper, San Francisco

Bordin, E S (1994) Theory and research on the therapeutic working alliance: new directions, in *The Working Alliance: Theory, research and practice*, eds A O Hovarth and L S Greenberg, (pp 13–37), Wiley, New York

Buber, M (1970) *I and Thou*, Scriveners, New York

Capra, F (1988) *The Turning Point*, Bantam, New York

Capra, F (1997) *The Web of Life*, Flamingo, London

Castelnuovo, G, Faccio, E, Molinari, E, Nardone, G and Salvini, A (2004) A critical review of Empirically Supported Treatments (ESTs) and common factors perspective in psychotherapy, *Brief Strategic and Systemic Therapy European Review*, pp 208–24

Cheung-Judge, M-Y (2001) The self as instrument: a cornerstone for the future of OD, *OD Practitioner*, 33 (3), pp 11–16

Clarkson, P (1989) *Gestalt Counselling in Action*, Sage, London

Clarkson, P (1995) 2,500 years of gestalt: From Heraclitus to the Big Bang, in *Change in Organizations*, ed P Clarkson, (pp 126–39), Whurr, London

Clarkson, P (2003) *The Therapeutic Relationship*, Whurr Publishers, London

Cox, C (1999) *Nietzsche: Naturalism and interpretation*, University of California Press, Berkley, Los Angeles and Oxford

Crocker, S (2005) Phenomenology, existentialism, and eastern thought in gestalt therapy, in *Gestalt Therapy: History, theory and practice*, eds A Woldt and S Toman, (pp 65–80), Sage, Thousand Oaks, CA

Drake, D B (2009) Evidence is a verb: a relational approach to knowledge and mastery in coaching, *International Journal of Evidence Based Coaching and Mentoring*, 7 (1), 1–12

Duckworth, A and de Haan, E (2009) What clients say about our coaching, *Training Journal*, 64–67

Ellison, R (unpublished case study) When the health professional gets sick, www.rachelellison.com

Findlay, J and Gilchrist, I (2003) *Active Vision: The psychology of looking and sensemaking*, Oxford University Press, Oxford and New York

Gendlin, E (2003) *Focusing: How to gain direct access to your body's knowledge* (Anniversary edn), Bantam Books, London

Gendlin, E (2012) Focusing: Short form. Retrieved 28 December 2013 from *Focusing Institute*: www.focusing.org/short_gendlin.html

Grant, F and le Roux, A R (2011, May) A gestalt approach to coaching: optimising individual and team wellness, *1st Congress of Coaching Psychology*, Southern Hemisphere

Grimley, B (2007) NLP coaching, in *Handbook of Coaching Psychology: A guide for practitioners*, eds S Palmer and A Whybrow, (pp 193–210), Routledge, London and New York

Hall, L (2013) *Mindful Coaching: How mindfulness can transform coaching practice*, Kogan Page, London and Philadelphia

Heidegger, M (1962) *Being and Time* (J Macquarrie and E Robinson, Trans), Harper and Row, New York

Herman, S M and Korenich, M (1977) *Authentic Management: A gestalt orientation to organizations and their development*, Addison-Wesley, New York

Houston, G (2007) *The Now Red Book of Gestalt*, Gaie Houston, London

Kabat-Zinn, J (2003) Mindfulness-based interventions in context: past, present, and future, *Clinical Psychology: Science and Practice*, **10** (2), pp 144–56

Köhler, W (1929/1947) *Gestalt Psychology*, Liveright, New York

Krishnamurti, J and Bohm, D (1999) *Limits of Thought: Discussions*, Routledge, London

Leahy, M and Magerman, M (2009) Awareness, immediacy and intimacy: the experience of coaching as heard in the voices of gestalt coaches and their clients, *International Gestalt Journal*, **32** (1), pp 81–144

Lewin, K (1946/2008) *Resolving social conflicts and field theory in social science*, American Psychological Association, Washington DC

Long, K (2011) The self in supervision, in T Bachkirova, P Jackson and D Clutterbuck, *Coaching and Mentoring Supervision* (pp 78–90), Open University Press, Maidenhead

Mandelbrot, B (1982) *The Fractal Geometry of Nature*, Freeman and Company, New York

Mann, D (2010) *Gestalt Therapy: 100 key points and techniques*, Routledge, Hove and New York

Maturana, H and Varela, F (1973/1980) *Autopoiesis and Cognition: The realization of the living*, D Reidel, Boston

Maturana, H R and Varela, F (1987/1998) *The Tree of Knowledge: The biological roots of human understanding*, Shambhala, Boston and London

McLeod, L (1993) The self in gestalt therapy theory, *British Gestalt Journal*, 2 (1), pp 25–40

McNamee, S and Gergen, K J (1990) *Relational Responsibility*, Sage, Thousand Oaks, CA

Nevis, E C (1987) *Organizational Consulting: A gestalt approach*, Gardner Press, New York

Newton, T and Napper, R (2010) Transactional analysis and coaching, in *The Complete Handbook of Coaching*, eds E Cox, T Bachkirova and D Clutterbuck, (pp 172–86), Sage, London

Nichol, L (1996) *On Dialogue*, Routledge, London

O'Broin, A and Palmer, S (2010) Exploring key aspects in the formation of coaching relationships: initial indicators from the perspective of the coachee and the coach, *Coaching: An international journal of theory, research and practice*, **3** (2), pp 124–43

Palmer, S and Whybrow, A (2007) Coaching psychology: an introduction, in *Handbook of Coaching Psychology: A guide for practitioners*, eds S Palmer and A Whybrow, (pp 1–20), Routledge, London and New York

Perls, F (1965) Three approaches to psychotherapy: Gloria. Part II: Frederick Perls. Retrieved 22 January 2014 from www.youtube.com/watch?v=8y5tuJ3Sojc

Perls, F S (1957) Finding self through gestalt therapy. From the Cooper Union Forum Lecture Series. New York. In *From Planned Psychotherapy to Gestalt Therapy: Essays and lectures of Frederick Perls* (2012) The Gestalt Journal Press

Perls, F S, Hefferline, R and Goodman, P (1954/1991) *Gestalt Therapy: Excitement and growth in the human personality*, The Gestalt Journal Press

Pinna, B (2010) New gestalt principles of perceptual organization: an extension from grouping to shape and meaning, *Gestalt Theory*, **32** (1), pp 11–78

Resnick, R W (1984) Gestalt therapy east and west: bi-coastal dialogue, debate or debacle? *Gestalt Journal*, Vol 7 (1), pp 13–32

Rowan, J and Jacobs, M (2002) *The Therapist's Use of Self*, Open University Press, Buckingham

Senge, P, Scharmer, C, Jaworski, J and Flowers, B (2004) *Presence: An exploration of profound change in people, organizations and society*, Random House, New York

Simon, S (2009) Applying gestalt theory to coaching, *Gestalt Review*, **13** (3), pp 230–40

Spoth, J, Toman, S, Leichtman, R and Allan, J (2013) Gestalt approach, in *Handbook of the Psychology of Coaching and Mentoring*, eds J Passmore, D B Peterson and T Freire, (pp 385–406), John Wiley and Sons, London

Sun, B J, Deane, F, Crowe, T P, Andresen, R, Oades, L and Ciarrochi, J (2013) A preliminary exploration of the working alliance and 'real relationship' in two coaching approaches with mental health workers, *International Coaching Psychology Review*, **8** (2), pp 6–17

Tang, Y Y, Ma, Y, Wang, J, Fan, Y, Feng, S, Lu, Q, *et al* (2007) Short term meditation training improves attention and self-regulation, *Proceedings of the National Academy of Sciences of the USA* (pp 17152–56)

Whybrow, A (2013, December) *Taking a Look at Super-Vision*, Edinburgh

Yalom, I D (1991) *Love's Executioner and Other Tales of Psychotherapy*, Penguin, London

Yontef, G (1999) Awareness, dialogue and process: Preface to the 1990 German Edition, *The Gestalt Journal*, **XX11** (1), pp 9–20

Yontef, G (1980) Gestalt therapy: a dialogic method, Unpublished manuscript

Zinker, J C (1977) *Creative Process in Gestalt Therapy*, Vintage Books, New York

Neurobehavioural modelling

06

Applying neuroscience research to the development of coaching practice

PAUL BROWN AND DENYSE BUSBY-EARLE

Introduction

The emergence of neuroscience into the practice of coaching is a relatively new phenomenon.

The knowledge base for neuroscience-based coaching relies upon a number of sources. In no special order of significance these include Allan Schore's integrative writings on the development of the self (Schore, 1994, 2003a, 2003b); Daniel Goleman's *Emotional Intelligence* (1995); the developments in interpersonal neurobiology led by Dan Siegel, with special reference to attachment theory (eg Siegel, 1999); the developing brain imaging (fMRI) research in the social cognitive neurosciences, especially at UCLA (eg Eisenberger *et al*, 2003; Eisenberger and Lieberman, 2004; Lieberman, 2007; Lieberman *et al*, 2007); McGilchrist's magisterial synthesis of the research that underpins an understanding of the way the two halves of the brain are different (McGilchrist, 2009); and the varied writings of the newly-emerging neuro-philosophers of the mind (eg Damasio, 1994, 1999, 2003; LeDoux, 2002).

The application of neuroscience to coaching was especially encouraged by the founding of the NeuroLeadership Institute (NLI) by Rock and Ringleb in 2007 in the United States, Australia and Europe (Rock and Page, 2009) and the setting up of Masters level degree studies through distance learning in its field of interest. The Institute's objectives and purpose were established from the outset, and remain, 'to encourage, generate and share neuroscience research that transforms how people think, develop and perform'. It structured its field of interest into four domains – how people:

- make decisions and problem solve;
- regulate emotions;
- collaborate with others; and
- facilitate change.

Although this list might now have a slightly early 21st-century Westernized-culture 'corporate agenda' feel about it, as being organizational demand driven rather than neuroscience research driven (see Passmore, 2013, for a wide-ranging discussion on diversity issues in coaching), the NLI began the now well-established trend for coaching to make available to the corporate world the increasing accumulation of knowledge about the brain and corporate behaviour.

One limitation of Rock's approach, however, is that it seems to ask not how coaching might develop out of neuroscience but, with particular regard to leadership, how neuroscience might be used to smarten up coaching. Brown and Brown (2012), on the other hand, have taken a starting point that says, in essence, *if* coaching in practice and as a profession were to develop based on experimental method and knowledge, not just practice smartened up by bits of knowledge, then what would the art and practice of coaching look like when informed by such a body of knowledge?

The purpose of this chapter is to expand on that question. It focuses on how practice can be derived and, in principle, tested. It relies upon a working definition of coaching exemplified by the practice of neurobehavioural modelling (NBM) (Brown *et al*, 2009; Brown and Brown, 2012). From this perspective coaching becomes an interpersonal laboratory in the neurobiology of experience where the brain, as the organ of relationship and within a coaching relationship, is helped into a state in which it can create for itself the first tentative pathways that the goals of any particular coaching contract require.

At its best, the coaching encounter of itself creates what Scharmer and Kaufer (2013: 147) have called 'generative listening'; which 'means to form a space of deep attention that allows an emerging future possibility to "land" or manifest itself ... [great coaches] ... listen deeply in a way that allows you to connect to your future emerging self'. This is very akin to Nancy Kline's concept of creating 'generative attention in uncontaminated silence' through the structuring of time to think (Kline, 2009) although Scharmer and Kaufer make no reference to Kline's work.

It seems to be the case that neuroscientists in general are not very interested in people – their field of specialization is, after all, the brain. In contrast coaches, who are profoundly interested in people, see neuroscience as a complex area into which they should not trespass. But while neuroscience, as an applied field, may not be known to most coaches it is far from unknowable.

And there is, arguably, some urgency for coaches to know it. For the fact of the matter is that it is now possible to say with high levels of confidence that there can be no changes in behaviour without there being a prior and corresponding change in the neurochemistry and circuitry of the brain – in its neurobiology. So if what coaches see themselves doing professionally is, with agreed goals, creating developmental change in individuals, then there is a strong case easily made for suggesting that coaches do need an effective grounding in how the brain works and how the self and the individual come to be who they are (let alone who they might be); so that as professionals coaches can target their coaching interventions all the better and develop techniques and methods for which there is some justification in an underlying science.

Although the pathways of the brain are now, through the developments of connectomics (eg Seung, 2012), subject to scrutiny of a kind that was not previously possible, the three-part evolutionary structure of the brain described by MacLean (1985) – reptilian complex, paleomammalian complex (limbic system) and neomammalian complex (neocortical system) – is the best working model currently available. It makes it possible to equip executive coaches with the necessary and sufficient knowledge for them to be appropriately and professionally mindful of the brain. Coaches who are otherwise mindless of the brain may do themselves and their clients no service now in ignoring a body of knowledge that, even if embryonic, is formed enough to be of great value.

In the growth of the scientific evidence for how the brain works, MacLean (1985) asked the profoundly simple but crucial question: What happened to the development of the brain when mammals first appeared in the evolutionary record? If dependent young require some care then, MacLean reasoned, the brain must have developed in order to provide the kind of infant care that egg-laying reptiles – the evolutionary predecessors of mammals – do not show. In consequence there should be some development in the evolution of the brain that makes caring-for-young possible.

Already in his early sixties when he formulated that question, MacLean spent the rest of a long research and writing career answering it. In 1952 he had coined the term 'limbic system' to describe the central area of the brain responsible for managing emotions and by 1985 had started formulating the concept of 'the triune brain' – the three-stage evolutionary development of the brain from reptile to mammal to cognizant human being (MacLean, 1985, 1990). Knowledge of the workings of the triune brain is critical to the executive coach's neurobiological understanding of the client.

This chapter sets out, therefore, to bring to the attention of experienced coaches a means of incorporating modern applied neuroscience into their everyday professional practice.

Evidence-based approach to neurobehavioural modelling (NBM)

The formal evidence for the benefits of a brain-based approach to coaching is, at this stage, nil. No systematic comparative studies have as yet been conducted. The field is right at the beginning of its early development.

There are, however, moments in history where developments in a clinical science knowledge create an applied paradigm shift. The Western discovery of the circulation of the blood was one such (Harvey, 1628) – though for many centuries it led to many misapplications, of which blood-letting and cupping were two, in the mistaken belief, and in the absence of any knowledge about the workings of an immune system, that if disease was carried by the blood it were better that the blood was evacuated from the body.

Nearly 350 years later in the second half of the twentieth century, and by direct observation using appropriate transducers, Masters and Johnson (1966) described scientifically for the first time the fact that the human sexual response system in both male and female also relies substantially for its procreative powers as well as its pleasures on the effective circulation of the blood. From such observations new treatments developed.

This is the kind of applied paradigm shift that a brain-based approach to coaching offers the coaching profession. The development of coaching, it is suggested, is at a point in time when pragmatism (technique that seems to work) has the opportunity to be the beneficiary of empirical science; for that science to question the prevailing pragmatism; and for practice to be (re-)developed from a new knowledge base.

Looking back upon the twentieth century and a hundred years of the psychotherapy in various guises from which coaching has been derived, it can now be seen that many of the psychotherapies are belief systems, not scientific systems: and adherents of one system or another have been trained as acolytes, not applied scientists.[1] Dissent – Jung against Freud, to note the most obvious of many dissentient couplings – resulted in the need to found another church ('school of thought') and attract adherents (Jungian vs Freudian, and so on). No underlying model appeared that would unite the schools of thought in shared discussion.

So we are at a point in time where psychotherapy can now be seen as a set of belief systems and its founder, Freud, as an extraordinary explorer and observer but a very poor model builder. There is no id, ego or superego to be discovered in the architecture of the brain. They are descriptive, not definitive, states.

Will the same be being said of coaching in 20 years' time? Or will a profession have been developed that is firmly grounded on research?

Parsons (2013) makes a similar point:

> The 20th century was not short of models of human behavior. What it lacked was *facts*. In the absence of facts the vacuum got filled by theories being asserted as facts. Many coaches and leadership development consultants have

been trained to use these assertions developed more as a matter of personal attachment to an idea and belonging to one school of thought or another than the pursuit of a common body of evidence founded in science that had, at its heart, a common set of assumptions.

So here are some of these, sometimes surprising, assumptions:

The brain hates change. The best bet for the brain is always to trust its own experience. Intellectually, change might sound challenging or exciting but to the brain it spells danger. The brain that got me here is the one most likely to get me there, if you will. The brain is an error-detection system. The Orbital Frontal Cortex (above the eyes) detects any unexpected change and is closely linked to the amygdala, the brain's fear circuitry within the limbic system, the brain's emotional command centre. When activated, the limbic system draws precious energy away from the frontal areas of the cortex responsible for decision making and executive function. Error detection signals can push people to become more emotional and act more impulsively; animal instincts taking over. But with a cycle of perpetual change now a reality, even if change is well explained and implemented, the associated uncertainties can still trigger strong threat responses in people.

Emotions are everything. These threat responses need to be understood. All sensory input first comes into the brain via this limbic system, where every event is given an emotional loading. Emotions and feelings attached to experiences create meaning. This happens before information is distributed into the cortex for decision or action. Think about that for a minute because it's a pretty explosive statement: *emotions underpin all decisions*. The emotional patterning laid down in childhood has been shown to have far-reaching consequences in adult life. The coach's task is to pick up on the energy of the client's emotions and use that energy to create a shift in direction that the coaching contract has described.

The social brain, an organ of relationship. The brain is predominantly social, a fact we forget all too easily at work. Social pain activates the same regions in the brain as physical pain. When someone is put down, barked at or on the end of an abrasive management style, threat responses are activated by the limbic system impairing the ability to think clearly. You know that feeling – 'I'm just too stressed, I can't think straight!' – what's happening is the frontal cortex is drained of energy as the limbic system lights up like a Christmas tree and absorbs all of the energy itself.

Insight requires a quiet brain. What do most of us do when we are trying to think? Hold our heads and say to ourselves, 'Come on, think harder!' Problem is, insight comes from having weak associations. You have to quieten down the narrative circuitry in the brain to allow insight to come. Most people would seem to find insight coming when away from work or the situation to be dealt with. Some companies such as Google have experimented by allowing engineers time away to work on completely different things. Most problems are not solved rationally (we can't explain 60% of problems we solve). Anxiety is inversely related to ability to spot them, ie the more anxious you are, the less likely you are to get insight and vice versa. What does this suggest you do now versus what might you do differently?

Giving people ownership is key, telling them what to do just doesn't seem to work. There is a significant body of clinical and work-based evidence now that attests to this fact. If someone always late for meetings is reprimanded, the short term threat of sanction might work for a while but it simply heightens anxiety and diverts attention away from work and back to problems that led to lateness in the first place. Even rewarding punctual attendance at meetings (say with better assignments) reinforces neural pathways associated with the habitual problem. However when people solve things themselves, the brain makes patterns and emits a rush of adrenaline. The reward response from ownership can be stronger than a pay rise.

Expectation shapes reality. Mental maps play a bigger part than we ever thought in human perception. Take the placebo effect: tell people they have been administered a pain-reducing agent and they experience a marked reduction in pain, despite receiving a completely inert substance like a sugar pill. A study by Robert Coghill (Coghill *et al*, 2003) found that 'expectations for decreased pain produce a reduction in perceived pain (28.4%) that rivals the effects of a clearly analgesic dose of morphine'. People are clearly more focused on the pain relief, activating the brain's pain relief circuits, ie they experience what they expect to experience. The influence of expectations, whether conscious or not, on perception has significant implications. Two call centre workers might have different views of an irate customer, one seeing an obstructive child to be overcome, the other seeing an intelligent grown-up with useful suggestions.

Attention and focus are key. Cognitive scientists have known for years that the brain can change significantly in response to changes in the external environment. We also now know that the brain changes according to where it focuses its attention. Attention changes the brain – very quickly. The aim is to develop ability to control attention and make attentional choices. The more you can understand the brain, the more you can be solution not problem-focused. Tremendous benefits can be had from short bursts of practice (a few minutes a week), noticing your brain and assessing where its energy is flowing. In this way, you quieten down your brain, reduce any threat response, maximize prefrontal cortex activity therefore optimize insight and problem solving.'

Rock (2006a) sets out a stall of some of the attractions of a more rigorous neuroscientific approach for coaching. 'Senior executives,' he writes (though it is not a statement with which all would agree):

> being academically trained and analytical, will want a theory base, evidence and research to support the introduction of any new way of thinking into their organization. A brain-based approach to coaching may provide an answer to this challenge, for a number of reasons.
>
> First, every event that occurs in coaching is tied to activities in someone's head. This means that a brain-based approach should underpin and explain every good coaching model and provide the field with an underpinning science. A brain-based approach is going to be inclusive and bring the disparate field (of coaching) to greater cohesion.
>
> Second, a brain-based approach to coaching looks attractive when you think about the other contenders for a foundational discipline, the obvious one being psychology. From an organizational perspective, psychology suffers from a mixed history and a perception of being unscientific. While psychologists are the first people called on if someone is in crisis, most senior leaders would not consider them for improving performance because of the bias they assume psychologists have for therapeutic languages and models... We live in a materialistic world where organizations respect things that can be measured. To bring about the wide-scale use of coaching as a learning or transformation tool, we need to speak to organizations in a language they understand.

In thinking very widely about old paradigms having limiting effects, and with special reference to classical physics and quantum mechanics as being different ways of understanding causality, Schwartz, Stapp and Beauregard (2005: 3) have suggested (by way of parallel to the challenge facing executive coaches) that:

> Surmounting the limitations imposed by restricting one's ideas to the failed concepts of classic physics can be especially important when one is investigating how to develop improved methods for altering the emotional and cerebral responses to significantly stressful external or internally generated stimuli. An incorrect assignment of the causal roles of neurophysiologically and mentalistically described variables can impact negatively on a [coach's] selection of a course of ... [appropriate action].

Although the prospect of taking a quick trip into quantum mechanics may be concerning to many coaches, the special aspect of this statement is that it challenges the coach to consider the reference point(s) guiding professional actions. This is the essential challenge needed in the development of a knowledge-based profession – knowledge of what happens in the way how things work. The question of whether any particular coach can make that happen is then a matter of specific skill and the development of method and technique.

Coaching and the practice of NBM

A standard and unexceptional definition of coaching is provided in the *Executive Coaching Handbook*:

> Executive coaching is an experiential and individualized leader development process that builds a leader's capability to achieve short- and long-term organizational goals. It is conducted through one-on-one and/or group interactions, driven by data from multiple perspectives, and based on mutual trust and respect. The organization, an executive, and the executive coach work in partnership to achieve maximum impact.
> (Executive Coaching Forum, 2012: 10; 2004: 7)

The limitation of such a definition is that it says nothing of the specifics of content, only of process. In a similar manner Peltier (2010) notes that the Center for Creative Leadership at Greensboro, North Carolina, has defined the executive coach as 'a consultant who uses a wide variety of behavioral techniques and methods'. It tells us nothing of a shared common discipline, and he lists no reference to neuroscience or the brain at all. In *The Complete Handbook of Coaching*, Cox and her colleagues have less than six lines of reference to neuroscience in more than 400 pages of text (Hawkins and Smith, in Cox *et al*, 2010). In 13 chapters of 'Theoretical Approaches' to coaching, they demonstrate decisively from the perspective of this chapter how coaching is at risk of going down exactly the same developmental route as psychotherapy – a pragmatic set of modes of practice without an underlying experimental body of knowledge.

In contrast neurobehavioural modelling is a deliberate attempt to derive practice from science, not attach science to justify practice. There are six main elements to the practice of NBM:

1 Establishing a relationship that has limbic resonance in it.

2 Biographical enquiry.

3 Creating wonder as part of mobilizing the whole emotional system, but especially its attachment side.

4 Establishing and rehearsing contractual goals within the privacy and privilege of the professional setting of the coaching sessions.

5 Setting objectives for inter-sessional experience.

6 Monitoring the outcomes of inter-sessional experience.

These elements are not necessarily sequential in the manner listed above. And in any particular coaching encounter not all may be apparent all of the time though must have been apparent some of the time. It is contended, however, that for NBM coaching to be successful all these elements must necessarily be (have been) in play.

It is axiomatic, therefore, that the coach must have some working knowledge of the brain in order to keep these elements in active play: and in particular must have an easy familiarity with the basic emotions, the way they drive all behaviour, are the source of all motivation, and are expressed as feelings. Being able to distinguish between specific emotions and generalized states such as 'happiness' is also important.

Coaching within the disciplines and structure of NBM relies especially on the natural and developed capacity of the coach to create limbic resonance with a client in such a way that the client's brain starts tuning to (resonating with) the coach's brain. The client's brain then opens itself to the possibility of structural development. Schore (2003a) says that 'resonance' requires that the participants be 'psychobiologically attuned' (77):

> In physics, a property of resonance is sympathetic vibration, which is the tendency of one resonance system to enlarge and augment through matching the resonance frequency patterns of another resonance system. It is well established that the transfer of emotional information is intensified in resonant contexts, and that the moment when a system is tuned at the 'resonant' frequency it becomes synchronized. Such energy-infused moments allow for a sense of vitalization, and thereby increased complexity and coherence of organization.
>
> (Schore, 2003a: 76)

> Resonances often have chaos associated with them, and thus they are characterized by nonlinear dynamical factors – relatively small input amplitudes engender a response with a surprisingly large output amplitude.
>
> (Schore, 2003a: 141)

With resonance working the objectives of the coaching contract can properly start, or continue to be worked towards, by being modelled in the session so that new neural pathways start to be shaped. The best outcome of any session is awareness in the client that new options that are to be tested out in the real world are becoming possible. So the coaching session itself is a laboratory in which the self is being modified and new options tested for consolidation or revision as a result of continuing experience. This gives rise to the possibility of developing a working concept of 'the limbic leader' (Brown, Swart and Meyler, 2009).

Brown and Brown (2012: 14) describe the coaching session as follows:

> There are two brains at work in a coaching session. One belongs to the coach and one to the client. Both are trying to make sense of the other. Each is sending signals that will materially affect the way the other is working. Both function in the same way but each is quite unlike the other in the detail of the way it as constructed. Both were constructed by and through relationship, and both continue to be hugely influenced by and be the influencer of relationship.
>
> The brain is organized through an extraordinarily complex number of neurochemical connections created by electrical charges between brain cells –

86 billion of them each with the possibility of 10,000 connections. Through repeated firing of the same pathways, networks and circuits, patterns are established which encode experience, establish the individuality of each person, and control how people express themselves in all aspects of their lives.

Although the brain is a whole system it is useful to distinguish three major parts – the reptilian brain, also frequently called 'the snake brain', the mammalian brain and the neocortical cognitive brain. The way they operate together – and especially the mammalian and cognitive – is what the modern neurosciences are revealing. The way the mammalian brain and the cognitive brain interlink is the key to the practice of coaching based on the science of the brain. Change and development happen essentially through the mammalian brain. All information impinging on the brain – from outside sources as well as inner experience and thoughts – is assessed by the mammalian brain for its emotional significance and distributed into the rest of the brain once the significance has been assessed. The practice of brain-based coaching relies essentially on knowing enough about the brain to use that knowledge to know about the person. The way into knowing about the person is to build a picture of the key influences – and influencers – that shaped the emotional structure of the person you coach.

The first three elements of the six listed above are perhaps the most specific to NBM and are worth considering in some detail. Elements 4, 5 and 6 will be familiar from many evidenced based coaching trainings. In the NBM framework it is the content, context and intent that is specific to NBM.

Element 1: Limbic resonance

In their seminal book *A General Theory of Love*, Lewis and his colleagues (Lewis *et al*, 2000) define limbic resonance in the following way:

> Within the effulgence of their new brain, mammals developed a capacity we call limbic resonance – a symphony of mutual exchange and internal adaptation whereby two mammals become attuned to each other's inner states. It is limbic resonance that makes looking into the face of another emotionally responsive creature a multi-layered experience. Instead of seeing the eyes as two bespeckled buttons, when we look into the ocular portals to a limbic brain our vision goes deep: the sensations multiply, just as two mirrors placed in opposition create a shimmering ricochet of reflections whose depths recede into infinity. Eye contact, although it occurs over a gap of yards, is not a metaphor. When we meet the gaze of another, two nervous systems achieve a palpable and intimate apposition. (16)

The precise mechanisms of limbic resonance are not entirely understood. But they are as crucial to individual relationships and a sense of well-being as was Bach's *Well-Tempered Clavier* to the development of harmony in Western music.[2] In the way that an instrumentalist needs a keyboard that is in tune to be able to create music, so a coach needs a brain that is well-tuned, *wohltemperierte*, to be able to create the harmonies, however tempestuous, that effective coaching requires as the client learns to flow with the coach while the coach is simultaneously learning to flow with the client.

Boyer (2011) has suggested the following ways in which a chief executive can develop limbic resonance:

- **Monitor emotions** – learn to monitor your own emotions when with others. What are you experiencing? Is it coming from you or from someone else?

- **Be present** – be mentally present and emotionally available so that others feel emotionally connected to you.

- **Conduct emotional scans** – do an emotional scan before, during and after events that can trigger emotional reactions to prevent your own emotional hijacking and to convey the emotional attitude you want to convey.

- **Choose which emotions to convey** – before presenting important or possibly emotion-laden topics, consider what emotions you want to communicate and practise getting into the body that will convey them.

- **Listen with and for emotion** – to be a better listener, recognize the emotions and body of the speaker, both of which give clues to the speaker's perspective. What emotions surface? What impressions come to mind?

- **Discuss and promote emotional health** – make people aware of emotions and help them learn positive emotional reactions.

- **Create a healthy emotional climate** – develop a specific plan to foster an emotionally healthy and productive culture. Promote and implement that plan.

- **Practise lightness** – become aware of the importance of lightness in interaction. People enjoy being around lightness because it, like other emotions, is contagious. Daniel Goleman (2006) said, 'Laughter may be the shortest distance between two brains, an unstoppable infectious spread that builds an instant social bond.' Use it and enjoy it.

It is probable that in her *Time to Think* writings, teaching and consulting Nancy Kline (1999, 2009) has created the so-far most developed practical methodology for inducing a resonant limbic state that can be put to coaching (and other organizational) uses in a systematic manner. Although not conceptualized as such, she has created a style of practice that appears to maximize the capacity of the client to respond constructively and creatively through having created the conditions where the amygdala – the guardians of the emotional system and the assessor/distributor of all incoming stimuli – judge the (coaching) situation as safe so that the brain can explore its own interstices with a highly-focused but minimalist guidance from the coach: and from such an exploration to arrive at its own best solutions with regard to whatever it is that is under consideration in the time-to-think coaching session.

Although the neuroscientific data for these observations is not yet fully developed with reference to coaching, they are in principle all testable observations. So what we are seeing at this stage of development of applied neuroscience in coaching is informed pragmatism paving the way for experimental method to confirm, disconfirm or otherwise enlarge our understanding of the precise neural underpinnings of individual development as a consequence of coaching.

Element 2: Biographical enquiry

Although all brains are essentially the same, all are profoundly different. It is experience (nurture) that is essentially responsible for the working arrangements of any particular brain, given the specifics of its genetic potential and structural origins (nature). Were we able to see a brain as readily as we can see another human being we would readily see that the brain of each person is as unique as we know individuals to be from the way we recognize them in a wide variety of smaller and larger ways.

What this means for the skilled practice of coaching is that no assumptions can be made about the client based upon achievements (CV) without having the proper support of the specifics of the developmental interpersonal environment in which the person grew up. Nor, more importantly, can any safe assumptions be made about the client from the coach's presumed familiarity with aspects of the client's organizational, career or social history. All this requires coaches to have the skill of biographical enquiry which permit some understanding of the motivational 'why?' of human endeavour, not just the performance 'what?'

Within the developmental environment the emotions sculpt the pathways of the brain – as they do for the whole of life; so that 'developmental' refers to any process of development at any stage of life, not just early life. Although it is in the first 24 years of life that most of the sculpting takes place (and more so at some developmental stages than others, some developmental phases being triggered biologically and genetically for the specifics of what happens), the capacity of the brain to change itself through the mechanisms of neuroplasticity is one of the discoveries of modern neuroscience (Doidge, 2007). The fact that it can be hard work changing well-established patterns of thought, feelings and behaviour (for all of which the brain is responsible), as well as extraordinarily easy, should only serve to increase a coach's fascination with the possibility of structural change being possible.

'Change' is a word used here with some caution, however. The brain prefers not to change. It is a time-consuming, energy-demanding and distracting business. But what the brain seems to be very good at doing is *adapting*. 'Change' creates resistance. 'Adapting' creates possibility. Adaptation builds on what the (individual, unique) brain knows. 'Change' confronts the brain with the prospect of something unknown and therefore potentially fearful. And adaptation has within it the possibility of 'wonder'.

So biographical enquiry requires the coach to become familiar with not only the events of a person's life but the surrounding emotional circumstances too. As all behaviour is motivated (focused) by the attaching of event to emotion that is then constructed as meaning, biographical enquiry that focuses on what the emotional themes are that underpin particular behaviours, and how and when such themes were established, will give both coach and client a level of understanding about how to address the coaching contract that cannot otherwise be obtained.

Element 3: Wonder

The NBM working model for using knowledge about the brain in executive coaching relies upon the fact that as the primary emotions are the effective source of energy within the brain, and the client has the stated intention of wanting to develop or change some aspect of his or her Self, then the emotional system has to be mobilized to make change possible. It is entirely possible for a client to like the idea of difference or change without in any way changing the underlying emotional patterns that are responsible for current behaviour: but without the underlying patterns changing, no behavioural change will take place.

So an effective coach has to mobilize the emotional system. The surprise/startle emotion, of which wonder is a component, is a useful starting point.[3]

The quality of 'wondering' will vary from client to client because its associated components will be particular to the individual client. And there are clients – technically called 'anhedonic', which is a lack of capacity to feel pleasure from normally pleasurable activities – in whom spontaneous wondering seems such a foreign possibility.

A good way to try out whether 'wonder' will be the right way for mobilizing the emotions of a client is at the very beginning of the first encounter. An introduction that says:

> We don't know anything much about each other. My task, as your coach, is to get to know you as well as I possibly can so that I can look at the world through your eyes. But while I am trying to make sense of you, you are also inevitably trying to make sense of me. That's what we do as human beings. So I would want you to feel free to ask me anything about me that you want to while we are engaged professionally together. In the privileged circumstances of our coaching we both keep our knowledge of each other confidential (save for the normal boundaries to confidentially, such as risk of harm or serious illegality). But as I get to know you, and help you get to know yourself, it's only fair that if you want to balance up our understanding of each other by asking me questions than please do.

This is an unusual enough introduction to a professional encounter for it to have the possibility of triggering wonder and surprise in the other person. How the client reacts will tell you immediately an enormous amount about their emotional system and interpersonal style. What you have done as coach is offer a situation that implies the possibility of a great deal of mutual trust. The way it is welcomed, rejected, misunderstood or ignored or anything else starts your understanding of the client's emotional landscape.

This then leads on easily to the more familiar coaching tasks contained in the remaining three elements:

4 Establishing and rehearsing contractual goals within the privacy and privilege of the professional setting of the coaching sessions.

5 Setting objectives for inter-sessional experience.

6 Monitoring the outcomes of inter-sessional experience.

In 1949 the Canadian neuropsychologist D O Hebb formulated the proposition that the brain is organized as an associative learning mechanism – the cells that fire together, wire together. It was a huge imaginative leap for which the evidence has increasingly emerged over the subsequent decades. It is now understood additionally that the mechanism of getting the cells to fire together in all their complex neurochemical processes of creating new or extending old pathways relies upon the emotional system which also results in establishing meaning. Consequently, for coaching, the workings of a client's emotional system are paramount.

In Element 3 the idea was introduced of an immediate approach to understanding the client's emotional system, for which biographical enquiry as described here and used in NBM is the more formal process. In Elements 4, 5 and 6 the effectiveness of what is accomplished relies equally upon the continued mobilizing of emotional energy – really attaching to the goals of coaching, setting meaningful inter-sessional objectives, and monitoring the actual experiences and outcomes. While this monitoring may well take place in subsequent coaching sessions it is by no means limited to such time and place. Appropriate contact with a client by telephone, text, e-mail or Skype in-between formal coaching sessions not only strengthens the relationship but keeps the emotional energy needed to create effective change alive within the client when all pressures will mitigate against effective change.

One key emotional experience common to many coaching sessions also needs putting in context.

It is not unusual for a client to leave a coaching session profusely appreciative of the session, saying how helpful it has been, and creating a warm and rewarding feeling in the coach of a professional job well done. Coaches need to be very humble about such occasions, and remember context. For many executives the opportunity to spend private time talking essentially about themselves with an involved yet professionally detached person is a situation in which the attachment emotions flow intensely and with great delight.

But if a coach considers this a job well done, when such emotions appear, it is worth asking whether the *direction* that coaching needs to be taking is being properly accomplished. Has the emotional energy in the session been properly focused on the contractual goals? If it has not, but only on the immediate experience, then the coach is using the special qualities of the coaching relationship as a means of boosting a sense of professional competence that might well be misplaced. It is to be guarded against. The coach's special responsibility is to mobilize the attachment emotions in the service of the client, not the boosting of the coach's professional satisfactions.

CASE STUDY

Meet Cassie... a busy, middle-aged senior executive who had joined a high profile team of a large multinational as an expatriate, eight years prior to her venturing into our coaching relationship which she came into as she struggled with a new and more senior role.

Originating from a developing country, Cassie, the prime breadwinner of her family, faced with dignity, and modesty, the cultural, climatic and social challenges of working and living in the testing environment of an England that she and her family had initially found quite alien.

With a commercial focus, her job was to stimulate and maintain others' inputs to a remit that spanned disparate, geographically spread teams which together were being held accountable for delivering a unique, large scale, highly visible project on time.

Faced with unfamiliar negative feedback at an annual appraisal a year into her new role, Cassie's brain fought to make sense of elements of her 360° review. In thinking about embarking on our coaching relationship, she expressed a desire to learn to:

- manage conflict at work (desperately wanting to learn to tackle this pragmatically, she was finding that when the 'voice in her head' constantly said, 'that's nonsense' about something she knew indeed was nonsense she avoided interaction and withdrew from difficult situations for days on end);

- be better attuned to the needs of others; and

- initiate rather than stand back and observe.

A logical and objective thinker with a preference for introversion, Cassie was unlikely to be impressed or convinced by anything other than reasoning based on solid, concrete facts. Her academic, analytical style needed coaching that could help her experience that feelings were observable facts, and that they control behaviour, which is the premise of a brain-based approach.

In the conversation that prefaced our coaching relationship, we explored Cassie's concern about the unknown, highlighting her reluctance to divulge deeply held confidences. With moist eyes, she coolly emphasized the importance of trust as she reflected on whether to commit to embarking on our voyage together. The window of opportunity for change had been opened through a degree of limbic resonance between coach and client, and the boundaries of 'the self' had already begun to become fluid as her eyes testified.

The cumulative six hours of the first two coaching sessions revealed the depth of her inward, meditative and reflective style. Most significantly it offered telling insight not just into her preferred behaviours, 'the how', but also 'the what', ie the environment of family, career and social history.

The real key to change lay in using the intimacy of the coaching courtship to delve into the previously unexplored yet wonderfully revealing depths of Cassie's world. Dilts' iceberg model (Dilts and Bonissone, 1993) was used as a framework for guiding the conversation as Cassie explored her hitherto hidden/less articulated beliefs, values, identity and her spiritual drive – 'the why' – that had sculpted the pathways of her brain – the connectome which to that point had defined her.

Married, with an academically gifted child, Cassie never knew her own mother, who died in childbirth. Against this atypical backdrop, her formative years had nevertheless defined her developmental interpersonal environment with intellectual, cultural and religious stimulation from those who nurtured her. Left without the usual prime 'interior decorator of one's life... a mother', Cassie's father and devoted relatives espoused and constantly reinforced opinions of everything being done 'the right way' within the prevailing family ethos of 'private, emotional matters never being aired in public'. What happened in the home and within the family was, as Cassie recalled, 'nobody's business'.

Concerned about precision, privacy and discipline, the client had therefore developed high standards and expectations of herself and others. With an insatiable appetite for learning, learnt and rewarded through her childhood, Cassie had self-created rules for her life, which included a very strong belief that 'head must always rule over heart' supported by her stated life motto: 'Think – Process – Act' (left brain dominance).

From these exploratory conversations about the work, home and social contexts emerged a logical thinker, with a preference for clear direction in the form of strict agendas, procedures and regulations. Indeed, her success to date had been fostered by elements of creative insight firmly backed by logical reasoning combined with a practical step-by-step approach to tackling work diligently.

While appearing outwardly to do so confidently, in her new work environment she was plagued by a self-limiting belief that having grown up in the developing world she was less capable than those with whom she now worked. This, combined with a reduced inclination to trust, the legacy of a prior traumatic and dysfunctional relationship with a colleague, was compounded therefore by the negative 360° feedback leaving the client disappointed, disinclined to initiate activity and demonstrating passive avoidance of conflict at work.

Preferring conformity as her customary way of doing things and driven by the escape/avoidance emotions of some fear and shame, Cassie distanced herself from the team. Impatient with some who were disorganized or inconsistent in their performance, she avoided conflict at work by withdrawing when stressed, quietly 'retreating into her cave' to become the diligent but silent observer over periods of three–five days.

In stark contrast, at home, in the moment, Cassie seldom hesitated in displaying and voicing anger and disappointment, saying what she felt rather than dwelling on it.

Indeed, in exploring the concepts of emotion and feeling, she initially balked at the suggestion that there was a discussion to be had, implying that it meant the same to her as thinking.

Stimulated by inviting her to reflect using the metaphor of colour, she eventually shared 'emotion, if any, was kept in a box in my head. On a good day, the box is a pale whitish blue hue filled with ideas, concepts, facts and processes'.

Cassie went on to volunteer that 'felt fairness' in the past had been the trigger to her experiencing the emotion of her 'whitish blue box'.

She added: 'I feel sunshine and warmth when I am doing stuff with my son. Then it's a fuzzy, warm feeling. It's like a tennis ball with a protective outer shell and a soft centre.' We had begun to create meaning through attaching a pattern and language for emotional themes that the client had never before been cognizant of, let alone identified.

A committed Christian, Cassie recognized that additionally her spiritual connection and religious activities had provided her only other recognized outlet fuelling catharsis, enjoyment and a sense of inner peace.

Over time, recognizing possibilities, she began to look excitedly towards exploring additional themes for growth. Through a wellness audit with her coach she decided that sleeping more than four hours per night would be a great start to calming her mind. She chose to focus additionally on wellbeing, enjoying new gastronomic experiences, and travel.

Biographical enquiry also revealed her desired legacy … 'the Coke effect'. Cassie wanted to be experienced and perceived as effervescent, bubbly and energetic – and recognized that though that adaptation would demand some significant change, it was exciting and filled her with wonder!

This newfound vitality proved to be a significant catalyst for change. Recognizing the risk of stifling more creative or innovative approaches she relaxed from expecting and demanding conformity to her customary way of doing things.

In her intra- and inter-sessional feedback Cassie began to consider more frequently other people's ideas and explored feelings. Bit by bit snippets about her family and personal circumstances at work, emerged and her coach sensed a relaxing of the rigidity and inflexibility that for many years had defined her.

Six months following the end of the nine-month coaching relationship the coach received this:

> *... had my appraisal!!! I used the language of my coaching, including the 360 Leadership article. It went really, really well – 'Exceeding Expectations all the time' was the summary comment and 'needed in the team to drive projects/actions, because of energy and motivation'!!!* The email continued:
>
> *Take some credit for this as a proof point of your great coaching. During my appraisal, I referred to my coaching as an enabler, complimented my director loads, shared my plans to work with 'Little Ms Yellow' (the strong, direct, very energetic colleague with the high-pitched voice that filled the open plan office) and how I have begun already to move into action.*

The coach had stimulated and mobilized attachment emotions in service of the client and her contractual goals: better attunement to the needs of others; and initiating rather than standing back and observing.

Attention had been focused on the connection between emotion, physiology, beliefs, actions and results in a manner that inspired the client to allow herself to feel properly. She began to recognize her amygdaloid triggers and consequent reactions, particularly as they related to conflict in the workplace. She recognized that she could choose instead to respond in a manner than avoided her former retreating puzzled avoidant victim mindset.

Two years later her focus of attention was once again drawn to conflict in the workplace. Having been promoted into a role that she had wanted desperately and prepared well for, she was beginning to feel bruised by what she had described as a colleague's 'egotistic militaristic style'.

Committed to self-protection, on this occasion, rather than retreating as she had done in the past, she focused her attention on making sense of the 'paralysis' that she felt in the moment as if 'pinned against a wall' and sought help to deal with it through a couple of top-up coaching sessions.

Using the analogy of space and perceptual positions as we had a year prior in exploring the relationship with her husband, Cassie revisited the work issue, shocked and surprised that we were reusing a technique that she had 'disliked intensely' the first time!

She felt discomfort as it boosted her ability to see, to hear and to feel the relationship through the eyes, the ears and the emotions of the other person.

Once again she was moved to tears exploring this new work relationship through the eyes and ears of a neutral observer, a fly on the wall. As she moved through each position, the coach's silence, said Cassie, 'made it worse'. NOTE: The coaching relationship will not always feel comfortable, *in the moment*!

Startling Cassie in this way proved to be pivotal within the safety of the coaching session. She identified not just with what she felt, but it also invited her to experience what she was doing with her emotions, take responsibility for them and release associated toxicity.

In the intervening gap between the two sessions, the coach invited her to continue to witness and define the emotions in her body (a different take on 'FACTS' ... a focus that she had always enjoyed). Cassie defined and recorded them by:

- naming the behaviours that she was witnessing in herself;

- being clear on how they had worked against her;

- witnessing her emotions 'fear, anger, disgust' and the physiology associated in their manifestation as feelings; and

- sharing them in the follow-up coaching session three weeks later.

The coach had created a climate that invited Cassie to listen and notice mentally, physically, and emotionally – the toughest for her to do.

Focusing her attention in this way heightened her understanding as she allowed herself to explore her emotional landscape and in so doing make deliberate attentional choices when future conflict arose.

Over the period of the coaching relationship Cassie had shifted from avoidant 'immunity' to change to conscious 'attachment' to change, which paved the way for her to eventually establish and consolidate a different way of being.

An unplanned bonus was that this healthier emotional state had inspired her to address a concern that had defeated her for two decades.

Her new awareness inspired her to test a more holistic approach to wellbeing (mind, body and spirit). Her closest friends and relatives for many years had told her to take action, which she had resisted hotly. She attested to making herself 'physically invisible', avoiding corporate and social photos by hiding behind others.

Cassie had made a winning connection! Yes she had been hiding from interpersonal conflict, but her intra-personal battle pre-dated it.

Inspired to create a healthier physical state she embarked on a systematic approach to becoming fitter. Combining a healthier diet with exercise and six rather than three hours' sleep, the client sustained weight loss with a consequent shift to four dress sizes lower, and an improvement in her energy levels.

Cassie had solved the problem herself by owning what was already within her. She brought it into conscious awareness where it became possible to appreciate it within her own understanding of herself.

Her brain had created new patterns, emitting a rush of adrenaline which then fuelled excitement of the possibilities that lay ahead, importantly leaving her in control of the changes that she continues to choose to sustain.

Discussion

This account of Cassie in coaching illustrates the essential tenet of brain-based coaching, which is that there is no other way in which to engage in coaching. It is not that other techniques or models might not be useful. There are many ways of engaging with a client. But no other coaching approach offers an explanatory view of what is happening within the client, though many others offer a descriptive view.

If this appears a large claim for brain-based coaching – that there is no other way in which to engage in coaching – then the apparent arrogance of such a claim can perhaps be mitigated by acknowledging the certainty that, as all behaviour is underpinned by neurochemistry and the relevant neural structures, nothing can happen in coaching that is not related to the brain: and if change of any kind is the goal of coaching, then it must be underpinned by changes in both neurochemistry and brain circuitry. So coaching from a brain-based point of view, using what is currently known about how the brain works, carries with it the possibility that the client is served by the best knowledge available being used in the service of the shared goals of the coaching contract. And that cannot be other than a proper professional objective.

When might this approach be most suitable?

We have suggested so far that coaching is at a crossroads. Modern developments in neuroscientific knowledge offer the possibility of applying that knowledge to enhance coaching practice. We would contend, based on the research evidence from neurobiology, that all behaviour is underpinned by neurochemical processes. Given this understanding, we believe coaches should take account of this in their practice.

The extent to which neurobehavioural modelling will be an approach of choice will depend upon the development of competing models and a gradual increase in an experimental literature that creates the evidential framework for specific choices about intervention models, of which NBM is the first to be proposed within the coaching literature. As matters stand at the time of publication of this book, NBM is the only neuroscientifically-derived model available and, whatever its limitations at this first stage of its development and increasing use in the field, is applicable in all coaching circumstances.

Conclusion

This chapter has presented an outline description of coaching using neurobehavioural modelling. It relies upon an understanding of the detail of the emotional system as the main source of all directed energy within the human system: the way – through biographical enquiry – that the emotional system has been developed within the unique structures of the individual client: and the nature of the coach's interaction with the information that the client brings – everything about him- or herself – that makes sense for the client in such a way that the client becomes accessible to him- or herself as the means of re-structuring aspects of the Self.

Coaching through NBM is seen not as a set of techniques or practices but the use of a body of knowledge from which technique and practice are continuously derived in a creative and continuous manner as a unique response to the individuality of the client. At the core of this approach is the coach's capacity to establish a trust-based relationship with the client – itself an art form – based upon the coach's developed and tuned capacity to trust him- or herself.

Developing yourself as a neurobehavioural coach

Developing your skills

Neuropsychology for Coaches: Understanding the basics (see below) has been written specifically as a practical guide to coaching and takes into consideration how the brain (of the coach as well as the client) is likely to be working. The structure of the process in coaching is described by the term 'neurobehavioural modelling' (NBM). It lays special emphasis on understanding, through biographical enquiry, the patterns of emotional experience that are embedded as the basis of current behaviour.

Lanz and Brown have discussed the NBM model with specific reference to supervision.

- Brown, P and Brown, V (2012) *Neuropsychology for Coaches: Understanding the basics*, Open University Press / McGraw-Hill Educational, Maidenhead
- Lanz, K and Brown, P (2014) *Brain-based Supervision – Neuropsychology in Coaching Supervision.* Fourth International Coaching Supervision Conference, Ashridge, 27 June

Deepening your understanding

The material coming out of neuroscience laboratories around the world is increasing at a great rate. Applied neuroscience – finding ways of making use of such information in real-life situations – is only just beginning to develop as a new academic and applied field in its own right. Keeping a conscious awareness of the fact that all behaviour is motivated and that motivations arise and are directed from the energy contained in the emotions (e-motions), as described in this chapter, will help you refine your own way of understanding what is happening within yourself and in others.

- For a way of keeping in touch with thinking about how the brain works, track the work of Henry Markram in what used to be called the Blue Brain Project at Lausanne but is now the Human Brain Project in Geneva (eg **http://www.youtube.com/ watch?v=LS3wMC2BpxU**).
- Follow the monthly Brain Gain pieces in the management journal *Developing Leaders*, published by IEDP and available online.

Web resources

- Try the free app *3-D Brain* for an elegant display of the main regions of the brain.
- For some thoughtful discussion about why we have brains at all, see Daniel Wolpert on **http://www.youtube.com/watch?v=7s0CpRfyYp8**
- For a way of creating a sense of why attention is so important – energy flows where attention goes, see **http://youtu.be/xv4P09L-uzk** and start following The Brain Club.

References

Boyer, L (2011) *What is limbic resonance and how can leaders use it?* www.lynboyer.net/what-is-limbic-resonance-and-how-can-leaders-use-it-2/ (accessed 28 August 2013)

Brown, P T and Brown, V (2012) *Neuropsychology for Coaches: Understanding the basics*, McGraw-Hill/Open University Press, Marlow

Brown, P T, Swart, T and Meyler, J (2009) Emotional intelligence and the amygdala: towards the development of the concept of the limbic leader in executive coaching, *NeuroLeadership Journal*, **2**, pp 67–77

Coghill, R C, McHaffie, J G and Ye-Fen, Y (2003) Neural correlates of interindividual differences in the subjective experience of pain, *Proc. Nat. Acad. Sciences*, **100** (14), pp 8538–42

Damasio, A (1994) *Descartes' Error: Emotion, reason and the human brain*, Grosset/Putnam, New York

Damasio, A (1999) *The Feeling of What Happens: Body and emotion in the making of consciousness*, Harcourt, Brace, New York

Damasio, A (2003) *Looking for Spinoza: Joy, sorrow and the feeling brain*, A Harvest Book, Harcourt, Inc, New York

Dilts, R and Bonissone, G (1993) *Skills for the Future*, Meta Publications, Capitola, CA

Doidge, N (2007) *The Brain That Changes Itself*, Penguin, London and New York

Eisenberger, N I and Lieberman, M D (2004) Why rejection hurts: a common neural alarm system for physical and social pain, *Trends in Cognitive Sciences*, **8**, pp 294–300

Eisenberger, N I, Lieberman, M D, Kipling, D and Williams, K D (2003) Does rejection hurt? An fMRI study of social exclusion, *Science*, **302** (5643), pp 290–92

Executive Coaching Forum (2004, 2012) *The Executive Coaching Handbook*, www.theexecutivecoachingforum.com/docs/default-document-library/echb5thedition2_25.pdf (accessed 25 August 2012)

Goleman, D (1995) *Emotional Intelligence*, Bantam Books, New York

Goleman, D (2006) *Social Intelligence: The new science of social relationships*, Bantam Books, New York

Harvey, W (1628) *De Motu Cordis*, Frankfurt

Hawkins, P and Smith, N (2010) Transformational coaching, pp 231–34, in *The Complete Handbook of Coaching*, eds Cox, E, Bachkirova, T and Clutterbuck, D, Sage Publications Ltd, London

Hebb, D O (1949) *The Organization of Behaviour*, London: John Wiley and Sons

Kline, N (1999) *Time to Think: Listening to ignite the human mind*, Ward Lock, London

Kline, N (2009) *More Time to Think: A way of being in the world*, King Fisher Publishing, Poole-in-Wharfedale, England

LeDoux, J (2002) *The Synaptic Self: How our brains become who we are*, Viking, New York

Lewis, T, Amini, F and Lannon, R (2000) *A General Theory of Love*, Random House, New York

Lieberman, M D (2007) Social cognitive neuroscience: a review of core processes, *Annual Review of Psychology*, **58**, pp 259–89

Lieberman, M D, Eisenberger, N I, Crockett, M J, Tom, S M, Pfeifer, J H and Way, B M (2007) Putting feelings into words: affect labelling disrupts amygdala activity to affective stimuli, *Psychological Science*, **18**, pp 421–28

MacLean, P D (1985) Evolutionary psychiatry and the triune brain, *Psychol. Med.*, **15**, 219–21

MacLean, P D (1990) *The Triune Brain in Evolution: Role in paleocerebral functions*, Plenum Press, New York

Masters, W H and Johnson, V E (1966) *Human Sexual Response*, J and A Churchill, London

McGilchrist, I (2009) *The Master and His Emissary: The divided brain and the making of the Western world*, Yale University Press, New Haven

Parsons, J (2013) *Why brain-based coaching works*, Untapped Talent Career Coaching blog, 21 August, http://untappedtalentcareers.com/wp/?p=423andgoback=%2Egde_2964870_member_267726363#%21 (accessed 23 August 2013)

Passmore, J (ed) (2013) (2nd edn) *Diversity in Coaching: Working with gender, culture, race and age*, Kogan Page, London

Peltier, B (2010) *The Psychology of Executive Coaching*, (p xxv), Routledge, New York

Rock, D (2006a) *A Brain-Based Approach to Coaching, based on an interview with Jeffrey M Schwartz MD*, www.workplacecoaching.com/pdf/CoachingTheBrainIJCO.pdf (accessed 23 August 2013). See also *International Journal of Coaching in Organizations*, 2006, **42**, pp 32–43

Rock, D (2006b) *Quiet Leadership: Six steps to transforming performance at work*, HarperCollins, New York

Rock, D (2009) *Your Brain at Work: Strategies for overcoming distraction, regaining focus, and working smarter all day long*, HarperCollins, New York

Rock, D and Page, L (2009) *Coaching with the Brain in Mind*, John Wiley and Sons Ltd, London

Scharmer, O and Kaufer, K (2013) *Leading from the Emerging Future: From ego-system to eco-system economies*, Barrett-Koehler Publishers, Inc, San Francisco

Schmidt, E, Castell, D and Brown, P T (1965) A retrospective study of 42 cases of behaviour therapy, *Behav.Res.Ther.*, **3**, pp 9–19

Schore, A N (1994) *Affect Regulation and the Origin of the Self: The neurobiology of emotional development*, Lawrence Erlbaum Associates, Hillsdale, NJ

Schore, A N (2003a) *Affect Dysregulation and Disorders of the Self*, W W Norton and Company, New York

Schore, A N (2003b) *Affect Regulation and the Repair of the Self*, W W Norton and Company, New York

Schwartz, J M, Stapp, H P and Beauregard, M (2005) Quantum theory in neuroscience and psychology: a neurophysical model of mind-brain interaction, *Philosophical Transactions of the Royal Society of London, Series B*, **360** (1458), pp 1309–27

Seung, S (2012) *Connectome: How the brain's wiring makes us who we are*, Houghton Mifflin Harcourt, Boston

Siegel, D J (1999) *The Developing Mind: Toward a neurobiology of interpersonal experience*, Guilford Press, New York

Notes

1 Although there were varied attempts to apply learning theory psychotherapeutically – Pavlovian, Skinnerian and so on – only one strand of development had rigorous clinical experimental method attached to it. In his highly original book of 1958, *Psychotherapy by Reciprocal Inhibition* (Stanford University Press), Joseph Wolpe, a South African physician, described the experimental induction of fear in cats and its alleviation in humans. It led to the active and highly successful treatment of phobias. Learning theory and behaviour therapy models in general, however, lacked a working model of what 'learning' was and had no understanding of the functional structure and purpose of the emotions. Nevertheless Schmidt *et al* (1965) showed that a relationship effect appeared to operate when similarly skilled therapists used behavioural techniques.

2 J S Bach's *Das Wohltemperierte Klavier*, Books I and II of 1722 and 1742 respectively, are of profound significance in the development of Western classical music, requiring fine tuning or 'tempering' of the keyboard. See *Play Your Brain; Adopt a musical mindset and change your life* (2011). Prehn, A and Fredens, K, London; Marshall Cavendish International.

3 Any of the eight emotions will do, though mobilizing change via the escape/ avoidance emotions of fear, anger, disgust, shame and sadness is not an easy route to development. The attachment emotions of excitement/joy and trust/love are much better at creating new pathways that will result in desired behaviour change.

Cognitive behavioural coaching

07

HELEN WHITTEN

Introduction

Cognitive behavioural coaching (CBC) has been a growing practice since the early 1990s and is now frequently applied in business contexts. It is also beneficial for individual clients seeking help with personal issues, such as anxiety and anger management. CBC is underpinned by the theory that thoughts and beliefs about a situation shape emotions and that the emotions generated by the beliefs shape behaviours and actions.

In the context of this chapter I shall use the following definition of CBC as: 'An integrative approach which combines the use of cognitive, behavioural, imaginal and problem-solving techniques and strategies within a cognitive behavioural framework to enable clients to achieve their realistic goals' (Palmer and Szymanska, 2007: 86).

CBC evolved from the practice of cognitive behavioural therapy (CBT). Whereas CBT focuses on remedial work for disorders, usually within a clinical context, CBC developed from a growing demand from clients to provide a future-oriented problem-solving approach to the practical and emotional challenges being experienced in life and work. CBC integrates cognitive-behavioural psychology from the theories of Aaron Beck (Beck *et al*, 1979) with Albert Ellis' rational emotive behavioural therapy, REBT (1994). It combines goal-focused coaching methodology with CBT/REBT strategies to help clients achieve their defined outcomes. These could be anything from developing self-confidence to taking action towards a work promotion.

In this chapter, I aim to give an overview of the approach and its practical application for experienced coaches, as well as a critical review of the literature on the efficacy of CBC. In analysing what is effective about CBC I have drawn on research evidence and also my own practice over 20 years. The role of the CBC coach is to combine solution-focused behavioural methods with cognitive strategies and awareness. This includes cognitive reframing, disputational questioning, imagery, problem-solving, an understanding of the impact of the relationship between mind and body chemistry, and the emphasis on the need for the client to reinforce new habits through rehearsal and repetition.

CBC is a cooperative model between coach and client. This collaboration is essential as, for change to occur, the client needs to accept responsibility for their part in the process. Effective contracting and objective-setting ensures that both client and coach are travelling in the same direction. The coach introduces models to enable the client to recognize negative or limiting thoughts, beliefs, emotions and behaviours. Between sessions, the client practices replacing limiting thoughts and behaviours with rational and constructive approaches to their problems. This process provides a measurable method for change.

Behavioural change alone goes some way towards achieving a goal but goal setting can be a deceptively simple task. Achieving the outcome identified may well be hampered by unconscious negative thoughts and emotions that keep the client stuck in old habits. Cognitive models demonstrate the impact of thoughts on behaviours, enabling the client to understand how they may be sabotaging their own efforts through unconscious rumination that may directly contradict the result they are trying to achieve. Socratic questioning challenges the client to analyse whether current perspectives are rational and helpful. Developing problem-solving skills enables the client to gain flexibility of thinking and enhances creativity. Behavioural skills such as assertiveness can be practiced during home assignments to support the client's progress towards their goals, through measurable steps.

Changing thoughts, beliefs and behaviours requires hard work and reinforcement. I liken it to learning a new language – it takes repetition to build up a new vocabulary. Similarly, changing habits requires repetition and can be uncomfortable. The neural pathways of mental and muscle reactivity have been well-trodden grooves for some time and, like driving a new car, helping clients 'reprogramme' their mind and body to respond in new ways can feel awkward at first. But, just as one gets used to the latest technology on a mobile phone, so clients are able to adopt new viewpoints that can make profound changes to their life. As a 40-year-old client said to me recently 'I found the session really interesting and am already working hard on my "homework". Most revelatory for me was the need to slow down mentally which had never occurred to me and yet now I am aware of this need, it is so unbelievably obvious!' As this comment highlights, although the outcome is indisputable, many people are simply unaware that they have the capacity to tune in to thoughts and change the nature of them.

The practicality of the cognitive behavioural coaching methodology makes it accessible to people in all walks of life. By changing the way they think about situations a client comes to realize that the main freedom they have is in how they respond to events. So even if they can't alter the external environment they gain a sense of personal control by developing a more self-supportive perspective of themselves within it. The responsibility of the coach is to support this process by providing them with tools and techniques for change, together with realistic and compassionate encouragement.

This chapter will introduce examples of models and methods of cognitive behavioural coaching and how they are being applied in both business and personal life. I will include some theoretical background and cover the evidence-based research that is being undertaken to demonstrate the effectiveness of this approach. Examples of CBC models will be provided to demonstrate their practicality in achieving results. The case study aims to give you a journey through a client's ability to change behaviour and outcomes through challenging his inflexible perceptions of himself and others, developing new perspectives that enable him to manage his anger, thereby enhancing both his personal and business relationships. I shall also suggest situations where the CBC can be relevant.

Evidence-based approach to CBC

There is a great deal of literature on cognitive behavioural therapy and an expanding collection of books, articles and journals on cognitive behavioural coaching. In this section I shall aim to introduce you to some of the research studies that have been undertaken to demonstrate the effectiveness of CBC. I shall draw attention to written data on CBC that supports the effectiveness of client outcomes.

Background research

Cognitive behavioural therapy has become well recognized as a validated therapeutic approach (Neenan, 2008) within clinical settings and is the recommended treatment classified by National Institute for Health and Clinical Excellence (NICE) guidelines since 2005 for a wide range of psychological problems. It has become the single most important and best validated psychotherapeutic approach. It is the psychological treatment of choice for a wide range of psychological problems (NICE Guidelines to NHS Commissioning bodies, April 2008).

Evidence of the effectiveness of positive future-focused psychology has been building for several years now. The research into cognitive behavioural coaching for non-clinical problems is more recent and is still building up to demonstrate its effectiveness for use in both coaching at work as well as for personal life problems. I believe one can also argue that as the CBC coach utilizes the same theories, philosophy, methodology and models as CBT, though in a non-clinical setting, these models can be said to be equally effective wherever they are applied. I cover below those aspects of evidence that I have personally found to be most effective within my own practice and which are supported by evidence.

There is a body of research demonstrating the effectiveness of both CBT and REBT, supporting the case that it is successful in:

- helping clients to manage emotions such as fear, anxiety, anger, rejection;

- transforming pessimistic or negative thinkers into optimistic and rational-constructive thinkers with a beneficial impact on positive affect and health;
- goal striving and attainment with measurable changes in performance and motivation;
- sales results;
- study and revision for both young and adult students;
- confidence, self-esteem, authenticity; and
- psychological wellbeing.

Contracting and client–coach relationship

The success of CBC depends greatly on the relationship that develops between the coach and client at the offset. Clarity of expectation, roles and responsibilities enables each person to know what action they personally need to take. In this way the client understands boundaries, timescale and their own commitment to change by accepting the necessity to undertake home assignments between sessions.

Surprisingly little is written about this in the general literature on CBC. However Alanna O'Broin and Stephen Palmer have offered some interesting insights (Neenan and Palmer, 2012). They note that studies on the coaching relationship remain scarce (Gyllensten and Palmer, 2007; De Haan, 2008; O'Broin and Palmer, 2012), although it is acknowledged as an important element within most coaching models. The focus on collaboration, a specific feature of the CBC alliance, enables the client to become their own coach by learning models and theory as the coaching programme develops.

The attributes of a CBC coach are relevant to the effectiveness of a coaching programme. Coaching outcomes have been shown to be enhanced when provided by a professional coach rather than a peer (Spence and Grant, 2007; Passmore, 2010: 112). The role of coach competencies and accreditation is currently being researched and is reviewed in detail in 'The State of Play in Coaching' (Grant *et al*, 2010). This paper examines current coaching practice and efficacy and argues that ROI from executive coaching is difficult to calculate due to the multiple contaminating variables that exist within an organization.

The need for the coach to self-coach and consider the 'views' held by themselves and the coachee (Dryden, 2006, 2008a; Whitten, 2009) is essential for monitoring prejudice or collusion. This focus keeps the direction on the client's agenda and not that of the coach.

Research has been carried out on therapist empathy and a nine-item observer rating scale called the Therapist Empathy Scale (TES) was developed based on Watson's (1999) work to assess affective, cognitive, attitudinal and attunement aspects of empathy. There is a need for a balance between empathy and objectivity so that the coach does not become too closely involved with the client's problem. More studies are required to evaluate the impact of therapist/coach empathy on client outcomes.

Developing positive affect and wellbeing

There have been several studies that have demonstrated the benefits of helping clients to tune into and develop more constructive and positive thought patterns (see, for example, Seligman, 1990 and Garland et al, 2010).

Neuroscience is also supporting the theories underlying cognitive behavioural coaching by demonstrating the plasticity in the neural circuitry between the brain and emotions. Brain imaging techniques (Kaisera et al, 2009; Solo et al, 2009) are explaining the process by which the brain prunes neural pathways on the basis of 'use it or lose it' methodology. Those thoughts that are repeated become automatic habits but the client can identify thoughts that may be described as a 'thinking error' and learn to generate thoughts and behaviours that are constructive and supportive of positive emotions. In fact, neuroplasticity appears to trigger durable change in the structure and function of the brain (Garland and Howard, 2009; Michael Mosley, BBC Horizon, 10 July 2013, citing the work of researchers such as Professor Elain Fox (see **www.psy.ox.ac.uk**); Dr Becca Levy (see: **www.publichealth.yale.edu**); Michael Meany (see: **www.douglas.qc.ca**); Professor Rosalind W Picard (see: **www.media.mit.edu**) and Professor Tim Spector (see: **www.kcl.ac.uk**). Deliberately focusing on positive thoughts and events has been shown to develop resilience to the challenges and stresses of life, acting as a buffer.

Socratic questioning to develop greater self-awareness, critical thinking and goal attainment

Questioning is an integral part of the coaching process, aimed to enable the client to challenge their own perceptions and shape new perspectives. CBC coaches therefore frequently apply Socratic questions to unearth the client's own answers to the challenges they face.

This style of questioning is fundamental to cognitive behavioural therapy (Padesky and Greenberger, 1995) and is also applied in CBC (Neenan, 2006; Neenan and Dryden, 2002) to enable the client to understand how their thoughts and beliefs may be limiting their achievement of personal goals. When used in a disciplined and also compassionate way it can uncover misperceptions of situations, or the way in which the client has simply adopted a viewpoint without checking whether they have simply absorbed a view from a parent or other authority figure.

Yang et al (2005) examined whether Socratic questioning promotes critical thinking skills. They argued that asking thoughtful questions develops the ability to self-reflect and question concepts, which is an essential part of critical thinking function.

Christine Padesky (1993) delivered a paper at the European Congress of Behavioural and Cognitive Therapies in London in 1993 in which she argued that some questions are more useful than others. Michael Neenan has also built on this idea (Neenan, 2012). He explored the difference between using questions in order to change a client's mind, for example 'Don't you think it's a mistake to ask questions without a goal in mind?', which could be steering them to give an answer the coach wants to hear. Or to guide discovery, such as 'What do you know now that you didn't know then?'. Guided discovery enables the client to gain insight into the meaning they are attaching to the situation (Padesky, 1993: 11). Such an approach, it is suggested, is more powerful in enabling the client to view the diverse perspectives that are available to them, potentially opening up new options for managing their challenge.

Studies have shown that the CBC approach increases a client's goal-striving, wellbeing and hope (Green, Oades and Grant, 2006; Passmore, 2010: 112).

Developing flexibility to manage a changing environment

The challenges of life demand that individuals continually adapt to changing circumstances. As Charles Darwin said, 'It is not the strong or intelligent who survive, it is those who adapt to change.' Flexibility of thinking is an essential ingredient to managing change; and emotions arise within situations, shaped by cognitions (Lazarus, 1991). All emotions shape adaptive behaviours but negative emotions have been shown to lead to dysfunction, including negative social interactions and reactivity. Barbara Fredrickson's broaden-and-build theory of positive emotions (Fredrickson, 1998, 2003, 2009) enables clients to develop an expanded repertoire of desired action, which is an integral part of cognitive behavioural coaching, enabling individuals to see that they have many more options as to how they approach situations than they may have previously realized they had (Rowe *et al*, 2007). Meta-cognition, where the client is taught how to think about thinking, therefore improves problem-solving capacities, leading to decisions that are more authentic and have been thought about critically (Yang, 2005).

A laboratory experiment demonstrated that people who are coached to reappraise a stressful situation more positively as a 'challenge to be met and overcome' show faster cardiovascular recovery (Tugade and Fredrickson, 2004).

Enhancing student performance

Tony Grant (2001) carried out research on trainee accountants to investigate whether CBC helped reduce test anxiety. He found that combined cognitive and behavioural approaches were associated 'with an increase in academic performance, deep and achieving approaches to learning, enhanced self-concepts related to academic performance' as well as a reduction in test anxiety.

Studies have shown that the combination of cognitive and behavioural models is more effective than either strategy applied on its own. In 2006 Grant involved trainee accountants in another research study to examine the impact of three types of coaching approaches on study-related goal attainment: ability to self-regulate emotions and behaviours; ability to self-reflect and develop insight. The three interventions included:

1 Behavioural coaching.
2 Cognitive coaching.
3 Combined cognitive behavioural coaching.

Each group received 17 hours of programme time starting with one seven-hour seminar followed by five two-hour workshops. A control group received no coaching.

The group who received only behavioural coaching with no cognitive input showed a positive change in academic performance and reduced test anxiety but the change was not lasting. In the group who were trained only in the cognitive techniques there was a change in how the trainee accountants perceived themselves but with no behavioural element there was a decrease in academic performance. In the group who received both cognitive and behavioural input there was a significant impact on both academic perform-ance and how the trainee accountants saw themselves, in comparison to the control group. This effect was lasting to the follow-up one term (approxi-mately 12 weeks) later. The cognitive behavioural coaching intervention was also shown to enhance overall well-being as well as performance.

In further research CBC has been linked to increased student achievement, greater teacher efficacy and satisfaction, higher levels of conceptual thinking among teachers and more professional, collaborative cultures (Edwards, 2001).

The Emotional Intelligence quotient (BarOn EQ Inventory Youth Version, 1997) was enhanced in a group of students provided with cognitive-behavioural models of stress management. The study programme included 120 young people aged 16 years plus attending four weekly lessons to develop emotional intelligence and problem-solving capacity. A control group did not attend any lessons (Carrington and Whitten, 2005).

CBC efficacy in the treatment of perfectionism and self-handicapping in a non-clinical environment

Perfectionism can result in depression and a sense of never being satisfied with self, others or work performance. This is stressful and exhausting for the individual and can be frustrating for those around them. Perfectionism can result in procrastination due to a reluctance to start or finish a task in case it proves to be imperfect. In my own experience of working as a CBC coach it can be a frequent issue for some clients in the business world. Perfectionism in this context is defined as the setting of high standards and a critical self-evaluation. This can lead to lower self-esteem and a sense of failure. As the perfectionist is dependent on external approval they can tend to over-commit by endeavouring to achieve a perfect result.

Dr Randy Frost's conceptualization of perfectionism, now defined in the Frost Multidimensional Perfectionism Scale, highlights two cognitive inaccuracies on the part of the perfectionist. Firstly the standards set are excessively high, and secondly the self-evaluation is overly critical. This implies two cognitive errors on the part of the perfectionist: setting standards that are not appropriate or reasonable for the circumstances; and that the level of self-evaluation they undertake is out of proportion to the evidence (Shafran, Cooper and Fairburn, 2002). Cognitive behavioural coaching models have been used to challenge distortions to gain a more rational and balanced perspective related to standard setting. It has proved possible to reduce the level of perfectionism and self-handicapping and this change was sustained for the one-month follow-up, although there continued to be an element of self-doubt about actions taken.

Windy Dryden and Michael Neenan (2004) investigated the impact of perfectionism on procrastination styles and found that it is likely that both ego disturbance and discomfort disturbance beliefs are active. Ego disturbance relates to the demands a perfectionist imposes on themselves and a critical self-evaluation when they fail to live up to these demands. A typical belief might be 'If I can't do this task perfectly then I won't do it at all' or a self-critical evaluation such as 'if I don't complete this task perfectly I am a failure'. The discomfort belief would be 'I shouldn't have to push myself to do things that aren't comfortable', which results in a client being stuck and unwilling to try new behaviours or approaches.

In Australia, Hugh Kearns, Angus Forbes and Maria Gardiner (Kearns *et al*, 2007) carried out research into perfectionism. Twenty-eight Research Higher Degree students participated in an intensive workshop series held over six weeks. Perfectionism and self-handicapping were measured at the commencement and conclusion of the workshop series, and again four weeks later. Levels of perfectionism fell during the workshop series and this reduction was sustained at follow-up. Levels of self-handicapping did not fall during the workshop series but had fallen significantly by follow-up. Participants' level of satisfaction with their progress also improved.

CBC for sales training

Brian McCrae tested CBC as an objective for enhancing sales performance with 166 participants within a large major UK insurance corporation (McCrae, 2007). The participants:

- achieved a 20 per cent improvement in the proportion of salespeople 'on target';
- demonstrated a 27 per cent reduction in the proportion that showed signs of stress;
- showed a rate of resignations reduced by a factor of three; and
- all felt very positive about the programme.

Literature on CBC

Many of the books on the market are useful both for theory and also for the practical application of CBC models in the coaching room. *Cognitive-Behavioural Coaching in Practice (*edited by Neenan and Palmer, 2012) covers information on evidence-based approaches to CBC with a variety of contributors from the field. This includes topics such as procrastination, motivational interviewing, coach relationship, Socratic questioning, self-esteem, developing resilience, stress and performance coaching, mindfulness-based CBC and work culture. Each contribution covers theory and also examples of models in practice, together with reference papers covering effectiveness of the approach.

Cognitive-Behavioural Coaching Techniques for Dummies (Whitten, 2009) includes practical examples and a diverse variety of models that coaches can add to their toolkit, together with case studies. It also includes principles underpinning CBC and how the coaching process develops within workplace settings. *Life Coaching: A cognitive-behavioural approach* (Neenan and Dryden, 2006) provides several case studies underpinned by explanations of the models and theories specifically relevant to life coaching.

Chapters in *Handbook of Coaching Psychology* (Palmer and Whybrow, 2007) and *Excellence in Coaching* (Passmore, 2006 and 2010) include detailed descriptions of CBC in practice, covering the ABCDE, SPACE and PRACTICE models and providing examples of the Downward Arrow and inference chaining in practice.

The Wiley Handbook of the Psychology of Coaching and Mentoring (Passmore, Peterson and Freire, 2013) provides an in-depth analysis of a number of different models including CBC. The book provides details of the theory and research underpinning each model.

There are also useful books on specific topics experienced by CBC coaches, such as *Overcoming Anxiety* (Kennerley, 1997), *How to Control your Anger Before it Controls you* (Ellis and Tafrate, 1997), and Dr Windy Dryden's books on *Overcoming Anger* (1996) and *Coping with Guilt* (2013). These books build on the already extensive literature that has been written on both CBT and REBT in clinical settings.

Practice: CBC tools and techniques

The practice of cognitive behavioural coaching translates into practical coaching models that can be applied with a wide range of clients. It is a psycho-educative approach where the coach shares the knowledge, theory, philosophy and practice of CBC in order that the client can apply the strategies in their own life. I have divided the strategies I have found most effective for CBC success into the following five topic areas:

- initiating the coaching programme;
- developing client awareness of cognitive habits;

- challenging and reframing unhelpful thoughts and behaviours;
- developing new approaches to problem situations; and
- reviewing and integrating change.

CBC is time-limited coaching, generally involving between three and 12 sessions, driven on client needs. The focus is on awareness of how behaviours and actions taken by the client lead them towards, or away from, their outcomes. How the coaching programme is set up is integral to its success.

Initiating the coaching programme

Explaining CBC

The way that the coaching programme is initiated is important. The client needs to understand the underlying philosophy and principles of CBC – that the way they think about a situation determines the meaning and emotion they attach to it, which in turn shapes outcomes.

The philosophy underpinning cognitive behavioural psychology can be tracked to Stoic principles and specifically to Epictetus' statement in the first century AD that 'people are disturbed not by things, but by the views which they take of them'. This was developed further by the psychiatrist Adler who argued, in 1958, that people determine themselves by the meaning they give to situations, not by the situations themselves.

Both Aaron Beck's cognitive therapy and Albert Ellis' rational emotive behaviour therapy have evolved from the understanding that beliefs are not fixed immutable things but that people can learn to choose a viewpoint of events that is supportive of the emotional state that promotes constructive behaviours and actions. For example, a person who is made redundant can review whether a thought such as 'this means I am a complete failure' is helpful to their goal of finding a new job. They can learn to develop a more helpful thought such as 'I would rather this had not happened but I can manage it and will remind myself of the skills and experience I have built up in my last role. It does not mean I am a complete failure.' By changing the thought they change their sense of themselves emotionally and this can motivate them to have the confidence to go forwards towards their goal.

They are not tricking themselves into imagining that the event was an easy one but they are not allowing themselves to be sucked into the negativity of the experience. This concept has a powerful and practical relevance for coaching clients living in the fast-changing world of the 21st century.

The philosophy of self-acceptance and acceptance of human fallibility underpins the values by which the CBC coach and client will be working. For those who have perfectionist tendencies, or a habit of self-critical internal dialogue, the concept of self-acceptance can be both comforting and empowering. Understanding that perfection is subjective prepares the client to recognize that life is a learning process, where self-awareness is helpful but self-criticism unproductive. When the client is able to acknowledge that both they and those around them make mistakes, it enables them to see others as equals. They learn to evaluate situations rationally rather than be paralysed by fear of failure. Reflecting on actions with a compassionate eye can help clients move out of a rut to see new options they have previously been blind to noticing.

The coaching contract

Alongside explaining the principles, values and theory of CBC in initial meetings, the coach and client discuss and agree roles, responsibilities and expectations of the coaching programme, and a contract can be signed. A person's manager, or HR representative, may be involved in a triangular discussion to clarify the expectations. The client is asked to commit to collaborate and to accept their own role in practising new ways of thinking and behaving between sessions. An example form of contract is:

> **Terms of working together:** Coaching is an 'alliance' of cooperation between client and coach. The coach supports the client in developing the specific goals and objectives identified by the client at the outset by introducing models, methods and tools that support the client's objectives. The coach may share case studies, challenge perspectives, and provide theoretical strategies with a view to enhancing the client's ability to achieve their defined outcomes. The client agrees to undertake home assignments between sessions on the understanding that coaching is a collaborative process.
>
> All recommendations made in any form are made in good faith and on the information available at the time. Payment is due as per proposal agreement. A cancellation fee is due should a session be cancelled less than x working days in advance of an appointment. The Coach follows the best professional practice in protecting the confidentiality of client information. I understand and accept these terms.

The client's commitment to working on the coaching programme outside the consultancy room enables them to practise new thoughts, behaviours and actions. Bringing their home assignments and experiences back to the coach every session ensures that the objectives and learning from coaching sessions remain at the foreground of the client's mind.

Preparing the ground for coaching

A pre-coaching questionnaire can provide a head-start to the coaching programme by prompting the client to begin the coaching process before their first session. They can be asked to identify the specific situations they find difficult and begin to tune into the thoughts experienced when they face these challenges. In this way the client can come to understand how their thoughts are shaping feelings and how feelings are influencing behaviours and actions. Table 7.1 offers an example of a pre-coaching questionnaire.

TABLE 7.1   Pre-coaching questionnaire

Please start to notice and list:

A. The situations that cause you difficulty:

eg changing goal posts, feeling judged or criticized, speaking up in front of dominant people.

B. When you think about these situations, what are some of the beliefs, expectations or negative thoughts that come into your mind when you are in these situations? Please list these in sentences:

eg I am not good enough. I'm not doing things properly. I might say something stupid.

C. What are the emotions and behaviours that stem from the way you are currently thinking about and approaching these difficult situations? eg What is the consequence of your current response?

eg fear, helplessness, feeling overwhelmed. Leads me to be shy, not speak up, want to give up.

D. Under what conditions are these situations improved? When do you find a situation easier to manage than at other times, and what makes that difference?

eg when I relax, when I know the other people at the meeting, when I stop over-analysing and just act.

E. What are any physical conditions, symptoms or complaints you have that might be related to these difficult situations?

eg indigestion, tearfulness, insomnia, comfort eating and drinking.

F: What will 'success' look like? If you could manage the situations more effectively what would be different? What thoughts would impact how you felt within these challenges?

eg Success would be feeling in control of my workload. I would be thinking I was capable and feeling more confident about expressing my opinions to senior managers and my direct reports. I would be assertive about saying no and ensure I got home feeling relaxed for my partner and children.

Both the pre-coaching questionnaire and the coaching contract enable the coach and client to understand some of the key issues right at the onset of the coaching programme. Expectations are clarified. Well-defined problems, goals, roles and responsibilities enable the development of trust within the relationship. The use of these elements can both save time and help client misunderstanding. In my experience, when this part of the process is not given sufficient consideration, the coaching programme is less effective.

Developing client awareness of cognitive habits

Thinking errors and Socratic questions

In CBC the coach helps the client identify the 'thinking errors' that could be distorting reality and unconsciously sabotaging their actions. Working with the ABCDE model in the first session becomes straightforward once the client has begun to notice, in the pre-coaching work, how their limiting thoughts are impacting their feelings and behaviours. They may argue that this is the only 'right' way to think and act within it and the coach can help them broaden perspectives through disputation.

Applying ABCDE questioning can enable clients to develop greater flexibility of thinking. Clients may come to realize that they have become attached to their own viewpoint within the challenges they are facing and realize that they can develop more options than they had previously considered.

Challenging and reframing unhelpful thoughts and behaviours

The ABCDE model

The coach supports the client in developing the thoughts and behaviours that best achieve success. The ABCDE model can be excellent both in order to help a client see how they have been hampering their happiness or performance and also as a model to help them plan how to achieve success in the future. Table 7.2 is an example of a client who was facing possible redundancy, and demonstrates how he changed from sabotaging his success to becoming confident of his ability to keep his job.

Socratic questioning

Socratic questioning provides a method by which the coach can challenge the client's perspectives and help them develop approaches that are both rational and supportive of their efforts, whether the goal is to overcome anxiety, seek work promotion or become a world-class pianist.

Socratic questioning, based on the philosophy of Socrates, is a series of open questions that aim to help the client discover which thoughts or beliefs lie at the root of their problems and learn how to change them. It is a form of questioning that is systematic and disciplined, aiming to get to the specific truth and reality of a problem, to uncover assumptions and check evidence of perspective.

TABLE 7.2   ABCDE model applied

Activating situation	Beliefs, thoughts and expectations of the situation	Consequences of feeling behaviour and impact	Disputing whether current approach was: Logical? Helpful? Empirical?	Exchange response to new: thoughts feelings behaviours images
Fear of redundancy during the banking crisis of the credit crunch where colleagues were being made redundant.	'I'm 55 and I am bound to be the first person chosen to be made redundant.'	Anxiety, 'flight' mode of hiding away, less social and avoiding key colleagues and boss.	Recognized that there was no specific evidence that he would be made redundant, that others would not necessarily respond in this way and that this thought was not helpful. He realized that this approach could become a self-fulfilling prophecy.	'I am skilled and experienced and can be part of the solution.' Feelings of confidence, behaviours of ensuring that ideas and knowledge were shared with colleagues and key relationships. Visualizing image of people acknowledging expertise.

For example, the coach would ask:

- 'Might other people hold a different viewpoint of this situation?' in order to broaden perspectives.
- 'You say x. What evidence do you have to support this viewpoint?' in order to get to the specific truth and reality within a situation.
- 'What is the worst that could happen?' in order to help the client put the situation in perspective, and explore potential outcomes that are realistic.
- 'When you think this way how does it impact how you feel and act?' in order to evaluate the impact of this style of thinking and check whether it is helping or hindering the client to achieve their goals.

- 'Can you think of someone else you know who is experiencing a similar situation? How might you advise them to manage it?' in order to help the client distance themselves and gain greater objectivity.

The compassionate but systematic use of Socratic questioning can enable a coach to help the client identify where their thinking has become illogical or where they may have absorbed another person's opinion without reflection. Questioning enables the development of critical thinking (Yang *et al*, 2005) and the development of the cognitive habit of checking the helpfulness and rationality of specific thoughts, assumptions and beliefs.

The focus in CBC on specific outcomes incorporates a motivational element and keeps clients working towards an objective that they themselves have defined as attractive. However, there are plenty of people who pinpoint a goal but take no action towards it. The process of applying the ABCDE model combined with Socratic questions helps the client become aware of how they may be disturbing themselves or sabotaging their own efforts through underlying negative automatic thinking.

In order to assist this process the coach can provide handouts that introduce examples of thought disputation. The client can be asked to begin to develop their own ability to check that their cognitive approach is helpful (Table 7.3).

TABLE 7.3 Thoughts and questions

Thought	Socratic question
'I must not make a mistake or I shall be fired.'	What is the evidence that you will be fired if you make one mistake?
'I can't stand it if I am late for a meeting.'	Just because you prefer to be on time how is it logical to believe you must be on time even if your train has been cancelled?
'My boss wants me to be organized but I am not an organized person. This is not who I am and I can't change.'	Can you think of a time when you have previously managed to change a way of behaving?
'I'll never be happy because I was abused by my step-father.'	Can you think of a time when you have managed to be happy? How does holding onto this belief help you become happy in the future?

TABLE 7.3 *continued*

Thought	Socratic question
'I've had enough of this. I'm giving up.'	How does your low frustration tolerance help you keep your job? What would help you stay with the task to completion?
'My boss doesn't listen to me. She never gives me credit for my achievements.'	Can you think of a time when she did give you credit? What else could you do to ensure she does hear you in future?
'I must clear all my e-mails every night before I go home.'	Who says you must? Is there a law written that you must? How might others manage their emails? How does it help you with your goal of getting home to read a story to your daughter?
'I want to say "no" to demands but I'm worried that others might think badly of me.'	What's so awful about having the disapproval of others? Can you think of any one person who has the approval of 100% of the population?

When the questioning is offered with compassion, the coach can help the client develop their own sense of amused self-observation. Often a client will get an 'Aha' moment where they realize how they have been setting specific demands of themselves and others which are arbitrary, irrational and unhelpful. They realize that their thoughts and behaviours are sabotaging their efforts to achieve their objectives. They can develop the ability to say to themselves 'Here I go again. What do I need to do differently now?' They don't criticize themselves but feel encouraged to find new ways of approaching situations.

Hyperarousal interferes with thinking

Certain circumstances can impair a client's ability to think clearly and rationally. Prolonged physiological arousal is associated with disturbing emotions such as stress, anger or anxiety. This can interfere with a client's clarity of thought, as limbic system hyperarousal triggers a state of heightened reactivity. In these situations, the brain pattern-matches to previous experiences, and generates an emotional and behavioural response to an event can be instantaneous. The body goes into fight-flight-freeze or fold mode, and when there is no physical outlet for the build-up of stress chemistry, this can result in dysfunctional breathing (Wilhelm, Gervitz and Roth, 2001), impacting higher-function thinking and also the immune system.

A client who has anxiety around a bullying relationship, based on previous events, will immediately become hyper-aroused when meeting with that individual. This can lead to habitual ways of responding to old problems. It can signify defensive or aggressive behaviour taking over before the client has had a chance to understand what is happening.

Incidents such as road rage can occur when a person has a set of un-conscious demands that have become entrenched concerning how other drivers 'should' treat them. Should another driver unwittingly threaten these demands the individual can react with violence. This reaction occurs before they have had a chance to stop and think or consider the consequences of a moment's anger.

Helping the client to understand the mind–body responses to prolonged or chronic stress can enable them to understand what they need to do. It is easy to assume that clients are familiar with the physiological responses to stress and yet I have found that many people have never been taught the process of biological change that occurs in the mind and body under pressure. Learning to ask about physiological symptoms can be revelatory as many clients are experiencing insomnia, IBS and other problems that may well be related to the challenges they are presenting to their coach.

The coach can teach the client to become 'breath aware', by monitoring whether the breath is in the upper chest, which would signify stress, rather than using diaphragmatic breathing. The client can learn to take a breathing space of a few minutes, to shift breath to the diaphragm and learn to focus on a longer outbreath, which reduces hyper-arousal, raises CO_2, and lowers blood pressure. Teaching relaxation methods can be helpful, and there is research to show that practising mindful breathing techniques at around six breaths per minute for 10 minutes (Bernardi *et al*, 2001, Lehrer, Sasaki and Saito, 1999) a day for a period of two–four weeks can reset the limbic system hyperarousal (Lehrer, Woolfolk and Sime, 2007) and aid restoration of both mental and physical health.

Learning to plan responses to difficult situations can help the client switch off the spontaneous reactivity of previous behaviours, enabling them to access a more empowered emotional state where they feel capable of managing the challenge. Developing and rehearsing constructive thoughts and behaviours reprogrammes the mind–body response so that when they meet a similar situation again in the future they choose to react differently. If you study the four images in Figure 7.1, overleaf, you will see that as you change focus, the brain develops new chemical networks of neural pathways and prunes those that are no longer used.

Those clients who are of a scientific frame of mind find it helpful to see cognitive behavioural coaching practice in action through these changes

FIGURE 7.1 Changing focus and developing new neural pathways

1. Habit patterns of behaviour: Wiring the brain

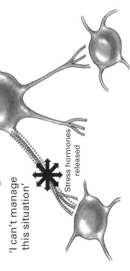

'I can't manage this situation'

2. Habits – which could hold you back?

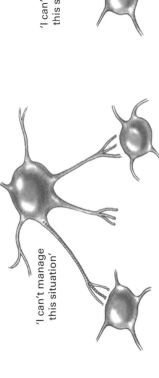

'I can't manage this situation'

Stress hormones released

3. Switch the circuitry

'I can – it may work'

'I can't – it won't work'

4. Accentuate the positive: Which thoughts will help you?

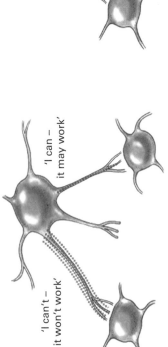
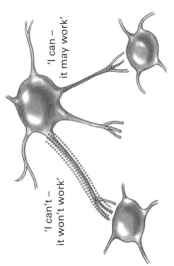

'I can – it will work'

Endorphins released

in the brain. It also helps clients realize that switching circuitry of neural pathways can be difficult and uncomfortable – just like learning any new skills or subject. Clients relate well to the metaphor of driving your own car and getting used to the instruments. For example, remembering that they have an automatic response to changing gear or moving the indicator switch in their own car, then going on holiday and hiring a car where the indicator switch is on the other side. This feels uncomfortable but gradually their brain learns new responses so that the new way becomes the natural reaction and the old way then creates discomfort.

The impact of thoughts on feelings and behaviour

CBC is sometimes accused of ignoring emotions but the ABCDE model and the theory of healthy and unhealthy emotions provide tangible models that help the client review their emotional state and how it is impacting their behaviours.

The coach needs to check whether the client has become stuck in unhealthy emotions such as anger, anxiety, guilt, depression, or morbid jealousy. Distorted thinking can shape these emotions. For example, a person who has created a personal rule that 'other people should never talk down to me' would immediately respond with anger should this occur. However, once they replace that rule with 'I would rather people didn't talk down to me but I can manage it if they do' they are more likely to experience annoyance, which is described as a healthy emotion.

Or someone may become depressed after a bereavement because they have created a rule that says 'I can never feel happy again without this person or I would feel guilty'. Whereas if they are able to replace this thought with 'I am very sad but I am going to try to find ways to be happy now' they will experience sadness, which is a healthy emotion, but not sink into depression, which is an unhealthy emotion. The client can also be asked to consider whether there are any secondary emotions underlying their experience – for example feeling angry at feeling anxious. In this way they become familiar with their own emotional experiences. This can enable them to acknowledge, understand and manage their emotional state more effectively.

There are a number of methods that aid the client's ability to tune into and analyse the helpfulness of their thinking patterns and their impact on feelings, including a thinking log. Table 7.4 is an example of a handout that provides a record of the various cognitive distortions together with space for the client to record how they are responding to specific situations or relationships in their own lives. The handout sheet also enables them to assess the consequences and impact of their current thinking patterns on their life, work and relationships.

I have found that clients develop the ability to observe themselves with compassion, discovering for themselves how their thinking may be distorted and how these distortions are impacting their behaviours, frequently blocking their ability to resolve the situation.

TABLE 7.4 Thinking style sheet

Thinking style	Record of situations that trigger this style of thinking	Personal experience (thoughts, physiology, emotions, behaviours, consequences)
Overgeneralization: *'This will never work'* eg drawing some general as a result of one or two isolated experiences or events.	eg experiencing a restructure at work.	'Not another restructure.' Leads to anxiety and resentment. Behaviours in the new regime become defensive and unhelpful.
Selective Abstraction: *'No-one appreciated my efforts'* eg concentrating on a detail from an event or experience while other factors are ignored.	eg being left off an e-mail cc list.	'I am being overlooked. No-one takes me seriously.' Leads to anxiety, challenging behaviour with boss to understand why, which was not appreciated.
Magnification: *'This is the worst thing that could possibly have happened'* eg grossly magnifying the importance of an event.	eg being 10 minutes late for a meeting.	'I can't stand being late.' Leads to self-blame and anger. Very stressed on entering the meeting, pink-faced and sweaty, not making a good impression.
Minimization: *'It's not really a problem'* eg playing down the importance of an event.	eg staying in a job where the client is being bullied.	'I can manage this. It will be ok tomorrow.' Leads to stress and ill-health, gradual deterioration of self-esteem through adopting passive behaviour.
Arbitrary Inference: *'They're planning something against me'* eg inference about a situation or person without evidence to support their conclusion.	eg a colleague is not returning a phone call.	'They don't like me. They're going to leave me out of the deal.' Leads to defensive behaviour, being huffy, which makes the relationship deteriorate.

TABLE 7.4 *continued*

Thinking style	Record of situations that trigger this style of thinking	Personal experience (thoughts, physiology, emotions, behaviours, consequences)
Mind Reading: *'I know she doesn't like me'* eg making assumptions about another person's behaviour.	eg paranoia that a new colleague wants to usurp the client's position.	'They are a threat. I think they want my role.' Leads to unhelpful and uncollaborative behaviour. Annual appraisal states that the client is not a team player.
Fortune Telling: *'He's going to dump me'* eg imagining an outcome despite many different potential outcomes.	eg the new manager is not going to be any good.	'I'm fed up. I don't want a new boss.' Leads to defensive behaviour and does not get the relationship started on the right foot.
Dichotomous thinking: *'It's completely useless'* eg 'all-or-nothing' or 'black-and-white' thinking, missing shades of grey.	eg boss says they want the client to be more sociable.	'My role is dealing with facts. I can't be an expert in detail and also be friendly. I don't think being sociable is an important feature of my work.' Leads to a bad appraisal when client doesn't bother to be friendly.
Personalization: *'I must have done something wrong'* eg taking personal responsibility for an event despite others being involved.	eg the client's client is angry about the way a marketing campaign has been run.	'I must have got the wrong end of the stick. They are going to think I am no good at my job.' Leads to self-blame, despite the fact that the client is a member of a larger team and did not plan the campaign alone.

TABLE 7.4   *continued*

Thinking style	Record of situations that trigger this style of thinking	Personal experience (thoughts, physiology, emotions, behaviours, consequences)
Blaming: *'It's all his fault!'* eg whatever happens is always the fault of another person so that the individual feels victimized and does not take responsibility for their part.	eg perceived parental neglect.	'It's my father's fault. He always criticized me and has made me feel useless.' Leads to a pattern of being a victim in other situations accentuating the feeling of helplessness, pointing fingers at others for having more 'power'.
Shoulds, Musts, Oughts: *'I must get this promotion'... 'he should be able to get this right'... 'she ought to know that I need that information now'* eg demanding a certain set of random rules of behaviour.	eg spouse does not help in the house.	'He ought to know that I want him to vacuum the lounge.' Leads to anger and resentment if he doesn't, even if the subject has not been discussed.
Catastrophising: *'It's simply awful and I can't stand it!'* eg making more of a situation than you have evidence of.	eg getting lost en-route to a family occasion.	'I can't stand this. I'll never get there.' Leads to stress and lack of clarity of thought in trying to find the way logically.
Emotional Reasoning: *'I feel so miserable that I am sure this meeting won't go well'* eg coming to a conclusion because of feelings rather than facts.	eg client has experienced a row with his wife that morning.	'I feel fed up and misunderstood. Today will go badly.' Leads to assumption that others are in a similar mood. The day goes badly.
Labelling: *'I'm totally stupid'* eg branding self or others with a label as a result of one instance or perception.	eg a bad presentation where client couldn't answer questions.	'I'm totally hopeless. I can't even make a presentation to the Board. I'll never get anywhere.' Leads to hopelessness and giving up.

TABLE 7.4 *continued*

Thinking style	Record of situations that trigger this style of thinking	Personal experience (thoughts, physiology, emotions, behaviours, consequences)
Low Frustration Tolerance: *'I've had enough of this'* eg getting impatient so not finishing a task, even though it will be of benefit.	eg starting projects but not finishing them.	'I can't be bothered. I'm getting bored now.' Leads to demotivation and disappointment, resulting in boss and colleagues getting fed up that the projects aren't finished.
High Frustration Tolerance: *'It's ok, I can manage'* eg staying in a damaging situation too long.	eg being a martyr and taking on a colleague's work.	'It's ok if I stay late.' Leads to self-blame and resentment, pretending it's ok when in fact it isn't.
Imposter Fear *'If I don't succeed all the time I'll be found out for not being as clever as they think I am'* eg can lead to perfectionist and driven behaviours.	eg being promoted although the client doesn't have as many qualifications as another candidate.	'It was a fluke. They'll find out that I am not as clever as they imagine.' Leads to fear of failure and driven behaviour in attempt to prove self as capable.

Developing new approaches to problem situations

Solutions and decisions

In order for clients to make changes in their lives, the CBC coach helps them develop more flexible and creative ways of solving problems. Humans are deeply habitual and, when stressed, people tend to revert to old patterns. This can occur within many situations from a relationship that is not working well to someone who procrastinates or is a perfectionist.

The PRACTICE problem-solving model (Palmer, 2007a) is a useful and practical process to follow (Table 7.5).

Clients tend to find following a defined process such as the PRACTICE model on a handout helps them to stay on target. The PE-P Model (Israel,

TABLE 7.5 PRACTICE problem-solving model – developing creative and flexible thinking

Steps	Good questions to stimulate best solutions and actions
1 Problem identification.	What is the real concern? What would you like to change? When is it not a problem? Could your viewpoint or perspective be distorted? Might others manage the situation differently?
2 Realistic goals that are relevant and SMART (Specific, Measurable, Achievable, Results-Focused, Time-Bound).	What do you want to achieve? What would success look like? By what time would you like this outcome?
3 Alternative solutions and courses of action generated.	What are your options? In how many different ways might you achieve this outcome?
4 Consideration of consequences of each alternative solution, considering pros and cons.	What could happen if you put these solutions into action? How practical is each solution? Rate on scale of 1–10. How might each solution impact others? What are the benefits?
5 Target the most feasible and desirable solution(s).	What is the most feasible solution? What do you need to do in order to put it into action? When will you start?
6 Implement the **C**hosen solution(s) by rehearsing strategies and behaviours by means of imagery and practical actions.	Act on the solution, first by rehearsing it mentally or in role play, and then by doing it, in manageable steps.
7 Evaluate methods, actions and efforts, review what has been learnt and reconsider the problem in the light of specific approaches and solutions.	How did it go? How successful was it on a rating scale of 1–10? What can you learn? What might you alter next time you try? Would one of the other options you generated work better? Do you feel ready to complete the coaching programme now?

Shaffran and Whitten, 1995) integrates multi-modal approaches with problem-solving, planning and imagery.

PE-P (Problem Emotion – PLAN)

Stage One: Problem

Clearly identify the problem you want to solve.
Consider why you want to solve it.

Stage Two: Emotion

Recognize and accept the emotion inspired by the problem.
Identify the thoughts, images, beliefs and expectations that trigger the emotion.
Use the ABCDE Model to develop more rational thinking patterns.

A = Activating Event
B = Belief/Expectation of Self/Other people and the World
C = Consequence – emotion and behaviour
D = Disputing:
How logical is it for you to hold the belief/expectation?
How realistic is it for you to hold the belief/expectation? (eg: is there empirical evidence that everyone holds this belief?)
How is it helpful to you to continue to hold this belief/expectation?
If it is logical, realistic and helpful then you can choose to continue the belief.
If it is not, then you can begin to decide what might be a more helpful belief or expectation to hold.
If you realize at point (b) that not everyone would react in the same way you can become aware that you are making a choice (albeit, possibly, a subconscious one) and can take personal responsibility for your individual reaction. This realization of responsibility then frees you to change should you choose to do so.
E = Exchange the belief for a more constructive thought that is support-ive of your goal.
Changing your thinking can therefore enable you to change your emo-tional response, which in turn affects your behaviour.

Stage Three: Plan

Develop a practical and achievable plan including:

- setting realistic and achievable goals with a step by step plan of action;
- plan in advance how you would like to think, feel and behave;
- take necessary practical steps to alleviate or solve the problem;
- plan and practise the new behaviour, including: thinking skills, imagery techniques, breathing techniques, emotion recognition, acceptance and management, interpersonal responses;
- consider the consequences of changing your behaviour;

- focus on the plan and let go of the problem; and
- believe in your ability to change and achieve your goals.

Here is an example of a client working through the PE-P process:

PE-P WORKSHEET

1. **Problem:** Clearly define the general problem: *Not speaking up in meetings. My colleagues taking my ideas and results as if they are their own.*
   Consider the consequences of continuing to have this problem: *My boss will not see that I am achieving results so I shall get neither a bonus nor promotion.*
   Consider the consequences of solving this problem: *I would feel more confident in myself. Others would realize that I am achieving good results and would respect me more. I would be more likely to receive promotion and a bonus.*
   Is there any part of you that wants to maintain the problem? *If so, why? Well, I suppose that while I take no action I remain in my comfort zone of not drawing attention to myself. I can continue to sit quietly in meetings but I don't want to do this because it hampers my career.*

2. **Emotion:** What are you feeling in this situation? *Frustration at myself, resentment at others.*

   ABCD:

   A: specific activating event:
   (eg: may be a specific incident relating to the main problem detailed in Section One). *I signed a new client but my colleague took the credit.*

   B: belief/expectation:
   Write down any thoughts that were in your head about the activating event: what were you demanding of yourself/others/the world? 'shoulds' and 'musts'.
   I should/ought to have stood up for myself; I should not make a fuss
   Others should/ought to have behaved honourably and given me the credit

   C: consequence:
   Consider the emotion detailed at the beginning of Section 2 and define any secondary emotions (eg: feeling angry at being frightened). *Depressed at my frustration which leads to feeling hopeless.*

   D: dispute:
   Is it logical for you to hold the belief/expectation? *Logical to stand up for myself, not so logical to think I should not make a fuss.*
   Would everyone in this situation feel the same way? *No, I have seen colleagues row with others in order to stand up for themselves.*
   Is it helpful for you to continue to hold this belief/expectation? *It is helpful to allow myself to think I should stand up for myself but not helpful to think I shouldn't make a fuss.*

3. **Plan:** Develop a practical and achievable plan:
   What is a Positive outcome? *That I have a conversation with my colleague to state that I was disappointed when he took credit for my work. That I do stand up for myself in future and develop a successful career by being more assertive.*

Get creative: How might others manage this situation? *Some people would have had a row at the client meeting. Others might have sent an e-mail afterwards. Some people might have a meeting one-to-one after the meeting. Others might storm out and leave.*

Decide on a course of action: *My goal is to have a one-to-one meeting so that this doesn't happen again, and then to be more assertive at work and in meetings.*

Personal Management Plan:

In order to achieve your goal and manage the situation well how would you like to:

Behave? *Assertive. Able to state my feelings and needs for the future.*
Feel emotionally? *Confident and empowered.*
Feel physically? *Calm, strong and yet also flexible.*
What images would be helpful? *A tiger. I think of a tiger as strong but flexible.*
What thoughts would be helpful? *I have a right to be acknowledged for the good work I am achieving.*
What interpersonal skills would be helpful? *Being assertive means I respect myself and respect the other person. I'm ok, they're ok. I want to find out their reasons and how conscious they were of what they did. I will ask questions and listen to their responses. I would like to retain a good relationship with them and an agreement regarding how we work together in future.*
What biological interventions/lack of interventions would be helpful? (eg: less caffeine, slow breathing exercises) *I shall try to get to bed at a reasonable hour, wake up and do my yoga stretches and breathing before breakfast; walk from the tube rather than get the bus so that I have time to collect my thoughts.*
Create an action plan to rehearse these skills in order to help you manage the event (eg: training and/or daily practice) *I would like to do some role play please so that I can practice using assertive but collaborative language.*
Why do you want to change and take this action? *I shall feel a greater sense of self-worth if I address this situation. Even if my colleague doesn't agree with me I shall feel I am taking my life and future in my own hands rather than sitting and being walked over. That is really important to me for developing a successful career.*

Adopting new behaviour can mean taking risks. In the case study above the colleague might feel angry and take it out on the client, so the client had to be willing not to be attached to a specific outcome. By identifying the benefits and underlying reasons why the client is choosing to take action the coach can help them recognize that taking action is, in itself, life-changing, even if the specific goal is not reached. Tapping into the values beneath the client's targets is motivational. It also enables them to have the flexibility to know that all effort is, in itself, a step forward.

The client can learn to recognize Performance Interfering Thoughts (PITS) (Palmer and Dryden, 1995) such as 'this will never work' or 'I can't stand it if my boss doesn't listen to me', both of which inspire emotions of fear and anxiety. They can develop Performance Enhancing Thoughts (PETS)

(Palmer and Dryden, 1995) such as 'even if my colleague doesn't listen I shall feel better about myself for having expressed my disappointment at their behaviour' or 'even if the meeting doesn't go as planned I still have opportunities later to re-balance my relationship with them'. The PETS allow for flexibility of response.

Reviewing and integrating change

Change can be difficult. The client needs to buy into the value of the coaching programme in order to be persuaded to take action. Some clients respond negatively or can be sceptical of the process. This can happen particularly if a client has been 'sent' by a boss or HR. Coaching can then be perceived as remedial or a punishment rather than developmental. Should the coach observe that the client is defensive, or is not completing home assignments, it is of value to address the issue and try to understand their resistance. Applying inference chaining or the cost–benefit analysis might help the coach identify underlying beliefs about coaching, and also help the client to recognize the benefits of change.

CBC coaches will be checking in with clients on a regular basis over the coaching programme to review together what is working and what is not. The coach can adapt their methods to the client's learning styles in order to ensure that they are supporting the change process as effectively as possible.

Some clients comment 'I am the person I am, full stop'. Understanding the learning mechanism of the brain is useful to help them accept the ever-changing nature of mind and body. Neuroscience is supporting the theories of CBC by demonstrating how the brain's plasticity enables an individual to develop and change as they go through life.

Repetition and practice of new approaches is essential to the integration of change. Once desired thoughts and actions are identified, it is necessary for the client to undertake their home assignments in order to reinforce new habits. Sending short summaries of each CBC coaching session supports learning, reminding the client what was covered and what actions they committed to take between sessions.

Compassion and the reinforcement of fallibility supports clients to keep motivated through setbacks. Change is rarely a smooth process so the challenging of all-or-nothing thinking is important should mistakes or failures occur. Some clients create rules such as 'if I have broken my diet by Tuesday I shall wait until the following Monday before I start again' rather than recognizing that there is no logical reason not to re-start the new lifestyle practice immediately rather than wait.

Imagery

Imagery can be extremely effective in enabling a client to 'rehearse' their new behaviours before carrying them out in the real world. The coach can lead the client to relax and imagine what change will look like and how it will feel physically in the body. The coach takes the client through steps of change in mental visualization. This can start by suggesting they imagine scenes they may face in the coming weeks:

- Where will you be as you start to adopt new ways of thinking and behaving?
- Can you see the rooms and environments in which you will be taking action?
- Who might you be interacting with?
- What will it look like when you are achieving your goals?
- How might other people respond to you differently?
- How will you feel differently about yourself if you are successful?
- What is a word and image that can help to remind you of your successful behaviour?

Bibliocoaching

As the client is expected to be become their own coach, it can be effective to suggest that they read certain books alongside their coaching programme. These can be books on psychology or coaching, self-help, management, leadership, communication or motivation literature. Similarly providing the client with CDs or DVDs on related subjects to their goals can reinforce learning and development. There are many websites that have inspirational and educational talks that help to integrate the client's change behaviours.

As the coaching programme draws to an end the client understands that they have a large source of supportive literature and lectures to call upon to support their ability to be their own coach.

CASE STUDY

Alan worked in a large organization in London. He was head of the department responsible for overseeing accounts. The CBC coach was called in by his boss, as colleagues had complained that they found Alan explosive and unapproachable.

Objective setting

In a pre-coaching meeting, Alan shared that his objectives were to be able to control his anger and to resolve issues in a more assertive manner. He expressed a real motivation for change and agreed to sign a contract where he took responsibility for completing home tasks.

TABLE 7.6 Alan's thinking log for NATs

Activating situation	Beliefs and negative thoughts	Consequential emotions
Criticism of Alan's action or opinion.	*Why do you always block my ideas?* *I hate you for blocking me.*	*Anger and resentment.*
Making a mistake.	*I must be no good.*	*Self-doubt.*
I couldn't find a solution to a problem on the project I run.	*Why can't I come up with a good solution? People must think I am a failure.* *I am the loser here because I have lost my temper.*	*Disappointment in self and self-criticism.* *Defensive/aggressive when others question me.*
Trying to communicate but feeling others don't understand where I am coming from.	*Why can't you understand me? Why do you put me on the spot? I'd rather write it out.*	*On the back foot – feeling undermined so turn aggressive to hide vulnerability.*

Alan identified specific difficulty in managing situations where he sensed that others were blocking his progress or where he felt criticized. The coach explained the ABCDE model and demonstrated to Alan how his thoughts could lead to unhelpful behaviours. It was suggested that he complete a written log to identify the Negative Automatic Thoughts (NATs) he experienced and become conscious of whether his thinking was disturbing him (Table 7.6).

The coach disputed whether Alan's beliefs were limiting his management of the situations he was facing. Alan said he realized that they were driving his angry responses and shaping his aggressive behaviour. Anger had become his default position. He shared the fact that uncontrolled temper had been a problem throughout his life as he sought to bring people under his own control, through brute force if necessary. He explained that he never liked to back down as he felt that this showed weakness. He defended his position, blaming the other person for his own discomfort. Losing face himself was not an option.

Physiology

In checking any physical symptoms he experienced under these conditions he said that he suffered from insomnia and ground his teeth. He experienced chest pain when he lost his temper and felt tired, drained and isolated afterwards.

When asked what helped these situations to go more easily, Alan responded that he preferred to be in charge of events so that he could take action without involving others. He described his positive outcome as being able to feel jollier, more gracious, positive and able to arrive home calmer.

The coach taught Alan to relax physically and mentally by taking a breathing space to quieten his agitated thoughts. He learnt to relax his shoulders and breathe gently into his diaphragm, with a longer outbreath. He learnt that he could calm himself and reduce both blood pressure and hyper-arousal. A progressive relaxation technique was provided to him on a CD to reinforce the learning.

Perfection versus the pursuit of excellence

To understand the driving force behind his anger the coach explored an underlying theme of perfectionism, which came to light when Alan said several times that 'it should have been better than that' or 'I felt stupid and a failure when it didn't turn out the way I had anticipated'. The coach explained to him that there was a difference between the pursuit of perfection, which is subjective, and the pursuit of excellence, which is accepting that one is fallible and just doing one's best. Alan could see that his pursuit of a perfect result put him under pressure. He embraced the philosophy of fallibility, though realized that it might take him some time to integrate this concept into behaviours.

The coach asked Alan to consider the basic demands he might be making about:

- **Himself** – 'I ought to be able to get things right and convince other people'. This was leading to self-criticism and frustration, which in turn led to angry and impatient behaviour with others.

- **Others** – 'Other people should do things the way I want them to, otherwise it shows that they are hostile to me and are acting against me'. This was leading him to react angrily when others expressed differing opinions to his own.

- **The situations he was facing** – 'Meetings must have the outcomes I want them to have otherwise it shows that I am a failure in motivating other people to work with me'. This was leading him to be on edge and he was putting himself under pressure to come out with the rigid goals he set himself.

The coach suggested that he continue to monitor his thoughts and dispute his current approach by asking himself whether those thoughts were:

- helping him to achieve his goals;
- logical and rational – just because he wanted someone to respond in the way he demanded, was it logical to expect that they must do so?; and
- practical and realistic – would everyone respond in the same way as he did in this situation? If not, what were the options so that he could develop greater flexibility of response?

In exploring distorted thinking, Alan realized that he was making a thinking error when he made assumptions that other people were 'out to get him'. It was agreed that his homework would be to seek evidence of any assumption he might make. Similarly he would not allow his mind to create imagined scenarios of what might happen but had not yet done so. He agreed to watch out for making reactive decisions about colleagues without first seeking specific facts.

He started to plan new ways of responding to difficult situations where he would previously have responded with anger. Imagery helped him create a space before reacting. He visualized traffic lights being on Red for Stop before reacting; Amber for take a moment to think and reflect; Green for when he felt calm and ready to respond. He developed the constructive and helpful thought 'I am in control of how I respond' and realized that instead of looking powerful in being angry he could actually end up looking foolish.

Behavioural changes

The coach shared with Alan the difference between aggressive and assertive behaviour by showing him the four different ways people transact so that he could observe when his behaviour was well adapted or maladaptive (Table 7.7).

Alan's home assignment was to practice breathing slowly and generating calm thoughts and physiology. He agreed to listen and allow others to question

TABLE 7.7   Types of behaviour

Aggressive: takes space from others and is disrespectful. Often defensive and bullying in order to avoid responsibility. Blaming and sometimes humiliating others. *Alan realized he spent much time in this quadrant.*	**Assertive**: mutual respect and collaborative style, seeking a working compromise that allows both parties to express opinions and needs, agree to disagree without blame or putting the other down. *Alan could see he needed to learn to be in this quadrant.*
Passive Aggressive: appear to be passive but are driven by anger that they are unable to express, so this leaks out through manipulation or emotional blackmail. They do not feel powerful themselves but equally are angry at others and disrespectful of their needs or views. *Alan could see that his behaviour would stimulate passive aggressive responses in others.*	**Passive**: timid and unable to stand up for themselves, can become a victim or martyr as make assumptions that others have more power than them. *Alan could see that his behaviour could stimulate passivity in some colleagues.*

him without becoming aggressive, to stop seeing work as a battlefield and reassure himself that 'I can listen to other opinions without feeling criticized and can work in a more collaborative and assertive way now'.

Alan shared the fact that he had previously seen himself as the Incredible Hulk but now realized that this was not a helpful image. When prompted, he suggested he would think of himself as James Bond. He felt that this image would remind him that he could be strong but self-contained and cool, expressing his thoughts without being aggressive.

As the coaching programme continued Alan reported that he had managed to respond in new ways in several situations, feel calmer and more measured. He remained self-critical, especially when he felt he had not come up to his new standard. However, he and his coach reinforced the principle of step-by-step change. He learnt to develop the thought 'I would prefer it if this situation worked out the way I specifically want but I can manage if it doesn't'.

Measuring change

After four sessions Alan reported a 'radical shift' in the way he was responding to challenges where previously he would have lost his temper. He was more tolerant of others, including his wife. He had relapses but was learning to accept that he would not always reach his own high standards and nor would others. He accepted that anger did not have to be overwhelming. Both his wife and team commented on the difference in his behaviour. Alan had learnt to develop more flexible and compassionate ways of thinking and responding to others.

When might the CBC approach be most suitable?

The applications of the cognitive behavioural approach are many. I have personally practised these models with children in schools, young people in colleges preparing for their adult life and careers, managers and professionals managing everyday workplace challenges, people facing redundancy or retirement or recovering from illness, for teams to recognize how individual thinking is shaping the behaviour, actions and results of the whole team, and for people in old age who need to find constructive ways of thinking about themselves and their lives as they age.

The structure that is provided by cognitive behavioural models can be particularly useful in the workplace, where there is also an appreciation of the problem-solving and goal-focused methodology of CBC. There has also recently been a move to educate school children to adopt cognitive behavioural approaches to how they manage the challenges of their lives. This can provide young people with a life skill that supports their ability to develop emotional intelligence.

As the theories and methods of CBC have become increasingly integrated with the other approaches mentioned in this book, CBC provides the coach with a holistic and diverse selection of techniques to keep in their toolbox. This enables them to adapt their approach to the specific needs of the client.

Conclusion

In today's fast-paced world people want short sharp solutions to their problems. The fact that CBC is time-limited and focused on the client's goals makes it an attractive and also an effective proposition. A report by the London School of Economics in 2006 commented that a fixed course of task-oriented CBT sessions, rather than an open-ended programme that can extend over years rather than months, makes it practical for a large number of people. The effectiveness of CBT as a remedial intervention provides credibility to CBC as a developmental process because CBC adapts the techniques to help clients move forward and achieve their work and life goals. CBC is more empowering than some other forms of coaching as it doesn't just provide someone with an hour of introspection but provides the client with tangible tools that they can apply immediately in their own lives.

CBC provides information and strategies on a large range of aspects of human experience from challenging limiting beliefs, to managing stress, or to sharing the skills that enable the client to develop more assertive methods of communication.

The theories and models of cognitive behavioural psychology furnish individuals with a set of life skills that can help them manage the challenges of all phases of life. The ability to self-observe and challenge one's own beliefs and demands can free people from deeply held but unhelpful and out-dated perspectives on life. Knowing how to choose one's thoughts and responses to situations, even if one can't change the situation itself, is profoundly empowering.

Developing yourself as a cognitive behavioural coach

Developing your skills

Coaches wishing to learn more and develop their skills in cognitive behavioural coaching may wish to explore the following practitioner texts:

- Neenan, M and Palmer, S (2012) *Cognitive-Behavioural Coaching in Practice: An evidence based approach*, Routledge, London
- Whitten, H (2010) *Cognitive-Behavioural Coaching Techniques for Dummies*, Wiley, Chichester
- Passmore, J (Ed) (2010) *Excellence in Coaching: The industry guide*, Kogan Page, London
- Palmer, S and Whybrow, A (2007) *Handbook of Coaching Psychology: A guide for practitioners*, Routledge, London

Deepening your understanding

Coaches wishing to recommend CBC-based self-help books and workbooks for their clients may wish to consider the following:

- Dryden, W (2013) *Coping with Guilt*, Sheldon Press, London
- McMahon, G (2011) *No More Stress: Be your own stress management coach*, Karnac Books, London
- Dryden, W (1996) *Overcoming Anger*, Sheldon Press, London
- Burns, D (1990) *The Feeling Good Handbook*, Plume, New York
- Israel, R, Whitten, H and Shaffran, C (2000) *Your Mind at Work, Developing Self Knowledge for Business Success*, Kogan Page, London

Web resources

Useful websites for both coaches and clients include:

- Albert Ellis on rational thinking:
  www.youtube.com/watch?v=GyRE-78g_z0
- Aaron Beck on cognitive behavioural psychology:
  www.youtube.com/user/BeckInstitute
- Example of NHS resource information on CBT coaches:
  www.northtynesidebrighterminds.nhs.uk/resources/
- Training, tips and videos:
  www.centreforcoaching.com/#!video_tips/cdvr

References

Adler, A (1931) *What Life Should Mean to You*, Capricorn, New York

Beales, D and Whitten, H (2010) *Emotional Healing for Dummies*, Wiley, Chichester

Beck, A T (1993) Cognitive approaches to stress, in *Principles and Practice of Stress Management*, eds R Woolfold and P Lehrer, (2nd edn pp 333–72), Guilford Press, New York

Beck, A T, Rush, A J, Shaw, B F and Emery, G (1979) *Cognitive Therapy of Depression*, The Guilford Press, New York

Beck, J W (1995) *Cognitive Therapy: Basics and beyond*, Guilford Press, New York

Bernardi, L, Bandinelli, G, Cencetti, S, Fattorini, L, Lagi, A and Wdowczyc-Szulc, J (2001) Effect of rosary prayer and yoga mantras on autonomic cardiovascular rhythms: a comparative study, *The BMJ*, **323** (1446)

Burns, D (1980) The perfectionist's script for self defeat, *Psychology Today*, November, pp 34–51

Burns, D L (1990) *The Feeling Good Handbook*, Plume, New York

Carrington, D and Whitten, H (2005) *Future Directions: Practical ways to develop emotional intelligence and confidence in young people*, Continuum, London

Cooper, C L and Palmer, S (2000) *Conquer your Stress*, CIPD, London

Crane, R (2009) *Mindfulness-Based Cognitive Therapy*, Hove: Routledge

Curwen, B, Palmer, S and Ruddell, P (2000) *Brief Cognitive Behaviour Therapy*, Sage, London

Decker, S E, Nich, C, Carroll, K M and Martino, S (2013) Development of the Therapist Empathy Scale, *Behavioural and Cognitive Psychotherapy*, **41** (3), May 2013, pp 371–75, available on CJO2013. doi:10.1017/S1352465813000039

de Haan, E (2008) I doubt therefore I coach: critical moments in coaching practice, *Consulting Psychology Journal: Practice and Research*, **60** (1), pp 91–105

Dryden, W (1996) *Overcoming Anger*, Sheldon Press, London

Dryden, W (2008) The therapeutic alliance as an integrating framework, in W Dryden and Reeves (eds) *Key Issues for Counselling in Action*, pp 1–17, Sage, London

Dryden, W (2009) *Rational Emotive Behaviour Therapy*, Routledge, Hove

Dryden, W (2013) *Coping with Guilt*, Sheldon Press, London

Dryden, W and Gordon, J (1990) *What is Rational-Emotive Therapy?*, Gale Centre Publications, Loughton

Dryden, W and Gordon, J (1993) *Peak Performance: Become more effective at work*, Mercury, Didcot

Edwards, J (2001) Cognitive coaching SM: a synthesis of research, in *Cognitive Behavioural Coaching*, ed M Neenan, Chapter 7

Elder, L and Paul, R (1998) The role of Socratic questioning in thinking, teaching and learning, New York, *Clearing House*, 297–301: http://dx.doi.org/10.1080/00098659809602729

Elder, L and Paul, R (2006) *The Art of Socratic Questioning*, Foundation for Critical Thinking, Dillon Beach, CA

Ellis, A (1994) *Reason and emotion in psychotherapy: comprehensive method of treating human disturbances*, Citadel Press, New York

Ellis, A and Tafrate, R (1997) *How to Control your Anger Before it Controls You*, Citadel Press, New York

Essex, A (2004) *Compassionate Coaching*, Rider, London

Garland, E L, Fredrickson, B, Kring, A M, Johnson, D P, Meyer, Piper, S and Penn, D L (2010) Upward spirals of positive emotions counter downward spirals of negativity, *US Clinical Psychology Review*, **30**, pp 849–64

Garland, E L and Howard, M O (2009) Neuroplasticity, psychosocial genomics, and the biopsychosocial paradigm in the 21st century, *Health & Social Work*, **34** (3), pp 191–99

Grant, A M (2001) Coaching for Enhanced Performance: Comparing cognitive and behavioural approaches to coaching. Paper presented to the 3rd International Spearman Seminar

Grant, A M (2007) Past, present and future: the evolution of professional coaching and coaching psychology, in *Handbook of Coaching Psychology* (eds Stephen Palmer and Alison Whybrow), Routledge, London

Grant, A M, Green, L S and Oades, L G (2006) Cognitive-behavioural, solution-focused life coaching: enhancing goal striving, wellbeing, and hope, University of Wollongong, NSW, Australia and University of Sydney, NSW, Australia www.sfwork.com/pdf/jopp_green_oades_grant_2006.pdf

Grant, A M, Passmore, J, Cavanagh, M and Parker, H (2010) The state of play in coaching, *International Review of Industrial and Organizational Psychology*, **25**, pp 125–68

Gyllensten, K and Palmer, S (2007) The coaching relationship: an interpretative phenomenological analysis, *International Coaching Psychology Review*, **2** (2), pp 168–77

Hawkins, C C, Watt, H M G and Sinclair, K E (2006) Psychometric properties of the Frost Multidimensional Perfectionism Scale with Australian adolescent girls, *Educational and Psychological Measurement*

Howard, P J (1994) *The Owner's Manual for the Brain*, Bard Press, Texas

Irvine, W B (2009) *A Guide to the Good Life: The ancient art of Stoic joy*, Oxford University Press, Oxford

Israel, R, Shaffran, C and Whitten, H (2000) *Your Mind at Work: Developing self-knowledge for business success*, Kogan Page, London

Jeglic, E, Schaffer, M, Moster, A and Wnuk, D (2010) Cognitive Behavioral Therapy in the Treatment and Management of Sex Offenders, John Jay College of Criminal Justice, New York CUNY, *Journal of Cognitive Psychotherapy*, 04/2010, **24** (2), pp 92–103

Joseph, A and Chapman, M (2013) *Visual CBT*, Capstone, London

Kahneman, D (2011) *Thinking, Fast and Slow*, Allen Lane, London

Kaisera, A, Hallerb, S, Schmitz, S and Nitscha, C (2009) On sex/gender related similarities and differences in fMRI language research, *Brain Research Reviews*, **61** (2), pp 49–59

Kearns, H, Forbes, A and Gardiner, M (2007) A cognitive behavioural coaching intervention for the treatment of perfectionism and self-handicapping in a non-clinical population. Australia, *Behaviour Change*, **24** (3), pp 157–72 Staff Development and Training Unit, Flinders University, Adelaide, Australia, School of Medicine, Department of Psychiatry, Flinders University, Adelaide

Kennerley, H (1997) *Overcoming Anxiety*, Robinson, London

Lazarus, A A (1981) *The Practice of Multimodal Therapy*, McGraw-Hill, New York

Lazarus, R S (1991) *Emotion and Adaptation*, Oxford University Press, Oxford

Lehrer, P, Sasaki, Y and Saito, Y (1999) Zazen and Cardiac Variability, Philadelphia, *Psychosomatic Medicine*, **61** (6), pp 812–921

Lehrer, P, Woolfolk, R and Sime, W (2007) *Principles and Practice of Stress Management*, 3rd Edition, The Guilford Press, New York

McCrae, B (2007) Is cognitive-behavioural coaching your missing ingredient? London, *Training Zone*, 27 February 2013

McGilchrist, I (2009) *The Master and his Emissary*, Yale University Press, Yale

Neenan, M (2008) From cognitive behavioural therapy (CBT) to cognitive behavioural coaching (CBC), *Journal of Rational Emotive Cognitive Behaviour Therapy*, **26**, pp 3–15

Neenan, M (2012) Socratic questioning, *Cognitive Behavioural Coaching in Practice*, Routledge, London

Neenan, M and Dryden, W (2002a) *Cognitive-Behaviour Therapy, An A-Z of Persuasive Arguments*, Whurr Publishers, London

Neenan, M and Dryden, W (2002b) *Life Coaching: A cognitive-behavioural approach*, Routledge, Hove

Neenan, M and Dryden, W (2006) *Rational Emotive Behaviour Therapy*, Sage, London

Neenan, M and Palmer, S (2001) Cognitive behavioural coaching, London, *Stress News*, **13** (3), pp 14–18

Neenan, M and Palmer, S (2012) *Cognitive Behavioural Coaching in Practice, An evidence based approach*, Routledge, London

NICE (2008) Cognitive behavioural therapy for the management of common mental health problems, Commissioning guide: Implementing NICE guidance, NICE Guidelines to NHS Commissioning Groups, April, London, NHS, www.nice.org.uk/media/878/f7/cbtcommissioningguide.pdf

O'Broin, A and Palmer, S (2012) Enhancing the coaching alliance and relationship, *Cognitive Behavioural Coaching in Practice, An Evidence Based Approach*, Routledge, London

Padesky, C (1993) *Socratic Questioning: Changing minds or guided discovery*, European Congress of Behavioural Therapies, London

Padesky, C A and Greenberger, D (1995) *Clinician's Guide to Mind over Mood*, The Guilford Press, London

Palmer, S (1992) *Stress Management: A course reader*, Centre for Stress Management, London

Palmer, S and Dryden, W (1995) *Counselling for Stress Problems*, Sage, London

Palmer, S and Szymanska, K (2007) Cognitive behavioural coaching: an integrative approach, in *Handbook of Coaching Psychology: A guide for practitioners*, eds S Palmer and A Whybrow, Sage, London

Palmer, S and Whybrow, A (Eds) (2007) *Handbook of Coaching Psychology: A guide for practitioners*, Routledge, London

Palmer, S and Williams, H (2013) Cognitive behavioural coaching, in *Wiley-Blackwell Handbook of the Psychology of Coaching and Mentoring*, eds J Passmore, D Peterson and T Freire, Wiley-Blackwell, Chichester

Passmore, J (Ed) (2010) *Excellence in Coaching: The industry guide*, Kogan Page, London

Passmore, J, Peterson, D and Freire, T (eds) (2013) The *Wiley-Blackwell Handbook of the Psychology of Coaching and Mentoring*, Wiley-Blackwell, Chichester

Seligman, Martin, E P (1990) *Learned Optimism*, Knopf, New York

Shafran, R, Cooper, Z and Fairburn, C G (2002) Clinical perfectionism: a cognitive-behavioural analysis, New York, *Behaviour Research and Therapy*, **40** (7), pp 773–79

Smedley, K, and Whitten, H (2006) *Age Matters: Employing, motivating and managing older employees*, Gower, London

Snyder, C R and Lopez, S J (eds) (2002) *Handbook of Positive Psychology*, Oxford University Press, Oxford

Spence, G B and Grant, A M (2007) *The Journal of Positive Psychology: Dedicated to furthering research and promoting good practice*, **2** (3), pp 185–94

Tugade, M M and Fredrickson, B L (2004) Resilient individuals use positive emotions to bounce back from negative emotional experiences, *Journal of Personality and Social Psychology*, **86** (2), 320–33

Whitmore, J (2008) *Coaching for Performance*, Nicholas Brealey, London

Whitten, H (2009) *Cognitive Behavioural Coaching Techniques for Dummies*, Wiley, Chichester

Whitworth, L, Kimsey-House, H and Sandahl, P (1998) *Co-Active Coaching*, Davies-Black, Palo Alto California

Wilhelm, F, Gervitz, R and Roth, W (2001) Respiratory dysregulation in anxiety, functional cardiac, and pain, *Behav Modif*, 25 September (4), pp 513–45

Wills, F (2010) *Beck's Cognitive Therapy*, Routledge, London

Ya-Ting C Yang, Newby, T J and Bill, R L (2005) *The American Journal of Distance Education*, **19** (3), pp 163–81, Lawrence Erlbaum Associates Inc

Mindful coaching

08

LIZ HALL

Introduction

Mindful coaching (MC) is an emerging coaching approach that seeks in its widest sense to marry coaching with the principles, traits, state/s, processes and philosophy of mindfulness.

Mindfulness itself is nothing new. Its Buddhist roots go back more than 2,500 years and there is a history of contemplation and meditation in all the major religions. However, what is relatively new is its spread from the spiritual setting into a wide range of secular contexts, including education, medicine and therapy. In the United Kingdom, the National Institute for Health and Clinical Excellence has recommended Mindfulness-Based Cognitive Therapy (MBCT) for recurrent depression since 2004, for example, while mindfulness is being embraced in the workplace with employers including Transport for London and the US Army training employees in mindfulness skills. Other employers, such as GlaxoSmithKline, the BBC and Open University, have run mindfulness events for their internal coaches, while independent coaches are flocking to workshops and masterclasses on the topic of mindfulness and coaching.

One of the attractions of mindfulness as an approach is that it can be woven into everyday life. People do not have to eschew all contact with the outside world to meditate in a distant cave. It was this aspect that first attracted me to mindfulness many years ago as a highly stressed, working single mother (writing about work/life balance, an irony not lost on me at the time) and it is one that so many coaching clients find appealing – my clients and clients of others. Many of us live in such busy worlds, contactable 24/7, overwhelmed by choice and complexity, and in challenging uncertain times, where numerous crises including environmental and economical, are playing out. Mindfulness as a potential antidote to some of the mindlessness can seem highly appealing.

However, despite the widespread interest in mindfulness, and the impressive evidence base, there has been limited research and authorship relating specifically to mindfulness and coaching, and many coaches, even those with a well-established mindfulness practice, are unsure about how mindfulness can inform coaching.

This chapter offers an advanced perspective on mindfulness-based coaching or mindful coaching. It explores definitions and facets of mindfulness, and the evidence underpinning the approach. It explores common ground and potential tensions between mindfulness and coaching, arguing that powerful coaching can emerge as a result of exploring some of these tensions. It highlights how practising mindfulness can help coaches be more compassionate, more present, more attuned, and more resourceful, supporting clients around areas including stress management, resilience, emotional intelligence, cognitive functioning, work/life balance, and dealing with complexity, change and ambiguity, amongst others.

The practical section explores what MC looks like in practice, including how coaches might use the FEEL model for working with mindfulness in coaching along with a case study that illustrates the approach.

Evidence-based approach to mindful coaching

Despite the huge interest in mindfulness in general and the proliferation of mindfulness-related research papers in non-coaching arenas, only a small few authors and researchers have concerned themselves with mindfulness in relation to coaching, including Cavanagh and Spence, 2013; Hall, 2013; Passmore and Marianetti, 2007, 2009; Spence *et al*, 2008; Silsbee, 2010; Collard and Walsh, 2008. As Cavanagh and Spence (2013) have said, 'given that mindfulness seems to play a critical role in human functioning (particularly the process of purposeful positive change), its relative absence from scholarly coaching literature is somewhat strange.'

We will look at some of that research along with research in other arenas such as neuroscience, psychotherapy, and health with implications when considering how mindfulness might underpin coaching. First, however, let us define what we mean by mindfulness.

A multifaceted phenomena

Mindfulness is *not* about emptying the mind, as some mistakenly believe, and it does not merely involve the mind, but the body, the heart (some may say soul) and the wider environment. In a general sense, we can think of mindfulness as a way of training the mind.

When we get to specifics, however, there is widespread confusion about what mindfulness is. This is partly because mindfulness is experiential and thus hard to describe, and partly because, as Cavanagh and Spence (2013) suggest, there is 'an unwitting conflation of different categories of phenomena'. They distinguish between mindfulness as a philosophy (a set of beliefs about the nature of self, the world and experience), a deliberate intentional practice (deliberate process or set of behaviours), a present moment state (cognitive phenomena) and a trait (habitual predisposition toward experience). They argue that the aspects of mindfulness most likely to be responsible for the purported beneficial effects of mindfulness are the state of 'decentered awareness', and 'intentional attending', the process by which this state is attained. Thus their definition of mindfulness is 'a motivated state of decentred awareness brought about by receptive attending to present moment experience'.

In the mindful coaching approach explored in this chapter, mindfulness is viewed as is a way of being, a way of doing, and a way of *non-doing* – which Kabat-Zinn (1994) refers to as 'effortless effort'. Mindfulness is embraced in all its facets – state, traits, practice/process and philosophy.

I define mindfulness as 'a particular way of being, doing, and non-doing; of paying attention in and to the present moment, with non-judgment, curiosity and compassion'.

I choose to make explicit the element of compassion, which is absent in Kabat-Zinn's definition (1994), for example (although compassion is core to much of his work). He defines mindfulness as 'a way of paying attention in a particular way: on purpose, in the present moment, and non-judgmentally'.

The research

Mindfulness continues to be given much prominence in the psychological literature and other literature. The research covers many aspects of mindfulness, including its cultivation (eg Baer *et al*, 2006; Hayes, Strosahl and Wilson, 2003); definitions and theory (eg Bishop *et al*, 2004; Shapiro *et al*, 2006); measurement (eg Baer *et al*, 2006; Cardaciotto *et al*, 2008); outcomes in therapy and counselling (eg Brown *et al*, 2007; Shapiro *et al*, 2006); and the role of mindfulness in supporting therapeutic relationships (Bruce *et al*, 2010; Martin, 1997).

Cavanagh and Spence (2013) identify first, second and third order effects which come from the state of decentred awareness. The first order effects include an increased control over one's attention (attentional control), decreased emotional reactivity, heightened intrapersonal attunement, and increased access to new sources of information.

Increased attentional control has been linked with an enhanced sense of self-efficacy and self-regulation (Cavanagh and Spence, 2013). Decreased emotional reactivity means the person chooses their emotional responses, rather than the other way round.

Some affective states such as anxiety can bias the selection and recall of information, impairing judgement and evaluation but mindfulness practice can counteract the tendency to egocentric processing, suggest Cavanagh and Spence. It does this by helping us notice more information, and allowing us access to more choices for how we respond.

The second order effects they identify include perceived self-efficacy, interpersonal attunement and a wider range of effective behavioural choices, and the third order effects, autonomous goal selection and effective self-regulation, which we will explore later.

Benefits attributed to practising mindfulness include improved well-being, resilience and stress management (eg Chiesa and Serretti, 2009; Bränström, Duncan and Moskowitz, 2011); improvement of psychological conditions including anxiety, insomnia, phobias and eating disorders (Walsh and Shapiro, 2006); reduction in emotional disturbance and psychological distress (Baer *et al*, 2006; Brown and Ryan, 2003); lifting of mood (Davidson, 2004); and greater vitality (Brown and Ryan, 2003). Mindfulness has been linked to improved medical conditions such as type 2 diabetes, cardiovascular disease, asthma, premenstrual syndrome and chronic pain (Walsh and Shapiro, 2006), decreased cortisol (Tang *et al*, 2007*)*, and a boosted immune system (Davidson *et al*, 2003; Tang *et al*, 2007).

There are clear indications that mindfulness improves cognitive functioning, for example: less cognitive rigidity (Greenberg *et al*, 2012a; Moore and Malinowski, 2009); heightened focus and ability to stay on task (Mrazek *et al*, 2013); the ability to think clearly, and reduced 'sunk cost bias' tendency (where we stick with something because we have already made an investment, in a bid to recoup or justify the investment) (Hafenbrack *et al*, 2013). It promotes more rational and faster decision-making (Kirk, Downar and Montague, 2011; Langer, 2000, cited in Langer 2005); improved ability to think more divergently (Colzato, Ozturk and Hommel, 2012); and improved insight problem-solving and creativity (Ostafin and Kassman, 2012). It boosts working memory capacity (Mrazek *et al*, 2013; Jha *et al*, 2010), reduces mind-wandering (Mrazek *et al*, 2013; Kerr *et al*, 2013), and promotes metacognition (Kerr *et al*, 2013; Rimes and Wingrove, 2011). Mindfulness practice improves backward inhibition (the inhibition of information that has been relevant in the past and is no longer relevant in the present moment), considered to be one of the purest measures of task set inhibition (Greenberg, Reiner and Meiran, 2012b). Impaired backward inhibition has been linked to depressive rumination.

Much of the research highlights how practising mindfulness can improve emotional intelligence (eg Boyatzis and McKee, 2005; Chu, 2010): self-awareness (Creswell *et al*, 2007) and self-management, and awareness of others and relationship management; improving empathy (Lazar *et al*, 2005; Rimes and Wingrove, 2011); enhancing compassion for self and others (Lutz *et al*, 2008; Rimes and Wingrove, 2011; Neff, 2003); improving emotion regulation (eg Boyatzis and McKee, 2005; Teper and Inzlicht, 2012; Lutz *et al*, 2008) and improving working memory capacity, linked to better emotion regulation (Schmeichel, Volokhov and Demaree, 2008), and greater relationship satisfaction, lower emotional reactivity, and more constructive responses to relationship stress (Barnes *et al*, 2007).

One potentially interesting development is in the field of epigenetics. Kaliman *et al* (2014) report what is thought to be the first evidence of specific molecular changes in the body following mindfulness meditation. The study compared the effects of eight hours of mindfulness practice in experienced meditators with those of quiet non-meditative activities in non-meditators. After the intensive mindfulness practice, the meditators showed genetic and molecular differences including altered levels of gene-regulating machinery and reduced levels of pro-inflammatory genes, which in turn correlated with faster physical recovery from a stressful situation. Perhaps surprisingly, according to the researchers, there was no difference in the tested genes between the two groups of people at the start of the study. The observed effects were seen only in the meditators following mindfulness practice. In addition, several other DNA-modifying genes showed no differences between groups, suggesting that the mindfulness practice specifically affected certain regulatory pathways. The key result, say the researchers, is that meditators experienced genetic changes following mindfulness practice that were not seen in the non-meditating group after other quiet activities – an outcome providing proof of principle that mindfulness practice can lead to epigenetic alterations of the genome.

Coaching-related research

My own research (Hall, 2013) was prompted by what I saw as a dearth of material on mindfulness and coaching. Thus far it has consisted of interviews with more than 50 coaches, coaching psychologists, coach trainers, coaching clients, mindfulness practitioners/trainers, psychotherapists and neuroscientists; a literature review including almost 1,000 research papers on mindfulness; an online survey of 156 coaches in 10 countries via SurveyMonkey (self-selecting respondents attracted via *Coaching at Work* magazine, LinkedIn groups including *Coaching at Work*, and the Association for Coaching), and reflections on my mindful coaching practice.

As part of this research, I looked at compatibility and commonality between mindfulness and coaching (Table 8.1), and areas of potential difference (Table 8.2). It is noteworthy just how much common ground there is between mindfulness and coaching.

When we look at potential tensions, some we can put down to differences in coaching style and approach, particularly given the increased diversification and growth in coaching forms (Bresser, 2013). Psychoanalytic coaches will explore a coachee's past, many coaches including those trained in the Nancy Kline Thinking Environment approach will embrace silence, and gestalt-informed coaches will work with the present, for example. However some areas present more of a challenge and can create resistance among coaches and clients to a mindfulness-based coaching approach: in particular, the last five in Table 8.2.

TABLE 8.1   Where mindfulness meets coaching: some areas of common ground/desired outcome

Category	Mindfulness	Coaching
BELIEF		
Person is 'whole'	✓	✓
Person is resourceful	✓	✓
We are interconnected (systemic lens)	✓	✓
PERSPECTIVE/STATE		
Beginner's mind	✓	✓
Observer's/Witness mind	✓	✓
Metacognition	✓	✓
Self actualization	✓	✓
Presence	✓	✓
Contemplation and reflection	✓	✓
Curiosity and enquiring-ness	✓	✓
QUALITY/ABILITY		
Compassion	✓	✓
Empathy	✓	✓
Non-judgement	✓	✓
Trust (in oneself, others, and the wider system)	✓	✓
Honesty	✓	✓
Authenticity	✓	✓
Intuitiveness	✓	✓
Wisdom	✓	✓
Clarity and focus	✓	✓
Co-creation	✓	✓

Particularly in the Western hemisphere, arguably, there is a very strong emphasis on being busy and getting things done. Often it really does not matter *what* we are doing, it is the *doing* that counts. Sometimes it is about seeking strokes from others – 'look how busy I am', or about running away from ourselves, or because we are caught in a system where burnout is rife and we

TABLE 8.2   Areas of potential difference/tension between a mindfulness approach and 'traditional' coaching

Category	Mindfulness	Coaching
Time focus	Present moment	Future orientation
Degree of recognition of inter-connectedness	Sense of one-ness	Focus on individual agenda whilst considering the system
Number of people	Solitary (not always)	Involves two or more people (apart from self-coaching)
Activity/mind mode	Being and non-doing	Doing
Stance in relation to striving	Non-striving/letting go	Striving
Attitude to goals	Non-goal-oriented	Goal-oriented
Attitude to change	Accepting 'what is'	Trying to change 'what is'
Stance in relation to attachment	Non-attachment	Attachment, eg to goal

find it hard to say 'no', or because of a merciless be-perfect driver, or because we have switched to hyper-threat vigilance and our 'on-off' button is not working properly. There are many reasons for what can be an unhealthy relationship with busyness and doing, but it is a relationship that can see some people unwilling to explore mindfulness because they associate it with doing nothing.

For ourselves as coaches in terms of self-care, and in service of our clients, it can be fruitful to step back and explore what is going on here. Sometimes the resistance some people bring to mindfulness in relation to coaching, for example, stems from dualistic thinking around the mental concepts of being and doing, and the closely associated concepts of non-striving and striving (Hall, 2013). There can be a fear that it's either/or; that becoming more mindful will mean nothing gets done.

With the emphasis on suspending judgements and evaluations, on just being open to whatever arises, mindfulness can free us from polarized thinking around being and doing. If there is an 'opposite' to doing relevant to mindfulness, it is non-doing:

> Non-doing doesn't have to be threatening to people who feel they always have to get things done. They might find they get even more 'done', and done better, by practising non-doing. Non-doing simply means letting things be and allowing them to unfold in their own way. Enormous effort can be involved, but it is a graceful, knowledgeable, effortless effort, a 'doerless doing', cultivated over a lifetime.
>
> (Kabat-Zinn, 1994: 45)

In addition, when it comes to the doing, as we have explored, mindfulness is likely to improve productivity and performance through boosting cognitive functioning and emotion regulation, for example.

Another lens on being and doing is that of being versus doing thinking modes (eg Williams, 2008). Williams highlights a number of differences between the discrepancy-based 'doing mode' of mind and the alternative 'being mode' of mindfulness. In terms of striving versus non-striving, doing mode focuses on monitoring and striving to close the gap between ideas of where we are now and where we want to be; or to keep as wide as possible the gap between ideas of where we are now and where we fear we might end up if we do nothing, while the being mode of mindful mind focuses on letting go of such striving towards or away from such ideas. In terms of avoidance versus approach, doing mode causes particular problems when it is motivated by avoidance of subjective experience, while mindfulness encourages remaining open, 'turning towards' the difficult and the unpleasant. In relation to thoughts as 'real' versus thoughts as mental events, doing mode uses ideas (thoughts and images) as its 'currency', taking such thoughts literally, while mindfulness sees thoughts as 'products' of the mind that arise, stay for a while then disperse. Williams also highlights how doing mode lives in the past and future, solving problems by switching between memories of the past and anticipation of the future, while being mode focuses on present-moment experience. Memories are recognized as memories that are arising now; future images are seen for what they are, images arising here and now. In relation to conceptual versus non-conceptual experience, doing mind is concerned with manipulating ideas, so the subjective experience is thinking about things, while mindful being mode focuses on direct, sensory experience, is non-conceptual, intuitive and experiential. And lastly, doing mind relies on habitual, over-learned routines that run automatically, while mindfulness involves intentionally paying attention to aspects of the self and the world.

Rather than seeking to promote polarization even further, this perspective clarifies some of the differences between a mindful and non-mindful mode, with the aim of fostering choice for the most appropriate responses at any given time. We can learn and help our clients learn to spot the difference between the different modes of mind. As Williams explains, in doing mode, our current state and our goals (and anti-goals) are expressed as representations – ideas, usually language-based. Once activated, this mode kicks off the range of available processes: analysing, remembering, anticipating, comparing and judging. If the thoughts and emotions are negative, we can take them literally, leading to experiential avoidance. Mindful mind, however, helps us to become aware of these habitual tendencies and of when they serve or do not serve us.

MC can help clients approach being, non-doing and doing in a very different way, helping them become more productive, creative and efficient, but also empowering them to take better care of themselves, putting the brakes on when they need to. Unpacking these concepts can foster a much healthier approach to work/life balance and help individuals manage stress and become more resilient.

Goal-free coaching?

For many coaches, the GROW (goals-reality-options-will/wrap-up) model popularized by John Whitmore (1992) or a similar goal-oriented framework, is core to coaching. Yet increasingly there is a school of thought that proposes that goal-setting is not always appropriate (eg Megginson and Clutterbuck, 2013). Encouraging clients through mindfulness to be more curious, more accepting, less attached to outcome and comfortable with not knowing, can be immensely fruitful, particularly when they are faced with ambiguous and complex worlds to navigate. Coaching is about opening up choices for our clients, and mindfulness supports this, be that inexplicitly via the coach role-modelling mindfulness, being more present and curious, for example, or explicitly through the sharing of mindfulness practices.

Particularly in the West, there is a focus on knowing, on prediction, on averting risks. However, as we have been reminded by recent economic and environmental crises, for example, it is not possible to know everything or to predict everything. When working with leaders, in particular, bringing a more emergent approach can be very helpful.

Yet it is not the case at all that mindful coaching need be goal-free or even 'goal-lite' coaching. Mindfulness-based coaching helps clients identify what truly matters to them, in line with their values (Hall, 2013; Cavanagh and Spence, 2013), helping them operate from being mode where helpful, and disengage from habitual patterns (eg Williams, 2008; Greenberg, Reiner and Meiran, 2012b).

Mindfulness also helps them to achieve their goals. In what seems to be the only study to directly examine the impact of mindfulness combined with coaching (Spence, Cavanagh and Grant, 2008), mindfulness training combined with solution-focused coaching was found to help clients attain their health-related goals, particularly if clients receive mindfulness training first. Mindfulness helped clients resist the temptation to sabotage their progress towards goals.

Improving self-efficacy is key (Cavanagh and Spence, 2013) – the more confident clients are about performing a behaviour, the higher their motivation, effort, performance and achievement (Bandura and Locke, 2003). Cavanagh and Spence (2013) argue that the combination of mindfulness, 'attentional control' and reduced emotional reactivity means people are better able to manage their emotional responses and use their cognitive resources more fully to self-regulate, noting that being able to effectively self-regulate positively impacts goal attainment (Carver and Scheier, 1998).

Practice: tools and techniques in mindful coaching

When exploring how coaches might work with mindfulness, we can distinguish between the following:

1 **Mindfulness skills training:** although coaching is typically non-directive, there can be a place for coaches imparting expertise where appropriate, with the client's permission. So, for example, if a client is suffering from pre-presentation nerves, or reports experiencing overwhelm, or cognitive overload, or a leader wishes to 'be more authentic', the coach may decide to explicitly teach the client some mindfulness practices which may be of help. This can be done within the coaching session or given as 'homework'.

2 **Coaching** *for* **mindfulness:** this is where the coach explicitly fosters mindfulness traits and behaviours in the client. For example, helping the client realize they are not their thoughts or notice more and pay more attention to what is in them and around them. This may even be via or combined with another approach, gestalt or somatic, for example, or cognitive behavioural coaching, and may be combined with the explicit sharing of mindfulness practices, or not.

3 **Coaching mindfully:** this may be explicit or implicit. Here the coach coaches from a state of mindfulness where possible, aspiring to show up with certain qualities, traits, behaviours and perspectives, and committing to certain strategies and practices to support themselves to be able to do this. In addition, they may teach mindfulness to the client *where appropriate.*

Here are some of the applications of mindfulness in coaching:

- Coach benefits personally from having a regular mindfulness practice, promoting self-awareness, self-care, resilience and happiness, for example (which impacts positively on how they coach).

- Coach uses mindfulness techniques to prepare for sessions, so they are more resourceful, creative and present right from the outset.

- Coach uses mindfulness techniques for themselves within sessions promoting their ability to use 'self as instrument', enhancing their ability to be intuitive, to notice and regulate their emotions, and distinguish between what are their own issues and those of the client, for example.

- Coach uses mindfulness techniques for reflection post-session, enhancing their ability to notice and capture data, and spark insights, for example.
- Coach shares mindfulness training/sharing mindfulness practices explicitly with the client within the session or as 'homework', helping the client be more resourceful, and helping them address specific issues/goals such as managing stress; preparing for meetings/presentations and so on; improving their ability to deal with change and transition; becoming more emotionally intelligent, and so on.
- Coach chooses to work with a mindfulness-informed coach supervisor.

Table 8.3 outlines some core principles and aspirations for coaching mindfully.

TABLE 8.3   Principles and aspirations for coaching mindfully

Not being overly attached to outcomes
Being non-judgemental
Exploring and reaching resolution with concepts of being/doing
Paying attention to being present for and to the client, attuning to the client and resonating with the client
Being curious and enquiring
Being comfortable with ambiguity and not knowing
Being empathic, and compassionate to self and others
Practising mindfulness (including meditation) regularly
Preparing mindfully for each coaching session
Reflecting mindfully after each coaching session
Approaching coaching systemically, 'being mindful' of the wider systems in which they and their clients operate
Attending (not solely) to what arises in the present in coaching interactions

Teaching mindfulness to clients is one of four areas where mindfulness can help coaches, along with preparing for coaching, maintaining focus in the session and remaining 'emotionally detached' (Passmore and Marianetti, 2007). In addition, Chaskalson (2011) highlights the ability to empathize with the client. Our ability to be present with, attuned to and resonant with the client; our ability to empathize with the client and feel compassion for them (and ourselves) are important factors in good coaching and are all enhanced by mindfulness.

In relationship

According to a report by the Ridler consultancy, the highest-rated characteristic sponsors seek in an external coach, by a significant margin, is 'personal chemistry' (Ridler, 2011). When Ridler drilled down further to establish what sponsors meant by personal chemistry, it found that it was about listening well (97 per cent of respondents) and the coach coming across as open and sincere (89 per cent) (Ridler, 2013). These are qualities to do with the coach making good use of their self as instrument.

Among the most powerful contributions mindfulness can make in coaching are helping coach and client make better use of their selves as instrument, and improving relationships. Bruce *et al* (2010) argue that mindfulness is a means of self-attunement that increases one's ability to attune to others and that this interpersonal attunement ultimately helps patients achieve greater self-attunement that, in turn, fosters greater well-being, and better interpersonal relationships. As we become more aware through mindfulness of our own emotional and bodily states, we also become more aware of those of others. The more aware we are of these states, the more our insula and anterior cingulated cortex activate and the better we are at reading others (Singer *et al*, 2004).

Presence

To become attuned with, and resonant to clients, coaches first need to have presence. At least two of the main professional coaching bodies – the Association for Coaching (AC) and the International Coach Federation (ICF) include presence as a core competency. However, there is very little in the coaching literature about how to actually develop presence. Along with others (eg Silsbee, 2010), I believe mindfulness is perfectly suited to the development of presence, helping us meet requirements such as those cited by the ICF for the coach 'to be present and flexible during the coaching process, dancing in the moment; access their own intuition and trust one's inner knowing – going with the gut, be open to not knowing and take risks, and to demonstrate confidence in working with strong emotions, being able to self-manage and not be overpowered or enmeshed by client's emotions' (ICF website, 2010).

Some 65 per cent of coaches surveyed in the Mindfulness in Coaching survey (Hall, 2013) say they practise mindfulness to become more present for their client. Other reasons include helping them be more self-aware (73 per cent), and manage/prevent stress (67 per cent).

Compassion and empathy

Compassion to others and to self, on the part of the coach and client, is arguably a core ingredient in coaching (eg Silsbee, 2010; Boyatzis *et al*, 2010; Hall, 2013) and is more fully explored in Chapter 9.

Compassion may be defined as: 'The motivation to empathize with another, to feel what they're feeling, to care deeply about their wellbeing, happiness and suffering, and to act accordingly... and the heartfelt emotions evoked within us when this motivation is activated' (Hall, 2013: 70).

The physiological changes that take place in our bodies through developing compassion boost our immune system and other systems related to health, while 'negative emotions' have the opposite effect, according to a number of studies (eg Rein, Atkinson and McCraty, 1995). Rein *et al* found that anger images and fantasies had a detrimental effect on the immune system's functioning, while compassion-focused ones had very positive effects.

Practising mindfulness helps us to develop compassion. Research indicates that developing the mental expertise to cultivate positive emotion alters the activation of circuitries previously linked to empathy and theory of mind in response to emotional stimuli (Lutz *et al*, 2008). Lutz *et al* argue that compassion meditation promotes more harmonious relationships of all kinds. So there are implications for conflict resolution in the workplace, for example.

Boyatzis *et al* (2010) have linked the adoption of a compassionate coaching approach to better coaching outcomes. They researched clients' neural reactions to a compassionate coaching style (where the coach intentionally encourages a positive future to arouse a positive emotional state) and a critical coaching style (which focuses on failings and what the person should do). When coaches use a compassionate approach, clients are more likely to learn and make behavioural changes, with activation in the parts of their brain associated with visioning, a critical process for motivating learning and behavioural change.

Specific compassion-development practices including the Loving Kindness Meditation (known sometimes as the Befriending Meditation) have been shared with clients by the author and others with positive outcomes, including helping clients be less harsh on themselves (Lee, in Hall, 2013) and promoting harmonious relationships (Hall, 2013).

Mindfulness increases self-compassion and empathic concern, as well as being associated with significant decreases in stress, anxiety and rumination, according to a study of trainee therapists (Rimes and Wingrove, 2011). Meanwhile, Farb and colleagues (2007) showed that after just eight weeks of mindfulness training, participants had increased empathy, with higher levels of insula activation, which is key in mediating empathy (Singer *et al*, 2004).

Practising mindfulness has been associated with higher self-esteem (Pepping, Donovan and Davis, 2013), helping clients become more aware of their negative automatic thoughts (self-awareness) and to develop self-compassion and self-forgiveness. Mindfulness is one of three components of self-compassion, along with self-kindness and common humanity (Neff, 2003). Developing self-compassion counters isolation, depression, anxiety, self-judgement and being harshly self-critical. For organizations, this can mean better relationships, higher productivity, and a more creative environment.

Transference and counter-transference

It is widely accepted that not being aware of or not being able to manage psychoanalytic processes such as transference and counter-transference can threaten the effectiveness of coaching outcomes. Effectively managing adverse reactions is positively associated with psychotherapy outcome (Hayes, Gelso and Hummel, 2011), which logically is likely to be the case in coaching too.

A study by Scheick (2011) points to how developing 'self-aware mindfulness' can help in the management of countertransference within relationships with clients (in this case, nurses). The depth and accuracy of self-assessment is directly proportional to one's present level of self-awareness, and requires introspection to appraise one's emotions. Fatter and Hayes (2013) associate the non-reactivity aspect of mindfulness with the facilitation of counter-transference management.

Mindful sessions

Of those coaches responding to the Mindfulness in Coaching survey, 74 per cent shared mindfulness practices with clients to do at home; 67 per cent used mindfulness for themselves in the session, and 64 per cent invited clients to do mindfulness practices within the session itself.

Many coaches will have their own way of preparing for a coaching session. Practising mindfulness before starting can help the coach be more present, more creative and more resourceful in general.

Cavanagh and Spence (2013) suggest mindful coaches will prepare for each coaching session by deliberately cultivating mindful qualities such as openness and acceptance, along with an overarching intention that provides a reason for such a stance. Having cultivated these qualities, such coaches are less likely to be emotionally reactive and more self attuned, which is likely to enhance coaching confidence or self-efficacy and lead to better attunement with the client and interpersonal attunement, they argue.

Ideally we will have allowed at least 10 minutes for quiet reflection and mindfulness. However, sometimes despite the best will in the world to leave enough time, we find ourselves hurrying to a coaching session with little or no time to spare. In such cases, we can engage in some mindful movement, walking (or running!) mindfully to our appointment. We can briefly bring our attention to our breath, for example practising the Three Minute Breathing Space, be that in the cloakroom, on the escalator, or even in the cloakroom.

Once in the session, we can suggest to our client that we begin with a short practice. We do not need to be too wedded to labelling this as mindfulness.

So, for example, rather than saying 'let's do a mindfulness practice' when a client arrives in a flustered state, we might gently suggest that to help both client and coach get into a more resourceful state, we/they take some time to 'settle' or 'land', closing their eyes, relaxing their shoulders and jaw, taking some gentle unforced breaths.

It is helpful to explain to the client that it will help us both be more creative and resourceful, and bring us into the present moment, helping us to focus and leave some of our baggage behind. It can be particularly helpful if either party has had to rush to the session.

Cavanagh and Spence (2013) also suggest starting each session with a mindfulness practice such as focusing on the breath, and they suggest modifying the physical space such as not having telephones and setting up cues to remind both parties to be mindful such as a mobile set to chime from time to time, and creating the expectation that both share internal states as an important source of data to assist understanding and decision-making processes. Of course, it is a good idea to contract for such processes.

Once the session is under way, the coach can draw on mindfulness explicitly and implicitly. For example, if the coach is 'triggered' by something the client says or shares, or how they act, they can intentionally and mindfully turn towards what is going on in and around them. If the coach has an established mindfulness practice in place, they will have honed their attentional control muscle, and be able to access much more data. Mindfulness too can help them regulate their emotions, for example, if they find they are becoming upset or angry, so they are better able to be neutral or emotionally detached. They have the option of sharing what they find with the client, which can lead to new insights for the client about how others experience them, or create more empathy, for example.

I developed the FEEL model (Figure 8.1) to guide those seeking to coach mindfully. It incorporates a number of facets of mindfulness including intentional awareness, attentional control, curiosity/enquiry, acceptance, compassion and letting go.

The model is as follows:

Focus

Explore

Embrace

Let go

FEEL can be used as a general prompt for coaching mindfully, explicitly with the client, or for self-coaching. Rather like the GROW model popularized by Sir John Whitmore, we might find we move through the model in a linear fashion in one session or we may move fluidly and back and forth between the different parts, or stay within one or two parts of the model – spending a whole session exploring, for example, or working with letting go. The model is particularly well-suited to working with emotions, but is very flexible – it can be used to help clients explore all sorts of issues or self-limiting beliefs. It is important to ensure there is sufficient rapport with

FIGURE 8.1   A model for working with mindfulness in coaching: FEEL (Hall, 2013)

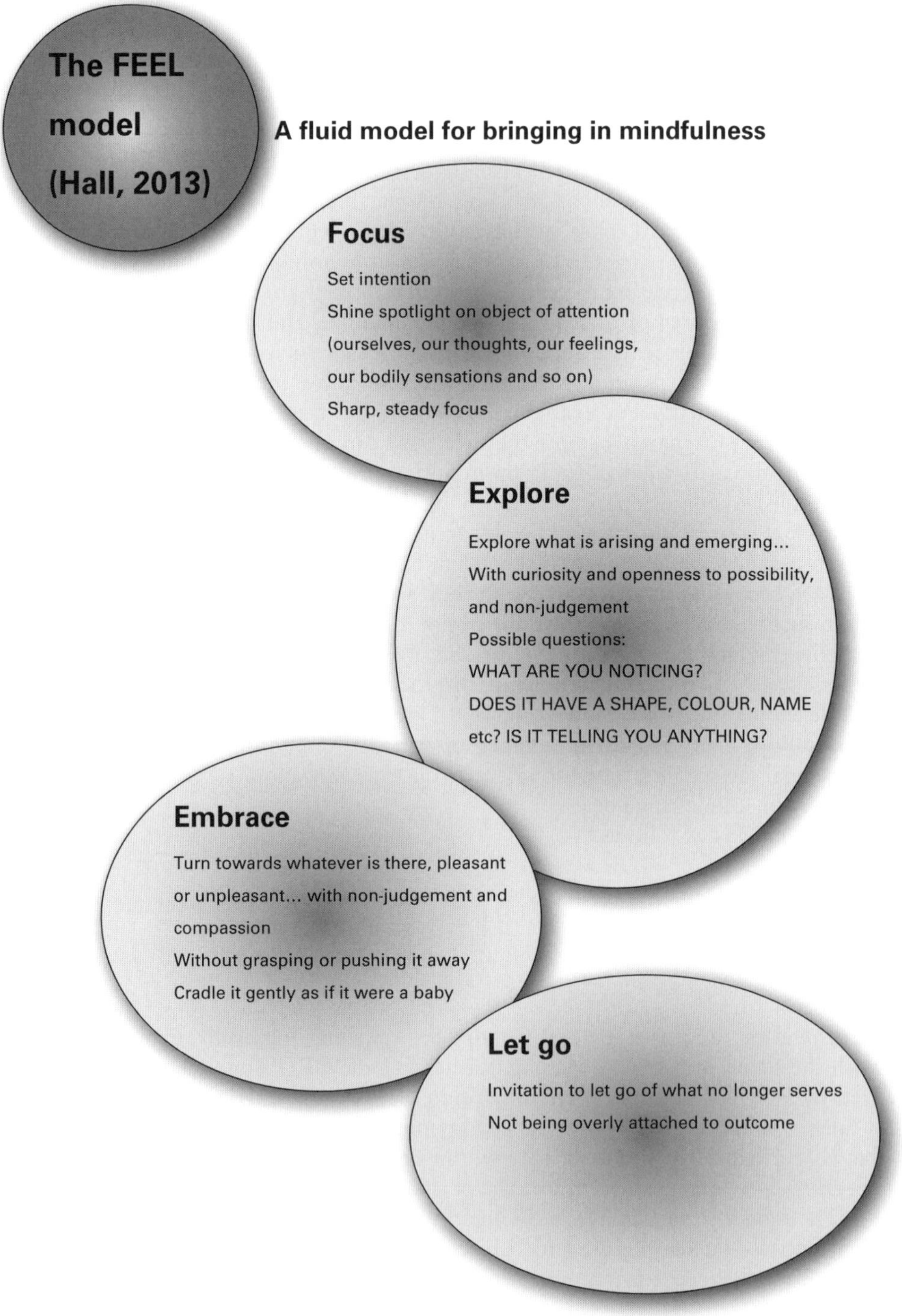

The FEEL model (Hall, 2013)

A fluid model for bringing in mindfulness

Focus

Set intention
Shine spotlight on object of attention
(ourselves, our thoughts, our feelings,
our bodily sensations and so on)
Sharp, steady focus

Explore

Explore what is arising and emerging...
With curiosity and openness to possibility,
and non-judgement
Possible questions:
WHAT ARE YOU NOTICING?
DOES IT HAVE A SHAPE, COLOUR, NAME
etc? IS IT TELLING YOU ANYTHING?

Embrace

Turn towards whatever is there, pleasant
or unpleasant... with non-judgement and
compassion
Without grasping or pushing it away
Cradle it gently as if it were a baby

Let go

Invitation to let go of what no longer serves
Not being overly attached to outcome

the client so they can have a deep sense of trust in you and your processes, as the model can go deep.

Let's look at the model in detail:

Focus

This is about setting our intention and identifying our object of focus, just as we might choose to look at a flower through a magnifying glass, or shine a spotlight onto something. We may choose to focus on our thoughts, our feelings, or our bodily sensations, or indeed an issue, just as we would normally do in coaching. The point here is that practising mindfulness helps us develop attentional control – as if it were a muscle we were honing with each activity. And we consciously seek to zoom in on whatever we choose to focus on. The invitation – to ourselves if self-coaching, or our clients – is to focus steadily and concentratedly, but with a lightness of touch. We can then expand to exploration, although we may at times re-focus.

One coach describes how she uses the Feel model 'to access those qualities people feel they have that could sustain their confidence and embrace them, and explore their limiting beliefs and let them go'. She goes on, 'Once they have accessed their sustaining beliefs I get them to be truly present with them and settle into a feeling of what their signature presence is, and both nurture it and draw strength from it.'

Example

Your client, John, is sharing the difficulties he is having with a particular work colleague and is providing a number of 'examples' of what he considers as unacceptable behaviour. He is getting rather heated. You see this as an opportunity to bring some mindfulness in, using the FEEL model (this could be done powerfully without making the model explicit too).

Coach: 'I can really hear how difficult you've been finding the situation with Boris of late. I wonder if you'd willing to work through a brief exercise to explore what's going on for you?'

John: 'Yes, that's fine.'

Coach: 'OK. If you're willing, please make yourself comfortable, with your back straight and eyes closed. And now take a few deep but unforced breaths. And when you're ready, I invite you to tune in and focus on your feelings around this Boris situation (Focus).'

John: 'Righto.'

Explore

Still maintaining our focus, we now gently explore whatever is arising and emerging, with compassion, curiosity, non-judgement and openness to possibility. It may be that we stick with the original topic/object, or that other hitherto-hidden information, insights, data come to light. We continue to explore, without seeking to interpret, just as a child might when playing with something new. We're seeking here to activate the 'approach system', to help the client be as resourceful as possible.

We can prompt the client to explore with the kind of questions we find in clean language and gestalt including:

- What are you noticing about X?
- Where do you feel it/them in your body?
- Is it/they familiar or new feelings?
- Does it/do they have a shape?
- A colour?
- A name?
- What else are you noticing?
- Are they telling you anything?
- What else?

If they are ostensibly finding the exploration difficult, you can gently re-mind them to evoke compassion towards themselves. If they find this hard, you can suggest they feel a sense of kindness towards themselves. If they are becoming distressed, you can invite them to attend to their breathing, bringing them back to the practice when and if they are ready.

Example

Coach: 'Now I invite you to gently explore the feelings that are there. Just being curious, just noticing what is there, rather than trying to work it all out.

Compassionate and curious.

And I may offer some questions up to help you explore.

You don't need to answer them out loud, and don't worry if no answer comes up. But by all means share anything you wish to.

What are you noticing?

I'll let you sit with this exploration for a little while.'

John: 'Lots of anger. Had no idea how much. Tightness in my chest.'

Coach: 'Does the tightness or anger have a colour? What about a shape?'

John: 'Red. Tightness in my throat. Been here before. Don't know about shape exactly, oh yes, big red dense foggy blob.'

Coach: 'What else are you noticing?'

John: 'Reminds me of my dad. Boris reminds me of my dad. He's so bossy. Never listens.' [John is breathing more shallowly]

Coach: 'So lots of anger, tightness, red. Stay with what you're noticing, without judgement. Just being really curious. Just focusing on your breath for a few breaths, that's it, just breathing in and out naturally. And then bringing your focus back to the feelings.'

Embrace

Here, what we're doing, while still maintaining focus and a sense of enquiry and exploration, is turning towards *whatever* is there – unpleasant or pleasant, without judgement and without grasping or pushing away. Vietnamese Buddhist monk Thich Nhat Hanh suggests having in mind the image of cradling a baby. So, for example, if anger arises, we turn towards and lightly embrace the anger, rather than moving to judgement and self-criticism. We're working with acceptance. We might label whatever it is, thus creating some distance – so that we are gently embracing rather than identifying with it or creating an unhelpful storyline about it.

Example

Coach: 'So the invitation is to try and witness what's there without getting caught up in the story. Turning towards these feelings of anger, for example, not hanging onto them or pushing them away. And noticing anything that shifts.'

John: 'That's interesting. The anger feels more distant now, less red.'

Let go

Building on Explore and Embrace further, continuing to just witness and accept what's there without grabbing onto it as something we desperately want to hold onto or seeking to reject it as something unpleasant, here we open up to letting go. It can be hard to let go, of course, and may not always be appropriate. The idea is not to force anything, but to issue the invitation. Transformation can occur at any time, and turning towards something with acceptance can often see it dissipate of its own accord.

It may be that what comes up for the client is highly uncomfortable, and we do need to be aware of boundaries. However, as I say, it is just about noticing what's there and seeing what can be let go of, what no longer serves, making space for the new.

Example

Coach: 'Is there anything you would like to let go of here?'

John: 'Well, I hadn't seen the connection between Boris and my father. I'd like to let go of that. There are similarities but Boris is not my father. There are lots of reasons why I'm angry with Boris, though.'

Coach: 'Ok, if you want to sit quietly for a while longer and when you're ready, open your eyes and we can explore this further.'

At certain points, it can be useful to share what you are noticing in yourself and in the client with the client, as potential additional data, as long as it is in service of their exploration, and does not interrupt their exploration.

As well as working with FEEL with clients, we can use FEEL to help us tune into what's happening within ourselves.

Core mindful practices

The suggested application of specific mindfulness practices contained within the standard eight-week mindfulness-based stress reduction (MBSR) or mindfulness-based cognitive therapy (MBCT) programmes (eg Williams and Penman, 2011) can easily be woven into coaching sessions, or given as 'homework' to clients.

As we have seen earlier, mindfulness in general has been associated with a vast array of benefits. Some researchers single out particular practices when looking at the impact of meditation, including the Body Scan (eg Ditto, Eclache and Goldman, 2006) and more widely, the Loving Kindness Meditation (eg Hutcherson, Seppala and Gross, 2008; Fredrickson *et al*, 2008; Johnson *et al*, 2009). However, much of the research considers the impact of a collection of mindfulness practices such as the Body Scan, sitting meditation and so on so it can be hard to pinpoint which practices work best when.

TABLE 8.4   Mindfulness practices

Practices	Applications
Three minute breathing space	Building self-awareness; stress management/resilience building through incorporating regular brief top-up practices through the day; well-suited to very busy clients as a way to 'press pause' at regular intervals.
Awareness of breath meditation	Stress management/resilience.
Mindful minute	Stress management/resilience building through incorporating regular brief top-up practices through the day; well-suited to very busy clients as a way to 'press pause' at regular intervals.
Mindful walking	Can be woven easily into everyday life, eg on the way to meetings; some clients prefer 'mindful movement' – it can feel less threatening.
Mindful eating	Can be woven easily into everyday life; addressing eating disorders/building a sense of self-nurture; stress management.
Body scan	Self-awareness; improving ability to use self as instrument including becoming more aware of what is coming from self or from outside; general relationship awareness; tackling insomnia.
Witness meditation	Becoming more aware/realizing that 'we are not our thoughts'; enhancing non-judgement; becoming more comfortable with 'not knowing' and staying with 'what is'; helpful when building client's capacity to cope with ambiguity and complexity.
Loving kindness/Befriending meditation	Improving relationships; increasing social connectedness; increased empathy; increased compassion to self and others; improving self-esteem and confidence; reducing harshness towards self; enhancing emotional intelligence; improving creativity (through being less harsh on self).

That said, and bearing in mind that there are common elements to the practices including attentional control, Table 8.4 offers some suggestions for specific practices which might be particularly useful, drawing on the general and specific research, and anecdotal evidence from my own and other coaches' practice.

Below is a description of the mindful minute practice, mentioned in Table 8.4.

The Mindful Minute

Find a minute where you won't be disturbed, get settled, and put a timer on for one minute (or get someone else to time you). You might like to close your eyes. Then without forcing your breath, just breathing naturally, count how many rounds (a round is one in-breath and one out-breath) there are in *your* minute. It doesn't matter at all how many. So just gently breathing and counting. At the end of the minute, you can stop and open your eyes. How many rounds? That is *your* Mindful Minute which you can practice anywhere – on the tube, at your desk, or whatever.

Introducing and adapting mindfulness to clients

When asked about concerns about using mindfulness with clients, 18 per cent of respondents agreed that the client might 'think the coach is 'woolly/fluffy/unprofessional' and 7 per cent that 'encouraging clients to practice mindfulness might expose (the client) to unpleasant feelings or buried experiences that will be difficult to deal with in the coaching, according to my Mindfulness in Coaching survey. 76 per cent had no concerns. However, lots of coaches who attend my mindful coaching workshops are unsure how and whether to introduce mindfulness to clients explicitly.

Obviously, mindful coaching is just one approach out of many and may not always be appropriate. However, often as not, the issue is about what to call it. We don't even need to use the word mindfulness. We can talk about improving emotional intelligence, or stress management, or building resilience, or resonant versus dissonant leadership (Boyatzis and McKee, 2005), or improving cognitive functioning.

As for stirring up unpleasant feelings, we all have to make a judgement call in coaching around how deep the client needs/wants to go, and how deep we can/want to go. A large part of coaching is about promoting self-awareness, and that can be uncomfortable. Practising mindfulness can help us confront ourselves, warts and all, and buried memories can come to the surface when we turn inwards. However, mindfulness is not about forcing anything, it is about being gentle and compassionate, and about turning towards whatever is there.

Cultural context

It is important to be culturally sensitive when considering any approach, and mindfulness is no different. We may want to explore mindfulness through a spiritual lens. The concepts of developing and enhancing the ability to be right here, right now consciously and to attain a higher state of awareness are common across many spiritual traditions, including Christianity, Taoism and Sufism.

Mirdal (2012) laments the lack of Islamic thought in much of the development of mindfulness, despite similarities in philosophy and the growing need for mental health support among Muslim populations. The study suggests that Sufism, in particular Rumi's teachings, shares much with mindfulness-based interventions, and that introducing concepts, images and metaphors based on the Persian mystic poet's worldview can offer a meaningful alternative to Buddhist-inspired practice when working with Muslim clients, for example. When working with Christian clients, we might want to reference Christian meditators such as St Teresa of Avila, the sixteenth-century mystic, and John Main who opened the first Christian meditation centre in Ealing Abbey in London in 1975.

However, one of the reasons why mindfulness has become so popular is that it has been embraced in many secular settings, as we have seen. Benefits from practising mindfulness can be gained for ourselves and for our clients, without 'spiritualizing' the approach. We do still need to pay attention to cultural suitability and accessibility, though. In Aotearoa (New Zealand), where coaching psychologists are required to demonstrate awareness and knowledge of Māori identity, values and practices, one Māori local government manager ended the coaching relationship because his coach suggested mindfulness as a stress reduction measure. Explorations more suited to Māori culture would have included a discussion of which of the four walls of Te Whare Tapa Whā needed attention to return the client to wellbeing, suggests Stewart (2012). Te Whare Tapa Whā is a model of Māori health and wellbeing embedded in Ministry of Health policy. The walls include taha wairua (the spiritual side), taha hinengaro (thoughts and feelings), taha tinana (the physical side) and taha whānau (extended family).

CASE STUDY

'Norman' came to coaching because he was 'disenchanted' with teaching and wanted to explore the possibility of changing career.

He was feeling overwhelmed and overloaded at work, and was having problems with his immediate boss. He felt unappreciated and unmotivated, and that he was being expected to do far too much, while acknowledging he wasn't giving his best. He said he wouldn't mind feeling happy again every once in a while.

Norman was receptive to the idea of mindfulness-informed coaching, explaining that he used to meditate and had found it beneficial.

Contracting

He and the coach contracted for six sessions each lasting an hour and a half, agreeing to meet where possible in locations which lent themselves to a more mindful approach (including walking outside) and to start each session with a short mindfulness practice. The coach explained that she might at times suggest mindfulness practices within the session or as 'homework'. They discussed mindfulness principles/qualities they could both bring to the coaching including openness, curiosity, compassion to self and other, and paying attention to what was coming up in the present moment, sharing where appropriate with one another as this could be useful data.

Beginning the sessions with paying attention to the breath for a few minutes helped both coach and client get started in a more resourceful place. On one occasion, there had been a miscommunication and the coach had been waiting in the wrong location – it was very helpful for the coach to take a few minutes on arrival. On another, Norman arrived in an agitated state after receiving a phone call from his boss and the mindfulness practice helped him calm down. In general, both parties felt the mindfulness practice at the beginning also acted as a ritual marking the beginning of their time together, and putting some distance between the coaching and whatever had gone before.

One of Norman's issues was the anger he felt towards his boss, who he experienced as 'nitpicking', 'hypocritical', 'unappreciative' and 'unreasonable'. Anger had been a theme in his life; he had felt both helpless and angry as a young child when he was being bullied by his older brother and had subsequently gone through an aggressive period at school. Running or martial arts had helped to keep the lid on the anger but he felt too tired to exercise these days. Although he didn't ever get outwardly aggressive with anyone any longer, he often felt the anger rise up, and did get snappy with his family sometimes. Most evenings he felt depleted, with little energy to spend quality time with his wife and children.

The coach shared a number of mindfulness practices with Norman (see list below) which he said sometimes helped him catch himself when he was about to get angry, so he had the chance to do something about it, or to calm himself down once he had got angry. Using the FEEL model (Focus, Explore, Embrace, Let go), Norman found it very helpful to turn towards his anger, approaching it almost like a wayward child rather than getting angry with himself for getting angry, thus adding another layer.

Another issue was how self-critical Norman was being, including beating himself up for getting cross. Although he had a strong sense that he was 'right', and his boss was 'wrong', at the same time, he was experiencing lots of self-doubt and was feeling very undermined. He was having lots of negative thoughts about himself. Working with mindfulness, including an exploration of core mindfulness principles and philosophy (including that we are not our thoughts, and that it is helpful to be compassionate to ourselves and others) was helpful here for Norman. The coaching looked at what it means to have an Observer's or Witness Mind (just noticing what is there) and a Beginner's Mind (approaching things as if they are new, rather like a child), supporting these perspectives with practices (see list below). Norman came to see that he was very much identifying with his thoughts (he liked the idea of imagining his thoughts as clouds passing by in the sky), which wasn't helpful.

Like most of us, Norman found it hard to be self-compassionate, although he was surprised to find he could evoke compassion and empathy towards his boss, which helped him be less 'black and white' in his thinking about her.

The coach also worked with aspects of the FEEL model to help Norman explore and embrace what he did like/love about himself, leading to insights, including that he could be strong and firm without relying on other people. He turned towards the idea that 'everything was actually alright', and in terms of the Letting Go aspect of the model, this was about Norman letting go of a whole bunch of his harsh storylines about himself, and the idea that he needed other people's approval for everything to be ok.

They also explored Norman's relationship to the concepts of doing and non-doing. He shared how guilty he felt just sitting around 'doing nothing', particularly as his wife also worked and they had three children. He started to realize that he was heading for burnout if he wasn't careful and that 'taking time out' meant looking after himself, not being self-indulgent. He had a long talk with his wife about how they could support each other to take time out.

In session number three, Norman shared how he was feeling very angry with his boss because yet again, she had asked him to do something 'unreasonable'. It was the beginning of the summer holidays and he had just received a series of e-mails from her, complaining that he had not done everything he was supposed to have done on a particular project, one he had thought had been signed off months before.

Exploration in this and the previous coaching session revealed that there was a repeated pattern of feeling bullied, and a sense that Norman may have 'handed over too much power in the past', been 'too loose' in accepting things and not telling people when he thinks they are being unreasonable. He felt that he had 'bent over backwards and have been taken advantage of', that he had 'brought it on myself a bit and not communicated clearly what is ok or not ok'.

Using elements of the FEEL model, the coach invited him settle into his chair, relaxing his shoulders and feeling his feet on the ground, closing his eyes, paying attention to his breath, then focusing and exploring, 'turning towards' whatever was there around this situation with his boss, with compassion and with curiosity. He found 'turbulence and fizziness'. He saw his boss's good intentions and felt that he had fallen victim to her clumsiness, lack of insight, lack of professional experience, and her being under pressure. He could feel himself getting dragged into this pressure but when he focused on her clumsiness, he felt 'less turbulence and more spaciousness'. 'It takes away the level of bullying. I'd got in my head that I was being bullied, but another way of looking at it is that it is another human being clumsy in her approach to me and me having my own baggage that responds to that clumsiness in an inevitable way.'

He realized that he was 'acting out' with his boss, reacting in a knee-jerk way, dashing off a childish e-mail to her.

At the end of the session, drawing on somatic coaching too, the coach invited him to tune mindfully into and embody a commitment around this particular issue/ situation: 'to being firm and strong, to not allowing people to influence me in a way that makes me feel bad'. She invited him a few times to re-ground himself, to scan his body and notice what was there, and she shared what she was noticing including what was going on in her too in response (including not feeling grounded, still feeling contracted, then noticing him stand taller and seem wider, hearing his voice deepen) until she could feel in herself and him that he was centred and calm and strong. His final commitment was to 'being strong and powerful and refusing to let other people influence me'.

He was later able to practice the Loving Kindness Meditation with his boss in mind, but at this stage it seemed important that he felt strong in himself. After having got more in touch with his internal benchmark of personal professionalism, he decided to do some of what his boss had asked, after all, feeling that actually he hadn't completed the task properly and had been acting like a child. His relationship with his boss improved and he found it easier to keep boundaries but he decided that overall, the relationship was unhealthy for him as she was not very good at appreciating people. He handed in his notice. However, he felt much more grounded and energized in general, renewed his commitment to working in education and subsequently got a much better paid teaching job.

Norman has started running again and has signed up to an MBSR programme. He feels that he is now much more able to respond, rather than react, to people as an adult, and is confident that should another relationship issue arise in his new place of work, he will be better placed to cope. The atmosphere at home has improved. And he reports feeling much happier.

Practices

Over the course of the coaching, the coach introduced Norman to a number of mindfulness practices, which she led him through initially during sessions.

She introduced Norman to the Mindful Minute (included earlier in this chapter) and the Three Minute Breathing Space to offer Norman some very brief practices he could punctuate his days with, even when he was extremely busy. The idea was for him to do these whether or not he felt he needed them so that he would naturally think to do them when he was angry or stressed. Norman committed to do these when he remembered at work or in response to a reminder in his smartphone. She also introduced a centring practice to help Norman become more grounded before, during or after encounters with his boss, for example, or before staff meetings, or during school inspections and other situations Norman found stressful.

Also she led Norman through the Body Scan, to help Norman get back in touch with his body, and to become better able to notice when he was getting triggered by his boss and needed to take remedial action, even if this was merely going off to the toilet to breathe calmly for a minute or two. The Witness Meditation helped Norman recognized that he is not defined by his thoughts, that there is an Observer aspect to his mind which is different to his thoughts while the Loving Kindness/Befriending Meditation helped Norman be less harsh on himself, and to improve relationships at work. One part of this meditation is to bring to mind someone we feel aversion towards and Norman chose his boss. He reported feeling more kindly towards her, and their relationship did improve.

When might the mindful coaching approach be most suitable?

Mindfulness is an approach that is adaptable and applicable in many settings, as has been evidenced in the successful adaptation of the eight-week Mindfulness-Based Stress Reduction programme for numerous contexts, including for education through the Mindfulness in Schools Project in the United Kingdom, for example. In the evidence-based section of this chapter, we looked at research from other arenas including psychotherapy and neuroscience, which showed many benefits associated with practising mindfulness. We can surmise that mindfulness-based coaching is likely to be particularly effective when working with clients in these areas, including stress management and resilience, emotional intelligence, and cognitive functioning.

TABLE 8.5   Issues mindful coaching is suited to helping with

Developing authentic leadership
Identifying and become more aligned with values
Acting more ethically
Developing intuitiveness
Developing presence
Enhancing self-compassion and compassion to others
Increasing self-esteem and confidence
Achieving better work/family balance
Living more in the present
Accepting how things are
Boosting health and wellbeing
Tackling sleeping problems
Improving resilience
Stress management
Management of mild depression
Boosting creativity
Enhancing cognitive performance

Table 8.5 lists some of the goals and issues MC is typically suited to helping with.

In terms of emotional intelligence, it can be used to help clients become more self-aware, more empathetic, more compassionate towards themselves and others, regulate their emotions, including anger, enhancing their ability to recognize, slow down or stop automatic and habitual reactions. It can help clients identify values/find 'meaning and purpose' and improve their social skills, including their ability to manage conflict.

An appreciation by coaches of the contribution mindfulness can make in helping clients manage stress and increase resilience, and become more emotionally intelligent was evident in responses to the Mindfulness in Coaching survey. Some 59 per cent of coaches said they were working with mindfulness to help their client be calmer/less anxious, and 55 per cent to help them manage stress. In the area of emotional intelligence, 70 per cent were working with mindfulness to help their client be more self aware, 51 per cent to manage reactions/responses; 39 per cent explicitly to help them be more emotionally intelligent; and 32 per cent to help them improve relationships with others.

There seems to be less awareness among coaches about the contribution mindfulness can make to boosting performance, although this does seem to be changing. Specifically, mindful coaching is well-suited to helping clients improve abilities in the following areas: clarity; focus/concentration; working memory capacity, planning and organization; problem-solving; speed and rationality of decision-making; ability to think strategically and long term; and being more creative.

Conclusion

Mindfulness may have been seen as peripheral to coaching. However, the tide has turned. More and more coaches are finding ways to make explicit use of mindfulness in their coaching sessions. Given the rapidly growing evidence base, which suggests strong benefits associated with mindfulness, it is likely that at least some clients will benefit explicitly from mindfulness. Even when it is not appropriate for coaches to work explicitly with clients in mindfulness, coaches can benefit from practising mindfulness, enhancing presence, for example, and their clients will benefit indirectly from the focus they bring to each and every session.

Developing yourself as a mindful coach

Developing your skills

Coaches wishing to learn more about and develop their skills in mindful coaching may wish to explore the following practitioner texts:

- Hall, L (2013) *Mindful Coaching*, Kogan Page, London
- Siegel, D (2010) *The Mindful Therapist: A clinician's guide to mindsight and neural integration*, Bantam Books
- Silsbee, D (2010) *Presence-based Coaching: Cultivating self-generative leaders through mind, body and heart*, Jossey-Bass, San Francisco

Deepening your understanding

Coaches wishing to recommend mindfulness self-help books, CDs and workbooks for their clients may wish to consider the following:

- Gilbert, P and Choden (2013) *Mindful Compassion: Using the power of mindfulness and compassion to transform our lives*, Constable and Robins, London
- Williams, M and Penman, D (2011) *Mindfulness: A practical guide to finding peace in a frantic world*, Piatkus
- Hanh, T N (1975) *The Miracle of Mindfulness*, Beacon Press

Web resource

A useful website for both coaches and clients is Be Mindful, a Mental Health Foundation website to raise awareness of mindfulness meditation, including details of MBSR and MBCT programmes: **www.bemindful.co.uk**

References

Baer, R A, Smith, G T, Hopkins, J, Krietemeyer, J and Toney, L (2006) Using self-report assessment methods to explore facets of mindfulness, *Assessment*, **13** (1), pp 27–45

Bandura, A and Locke, E A (2003) Negative self-efficacy and goal effects revisited, *Journal of Applied Psychology*, **88** (1), p 87

Barnes, S, Brown, K W, Krusemark, E, Campbell, W K and Rogge, R D (2007) The role of mindfulness in romantic relationship satisfaction and responses to relationship stress, *Journal of Marital and Family Therapy*, **33** (4), pp 482–500

Bishop, S R, Lau, M, Shapiro, S, Carlson, L, Anderson, N D, Carmody, J and Devins, G (2004) Mindfulness: A proposed operational definition, *Clinical psychology: Science and practice*, **11** (3), pp 230–41

Boyatzis, R E, Jack, A, Cesaro, R, Passarelli, A and Khawaja, M (2010) Coaching with compassion: an fMRI study of coaching to the positive or negative emotional attractor, in *Annual Meeting of the Academy of Management, Montreal*

Boyatzis, R E and McKee, A (2005) *Resonant Leadership: Renewing yourself and connecting with others through mindfulness, hope and compassion*, Harvard Business Publishing, Watertown, MA

Bränström, R, Duncan, L G and Moskowitz, J T (2011) The association between dispositional mindfulness, psychological well-being, and perceived health in a Swedish population-based sample, *British Journal of Health Psychology*, **16** (2), 300–16

Bresser, F (2013) Coaching across the globe: benchmark results of the Bresser Consulting global coaching survey with a supplementary update highlighting the latest coaching developments to 2013. BoD–Books on Demand

Brown, K W and Ryan, R M (2003) The benefits of being present: mindfulness and its role in psychological well-being, *Journal of Personality and Social Psychology*, **84** (4), p 822

Bruce, N G, Manber, R, Shapiro, S L and Constantino, M J (2010) Psychotherapist mindfulness and the psychotherapy process, *Psychotherapy: Theory, Research, Practice, Training*, **47** (1), p 83

Cardaciotto, L, Herbert, J D, Forman, E M, Moitra, E and Farrow, V (2008) The assessment of present-moment awareness and acceptance: the Philadelphia Mindfulness Scale, *Assessment*, **15** (2), pp 204–23

Carver, C S and Scheier, M F (1998) *On the Self-Regulation of Behavior*, Cambridge University Press, Cambridge

Cavanagh, M J and Spence, G B (2013) Mindfulness in coaching, in *The Wiley-Blackwell Handbook of the Psychology of Coaching and Mentoring*, eds Passmore, J, Peterson, D B and Freire, T, Oxford, pp 112–34

Chaskalson, M (2011) The mindful workplace, in *Developing Resilient Individuals and Resonant Organisations with MBSR*, John Wiley & Sons Ltd

Chiesa, A and Serretti, A (2009) Mindfulness-based stress reduction for stress management in healthy people: a review and meta-analysis, *The Journal of Alternative and Complementary Medicine*, **15** (5), pp 593–600

Chu, L C (2010) The benefits of meditation vis-à-vis emotional intelligence, perceived stress and negative mental health, *Stress and Health*, **26** (2), pp 169–80

Collard, P and Walsh, J (2008) Sensory awareness mindfulness training in coaching: accepting life's challenges, *Journal of Rational-Emotive & Cognitive-Behavior therapy*, **26** (1), pp 30–37

Colzato, L S, Ozturk, A and Hommel, B (2012) Meditate to create: the impact of focused-attention and open-monitoring training on convergent and divergent thinking, *Frontiers in psychology*, **3**

Creswell, J D *et al* (2007) Neural correlates of dispositional mindfulness during affect labelling, *Psychosomatic Medicine*, **69** (6), pp 560–65

David, S, Megginson, D and Clutterbuck, D (eds) (2013) *Beyond Goals*, Gower, Farnham

Davidson, R J (2004) Well-being and affective style: neural substrates and biobehavioural correlates, *Philosophical Transactions of the Royal Society*, **359**, pp 1395–411

Davidson, R J, Kabat-Zinn, J, Schumacher, J, Rosenkranz, M, Muller, D, Santorelli, S F and Sheridan, J F (2003) Alterations in brain and immune function produced by mindfulness meditation, *Psychosomatic Medicine*, **65** (4), pp 564–70

Ditto, B, Eclache, M and Goldman, N (2006) Short-term autonomic and cardiovascular effects of mindfulness body scan meditation, *Annals of Behavioral Medicine*, **32** (3), pp 227–34

Farb, N A, Segal, Z V, Mayberg, H, Bean, J, McKeon, D, Fatima, Z and Anderson, A K (2007) Attending to the present: mindfulness meditation reveals distinct neural modes of self-reference, *Social Cognitive and Affective Neuroscience*, **2** (4), 313–22

Fatter, D M and Hayes, J A (2013) What facilitates countertransference management? The roles of therapist meditation, mindfulness, and self-differentiation, *Psychotherapy Research*, **23** (5), pp 502–13

Fredrickson, B L, Cohn, M A, Coffey, K A, Pek, J and Finkel, S M (2008) Open hearts build lives: positive emotions, induced through loving-kindness meditation, build consequential personal resources, *Journal of Personality and Social Psychology*, **95** (5), p 1045

Greenberg, J, Reiner, K and Meiran, N (2012a) 'Mind the trap': mindfulness practice reduces cognitive rigidity, *PloS one*, **7** (5), e36206

Greenberg, J, Reiner, K and Meiran, N (2012b) 'Off with the old': mindfulness practice improves backward inhibition, *Frontiers in Psychology*, **3**

Hafenbrack, A C, Kinias, Z and Barsade, S G (2013) Debiasing the mind through meditation mindfulness and the sunk-cost bias, *Psychological Science*

Hall, L (2013) *Mindful Coaching: How mindfulness can transform coaching practice*, Kogan Page, London

Hayes, J A, Gelso, C J and Hummel, A M (2011) Managing countertransference, *Psychotherapy*, **48** (1), p 88

Hayes, S C, Strosahl, K D and Wilson, K G (2003) *Acceptance and Commitment Therapy: An experiential approach to behavior change*, Guilford Press, New York

Heifetz, R A (1994) *Leadership Without Easy Answers* (Vol 465), Harvard University Press

Hölzel, B K, Carmody, J, Vangel, M, Congleton, C, Yerramsetti, S M, Gard, T and Lazar, S W (2011) Mindfulness practice leads to increases in regional brain gray matter density, *Psychiatry Research: Neuroimaging*, **191** (1), pp 36–43

Hunter, J and Chaskalson, M (2013) Making the mindful leader, in *The Wiley-Blackwell Handbook of the Psychology of Leadership, Change, and Organizational Development*, eds H S Leonard, R Lewis, A M Freedman and J Passmore, John Wiley & Sons, Oxford

Hutcherson, C A, Seppala, E M and Gross, J J (2008) Loving-kindness meditation increases social connectedness, *Emotion*, **8** (5), p 720

INSEAD (2008) An overview of CSR practices response benchmarking report

Jha, A P, Stanley, E A, Kiyonaga, A, Wong, L and Gelfand, L (2010) Examining the protective effects of mindfulness training on working memory capacity and affective experience, *Emotion*, **10** (1), p 54

Johnson, D P, Penn, D L, Fredrickson, B L, Meyer, P S, Kring, A M and Brantley, M (2009) Loving-kindness meditation to enhance recovery from negative symptoms of schizophrenia, *Journal of Clinical Psychology*, **65** (5), pp 499–509

Kabat-Zinn, J (1994) *Wherever You Go, There You Are: Mindfulness meditation in everyday life*, Hyperion

Kaliman, P, Álvarez-López, M J, Cosín-Tomás, M, Rosenkranz, M A, Lutz, A and Davidson, R J (2014) Rapid changes in histone deacetylases and inflammatory gene expression in expert meditators, *Psychoneuroendocrinology*, **40**, pp 96–107

Kerr, C E, Sacchet, M D, Lazar, S W, Moore, C I and Jones, S R (2013) Mindfulness starts with the body: somatosensory attention and top-down modulation of cortical alpha rhythms in mindfulness meditation, *Frontiers in Human Neuroscience*, **7**

Kirk, U, Downar, J and Montague, P R (2011) Interoception drives increased rational decision-making in meditators playing the ultimatum game, *Frontiers in neuroscience*, **5**

Langer, E (2000) unpublished, cited in Langer, E (2005)

Langer, E (2005) *On Becoming an Artist: Reinventing yourself through mindful creativity*, Ballantine Books, New York

Lazar, S W, Kerr, C E, Wasserman, R H, Gray, J R, Greve, D N, Treadway, M T and Fischl, B (2005) Meditation experience is associated with increased cortical thickness, *Neuroreport*, **16** (17), p 1893

Lee, G and Robert, L (2010) Coaching for authentic leadership, *Leadership Coaching: Working with leaders to develop elite performance*, pp 17–34

Lutz, A, Brefczynski-Lewis, J, Johnstone, T and Davidson, R J (2008) Regulation of the neural circuitry of emotion by compassion meditation: effects of meditative expertise, *PloS one*, **3** (3), e1897

Martin, J R (1997) Mindfulness: a proposed common factor, *Journal of Psychotherapy integration*, **7** (4), pp 291–312

Mirdal, G M (2012) Mevlana Jalāl-ad-Dīn Rumi and mindfulness, *Journal of Religion and Health*, **51** (4), pp 1202–15

Moore, A and Malinowski, P (2009) Meditation, mindfulness and cognitive flexibility, *Consciousness and Cognition*, **18** (1), pp 176–86

Mrazek, M D, Franklin, M S, Phillips, D T, Baird, B and Schoole R J W (2013) Mindfulness training improves working memory capacity and GRE performance while reducing mind wandering, *Psychological Science*, **24** (5), pp 776–81

Neff, K (2003) Self-compassion: an alternative conceptualization of a healthy attitude toward oneself, *Self and Identity*, **2** (2), pp 85–101

Ostafin, B D and Kassman, K T (2012) Stepping out of history: mindfulness improves insight problem solving, *Consciousness and Cognition*, **21** (2), pp 1031–36

Passmore, J and Marianetti, O (2007) The role of mindfulness in coaching, *The Coaching Psychologist*, **3** (3), pp 131–37

Pepping, C A, Donovan, A and Davis, P J (2013) The positive effects of mindfulness on self-esteem, *The Journal of Positive Psychology*, **8** (5), pp 376–86

Rein, G, Atkinson, M and McCraty, R (1995) The physiological and psychological effects of compassion and anger, *Journal of Advancement in Medicine*, **8** (2), pp 87–105

Ridler Report 2011 (2011) Ridler & Co www.ridlerandco.com/ridler-report/

Ridler Report 2013 (2013) Trends in the use of executive coaching, Ridler & Co: www.ridlerandco.com/ridler-report/

Rimes, K A and Wingrove, J (2011) Pilot study of mindfulness-based cognitive therapy for trainee clinical psychologists, *Behavioural and Cognitive Psychotherapy*, **39** (2), p 235

Scharmer, C O (2009) *Theory U: Learning from the future as it emerges*, Berrett-Koehler Store

Scheick, D M (2011) Developing self-aware mindfulness to manage countertransference in the nurse-client relationship: an evaluation and developmental study, *Journal of Professional Nursing*, **27** (2), pp 114–23

Schmeichel, B J, Volokhov, R N and Demaree, H A (2008) Working memory capacity and the self-regulation of emotional expression and experience, *Journal of Personality and Social Psychology*, **95** (6), 1526

Scouller, J (2011) *The Three Levels of Leadership: How to develop your leadership presence, knowhow and skill*, Management Books 2000

Shapiro, S L, Carlson, L E, Astin, J A and Freedman, B (2006) Mechanisms of mindfulness, *Journal of Clinical Psychology*, **62** (3), pp 373–86

Silsbee, D (2010) *Presence-based Coaching: Cultivating self-generative leaders through mind, body and heart*, Jossey-Bass, San Francisco

Singer, T, Seymour, B, O'Doherty, J *et al* (2004) Empathy for pain involves the affective but not sensory components of pain, *Science*, **303**, pp 1157–62

Spence, G B, Cavanagh, M J and Grant, A M (2008) The integration of mindfulness training and health coaching: an exploratory study, *Coaching: An international journal of theory, research and practice*, **1** (2)

Stewart, L (2012) We say Kia Ora... *Coaching at Work*, **7** (6)

Tang, Y Y, Ma, Y, Wang, J, Fan, Y, Feng, S, Lu, Q and Posner, M I (2007) Short-term meditation training improves attention and self-regulation, *Proceedings of the National Academy of Sciences*, **104** (43), pp 17152–56

Teper, R and Inzlicht, M (2012) Meditation, mindfulness and executive control: the importance of emotional acceptance and brain-based performance monitoring (online), *Social Cognitive Affective Neuroscience*

Walsh, R and Shapiro, S L (2006) The meeting of meditative disciplines and Western psychology: a mutually enriching dialogue, *American Psychologist*, **61** (3), 227

Whitmore, S J (1992) *Coaching for Performance: A practical guide to growing your own skills*, Nicholas Brealey, London

Williams, J M G (2008) Mindfulness, depression and modes of mind, *Cognitive Therapy and Research*, **32** (6), pp 721–33

Williams, M and Penman, D (2011) *Mindfulness: A practical guide to finding peace in a frantic world*, Piatkus

Acknowledgement

To Michael Chaskalson (the Mindful Minute).

Compassionate mind coaching

09

TIM ANSTISS AND PAUL GILBERT

Introduction

Compassionate Mind Coaching (CMC) can be considered both a style or way of doing coaching, as well as a standalone, holistic, multi-modal coaching approach in its own right. Informed by evolutionary biology and neuroscience, compassationate mind coaching involves a progressive series of exercises and practices derived from mindfulness, compassion, Buddhism, and other therapeutic and coaching approaches. It suggests that in order for people to make progress in their lives it may be better if they get in touch with their own and other people's suffering and takes steps to alleviate and prevent such suffering in the future.

Compassionate mind coaching provides both the coach and coachee with a solid theoretical framework along with a range of activities and exercises to help clients reduce the strength and influence of their inner critic, talk with themselves in a more warm, accepting, soothing and understanding manner, and help clients change the way they think, feel, and behave in important and life-enhancing ways.

Coaches commonly work with clients who engage in excessive self-monitoring, are self-critical, are shame-prone and lack confidence. Excessive self-criticism – a form of negative self-monitoring – is common to a wide range of wellbeing and performance issues, and can get in the way of learning any new skill. Behaviours can become highly disrupted if people are constantly negatively monitoring their performance. Several years ago, one of us (PG) noted that while many of his depressed clients could identify the flow of their negative thoughts – eg, 'This is no good', 'I'm not doing this very well', 'other people are better than me', 'I'm a failure' – and even come up with alternative, more rational beliefs – eg 'well, it's a new skill, everybody struggles to begin with, with practice I will gradually improve and can't expect myself to be so good right now' – just focusing on the generation of alternative beliefs didn't seem to help them at the emotional level. They said things like, 'I can see the logic of this new belief, but it doesn't really help me feel any better or less inferior'.

Exploring the *emotional* textures of these alternative beliefs, PG found them to be harsh, even aggressive. The client's inner tone was more one of: 'for goodness sake! It's a new skill, everybody struggles to begin with, you have just got to practise. Obviously you're not good now, what do you expect stupid!'. His interventions evolved so as to help people stick with the alternative thoughts while deliberately creating and cultivating feelings of validation, support, kindness and understanding. He had people run through their alternative thoughts but to do it slowly, really focusing on the emotional textures – especially feelings of support and the kindness of the thoughts, getting patients to try to really *feel* them. What he found was that many clients actually resisted this for a number of reasons. Some felt they weren't worthy of kindness and some felt it was letting them off the hook. Others thought that being kind to oneself was a weakness and would not be helpful, and for others it opened up the grief process because they had never really felt kind to themselves.

This suggests it is important for coaches of all backgrounds to be familiar with the client's self-monitoring system, and the degree to which it is harsh, aggressive or even (at times) hating, and to get better at: helping their clients to start mindfully noticing the emotional tone of their self-monitoring system; and helping their clients to generate different emotions when they are trying to be helpful to themselves, including those associated with affiliation, acceptance, caring and kindness.

We feel that the more a coach understands the evolved nature of human minds, the better able they will be to help their clients and develop interventions for the above two processes. In this sense, compassionate mind coaching is not based upon any particular model of coaching, counselling or therapy, but on an understanding of the evolved psychological mechanisms and processes that underpin both the tendency to be self-critical and shaming and the ways in which our affiliative and caring emotions facilitate learning, change, personal development and growth.

Evidence-based approach to compassionate mind coaching

Humans brains are the result of millions of years of evolution (Buss, 2009; Panksepp, 2010). One behaviour that has been selected for is the ability to enter into and maintain relationships based on affection and caring, which is known to have many beneficial physiological and psychological effects, and can even influence genetic expression (Cozolino, 2007, 2008, 2013; Siegel, 2012). But humans don't just have relationships with others – they also enter into relationships with themselves, and these can be positive, eg self-care when wounded, learning to feed ourselves, positive self-talk when facing challenge, etc, or negative, eg getting angry with ourselves, hating ourselves, etc. These relationships we have with ourselves, especially those involving a sense of shame (Kim, Thibodeau and Jorgensen, 2011) and self-criticism (Kannan and Levitt, 2013), underpin a wide range of psychological health and wellbeing problems (Gilbert and Irons, 2005). Self-criticism is a powerful stimulator of threat processing in the brain (Longe *et al*, 2010). Two of the most pervasive problems in mental health are self-criticism and shame (Gilbert and Irons, 2005; Kannan and Levitt, 2013; Zuroff, Santor and Mongrain, 2005), and clinical levels of shame and self-criticism represent serious disruptions to the capacity for stimulating inner affiliative systems that are so important for emotion regulation and well-being. Self-criticism works through the threat system whereas compassion works with more affiliative brain systems (Longe *et al*, 2010; Weng *et al*, 2013).

There is also a growing body of evidence that self-compassion is linked to psychological health and wellbeing (Brach, 2003; Salzberg, 1997). Research suggests that individuals who are self-compassionate experience better psychological health than those lacking self-compassion, experiencing lower levels of anxiety and depression (Neff, 2012), lower cortisol levels, increased heart-rate variability (Rockliff *et al*, 2011), less rumination, perfectionism, and fear of failure (Neff, 2003; Neff, Hsieh and Dejitterat, 2005), less suppression of unwanted thoughts and a greater willingness to accept negative emotions as valid and important (Leary *et al*, 2007; Neff, 2003). Self-compassion also seems to be associated with such psychological strengths such as happiness, optimism, wisdom, curiosity and exploration, personal initiative and emotional intelligence (Heffernan *et al*, 2010; Hollis-Walker and Colosimo, 2011; Neff, Rude and Kirkpatrick, 2007) along with an improved ability to cope with such adversities as: academic failure (Neff, Hseih and Dejitthirat, 2005); divorce (Sbarra, Smith and Mehl, 2012); childhood maltreatment (Vettese *et al*, 2011); and chronic pain (Costa and Pinto-Gouveia, 2011). Self-compassion may also be associated with improved health behaviours such as persistence with dietary changes (Adams and Leary, 2007), smoking reductions (Kelly *et al*, 2009), seeking appropriate medical care (Terry and Leary, 2011), and physical activity (Magnus, Kowalski and McHugh, 2010), as well as improved relationship functioning (Neff and Beretvas, 2012; Yarnell and Neff, 2012), empathetic concern for others, altruism, perspective taking and forgiveness (Neff and Pommier, 2012).

Given these multiple benefits of self (and other) compassion, it make sense for coaches to explore its deliberate cultivation in some or most clients. But can different aspects of compassion, including self-compassion, be increased with training and practice? Several compassion programmes now exist, including: Compassion-Focused Therapy (CFT); Compassionate Mind Training (CMT) (Gilbert 2009, 2010); Compassion Cultivation Training (CCT) (Jazaieri *et al*, 2010); and a Mindful Self-Compassion (MSC) programme (Neff and Germer, 2012). Neff and Germer (2012) evaluated the effectiveness of an eight-week MSC programme designed to train people to be more self-compassionate, in which only one of the eight sessions specifically focused on mindfulness. They found significant pre/post gains in self-compassion, mindfulness and various wellbeing outcomes, with gains maintained at six and 12 month follow-ups. Jazaieri *et al* (2012) examined the effects of a nine-week Compassion Cultivation course in a randomized control trial using a community sample of 100 adults and found significant improvement in all three domains of compassion – compassion for others, receiving compassion and self-compassion. They concluded that specific domains of compassion can be intentionally cultivated in a training programme.

Another question is whether or not training people in compassion delivers any health and wellbeing benefits. A growing body of research indicates that training people in compassion is associated with a wide range of beneficial physiological and psychological benefits, including for both healthy people and people with severe health problems (Desbordes *et al*, 2012; Jazaieri *et al*, 2012; Weng *et al*, 2013; Hoffmann, Grossman and Hinton, 2011; Braehler *et al*, 2013). Pace and colleagues (2009) developed a six-week compassion meditation programme and found that in an undergraduate population, the amount of compassion-focused meditation practice was related to innate immune responses to a psychosocial stressor – eg decreases in interleukin 123(IL-6) and cortisol production. And in a pilot study, participation in Compassionate Mind Training yielded significant decreases in depression, self-attacking, shame and feelings of inferiority (Gilbert and Procter, 2006).

Participation in either mindfulness-based stress reduction (MBSR) or mindfulness-based cognitive therapy (MBCT) programmes is known to lead to significant improvements in physical and psychological functioning in a wide range of populations (Chiesa and Serretti, 2009; Grossman *et al*, 2004; Hofmann *et al*, 2010) and also seem to be associated with increases in self-compassion (Birnie, Speca and Carlson, 2010; Kuyken *et al*, 2010; Lee and Bang, 2010; Rimes and Wingrove, 2011; Shapiro *et al*, 2005; Shapiro, Brown, and Biegel, 2007; Shapiro *et al*, 2011). Some researchers have even suggested that increases in self-compassion may be a key pathway through which mindfulness-based interventions improve wellbeing (Baer, 2010; Holzel *et al*, 2011). For instance, Shapiro *et al* (2005) found that that self-compassion mediated the reductions in stress when health care professionals participated in an MBSR programme and Kuyken *et al* (2010) found that increases in mindfulness and self-compassion both mediated the link between MBCT and reduced depressive symptoms at 15-month follow-up, with increased self-compassion (but not mindfulness) reducing the link between cognitive reactivity and depressive relapse.

Still other lines of research inform our thinking about the benefits of training in compassion. For instance, there is increasing evidence that doing kind things for others and focusing on being helpful to others can promote happiness and reduce mild depression (Lyubomirsky, 2007), while practicing compassion for others seems to increase self compassion as well (Breines and Chen, 2013). Practising generating feelings of kindness (loving kindness meditations) for others has been shown to change brain systems (Lutz *et al*, 2008). Feeling cared for, supported and understood helps us to understand our own minds and emotions and shapes our motives (Cortina and Liotti, 2010; Trevarthen and Aitken, 2001), while feeling safe with, and connected to, others has been found to be a better predictor of vulnerability psycho-pathology than negative affect, positive affect or need for social support (Kelly *et al*, 2012). In addition, practising imagining one's 'best possible self' and relating to difficulties from that sense of self (one of the practices of compassionate mind coaching) is related to increased optimism and improved coping (Meevissen, Peters and Alberts, 2011; Peters *et al*, 2010).

Theoretical and practice

Core concepts

We think that coaches wishing to incorporate elements of the compassionate mind approach into their practice to better help their clients (and themselves) may wish to deepen their familiarity with the following models and concepts: the old brain, new brain model; the three circles model (of emotional regulation); it's not your fault; compassion; mindfulness; positive emotions; multiple selves; who is running the show?; and imagery.

The old brain, new brain model

The brain evolved over millions of years. Unable to go back and start again, nature tinkers with and makes use of what it has, adapting what is already there. This has resulted in a multi-layered structure sometimes referred to as the triune brain (McLean, 1990). The oldest part of the brain is shared with our reptile ancestors and comprises the R-Complex, a well-organized system supporting the functions, such as breathing, eating, drinking, mating, fighting, protecting territory (sometimes referred to as the four F's: feeding, fighting, fleeing and mating).

Evolution conserves processes that function well, or develops mechanisms for inhibiting those processes which are no longer helpful. It can't go back to the drawing board and start again. We share many of our basic drives and motives – be they for sex, status, belonging, tribalism, caring for our children, etc – with other animals, along with such basic emotions as fear, anger, disgust, joy and sexual lust. These are all hardwired (or hard-pathwayed) beneath the more recently developed cerebral cortex.

While many of the processes of evolution lead to advantages, some lead to disadvantages or trade-offs and this is very much the case with human brains. About 2 million years ago pre-humans started to evolve capacities for complex cognitive processes such as anticipation, imagination, perspective taking, mentalizing, language, symbols and a new sense of self. While these qualities gave rise to intelligence, science, culture, the arts and the modern world as we know it, they came with a downside. Other primates are not aware that they might die from a heart attack, nor do they ruminate about their appearance or how well they performed in some task. They probably don't stay up at night worrying about what other apes think about them, and most likely don't self monitor as to whether they are doing well or badly in life. Humans do, and do a lot. This capacity for complex reflection, thinking, imagination and mentalizing, along with having a sense of self and self-monitoring, can (and often does) spell serious trouble for humans (see Chapter 10).

One example we commonly use is that of the zebra running away from a lion. Once the zebra is away and safe it will calm down quite quickly and get back to grazing with the herd. For a human, however, after the flush of intense relief, the new brain will start to torment itself with all kinds of images – imagining what *could have happened* if one had got caught, imagining being choked to death by the lion, or having a leg bitten off, imagining what might happen tomorrow if there are two lions. And worrying about friends and relatives, and whether they will get chased and caught and killed. This is the brain of 'what if' and 'suppose that', a brain which creates loops in the mind, which ruminates about frightening things and about losses, a brain which monitors behaviours in threat focused ways and which gets stuck – constantly stimulating via the imagination difficult emotions and motives. A large chunk of human underperformance, struggle and suffering can be related to this disharmony between our old and new brains, between our basic, innate drives and emotions and our cognitions.

The skilful coach can use the old brain, new brain model to help their client understand that many of their problems stem from the way their brain has evolved, and that they (like all other humans) have 'tricky' brains containing different parts which are not well integrated and that can get them trapped in unhelpful loops and patterns. The coach can also use the old brain/new brain model to help underpin the 'it's not your fault' message (see later), as well as helping clients to understand why they can and do experience such a profound disconnect between their thoughts and feelings.

FIGURE 9.1   Old brain, new brain model

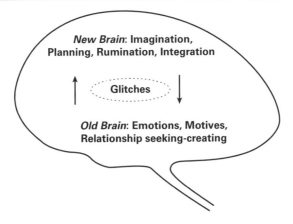

From Gilbert and Choden (2013) *Mindful Compassion*. With kind permission, Constable Robinson

FIGURE 9.2   Three types of affect regulation system

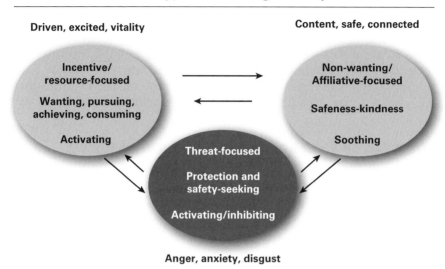

From Gilbert (2009) *Compassionate Mind*. With kind permission, Constable Robinson

The three circles model (of emotional regulation)

Compassionate mind coaches use the 'three circles model' to help clients understand how three evolved, basic functional emotional systems (or emotion regulation systems), interrelate and can become unbalanced (Depue and Morrone-Strupinsky, 2005; LeDoux, 1998; Panksepp, 1998). This three circles model is easily understood by clients who seem to readily identify with it. Coaches can use the model to help clients see in what way their emotional regulation system may have become unbalanced and to explore the benefits to them of spending less time in threat or drive mode and more time in safe, contented, recovery mode.

The threat and self-protection focused emotion system

This system evolved to attract attention, tune in to detect and respond to threats (LeDoux, 1998). There is a menu of threat-based emotions such as anger, anxiety and disgust and a menu of defensive behaviours such as fight, flight, submission, freeze etc. It is part of the 'fast brain' (Kahneman, 2011) and is one of the human brains dominant systems, running in the background, constantly monitoring for threats and ready to jump centre stage and grab the brain's attention at a moment's notice when serious actual or possible threats present themselves. This system is responsible for the 'negativity bias' (paying more attention to negative things that happen than positive things) and the 'smoke detector principle' (the tendency to overreact to ambiguous stimuli). It is much better for our survival to run away need-lessly 99 times from a harmless rustle of leaves than miss the one time when it was a predator hiding in the bush (Baumeister, Bratslavsky, Finkenauer and Vohs, 2001). This system activates the sympathetic nervous system, and many forms of therapy tend to work fairly directly with this threat system itself (Gilbert, 1993). In compassionate mind coaching, however, we tend to explore and help clients strengthen various 'positive' affect systems that help clients counteract and better regulate their innate threat system.

The drive, seeking and acquisition focused system

This system evolved to motivate and regulate our efforts at going and getting hold of resources, of desiring, seeking out, wanting and obtaining things which are to our advantage. It is involved in goal setting, striving and plan-ning, exploring and capturing resources for ourselves and others, of being competent, achieving and experiences of mastery. This system is involved in competitive drives and mental states in which individuals seek dominance and social position, and can involve striving to achieve motivated by fear of rejection and social exclusion. This system (like the threat system) also activates the sympathetic nervous system. Consumer capitalism, with its tendency to market and sell to people more than they need, may be con-tributing to the overstimulation of 'wanting', 'craving', 'acquiring', 'me focused', competitive behaviours, and such an overreliance on acquisition and achievement may increase vulnerability to feelings of depression – especially when people feel defeated, unable to reach their goals, or feel they are doing poorly in comparison to other people (Taylor *et al*, 2011).

Some clients spend a lot of time bouncing back and forwards between their threat and drive systems, unable to relax and simple be.

The contentment, soothing and affiliative focused system

This is a positive affect system linked to calming, resting and contentment, a state of inner peace and slowing where one does not feel threatened, is not seeking or striving and both the drive and threat systems are calmed (Depue and Morrone-Strupinsky, 2005). It evolved in mammals to enable states of peacefulness and quiescence when they are no longer threatened and are focused on recovering and consuming resources. It is particularly linked to the parasympathetic system, sometimes called the rest and digest system (Porges, 2007). Over evolutionary time this system of calming has been adapted for some of the functions of affiliative behaviour. So, for ex-ample, if a child is distressed, they can (re)turn to the parent who will hold, cuddle or reassure them and this has a calming effect on their distress. This capacity to experience others as caring and helpful is often the way in which feelings of threat are reduced, and there are very important brain systems that register the kindness of others and tone down threat systems.

The compassionate mind coach uses the 'three circles model' to help clients understand that some of their problems or issues might be best explained by an overactivity of one of these three emotional regulation systems, or a lack of balance between them. Perhaps they are excessively worried, anxious, fearful or concerned about their reputation, status, social standing, or chances of loss, etc. Perhaps they are excessively competitive, or materialistic and consumed with thoughts about winning and losing, about getting hold of money, property, objects, etc. Or perhaps they experience excessive feelings of inferiority, of 'not being good enough', or of being a 'loser', or somehow inadequate, perhaps spending excessive amounts of time either trying to 'prove' themselves (in their own eyes or in the eyes of important others) or ruminating about how they came to be the way they are. The coach can use the model to help clients see that – for whatever reason – perhaps an imbalance or overactivity has arisen, and that one aspect of the coaching work they will be doing will involve 're-balancing' their brain's basic emotional regulation systems, training them to more easily access and spend time in the contentment and soothing system as they make progress towards important life goals.

It's not your fault

Many clients experience unhelpful levels of self-blame, shame, regret, hurt, self-loathing and unhappiness about their current or past behaviours. They strongly feel that there is 'something the matter' with them. For such clients it can be helpful to provide an alternative explanation for their behaviour. That the reason they behaved the way they did, or behave the way they do, is not because they are 'bad' or because there is 'something the matter with them', but rather that they have inherited this tricky brain with its unhelpful loops which get in the way of wise living, combined with their exposure to early social environments they did not choose. Of course, we don't want the client to use the 'it's not your fault' message as an excuse to persist in undesirable behaviour, such as abusing others or drinking too much. They still have responsibility to change. It's just that some of their problems may be better explained by the fact that they own a tricky brain, doing the best it can in an environment for which it did not evolve.

Compassion

Like mindfulness, Buddhist concepts of compassion are being increasingly integrated into Western psychotherapy (Germer and Siegel, 2012). In compassionate mind coaching we use a Buddhist informed definition of compassion (Dalai Lama, 1995; Tsering, 2008) – compassion is 'a sensitivity to suffering, and the causes of suffering, with a commitment to try to alleviate and prevent it'. Compassion is linked to motives, emotions and abilities/competencies to be socially mindful, supportive, understanding, kind and helpful to others (Davidson and Harrington, 2002; Weng *et al*, 2013; Van Doesum, van Lange and van Lange, 2013). It overlaps with, but is slightly different from, concepts such as kindness (Phillips and Taylor, 2009; Gilbert and Choden, 2013).

Compassion has two psychologies or mental sets. The first is the ability to pay attention to suffering, to turn towards suffering and to start to notice the triggers and causes of suffering in our self and others. Here skills such as mindfulness and acceptance are very helpful – if we are to start to pay attention to suffering we also need to be able to tolerate it. The second element is action, because compassion without action is not very helpful. Imagine, for example, that you see somebody fall into a fast flowing river and immediately feel the urge to jump in and rescue them, to alleviate their suffering. And as you are in midair you remember that you can't swim! All that has happened is the amount of suffering in the world has increased. So intention without wise action is not necessarily compassionate. For instance, if you want to be a coach it helps to have a compassionate intention to help people, but then you also need to spend time studying and practising to develop your coaching skills. Simply having the intention to help people is not enough. Another important aspect of compassion is that it flows. There is the compassion we can feel for others, the compassion we feel coming from others to ourselves, and the compassion we can have towards ourselves – also known as self-compassion. Neff (2012) suggests such self-compassion comprises three interacting components: 1) self-kindness versus self-judgement; 2) a sense of common humanity versus isolation; and 3) mindfulness versus over-identification with painful thoughts and emotions.

Mindfulness

Compassionate mind coaching can be considered a fusion or integration of compassion development practices with mindfulness exercises. Mindfulness involves paying attention to the present moment in a non-judgemental way, and is not the same as 'quiet' mind or 'still' mind or 'empty' mind (a fuller description is given in Chapter 8 of this book). It involves noticing, and bringing the attention back to a particular focus, time and time again, without getting cross or frustrated. Quiet mind may result, but that is not what mindfulness is. Since the benefits of mindfulness and various practices for its cultivation are nicely dealt with elsewhere (eg Davis and Hayes, 2011), these will not be further explored here.

Positive emotions

Positively experienced emotions not only 'feel good' but they most likely help us to do good and stay well (Fredrickson, 1998). While negatively experienced emotions (fear, anger, hate, disgust, sadness, etc) tend to narrow our attention down onto a threat or something bad, positively experienced emotions (joy, curiosity, achievement, affiliation, etc) seem to broaden our perspective and help us protect and build resources (skills, friendships, knowledge, health, etc) which can help us survive and thrive in the future (Fredrickson, 2001). Compassionate mind coaches help their clients tone down their inner critic and experience increased feelings of acceptance, being understood, being cared for, being forgiven, being soothed and being loved, thus helping clients to experience more frequent, more intense and/or longer lasting positive emotions, and the benefits that flow from such experiences.

Multiple possible selves

The self you currently are is one of many that might have come into existence had your circumstance been different. Had you been born into a much more wealthy family, or from a mother addicted to alcohol, or been taken into care by the State, or had a bullying and sexually abusing older sibling – then a different you would have emerged. If either of the authors had been abducted as a baby and raised in a drug cartel, then as an adult we might have been comfortable with murder, assault, kidnapping and torture, and this chapter would not have been written. So our personal unfolding is strongly determined by our environment – hence the saying 'there but for the grace of God go I'. The good news is that our unfolding continues into adulthood. Each of us continues to contain 'multiple possible selves'. A key question the compassionate mind coach asks of their coachee is: Which of these possible selves do you wish to cultivate, or grow into? Which is your 'desired' self?

Who is running the show?

The idea that each of us contains a range of 'selves' within us is used in another sense. That we all have a 'critical' self (our inner critic), an 'angry' self, an 'anxious' self, a 'competitive' self, a 'jealous' self, as well as a 'wise' self and a 'compassionate' self. These different 'selves' can take centre stage when different situations arise, and that may not be the best thing from the perspective of living a happy, meaningful, engaged and fulfilling life. For example, one of us (TA) went for a nice long summer's walk with a group of about 30 friends a few months ago, and at the end of the walk we joined together in a game of rounders. TA was fielding, and a series of poor decisions by the referee ensued, combined with a series of 'made up on the spot' rules he felt were strongly to his team's disadvantage – despite his protestations. So he walked off and sat down with the spectators, deciding not to play. His 'competitive' self had taken centre stage, to be nudged off the stage by his 'childish' self. In due course his more grown up, 'playful' self emerged and he laughed at himself and returned to the game. Compassionate mind coaches can ask their clients which of their 'selves' do they want to be (generally) running their lives – their wise, compassionate, caring self, or any one of their other more blinkered, short-term selves. Assuming the client would choose their wise, compassionate, kind self to be generally running their lives, the coach lets the client know that that is the self that they will be working together on.

Imagery

Both a real snake and the thought of making a presentation to a group of strangers in someone scared of public speaking can powerfully stimulate the brain and the body – inducing changes in thinking, hormonal levels, heart rate, breathing rate, images of bad things happening, feelings of fear and urges/desire to escape. Similarly, lying in bed on your own and entertaining sexual images can stimulate some of the same cognitive, hormonal and physiological changes that having contact with a real sexual partner does. Compassionate mind coaches use this ability of mental images to bring about significant brain and body changes to help their clients bring about helpful, calming and healing brain and body changes in their clients. They use a progressive series of safeness and compassion-related visualization exercises to help clients access and spend time in the 'safe, content, affiliative' system, activating their parasympathetic nervous system and strengthening neural pathways that will enable the client to more easily access and spend time in calm, peaceful, non-striving, affiliative states in the future.

Tools and techniques

Compassionate mind coaching can be considered a style or flavour of coaching that can be layered onto existing coaching approaches – eg cognitive behavioural, humanistic – as well as a discrete, holistic, multi-modal approach in its own right.

Like many other coaches, compassionate mind coaches use a wide range of generic coaching tools and strategies to help their clients, including: psychoeducation; Socratic questioning; goal setting; visualization; empathic listening; self-assessment; feedback; behavioural experimentation; inference chaining; exposure; desensitization; letter writing; chairwork; in-session skills development; between session practice; reading assignments, etc. None of these are specific to compassionate mind coaching, but they are used by the compassionate mind coach to help their clients to both experience more compassion and grow into a more compassionate self.

Compassionate mind coaching is progressive, in that some elements may need to be understood and practised before others, with later sessions building on the skills and abilities developed in earlier sessions. These phases might be labelled:

- psychoeducation;
- motivation; and
- practice.

Let us look at each of these in turn and some associated techniques.

Psychoeducation

Many people view compassion as being nice, soft and forgiving, and perhaps also being weak. They typically won't know much about how their brain has evolved, or how the emotions they experience are regulated outside their conscious awareness. So some time will need to be spent exploring what compassion is and why the client might want to at least consider its deliberate cultivation. Some of the concepts, models and ideas compassionate mind coaches might share with clients include:

- That our brains have evolved over millions of years, that we all have an 'old brain' and a 'new brain' that don't work so well together, leading to 'tricky minds' that get us into trouble time and time again.
- That it is 'not their fault' that they are the way they are, given their evolved brain combined with their early childhood and personal history (that they did not choose).
- The fact that we are all in this together, that we all suffer – that this is part of our common humanity.
- That our brains have three main systems for regulating our emotions (the 'three circles' model) and these can become out of balance. Many of us have difficulty toning down our 'threat' and 'drive' systems and spending time in our 'soothing' system.
- That if we choose compassion as a focus for our motivation, then over time this may help to reorganize our brains (and minds) in a helpful way.
- The nature of mindfulness, and benefits of cultivating it.
- The nature of compassion, the benefits of cultivating it, of developing a compassionate self.
- The importance of practice.

Some clients feel that a compassion focused approach will not be helpful to them – perhaps believing it to be a form of weakness, softness and/or self-indulgence. Or they may feel that they are not worthy of compassion. These beliefs are best corrected by Socratic methods – perhaps having clients model a weak posture and asking them if that looks like compassion. Or asking them if they feel that certain historical figures noted for their compassion – eg Nelson Mandela or Ghandi – were weak. They may also be asked if they consider whether or not they feel that humanitarian workers working in high-risk situations to deliver life-saving care to others are weak, etc. If a barrier to compassionate mind work is feeling that they are not worthy of care, acceptance, understanding and even love, then the reasons for this can be explored in a empathic way. Model compassion. Acknowledge that this is sad. Other clients may feel that becoming more compassionate, including having more self-compassion, may undermine their motivation to make progress in life. That they need their harsh inner critic to motivate them.

Such beliefs around compassionate mind practices being unlikely to help, or of the client not being worthy of compassion, need to be explored and changed – or at least suspended – before the coachee will engage with the various compassionate mind practices required to change their brains and minds. For instance, the following story might be shared:

> Imagine two classrooms full of children. One class has a teacher who constantly criticizes the children, picking them up on their mistakes, putting them down in front of their classmates, and never giving out any praise. The other class

has a teacher who allows the children to express their thoughts, asks skilful questions to draw our their ideas, praises them for their contribution, and provides corrective information in a non-judgemental way – caring for the children. In which classroom do you think the children will be more motivated and make better progress?

Hopefully the client will agree the children in the second class, and their belief that they need a harsh inner critic to be motivated can be challenged.

Some clients, however, may actively resist compassionate mind practices due to difficulties with feelings of contentment and safeness. The feeling of slowing down may trigger aversive memories. One client described feeling 'safe and content' as lowering one's guard (vigilance), and remembered an occasion when she was relaxed and watching the television when her (alcoholic) mother would fly into a rage over something and beat her. The client said: 'You must never feel safe or settled, because that's when you get hurt.' From a classical conditioning perspective, pleasant and safe emotional states may have come to be associated with traumatic histories and memories. Other examples include where children have been resting in their rooms and the parent has come and abused them and then left them alone in their fear (Gilbert *et al*, 2012). If such issues surface, referral to a practitioner trained in, for example, compassion-focused therapy may be suggested.

Motivation

Information is important, but it is often not enough to bring about behaviour change (Miller and Rollnick, 2013). For the client to start, and persist, with compassionate mind practices, they need to be motivated to do so. Motivation varies in quality as well as quantity (Deci and Ryan, 1985). Intrinsic motivation is when people are motivated to do the behaviour since it is rewarding and perhaps pleasurable in and of itself. Extrinsic motivation is when people are motivated to do the behaviour because of something favourable that happens after the behaviour has taken place. People's motivation for engaging in compassionate mind exercises may initially be extrinsic – doing the exercises due to the improved emotional regulation and quality of life that they hope will follow. Over time, or after exposure to the practices, some intrinsic motivation may arise as they begin to enjoy the practices themselves.

Skilful coaches help their clients to discover their own motivations for doing compassionate mind work, and then strengthen these reasons while building client self-efficacy or confidence about changing. A range of motivation-enhancing tools and strategies might be used (examples are discussed in more detail in Chapter 11 of this book), including:

- exploring unhelpful and/or incorrect beliefs about the nature of compassion, while supplying corrective information (see above);
- helping clients to explore the advantages and disadvantages of experimenting with the approach, eg using decisional balance;

- helping clients explore the kind of person they wish to become, what their 'compassionate self' looks like;
- clarifying clients' goals for themselves, and then exploring where becoming more compassionate fits in;
- clarifying clients' values, and then exploring how compassion is consistent with or in harmony with their values;
- giving clients a taste of the approach, followed by a debrief and reflection;
- exploring two possible futures with the client – one in which they deliberately cultivated compassion for a few years, and the other in which they hadn't;
- modelling the approach, to help build client self-efficacy;
- exploring clients' strengths – perhaps using the VIA strengths classification system (**www.viacharacter.org/viainstitute/classification.aspx**) – and helping clients explore how compassion already underpins some of their strengths, and how compassionate mind practices may help them to further develop and apply their strengths in real-world settings. VIA strengths which seem particularly compatible with compassionate mind work include: curiosity, judgement, perspective, bravery, honesty, love, kindness and fairness;
- using open questions such as: 'what do you feel might be the advantages to you of experimenting with this approach?' or 'what are your three best reasons for becoming more compassionate towards yourself and others?';
- encouraging behavioural experimentation with compassionate mind exercises and activities in the session; and
- eliciting and strengthening client change talk.

Practice

Talking about compassion will only get clients so far. In order to derive the benefits of this approach, clients need to act, to do, to behave differently. To help, the coach guides and supports the client through a progressive series of exercises and practices – perhaps explaining the exercise, guiding the client through it, and then reflecting on the exercise after it has been performed. And just as a personal trainer does not overload a new, physically deconditioned client with too much exercise – recognizing it takes several weeks for clients to develop their strength, co-ordination, balance and exercise tolerance – so too the skilful coach does not overwhelm or overload their client with too much mindfulness and visualization activity too soon! It takes time to develop the skills, neural pathways and connections which underpin and enable compassionate mind practices.

These exercises involve attention to breathing, posture, voice and facial expression; recall of receiving compassion and being compassionate; method acting techniques (Cannon, 2012) to help have the experience of what it is like being a compassionate self; compassionate self-identity cultivation; the use of compassionate imagery; compassionate letter writing; as well as enacting compassionate behaviours on a regular basis. They are designed to stimulate the motivation, emotion and cognitive systems that underpin compassion (and its social mentalities) so that over time they become more integrated into the client's sense of self, their self-identity. A (more) 'compassionate' self evolves with associated ways of attending, feeling, thinking and behaving.

Here are some of the practices that help clients develop their compassionate selves and experience more compassion. (More detailed descriptions of these exercises, activities and practices can be found in the further reading section of this chapter, along with free templates, scripts, writing exercises and MP3 files.)

Soothing breathing rhythm

Have the client slightly slow and deepen their breathing to around five to six breaths per minute, in order to stimulate some parasympathetic calming that is associated with affiliation and the self-soothing system.

Body scan with compassionate focus

Have the client focus their attention on different parts of their body, in sequence. Help them focus on the sensations of slowing down and noticing what that feels like in their mind and their body. The body postures are one of finding a sense of inner stillness and inner groundedness and rootedness.

Mindfulness sitting practice and experiential acceptance

Help the client develop their mindfulness skills of focusing their attention and bringing it back to what is being attended to when the attention wanders. And doing this with gentleness, learning that wandering is one of the things that the mind does – it is not the being bad at mindfulness! Any thoughts about judging themselves or telling themselves 'I'm no good at this' are seen as the usual activities of the restless mind. Have them pay attention to various sensations which may come into focus, and allowing them to be as they are. Noticing them.

Creating a safe place

Have the client imagine a place where they feel safe. Imagine the place welcoming them. Encourage them to form an emotional connection with the place. Help them realize that this place is their creation and that it is always available to them – never more than a thought away. Encourage them to immerse themselves in their safe space imagery several times each week.

Visualizing a compassionate colour

Have the client imagine a colour, one that conveys a sense of warmth and kindness. Have them imagine the colour entering and slowly spreading throughout their body, imbued with qualities of strength, warmth, kindness and wisdom. Have the client holding a friendly facial expression during this exercise.

Cultivating a compassionate image

Have the client think about and imagine a compassionate other being, one that cares deeply for them. This imaginary compassionate other may be old or young, male or female, from any ethnicity, or perhaps a species other than human (one of us (TA) has an element of his calm, peaceful, loving Labrador in his compassionate other image). Have the client imagine the qualities they want their image to have – perhaps a complete acceptance of them as a person, a deep concern and care for them, a sense of belonging and kinship. Perhaps their compassionate other has experienced some of what the client has experienced. Then, while practising soothing breathing rhythm, have the client imagine their compassionate image saying the following words, in as warm a voice as can be imagined and with a full commitment to the person: 'May you be free of suffering [clients says own name in their head]', 'May you be happy, [name]', 'May you flourish, [name]', 'May you find peace and well-being, [name]'. Have the client practise this exercise several times each week.

Cultivating the compassionate self

Although we might practise specific skills such as golf, piano playing or painting, or take exercise to get physically fit, most people are unaware that they can practise cultivating a particular self-identity and that this will have an effect on their mind (Jazaieri et al, 2012; Weng et al, 2013). One way of doing this and of helping clients develop (and really experience) their compassionate self is to use method acting techniques (Cannon, 2012). Good method actors use imagery to stimulate different neurological and physiological systems to help them perform a particular role. Let's imagine they needed to act angry. They might bring to mind something that made them very angry, let that feeling fester for a while, create an angry face, adopt an angry voice, clench their fists and change other aspects of their physiology such as their breathing, their posture, their gaze, etc. Compassionate mind coaches help their clients use these same method acting techniques create their compassionate self. Have them start by imagining and creating a compassionate facial expression – one of friendliness, perhaps with a gentle smile. Then have them focus on imagining what a compassionate voice sounds like, one that is friendly, supportive and understanding. Have them sit quietly, slow down their breathing, and notice the difference in feeling between saying hello to themselves (eg 'Hello, Tim') using a neutral voice and saying the same phrase in a friendly voice. Reflect with the client on whether or not the deliberate creation of a friendly internal voice creates a different internal feeling. Then have the client imagine themselves having certain qualities, in particular wisdom, strength, sense of authority, and a commitment to being compassionate and helpful (Gilbert, 2010; Gilbert and Choden, 2013). Once this has been done, have the client imagine themselves being with others and undertaking activities from the perspective of their compassionate self. In addition to bringing about helpful psychological and physiological changes, these exercises can help create 'ideas' in the client's mind about the kind of person they might wish to become, over time.

Cultivating the wish to be well and happy

To help the client cultivate and experience more self-compassion, have them adopt a firm, rooted posture, cultivate the soothing breathing rhythm, and then have them say to themselves (in their mind) with a gentle smile on their face and a 'smiling' voice: 'May you be free of suffering [says own name]', 'May you be happy, [name]', 'May you flourish, [name]', 'May you find peace and wellbeing, [name]'. Have the client practise this exercise several times each week.

Cultivating compassion towards others

To help the client cultivate and experience more compassion for others, have them adopt a firm, rooted posture, cultivate the soothing breathing rhythm, and then have them bring to mind a particular person (or animal – eg a pet) and say to themselves (in their mind) with a gentle smile on their face and a 'smiling' voice: 'May you be free of suffering [says others name]', 'May you be happy, [name]', 'May you flourish, [name]', 'May you find peace and wellbeing, [name]'. Once the client has developed their ability to cultivate and experience the flow of compassion towards someone or something they love, they might progress to doing this exercise bringing to mind people they know but do not feel strongly about one way or the other. And there is the option to progress this 'compassion for others' exercise to people they mildly or strongly dislike.

Cultivating compassion for different aspects of oneself

As mentioned, it can be helpful to think of ourselves as being made up of different selves – eg the critical self, the anxious self, the angry self, the sad self, etc. This exercise involves developing compassion and understanding towards these different parts of oneself using chair work (Kellogg, 2004). Set out three chairs. Have the client sit in one chair and, being themselves, have them describe a particular issue that concerns or frustrates them, or which they beat themselves up about. Then have them sit in the 'critical self' chair, and have the critical self say things to the usual self. This is just 'externalizing' what their inner critic is already saying to them inside their heads on a regular basis. Then have the client return to the normal self chair, and ask them what they would like to say to their critical self. Sometimes you may notice a posture of defeat and submission as they agree with and give into the critical self. Then have the client sit in the third chair and, preparing themselves with breathing and postural exercises, adopt their compassionate self (previously practiced and cultivated) and have this compassionate self talk with their critical self. What is it that the critical self wants for the client? What is it that the critical self is scared of, such that it says the nasty things it does to the normal self? (For more detailed descriptions of cultivating compassion for different aspects of the self, see Gilbert and Choden, 2013.)

Exploring self-compassion through writing

The compassionate mind coach can have the client undertake one or more writing exercises to help them develop their compassionate mind, including having them write about an aspect of themselves they do not like, and then having them write an imaginary letter to themselves from a wise and compassionate friend, and having them keep a self-compassion journal.

As the reader might expect, we also recommend that the coach engages with and practises some of the above exercises for themselves (on their own or with the help of another), in order both to deepen their familiarity with the activities as well as to derive personal benefit from them.

CASE STUDY

The client is a 23-year-old semi-professional football player who is experiencing a loss of confidence in their skills, along with anger when they under-perform. They want to make progress in football, and are anxious that they may have reached their limit. They recognize that their anger is not helping them on the pitch or off of it.

Third session

Coach: 'In the last few sessions we've been exploring the way our emotions work in terms of the things that threaten us and how we deal with those threats, things we are trying to do and to achieve, and the way in which we can slow down, calm down and get help from others. Do those three emotion systems make sense too?' [They have previously looked at and explored the three circles model]

Client: 'Yes, I haven't seen them written out like that before but I can see how they work.'

Coach: 'And we have also been exploring the way you monitor your performance and how you relate to yourself when your performance isn't as good as you want.'

Client: 'Yes, I get quite frustrated and angry with myself really because I often make silly mistakes.'

Coach: 'And you have also told me that you drive yourself on by giving yourself a hard time and being critical on yourself, that you think compassion will actually make you weak.'

Client: 'Oh yes, my father was quite critical and taught me that only if you are hard on yourself are you going to achieve anything. So I can't really see how being kind to myself will help me really, and I don't want to lower my standards.'

Coach: 'I agree that if compassion was going to drop your standards that wouldn't be helpful, but in actual fact learning to be kind and compassionate to ourselves can be the very thing we need to help us keep going. Compassion is related to courage and slows us down sufficiently to understand why things went wrong and what we can do about it.'

Client: 'But compassion seems a bit soft. To me the idea of just being kind when actually you need to be tough doesn't make any sense.'

Coach: 'Let's explore this together. Imagine that you have something difficult to do like going for a worrying hospital appointments, or may be having to go through a divorce. What attitude would you want from one of your friends?'

Client: 'Well, I guess I'd want them to be supportive and understanding.'

Coach: 'Not harsh and critical?'

Client: 'No, I guess not.'

Coach: 'So what do you get out of them being kind, supportive and understanding in your time of anxiety or pain – what do you actually want them to help you do?'

Client: 'Well I guess to help me through it and help me face up to the difficulty – I suppose it does help to have a shoulder to cry on from time to time.'

Coach: 'Well yeah – maybe at times it's a shoulder to cry on. But most importantly we humans are a very social species and we can take a lot of courage from the support and kindness of others. And the thing is it's the same when we treat ourselves with kindness too.'

Client: 'Oh. I hadn't seen compassion as a source of encouragement.'

Coach: 'Well the basic definition of compassion is "being sensitive to the suffering of self and others with a commitment to do something about it". So if your suffering has been caused and you're struggling, then the thing to do is to find out why you're struggling and try to help you in your struggle, and you're much more likely to do this effectively if you do it from within the emotional system of soothing helpfulness and kindness. You literally become a good friend yourself. This isn't letting yourself off the hook, but genuinely finding ways to move towards your goals but in a way that doesn't constantly stress you out. After all, what system will you be staying in if you keep criticizing yourself in the way that you are?'

Client: 'Well, I suppose the stress system or threat system.'

Coach: 'Exactly. Self-criticism is usually fuelled by anger, anxiety or even contempt and if we look behind those we will see a degree of fear about failing or not doing well which is linked to the fear of rejection or not achieving one's potential.'

Client: 'I can see that.'

Coach: 'So when things are not going so well, the soothing, caring mindset can help you to stay reasonably mindful, observing what's happening in your mind, observing what's happening that you are not happy with and helping you to create an internally supportive approach to the difficulty. So this is why we are going to be practising compassionate voice tones and facial expressions along with some breathing exercises to give you an opportunity to notice and switch into your compassion system at times of difficulty. Would that be ok?'

Client: 'Sure.'

[Coach takes the client through some mindfulness and compassion related visualization practices, helping them discover/create their compassion self]

Coach: 'Would it be ok if we took a typical situation that might trigger your self-criticism, and explore how to adopt a more compassionate perspective? Can you tell me about one?'

Client: 'Well... it can be things like running past the ball and not getting it under control quickly, or having a very clear shot at goal and missing, or grossly over kicking my pass. I can be quite down on myself for a while.'

Coach: 'OK. Add some colour, tell me some of the things you say to yourself?'

Client: 'You [expletive]. How could you do that? You've been playing for over 10 years. You've practised the skills hundreds of times. What the hell is the matter with you? You shouldn't be missing easy chances like that. You're letting your team mates down. You're not making any progress. They are going to drop you from the side.'

Coach: 'OK. We will call that that your "critical and frustrated self". We can see that the underlying fear is "not getting anywhere and being left behind or not included".'

Client: 'Oh yeah, I very much want be part of the team and be a good contributor and valued by the team.'

Coach: 'OK, so now let's slow down the breathing and slow body process, and shift out of this angry frustrated self. Spend a few moments focusing on the wisdom of yourself, the recognition that this isn't intentional. We want to be able to pick ourselves up as quick as we can – to feel a sense of strength and power in your compassionate self and a real commitment to be helpful, supportive and bring out the best in you. So now with that warm voice tone we practised and those expressions, think about how you will respond to such a setback or disappointment as your compassionate self. What would you say?'

Client: 'Well, I have been practising my skills and unfortunately it's very common for even very talented professionals to make mistakes. Humans are not mistake free zones. It's understandable to be anxious and frustrated about this, but I can also remember some of the things I did okay, or even well. There are things are to build on. And I could ask the coach to help me practise where I tend to make mistakes.'

Coach: 'OK. So it's important to actually put your attention on those things and bring them to mind and hold them in line for a period of time. I would also like you to write down some of the things your compassionate self thinks, write them on a postcard and practise saying them to yourself in a generally compassionate and supportive kind of way. How do you feel about that?'

Client: 'Yes, that's something I will do.'

When might compassionate mind coaching be most suitable?

Regardless of the presenting issue or goal, many coaching clients might benefit from becoming less self-critical, less shaming, more self-accepting, more forgiving and more kind towards themselves and others. For optimum learning, change and growth within the coaching process, it is probably best that clients are open, non-defensive and prepared to set goals and make changes with minimum concerns about failure, rejection and critical self-judgement. In this sense, self-compassion may be seen as an accelerator or catalyst for the coaching process, and therefore something to be cultivated.

But there may also be some specific client issues for which the approach may particularly helpful, including:

- clients with a particularly strong or harsh inner critic, who beat themselves up a lot and find it hard to escape from negative self-talk. Including clients having CBT, perhaps able to generate alternative, more rational, more helpful beliefs, but not being able to have these penetrate their lives or change their emotional tone;
- clients who seem to have an overactive threat-focused system, experiencing unhelpful levels of fear, anger and/or anxiety;
- clients who seem to have an overactive drive-focused system, experiencing unhelpful levels of wanting, desiring, pursuing, consuming and competing;
- clients who seem excessively concerned with rank, status, doing well compared to others, or better than others, or needing to prove themselves to themselves, an important other, or a dead parent, etc.

Conclusion

Compassionate mind coaching is the coaching version of compassion focused therapy. It can be considered a fusion of coaching, mindfulness and compassion related practices and exercises, and is informed and underpinned by both evolutionary psychology and neuroscience. It is both a way or style of doing coaching, as well as a discrete, holistic and multi-modal coaching methodology in its own right – helping clients to achieve a better balance between three important emotion regulation systems, and toning down their 'threat' and 'acquisition' systems if these are interfering with their health, wellbeing and quality of life.

Compassionate mind coaching helps clients to think about and grow into more of the person they want to be. It provides clients with an alternative framework for thinking about their problems, their situation and their path forwards.

Finally, engaging in some of the practices and activities outlined in the chapter may help coaches themselves to become both better coaches and happier, healthier, more fulfilled human beings.

Developing yourself as a compassionate mind coach

Developing your skills

Coaches wishing to learn more about and develop their skills in compassionate mind coaching may wish to explore the following practitioner texts:

- Gilbert, P (2010) *Compassion Focused Therapy*, The CBT Distinctive Features series, Routledge, London
- Gilbert, P and Choden (2013) *Mindful Compassion: Using the power of mindfulness and compassion to transform our lives*, Constable and Robinson, London

Deepening your understanding

Coaches wishing to recommend compassionate mind based self-help books and workbooks for their clients may wish to consider the following:

- Gilbert, P and Choden (2013) *Mindful Compassion: Using the power of mindfulness and compassion to transform our lives*, Constable & Robinson, London
- Neff, K (2012) *Self Compassion: Stop beating yourself up and leave insecurity behind*, Hodder and Stoughton, London
- Tirch, D (2012) *The Compassionate-Mind Guide to Overcoming Anxiety*, Constable & Robinson, London
- Kolts, R (2011) *The Compassionate Mind Approach to Managing Your Anger*, Constable & Robinson, London
- Kolts, R and Chodron, T (2013) *Living With an Open Heart: How to cultivate compassion in everyday life*, Constable & Robinson, London

Web resources

Useful websites for both coaches and clients include:

- The Compassionate Mind Foundation: including lots of free training resources and resources for clients: **www.compassionatemind.co.uk/**
- Kristin Neff's site, also containing lots of free resources: **www.self-compassion.org/**
- Chris Germer's Mindful Self-Compassion site: **www.mindfulselfcompassion.org/**

- Centre for Mindful Self Compassion: **www.centerformsc.org/**
- A demonstration of a self compassion break:
  www.youtube.com/watch?v=Oe5nA0JdfvY

References

Adams, C E and Leary, M R (2007) Promoting self-compassionate attitudes toward eating among restrictive and guilty eaters, *Journal of Social and Clinical Psychology*, **26**, pp 1120–44

Baer, R A (2010) Self-compassion as a mechanism of change in mindfulness- and acceptance-based treatments, in *Assessing mindfulness and acceptance processes in clients: illuminating the theory and practice of change*, ed R A Baer, (pp 135–53), New Harbinger Publications, Oakland, CA

Baumeister, R F, Bratslavsky, E, Finkenauer, C and Vohs, K D (2001) Bad is stronger than good, *Review of General Psychology*, **5**, pp 323–70

Birnie, K, Speca, M and Carlson, L E (2010) Exploring self-compassion and empathy in the context of mindfulness-based stress reduction (MBSR), *Stress and Health*, **26**, pp 359–71

Brach, T (2003) *Radical Acceptance: Embracing your life with the heart of a Buddha*, Bantam, New York

Braehler, C, Gumley, A, Harper, J, Wallace, S, Norrie, J and Gilbert, P (2013) Exploring change processes in compassion focused therapy in psychosis: results of a feasibility randomized controlled trial, *British Journal of Clinical Psychology*, **52**, pp 199–214

Breines, J G and Chen, S (2013) Activating the inner caregiver: the role of support-giving schemas in increasing state self-compassion, *Journal of Experimental Social Psychology*, **49**, pp 58–64

Buss, D A (2009) The great struggles of life: Darwin and the emergence of evolutionary psychology, *American Psychologist*, **64**, pp 140–48, DOI: 10.1037/a0013207

Cannon, D (2012) *In-Depth Acting*, Oberon, London

Chiesa, A and Serretti, A (2009) Mindfulness-based stress reduction for stress management in healthy people: a review and meta-analysis, *The Journal of Alternative and Complementary Medicine*, **15** (5), pp 593–600

Cortina, M and Liotti, G (2010) Attachment is about safety and protection, intersubjectivity is about sharing and social understanding: the relationships between attachment and intersubjectivity, *Psychoanalytic Psychology*, **27**, pp 410–41

Costa, J and Pinto-Gouveia, J (2011) Acceptance of pain, self-compassion and psychopathology: using the chronic pain acceptance questionnaire to identify patients' subgroups, *Clinical Psychology and Psychotherapy*, **18**, pp 292–302

Cozolino, L (2007) *The Neuroscience of Human Relationships: Attachment and the developing brain*, Norton, New York

Cozolino, L (2008) *The Healthy Aging Brain: Sustaining attachment, attaining wisdom*, Norton, New York

Cozolino, L (2013) *The Social Neuroscience of Education*, Norton, New York

Dalai Lama (1995) *The Power of Compassion*, HarperCollins, India

Davidson, R and Harrington, A (2002, eds) *Visions of Compassion: Western scientists and Tibetan buddhists examine human nature*, Oxford University Press, New York

Davis, D and Hayes, J (2011) What are the benefits of mindfulness? A practice review of psychotherapy-related research, *Psychotherapy*, 48 (2), pp 198–208

Deci, E L and Ryan, R M (1985) *Intrinsic Motivation and Self-Determination in Human Behavior*, Plenum, New York

Depue, R A and Morrone-Strupinsky, J V (2005) A neurobehavioral model of affiliative bonding, *Behavioral and Brain Sciences*, 28, pp 313–95

Desbordes, G, Negi, L T, Pace, T W, Wallace, A B, Raison, C L and Schwartz, E L (2012) Effects of mindful-attention and compassion meditation training on amygdala response to emotional stimuli in an ordinary, non-meditative state, *Frontiers in Human Neuroscience*, 6 (292), pp 1–15

Fredrickson, B (1998) What good are positive emotions? *Review of General Psychology*, 2 (3), pp 300–19

Fredrickson, B (2001) The role of positive emotions in positive psychology, *American Psychologist*, 56 (3), pp 218–26

Germer, C K and Siegel, R D (2012) *Wisdom and Compassion in Psychotherapy*, Guilford Press, New York

Gilbert, P (1993) Defence and safety: their function in social behaviour and psychopathology, *British Journal of Clinical Psychology*, 32, pp 131–53

Gilbert, P (2009) *The Compassionate Mind: A new approach to the challenges of life*, Constable & Robinson, London

Gilbert, P (2010) *Compassion Focused Therapy*, The CBT Distinctive Features series, Routledge, London

Gilbert, P and Choden (2013) *Mindful Compassion*, Constable & Robinson, London

Gilbert, P and Irons, C (2005) Focused therapies and compassionate mind training for shame and self-attacking, in *Compassion: Conceptualisations, research and use in psychotherapy*, ed P Gilbert, (pp 263–325), Routledge, London

Gilbert, P P, McEwan, K K, Gibbons, L L, Chotai, S S, Duarte, J J and Matos, M M (2012) Fears of compassion and happiness in relation to alexithymia, mindfulness, and self-criticism, *Psychology and Psychotherapy: Theory, research and practice*, 85 (4), pp 374–90

Gilbert, P and Procter, S (2006) Compassionate mind training for people with high shame and self-criticism: overview and pilot study of a group therapy approach, *Clinical Psychology and Psychotherapy*, 13, pp 353–79

Gross, J J and Goldin, P R (2012) Enhancing compassion: a randomized controlled trial of a compassion cultivation training program, *Journal of Happiness Studies*

Grossman, P, Niemann, L, Schmidt, S and Walach, H (2004) Mindfulness-based stress reduction and health benefits: a meta-analysis, *Journal of Psychosomatic Research*, 57 (1), pp 35–43

Heffernan, M, Griffin, M, McNulty, S and Fitzpatrick, J J (2010) Self-compassion and emotional intelligence in nurses, *International Journal of Nursing Practice*, 16, pp 366–73

Hoffmann, S G, Grossman, P and Hinton, D E (2011) Loving-kindness and compassion meditation: potential for psychological intervention, *Clinical Psychology Review*, **13**, pp 1126–32

Hofmann, S G, Sawyer, A T, Witt, A A and Oh, D (2010) The effect of mindfulness-based therapy on anxiety and depression: a meta-analytic review, *Journal of Consulting and Clinical Psychology*, **78** (2), pp 169–83

Hollis-Walker, L and Colosimo, K (2011) Mindfulness, self-compassion, and happiness in non-meditators: a theoretical and empirical examination, *Personality and Individual Differences*, **50**, pp 222–27

Holzel, B K, Lazar, S W, Gard, T, Schuman-Olivier, Z, Vago, D R and Ott, U (2011) How does mindfulness meditation work? Proposing mechanisms of action from a conceptual and neural perspective, *Perspectives on Psychological Science*, **6**, pp 537–59

Jazaieri, H, Jinpa, G T, McGonigal, K, Rosenberg, E L, Finkelstein, J, Simon-Thomas, E, Cullen, M, Doty, J R and Jinpa, T (2010) Compassion cultivation training (CCT): instructor's manual. Unpublished, Stanford, CA

Jazaieri, H, Jinpa, G T, McGonigal, K, Rosenberg, E L, Finkelstein, J, Simon-Thomas, E, Cullen, M, Doty, J R, Gross, J J and Goldin, P R (2012) Enhancing compassion: a randomized controlled trial of a compassion cultivation training program, *Journal of Happiness Studies*, **14** (4), pp 1113–26

Kahneman, D (2011) *Thinking, Fast and Slow*, Macmillan, London

Kannan, D and Levitt, H M (2013) A review of client self-criticism in psychotherapy, *Journal of Psychotherapy Integration*, **23**, pp 166–78

Kellogg, S H (2004) Dialogical encounters: contemporary perspectives on 'chairwork' in psychotherapy, *Psychotherapy: Research, Theory, Practice, Training*, **41**, pp 310–20

Kelly, A C, Zuroff, D C, Foa, C L and Gilbert, P (2009) Who benefits from training in self-compassionate self-regulation? A study of smoking reduction, *Journal of Social and Clinical Psychology*, **29**, pp 727–55

Kelly, A C, Zuroff, D C, Leybman, M J and Gilbert, P (2012) Social safeness, received social support, and maladjustment: testing a tripartite model of affect regulation, *Cognitive Therapy and Research*, **36**, pp 815–26

Kim, S, Thibodeau, R and Jorgensen, R S (2011) Shame, guilt, and depressive symptoms: a meta-analytic review, *Psychological Bulletin*, **137**, pp 68–96

Kuyken, W, Watkins, E, Holden, E, White, K, Taylor, R S, Byford, S and Dalgleish, T (2010) How does mindfulness-based cognitive therapy work? *Behavior Research and Therapy*, **48**, pp 1105–12

Leary, M R, Tate, E B, Adams, C E, Allen, A B and Hancock, J (2007) Self-compassion and reactions to unpleasant self-relevant events: the implications of treating oneself kindly, *Journal of Personality and Social Psychology*, **92**, pp 887–904

LeDoux, J (1998) *The Emotional Brain*, Weidenfeld and Nicolson, London

Lee, W K and Bang, H L (2010) Effects of mindfulness-based group intervention on the mental health of middle-aged Korean women in community, *Stress and Health*, **26**, pp 341–48

Longe, O, Maratos, F A, Gilbert, P, Evans, G, Volker, F, Rockliffe, H and Rippon, G (2010) Having a word with yourself: neural correlates of self-criticism and self-reassurance, *NeuroImage*, **49**, pp 1849–56

Lutz, A, Brefczynski-Lewis, J, Johnstone, T and Davidson, R J (2008) Regulation of the neural circuitry of emotion by compassion meditation: effects of the meditative expertise, *Public Library of Science*, 3, pp 1–5

Lyubomirsky, S J (2007) *The How of Happiness*, Sphere, New York

Magnus, C, Kowalski, K and McHugh, T (2010) The role of self-compassion in women's self-determined motives to exercise and exercise-related outcomes, *Self and Identity*, 9, pp 363–82

McLean, P (1990) *The Triune Brain in Evolution: Role in paleocerebral functions*, Plenum Press, New York

Meevissen, Y M C, Peters, M L and Alberts, H J E M (2011) Become more optimistic by imagining a best possible self: effects of a two week intervention, *Journal of Behavior Therapy and Experimental Psychiatry*, 42, pp 371–78

Miller, W and Rollnick, S (2013) *Motivational Interviewing: Helping people change* (3rd edn), Guilford Press, New York

Neff, K (2011) *Self Compassion*, Morrow, New York

Neff, K D (2003) The development and validation of a scale to measure self-compassion, *Self and Identity*, 2, pp 223–50

Neff, K D (2012) The science of self-compassion, in *Compassion and Wisdom in Psychotherapy*, eds C Germer and R Siegel (pp 79–92), Guilford Press, New York

Neff, K D and Beretvas, S N (2012) The role of self-compassion in romantic relationships, *Self and Identity*, 12 (1)

Neff, K D and Germer, C K (2012) A pilot study and randomised controlled trial of the mindful self-compassion programme, *J Clin Psychol*, 00 pp 1–17

Neff, K D, Hsieh, Y and Dejitterat, K (2005) Self-compassion, achievement goals and coping with academic failure, *Self and Identity*, 4, pp 263–87

Neff, K D and Pommier, E (2012) The relationship between self-compassion and other-focused concern among college undergraduates, community adults, and practicing meditators, *Self and Identity*, 12 (2), pp 160–76

Neff, K D, Rude, S S and Kirkpatrick, K (2007) An examination of self-compassion in relation to positive psychological functioning and personality traits, *Journal of Research in Personality*, 41, pp 908–16

Pace, T W, Negi, L T, Adame, D D, Cole, S P, Sivilli, T I, Brown, T D, *et al* (2009) Effect of compassion meditation on neuroendocrine, innate immune and behavioral responses to psychosocial stress, *Psychoneuroendocrinology*, 34, pp 87–98

Panksepp, J (1998) *Affective Neuroscience: The foundations of human and animal emotions*, Oxford University Press, Oxford

Panksepp, J (2010) Affective neuroscience of the emotional brainmind: evolutionary perspectives and implications for understanding depression, *Dialogues in Clinical Neuroscience*, 12, pp 383–99

Peters, M L, Flink, I K, Boersma, K and Linton, S J (2010) Manipulating optimism: can imagining a best possible self be used to increase positive future expectancies? *The Journal of Positive Psychology*, 5, pp 204–11

Phillips, A and Taylor, B (2009) *On Kindness*, Hamish Hamilton Press, London

Porges (2007) The polyvagal perspective, *Biological Psychology*, 74 (2), pp 116–43

Rimes, K A and Wingrove, J (2011) Pilot study of Mindfulness-Based Cognitive Therapy for trainee clinical psychologists, *Behavioural and Cognitive Psychotherapy*, 39 (2), pp 235–41

Rockliff, H, Karl, A, McEwan, K, Gilbert, J, Matos, M and Gilbert, P (2011) Effects of intranasal oxytocin on compassion focused imagery, *Emotion*, **11**, pp 1388–96

Salzberg, S (1997) *Lovingkindness: The revolutionary art of happiness*, Shambala, Boston, MA

Sbarra, D A, Smith, H L and Mehl, M R (2012) When leaving your ex, love yourself: observational ratings of self-compassion predict the course of emotional recovery following marital separation, *Psychological Science*, **23** (3), pp 261–69

Siegel, D (2012) *The Developing Mind* (2nd edn), Guilford Press, New York

Shapiro, S L, Astin, J A, Bishop, S R and Cordova, M (2005) Mindfulness-based stress reduction for health care professionals: results from a randomized trial, *International Journal of Stress Management*, **12** (2), pp 164–76

Shapiro, J, Astin, J, Shapiro, S L, Robitshek, D and Shapiro, D H (2011) Coping with loss of control in the practice of medicine, *Family Systems Health*, **29** (1), pp 15–28

Shapiro, S L, Brown, K W and Biegel, G M (2007) Teaching self-care to caregivers: effects of mindfulness-based stress reduction on the mental health of therapists in training, *Training and Education in Professional Psychology*, **1**, pp 105–15

Siegel, D (2012) *The Developing Mind: How relationships and the brain interact to shape who we are*, Guilford Press, New York

Taylor, P, Gooding, P, Wood, A N and Tarrier, N (2011) The role of defeat and entrapment in depression, anxiety and suicide, *Psychological Bulletin*, **137**, pp 391–420

Terry, M L and Leary, M R (2011) Self-compassion, self-regulation, and health, *Self and Identity*, **10**, pp 352–62

Trevarthen, C and Aitken, K (2001) Infant intersubjectivity: research, theory, and clinical applications, *Journal of Child Psychology and Psychiatry*, **42**, pp 3–48

Tsering, G T (2008) *The Awakening Mind: The foundation of Buddhist thought: Volume 4*, Wisdom Press, London

Van Doesum, N J, Van Lange, D A and Van Lange, P A (2013) Social mindfulness: skill and will to navigate the social world, *Journal of Personality and Social Psychology*, **105**, pp 86–103

Vettese, L C, Dyer, C E, Li, W L and Wekerle, C (2011) Does self-compassion mitigate the association between childhood maltreatment and later emotional regulation difficulties? *International Journal of Mental Health and Addiction*, **9**, pp 480–91 www.viacharacter.org/viainstitute/classification.aspx [accessed 17 December 2013]

Weng, H Y, Fox, A S, Shackman, A J, Stodola, D E, Caldwell, J Z K, Olson, M C, Rogers, G M and Davidson, R J (2013) Compassion training alters altruism and neural responses to suffering, *Psychological Science*, **24**, 1171–80

Yarnell and Neff (2012) Self-compassion, interpersonal conflict resolutions and wellbeing, *Self and Identity*, pp 1–14

Zuroff, D C, Santor, D and Mongrain, M (2005) Dependency, self-criticism, and maladjustment, in *Relatedness, Self-Definition and Mental Representation: Essays in honour of Sidney J. Blatt*, eds J S Auerbach, K N Levy and C E Schaffer, (pp 75–90), London, New York

Acceptance and commitment coaching

10

TIM ANSTISS AND RICH BLONNA

Introduction

This chapter explores the theoretical underpinnings, empirical support, key concepts, tools and strategies for coaching people towards improved health, wellbeing and performance using acceptance and commitment coaching (AC coaching), the coaching version of acceptance and commitment therapy.

AC coaching is an holistic and multi-component approach to helping people. It is a pragmatic form of coaching, underpinned by functional contextualism and relational frame theory. The goal of AC coaching is to help clients increase their psychological flexibility – a state characterized by being clear about and living in harmony with one's values, spending time in the present moment, defusing and gaining separation from thoughts, accepting unwanted, unpleasant and unhelpful feelings and sensations and cultivating the perspective of the observing self.

In contrast to much cognitive-behavioural coaching, AC coaches help their clients change their relationship with their cognitions (thoughts, images, beliefs, memories, etc) rather than trying to change their form or content of their clients' thoughts. Clients are guided and encouraged to notice the rise and fall of unpleasant and unhelpful thoughts and feelings, and to take these thoughts, feelings and sensations with them as they go about living the kind of life they want for themselves. AC coaches consider experiential avoidance – the struggle with unwanted thoughts and feelings, including attempts to control or suppress them – to be at the heart of many people's problems with living and the opposite of acceptance and psychological flexibility.

In this chapter we introduce the Ramp Model of AC coaching, which emphasizes the need for clients to expend effort and take the time to practise (within and between sessions) and develop several key skills that are necessary for psychological flexibility, improved function, quality of life, thriving and flourishing.

Evidence-based approach to AC coaching

AC coaching is the coaching version of acceptance and commitment therapy or ACT (pronounced 'act' and not 'A C T'). ACT is an extensively evaluated approach to helping people, with proven effectiveness in a range of conditions. With its origins in the science of behavioural analysis and, more specifically, Relational Frame Theory (Hayes, 2004) ACT is sometimes considered to be part of a 'third wave' of behavioural approaches (which includes mindfulness-based CBT, DBT, and compassion-focussed therapy), to differentiate it from 'first wave' (eg Pavlov, Skinner and Watson, etc), 'second wave' (eg the REBT of Albert Ellis, the CBT of Tim Beck, etc) approaches to helping people change their behaviour. RFT explains why cognitive fusion (excessive identification with thought, beliefs, images and memories) and experiential avoidance are both so common and so unhelpful. AC coaching, like acceptance and commitment therapy, helps clients to reduce cognitive fusion and experiential avoidance, giving clients more freedom to take their lives in the direction of their choice, in line with their values.

Acceptance and mindfulness

Around 2000, exposure-based approaches to human change began to focus as much or more on contact with private internal events rather than external events (Barlow, 2002) and sought to alter the function of these internal events, without necessarily changing their content or form. A growing emphasis on understanding the context of events and experiences (eg, Bouton, Mineka and Barlow, 2001) combined with positive outcomes for dialectical behaviour therapy (DBT) (Linehan, 1993; Hayes *et al*, 2004) increased recognition of the value of acceptance and mindfulness in helping people change unhelpful or unwanted behaviours (Hayes, Follette and Linehan, 2004; Hayes *et al*, 1994). Attentional and metacognitive perspectives (eg Wells, 1994) suggested that trying to change the frequency and/or content of particular thoughts and beliefs may be less helpful than helping people cope better with them, and more emphasis on helping clients contact the present moment (eg, Borkovec and Roemer, 1994; Teasdale *et al*, 2002) yielded a growing body of evidence that the function of thoughts can be altered without altering their form.

Pragmaticism

ACT is based on a form of pragmatism known as functional contextualism (Biglan and Hayes, 1996; Hayes, Hayes and Reese 1988; Hayes *et al*, 1993). The unit of analysis is the 'ongoing act in context' – and the context in which a particular act takes place is key to a proper understanding of its function.

Psychological events are seen as interactions between organisms and their contexts. The truth criterion of contextual approaches such as ACT is what works (Hayes *et al*, 1988), and in order to know what works there must first be an understanding of what one is working towards, one's goals (Hayes, 1993). Acceptance and commitment practitioners do not waste time trying to discover what is true or real, realizing that we know the world via our interactions in and with it and that these interactions are historically and contextually limited. Instead, acceptance and commitment practitioners try to bring about helpful change, and their interventions are 'true' to the extent they do so. 'Truth' in ACT is about helpfulness, not logic or accuracy. Coaches encourage their clients to 'abandon any interest in the literal truth of their own thoughts or evaluations' (Hayes, 2004) and guide and encourage them to 'embrace a passionate and ongoing interest in how to live according to their values'.

Relational Frame Theory

ACT builds upon a functional contextual programme of basic research on language and cognition. Called Relational Frame Theory (Hayes *et al*, 2001), this approach to language and cognition attempts to provide basic principles for all forms of cognitive intervention. It maintains that at the core of human language and thought is the ability to learn to relate events under arbitrary contextual control. For instance, if one object looks the same as, or bigger than, another object, many animals can learn that relationship and show it with new objects that are related in the same way (Reese, 1968). Human beings are especially able to abstract the features of such relational responding and transfer the learning to events that are not formally related, or related on the basis of social whim or convention. For example, having learned that 'x' is 'smaller than' 'X' humans may later be able to apply this stimulus relation to events under the control of arbitrary cues (such as the words 'smaller than'). A young child may know that a nickel is bigger than a dime, but an older child will learn that a nickel is 'smaller than' a dime by attribution (even though in a formal, physical sense, it is not). And while animals tend to associate things only when they are presented in a particular order, humans (with our fantastic linguistic abilities) are able to associate all kinds of things together regardless of the order in which they are presented, and it is possible to teach even young children large and complex relational networks (Smeets, Barnes and Roche, 1997). Carefully controlled empirical studies on RFT have consistently demonstrated that relational responses can and do occur in a manner consistent with RFT principles (Hayes *et al*, 2001).

Relational Frame Theory explains human psychological problems as arising because derived relations dominate over other sources of behavioural regulation, and because human beings have difficulty detecting the ongoing process of thinking as distinct from the products and objects of thinking (ie thoughts). This 'cognitive fusion' leads to powerful evaluations becoming attached to internal events, and people predicting, fearing and attempting to regulate and avoid their inner experiences, thoughts, feelings and bodily sensations even when this 'experiential avoidance' process is harmful to them (Hayes *et al*, 1996). You may be able to run away from a dangerous predator, and indeed probably should – but you can't really run away from frightening thoughts, even though many people expend an awful lot of time and effort trying to do just that. Cognitive fusion also leads to people becoming overly attached to labels about themselves and to them becoming much less aware of the present moment. These processes result in 'psychological inflexibility' – which is the inability to persist with or change behaviour in the service of chosen values. AC coaching and ACT both aim to increase client psychological flexibility. What clients choose to do with their increased psychological flexibility is up to them.

Evidence

Correlational evidence

The Acceptance and Action Questionnaire (AAQ) (Hayes, Strosahl *et al*, 2004) measures the degree to which an individual fuses with thoughts, avoids feelings, and is unable to act in the presence of difficult private events. A large number of correlational studies have demonstrated an association between scores on the AAQ or a variant (eg the CPAQ) and measures of psychopathology and quality of life. For instance: perceived physical health, wellbeing at work, job-induced tension and depression symptoms (Bond and Bunce, 2000); performance, negativity and job satisfaction (Bond and Bunce, 2003); feelings of general health (Donaldson-Feilder and Bond, 2004); depression symptoms (Dykstra and Follette, 1998; Polusny *et al*, 2004; Strosahl *et al*, 1998; Toarmino Pistorello and Hayes, 1997; Tull *et al*, 2004); various fears and phobias (Dykstra and Follette, 1998); anxiety severity (Forsyth, Parker and Finlay, 2003); post-traumatic stress (Gold, Marx and Lexington, 2007; Marx and Sloan, 2005); deliberate self harm scores (Gratz and Roemer, 2004); parenting stress (Greco *et al*, 2005); depression about pain, anxiety about pain and medication taken for pain (McCracken, MacKichan and Eccleston, 2007; McCracken, Vowles and Eccleston, 2004).

Interventional evidence

ACT is recognized as 'empirically supported' by the US Substance Abuse and Mental Health Services Administration (SAMHSA, 2012) in their national registry of evidence-based programmes and practices in the areas of obsessive–compulsive disorder (OCD), depression, general mental health, and rehospitalization; and by the American Psychological Association

Division 12 Society of Clinical Psychology (APA Div 12 SCP, 2012) as having modest research support for depression, OCD, psychosis, and 'mixed anxiety' (a sample composed of panic disorder, social phobia, OCD, and generalized anxiety disorder (GAD), and strong research support for chronic pain. In a recent review of the evidence of effectiveness of ACT, Smout *et al* (2012) found that good-quality studies could be considered to offer National Health and Medical Research Council Level II evidence for chronic pain, obsessive-compulsive disorder, and a subset of other anxiety disorders (panic disorder, social phobia, and generalized anxiety disorder).

Evidence of varying quality also supports the effectiveness of ACT in the following conditions: tinnitus (Westin *et al*, 2011); cancer wellbeing (Rost *et al*, 2012; Branstetter *et al*, 2004; Montesinos and Luciano, 2005; Páez, Luciano and Gutiérrez, 2007); borderline personality disorder pathology (Morton *et al*, 2012); disordered eating (Weineland *et al*, 2012); pain (Wicksell *et al*, 2009; Wetherell *et al*, 2011; Mo'tamedi, Rezaiemaram and Tavallaie, 2012); psychosis (White *et al*, 2011; Shawyer *et al*, 2012); substance use (Smout *et al*, 2010; Stotts *et al*, 2012; Gifford *et al*, 2011; Hernández-López *et al*, 2009); epilepsy (Lundgren *et al*, 2006; Lundgren *et al*, 2008); weight loss (Forman *et al*, 2009; Lillis *et al*, 2009); diabetes (Gregg *et al*, 2007); multiple sclerosis (Sánchez, and Luciano, 2005); HIV prevention (Gutiérrez *et al*, 2007); Systemic Lupus Erythematosus (Quirosa *et al*, 2009); chess-players' performance (Ruiz and Luciano, 2012) and reducing prejudice and stigma (Hayes *et al*, 2004; Masuda *et al*, 2007).

Practice: tools and techniques

The effective AC coach will be familiar with the theoretical framework of the approach (RFT, functional contextualism, pragmatism and mindfulness) along with some core concepts and a range of tools, techniques and strategies to help clients become more psychologically flexible. They will also use one or more visual models or frameworks to guide their practice. In this chapter we introduce the Ramp Model of AC coaching, but coaches may also wish to familiarize themselves with the hexaflex model, which we omit here due to space considerations. Jumping in with isolated tools and techniques in an unfocused, ad hoc, unguided way will be unlikely to lead to the desired level of client improvement – so the following section and case study tries to show how to integrate theory, concepts, and tools and techniques in a unified, systematic, client-focused manner.

Core concepts

Core concepts in AC coaching include: private experience; experiential avoidance; psychological flexibility; cognitive fusion; workability; and common humanity.

Private experiences

Private experience refers to those things we experience inside our minds and which are not available for other people to experience. Harris (2010) nicely classifies these using the acronym EMITS:

- Emotions and feelings.
- Memories.
- Images.
- Thoughts.
- Sensations.

These private experiences can be pleasant or unpleasant, helpful or un-helpful, barely noticeable or overwhelming and insistent. One of the core tasks of the AC coach is to help their client to accept that however un-pleasant, unhelpful, confusing or painful these private experiences may be, they are not the client's main issue or problem. Their main issue, what is holding them back from reaching their goals and living the kind of life they want for themselves, is how they react to and try to deal with these private experiences.

Please notice the difference with traditional cognitive behavioural ap-proaches which, building on the Greek Stoic philosopher Epictetus (Oldfather, 1925), are guided by the dictum: 'It is not that which befalls man which upsets him, but the view he takes of things.' AC coaches go one further than this. They would say something like: 'It is not that which befalls man which upsets him, nor the view he takes of things. Rather it is how he deals with his private inner experiences which determines much of his quality of life and personal effectiveness.' Not quite as punchy, for sure, but putting emphasis on the client's relationship with their beliefs rather than the form of content of those beliefs.

One very common (and understandable) way in which people deal with unwanted private experiences is avoidance – either by avoiding doing the things which bring them on, or doing things to make the experiences go away as quickly as possible.

Experiential avoidance

As previously mentioned, much of what we experience inside our minds and bodies is unhelpful, unwanted and uncomfortable/painful. Naturally we may seek to avoid situations that seem to bring on these uncomfortable experiences, and/or to reduce the intensity and duration of these experi-ences once we have them. This is experiential avoidance and is considered by the AC coach as the client's main issue or problem, the thing on which they should be focusing their efforts. That is why a large chunk of what the coach does is psychoeducation and Socratic questioning – to help the client 'reframe' what it is that needs to change. The AC coach helps the client to see that is it not their unwanted experiences per se that are the main cause of their frustration, difficulty, struggle or dissatisfaction, but rather the strategies and tactics they have been using to avoid or attempt to control or reduce these experiences, troubling thoughts and painful emotions. For instance, a person who experiences anxiety about delivering a presentation at work may avoid doing this and may thus limit their career growth opportunities. A person who experiences anxiety when talking with (or thinking about talking with) members of the opposite sex may avoid this activity and be more lonely as a result. A person who experiences uncomfortable symptoms when exercising may avoid this and end up less fit and more heavy as a result. A person who experiences sadness or loneliness when alone at home in the evening may binge on food or consume too much alcohol to reduce those feelings.

These are all examples of experiential avoidance. You can perhaps see how this one common psychological process underlies many human problems – including career and relationship difficulties, underperformance in sports, arts and the bedroom, along with several chronic physical and psychological health problems. The range of things people do which – depending on the context – may be considered experience avoidance include: procrastination; becoming angry; promiscuous sex; drug taking; staying in bed; staying in unhelpful relationships; being unassertive; not leaving the house, etc. That is why AC therapy is referred to as 'transdiagnostic', maintaining that a common set of psychological processes underlie a wide range of 'diagnoses'.

Cognitive fusion and entanglement

Imagine frying an egg in an old frying pan without any oil. Chances are the egg will become stuck to the pan. Once cooked it won't slide off the pan onto the plate and bits may remain stuck even after using a spatula. The protein in the egg has become fused with the metal of the pan. This is a bit like what happens with some thoughts beliefs, rules, saying, words, phrases, images and memories. They can become 'stuck' to our minds and follow us around, forcing us to see the world through their often unhelpful perspective – 'you're a loser', 'people don't like you', 'all men are the same', 'I'll never be able to do this', 'there is something the matter with me', 'you're lazy', 'you're a coward' etc. However much we try, we can't seem to shake these thoughts off. Worse still, the more we struggle with these unwanted thoughts and feelings, the stronger and more insistent/persistent they sometimes become, and even if we can make them go away for a while (eg via distraction, medication, or some types of therapy) they seem to come back.

Workability

Clients will often have tried to 'fix themselves' or make progress before coming to coaching, perhaps for several years. But the strategies and approaches they have been using may not have been working for them, or may only have worked for a brief period of time before leading to other problems, eg excessive eating or drinking to avoid certain unwanted feelings which then cause other issues of their own. AC coaches call such strategies 'unworkable'. They have not been working. The concept of 'workability' applies not just to coping strategies but also to beliefs. Compared to a traditional cognitive behavioural practitioner, AC coaches are much less interested in whether or not a client's beliefs are empirically true. It is more important to explore with the client whether their thoughts or beliefs are helpful to them living the valued life they want for themselves. By way of example, imagine you are trapped in an upstairs room in an old building. A fire is raging outside the door and smoke is coming in. Stay put and you will die. You decide to open the window and climb 30 feet down the drainpipe to safety. You really need to concentrate on keeping hold of the drainpipe, slowly moving hands and feet down, one after the other, again and again and again. But the drainpipe is old. You think 'this pipe could break, or detach from the wall, and then I would fall and may die'. Is this thought true, factually correct? Yes. Is it helpful to have this thought at this time? Does it help with survival and the project of escaping to safety? Not really. In AC coaching we help clients focus on the workability and usefulness of their belief systems, not their truth or 'believability'.

One technique for helping clients change their relationship with some of their beliefs is to ask them: 'to what extent does that thought or belief help you in making progress towards your goals, towards the life you want to lead?'. Of course, it is important we do this with empathy and compassion, rather than sarcastically throwing out the comment 'and how's that working out for you?'.

Common humanity

We all struggle. In different ways, of course. But we all struggle and no one gets out alive. Struggle, frustration, anxiety, self-doubt, suffering, confusion, self-defeating behaviours, unfairness – these experiences are all part of our common humanity, things we share with every other human being on the planet. Yes, even the fabulously wealthy, famous, powerful and beautiful struggle – just open any newspaper to learn of their addictions, suicides and troubled and problematic relationships. Even AC coaches struggle and have unwanted, painful private experiences – and it is perfectly acceptable for the coach to share with the client some of the ways in which they themselves struggle, emphasizing our common humanity and the traps we are all prone to. Of course, the coach may also wish to model how they practice and try to cultivate psychological flexibility (see below) and in so doing help to develop client self-efficacy, one source of which is vicarious learning (Bandura, 1977).

So the AC coach helps their client accept that they are not alone in suffering and experiencing the frustrations that they do, and perhaps also that their struggle and their unwanted, painful, and unhelpful experiences and behaviours are not really their fault. That the language function we have in our brains, while immensely helpful in solving problems in the real world outside of ourselves (witness the many achievements of science) can be really quite useless – or worse than useless – when we try and use it to solve the problems inside our heads. That is why so much of what the AC coach does is to try to reduce the power and influence of words and thoughts on the person's behaviour and wellbeing.

Psychological flexibility

Psychological flexibility is something AC coaches want for both themselves and their clients. Psychological flexibility enables us to make progress towards valued goals and to live lives of better quality – more meaningful, more vital and more rewarding lives. A lack of psychological flexibility is the main reason clients get stuck (from an AC perspective). People who lack psychological flexibility:

1 tend to have a lack of clarity about what is important to them;

2 tend to take insufficient committed action in the direction of their values;

3 tend to avoid unpleasant or unwanted thoughts, feelings and sensations;

4 tend to 'fuse with' and get entangled with their thoughts, memories and images of the future;

5 tend to have a lack of contact with the present moment; and

6 tend to be over-attached to their 'narrative' self, their self story and various rules and assumptions that they have about themselves.

AC coaches seek to guide their clients from psychological inflexibility towards psychological flexibility. They use a mixture of psychological education, metaphor, experiential exercises, Socratic methods, modelling of helpful attitudes and behaviours, practice assignments, goal setting, reflection and feedback in order to help their clients:

1 clarify and live more fully in harmony with their values;

2 take effective (committed) action towards goals which are in harmony with these values;

3 disentangle, distance and defuse themselves from unhelpful, unwanted and uncomfortable thoughts;

4 accept, open up to, allow, tolerate and make room for unpleasant feelings and sensations;

5 pay attention with openness, flexibility and curiosity to what is happening in the present moment; and

6 cultivate and view the world from the perspective of the observing self – that silent, quiet part of oneself that persists through time, observing and noticing change in the world but which does not itself get caught up in those changes.

The Ramp Model of AC coaching

In this chapter we introduce the Ramp Model of AC coaching (Figure 10.1) to help the coach guide their client towards increased psychological flexibility. It shows how psychological flexibility is increased by making progress in each of six different domains or psychological processes, while suggesting a sense of direction or movement, a bit of a journey. The coach's role is to help the client make progress up the ramp – perhaps first working on one skill, and then another. In reality, the AC coach works with the client on several skills in any one particular coaching session, and the component skills are all interconnected. For instance, when you cultivate the perspective of the observing self you will most likely also defuse from some unhelpful beliefs. And as you learn to accept and make space for uncomfortable feeling and bodily sensations, you will also be more able to take effective action in the world. The Ramp Model also suggests that: a) effort is required to make progress (it won't happen spontaneously); b) 'backsliding' is not unexpected; c) the coach cannot do it for the client, or fix them, and; d) that there are multiple skills to be developed and practised, not just one. (Some clients think that insight alone will fix them: 'If only I knew why I am like this, why this happened, why this stuff keeps happening, then I will be better.' Not from the perspective of AC coaching. Insight may not be required at all.)

FIGURE 10.1   Ramp Model of AC coaching

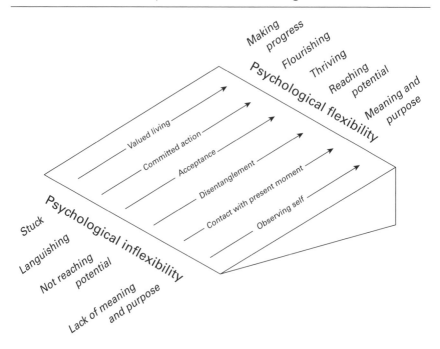

During each session, the coach helps nudge the client further up the slope of the wedge, towards a more vital, engaged, thriving, values driven life and way of living.

Let us look at each of these processes or skills in turn, and show how the AC coach helps the client to develop more psychological flexibility.

Tools and techniques

To help clients make progress, flourish, experience more psychological flexibility and live more meaningful, vital and rewarding lives, AC coaches help clients to:

- clarify their values;
- take committed action;
- accept unwanted thoughts and feelings;
- defuse and disentangle from certain thoughts, beliefs and images;
- contact the present moment; and
- cultivate the observing self.

Clarifying values

According to Blonna (2010), when clients are not clear about their values it is like they are in a sailboat without a rudder. They find it very hard to stay on course, especially when navigating the rough seas of their lives. Values are the rudder that allows clients to steer their ship along the course they've set to reach their goals.

AC coaches help their clients clarify their values and see how moving towards and living more fully in harmony with their values will likely bring about more meaning, purpose, vitality, engagement and wellbeing in their lives. Values are the things which are most important to us, which relate to and inform what we want our lives to be about. They inform and shape how we behave. Values are personally chosen, not imposed by others as 'shoulds' or 'musts'. They can be considered compass points – providing a direction for our lives and enabling us to check, from time to time, if our lives are going in the right direction. Values are not goals. Goals are things that can be 'reached' or 'achieved'. Values are things that can be 'lived in harmony with', 'expressed', 'turned towards' or 'moved in the direction of'. The question 'Am I done yet?' can be asked of goals, but not values (Hayes and Smith, 2005). Wilson and Murrell (2004) used the term 'valued living', emphasizing that this is an ongoing process and not an outcome. Living in harmony with our values provides us with multiple and sustainable sources of positive reinforcement, provides us with both intrinsic and autonomous sources of motivation and contributed to life satisfaction. AC coaches help their clients to see how clarifying and living more fully in harmony with their values can help them to flourish as a human being, to live the kind of life they want for themselves, and to reach their potential.

Values clarification may be one of the first things an AC coach does with a client, since until the coach knows what it is their client values it can be hard to identify in what ways their psychological inflexibility and experiential avoidance is getting in the way. The AC coach has a range of tools and strategies to help clients clarify what is important to them, including:

- selecting and prioritizing from a list of values;
- using a 'values card sorting' exercise, placing different value cards into different piles according to their relative importance;
- visualization exercises, such as asking the client to describe what their life will be like when it is going well, or the 'attending one's own funeral' exercise where the client is asked to describe what they would like people attending their funeral to be thinking and saying about them;
- having the client talk about their values in different areas or domains of life;
- using the 'values compass' exercise or worksheet (**www.thehappinesstrap.com/upimages/Values_Questionnaire.pdf**);
- using a questionnaire such as the Valued Living Questionnaire (**www.mindfulness-extended.nl/content3/wp-content/uploads/2013/07/Valued-Living-Questionnaire-EN.pdf**), the Personal Values Questionnaire or the Survey of Life Principles.

The AC coach also touches on values from time to time during ongoing coaching – asking such questions as 'does this move you in the direction of your values, or away from the life you want to be living?' or 'what would you like to do, to take you in the right direction for a meaningful life for you?'.

Taking committed action

Thinking and talking will only get the client so far – and perhaps not very far at that. For the client to make progress they need to act, to behave differently. Like many other coaches, the AC coach helps the client:

- set long-term and short-term goals in harmony with their values;
- make plans for new (values-consistent) behaviour, so that it is more likely to occur;
- publicly commit to a particular course of action;
- do the required behaviours; and
- be willing to experience uncomfortable thoughts, feelings and sensations as they make behaviour changes.

Blonna (2010) describes willingness as the internal part of commitment, and a willing mind is one that understands the need to act while accepting that you can't figure everything out in your head in advance. The external part of committed action is the physical act of doing something constructive. Taking construction action means behaving in values-congruent ways that help you meet your goals.

Some clients may need to develop or improve their skills in order to take committed action. For instance, a single person who values a warm, committed relationship may need to develop their dating skills; a person who struggles with anger at work but values being a good colleague may need to develop their anger management skills; and an overweight person who values their independence may need to develop their food selection, preparation and healthy eating skills, as well as their ability to tolerate unpleasant feelings that may have historically triggered overeating.

It is important that clients do not to feel overwhelmed by a commitment to live in harmony with their values, but rather to realize that, regardless of recent or previous behaviour, they can always choose – moment by moment – to turn towards their values, and have their values guide what they are going to do next. Like falling off a bicycle, the client can always choose to get back on and continue moving in a particular direction – towards a life that matters for them.

Accept unwanted and unhelpful thoughts and feelings

Acceptance involves a willingness to have what is being experienced right now (Flaxman, Blackledge and Bond, 2011), including uncomfortable thoughts, feelings and sensations. The client does not have to want these experiences, just be able to tolerate them, accept them and allow them to be. And, importantly, for the unpleasant, unwanted experiences to be experienced as they are, not as the mind says they are (Forsyth and Eifert, 2007). Acceptance is the opposite of experiential avoidance, and it involves a willingness to experience the unwanted and distressing thoughts and feelings that surface in one's life.

Since avoiding uncomfortable experiences (anxiety, anger, sadness, shame, fast heart rate, unpleasant images, etc) is natural, the AC coach may have to first explain to the client why learning to tolerate, be with and accept these feelings may be a good idea. This involves some psychoeducation about the fact that it is not the experience itself that is problematic and holding them back from the life they want to live, but the things they are doing to avoid or attempt to control the experience. A range of metaphors exist to help the client 'get' the importance of acceptance rather than avoidance, including:

- *Passengers on the bus.* The client is a bus driver, and whenever they turn the bus in the direction they want to go, passengers become noisy and come up to the front and threaten the driver, telling him to change direction. Often the driver does what the passengers say, and turns the bus away from the direction he or she wanted to take it. But the passengers can never actually harm the driver. If the driver keeps going in the direction they want, the passengers will make some noise but will not ever touch or harm the driver. In this metaphor, the passengers are the client's thoughts and feelings, and the bus is their life.

- *Unwanted visitor at a party.* You're having a party with friends, and an unpleasant neighbour turns up and barges in. You spend time trying to get him to leave, with little success. You get angry with him, spend less time with your friends, and begin to feel that the party is spoiled. Alternatively, you could choose to spend time doing what you want to do at your party with your friends, and just let the unwanted visitor be – not wanting them, but allowing them to be present, accepting and making space for them.

Once the client accepts (or accepts the possibility) that giving up their struggle with, and learning the skills of tolerating and allowing unwanted thoughts and feelings can help them get on with their lives, the AC coach helps them learn how to more fully notice, experience, take in, tolerate and be with the unwanted feelings, using various mindfulness, visualization and breathing exercises. They encourage the client to be open and curious about their inner experience and sensations, like a scientist – trying to locate in it their body, to describe it as a colour or an object, and to try to 'breath into' the sensation or experience, and to 'soften' around it. This is a form of exposure therapy. Once clients are more able to accept and tolerate their unwanted experiences, they are often able to see how they are now in a better position to get on with their lives – taking their unwanted experiences and sensations with them.

Disentangling and defusing from thoughts

The AC coach uses a variety of tools and strategies to help their clients (and themselves) become less entangled and fused with their unhelpful thoughts, beliefs, rules, saying, words, phrases, images and memories. Different metaphors are used to help clients get the idea of fusion – such as the egg stuck to a frying pan, or 'radio doom and gloom' always playing in the background telling the client unhelpful stuff, or 'getting hooked like a fish' in which the more you struggle with a particular thought or belief, trying to change it, the more it hooks you and prevents you from moving on. Some coaches invest in some Chinese paper finger traps. Once both index fingers are inserted the more you pull your hands apart the tighter they grip the fingers. In order to free yourself you need to stop struggling and push the fingers towards each other so the grip lessens. Another experiential exercise to help clients get the importance of noticing thoughts rather than seeing the world through them includes having the client write down some of the unhelpful thoughts and words they use about themselves on a sheet of paper. Then having them hold this piece of paper up in front of their face and asking them to walk around the room. They will, of course, experience some difficulty with this task as a result of having their view obstructed. Then ask the client to take the piece of paper away from their face and hold it lower down their body and perform the same task of walking round the room. Asking them what they noticed may evoke something like 'well, it's a lot easier now' – and the parallel can be made with how holding onto our thoughts and beliefs too tightly and closely can lead to problems with navigating one's life and making progress in the world.

There are a large number of exercises the coach can use with clients to help them develop their skills in distancing and defusing from their thoughts and images, including:

- leaves on a stream;
- seeing thoughts as if on a blank TV screen;
- singing the thoughts or saying them in a funny voice;
- repeating the word 50 times;
- thanking the mind for having the thought; and
- saying 'I'm having the thought that...'

The interested coach will be able to find instructions for these and other experiential exercises in the further reading section at the end of this chapter.

Of course, the reason to help the client defuse and distance from un-helpful thoughts and beliefs is to increase their freedom to act in a desired way, to give them more control over the direction of their lives, to give them more choice on a moment to moment basis. It helps them to more fully engage with the world as it is, via the senses, rather than experiencing the world through filters of words, images and other cognitions. Thoughts, images and memories come to be seen as things that come and go, which rise and fall, of their own accord and in their own time – rather than things that are to be struggled with, fought, suppressed, argued with or blotted out.

Spending more time in contact with the present moment

Unhelpful and unwanted thoughts and images are commonly about the past or the future – not about what is happening in the immediate moment. Many emotions and feelings have a past or future orientation – for instance sadness, regret, anger, shame, guilt, bitterness and hurt tend to be 'back-wards looking' emotions, while anxiety, fear and dread tend to be 'forward oriented' emotions. But the past and the future have no independent exist-ence outside of a human brain, they are not 'real'. By helping clients connect with, experience and spend more time in the present moment the AC coach helps reduce some of the power of the client's recalled past and anticipated future. It also helps the client who is experiencing some anxiety or other intense unwanted feelings in the session become more grounded and less distressed and distracted.

Blonna (2010) (building on Germer, Siegel and Fulton (2005)) outlines four aspects of mindful moments:

1 They focus on the present moment.
2 They are non-judgemental, accepting the present moment for what it is.

3 They are non-verbal. Adding speech to describe the present moment adds a level of interpretation and is one step removed from the here and now.

4 They are non-conceptual. During mindful moments nothing gets figured out, worked on, analysed, or solved.

The AC coach helps the client spend time in the present moment in a non-judgemental, non-labelling way – just paying attention to the raw sensations that change, rise and fall both outside and inside their skin. Wilson and colleagues (Wilson *et al*, 2001) emphasize that evaluative language – our ability to label, rate, judge things as good or bad, wanted or unwanted, acceptable or unacceptable, forgivable or unforgivable, etc – is at the heart of much psychological distress, poor wellbeing and poor performance in various life roles. And importantly that none of these labels or judgements apply to the thing itself, as experienced through the senses or sight, touch, smell, hearing or feeling. Focusing on the present moment puts one in closer contact with raw, unmediated sensations and can help clients to notice and thus gain some separation from the judgements, evaluations, commentaries, beliefs and stories that they add to the mix – noticing as these things come and go, rise and fall, appear and disappear.

Tools and strategies AC coaches use to help the client get in contact with the present moment include:

- *Noticing one's hand.* Have the client hold up their hand in front of them, and guide them for a few minutes to really pay attention to it in detail – the contour of the fingers, the patterns of any veins, the presence of any hairs, the nails, the lines, any scars that may be present, etc.

- *Focusing on one's breath.* Having the client pay attention to the breath coming in and the breath going out. To what happens to the stomach and shoulders with each in breath and out breath. Noticing the sensation of the breath entering the nose or the mouth. Noticing any temperature difference between the breath coming in and the breath leaving.

- *Listening to sounds.* Have the client close their eyes and pay attention to the sounds in the room. To really listen for sounds, and any sounds behind sounds. To notice them, and how the mind tries to label them. And then to bring the mind back to just noticing the sounds. Sounds far way, sounds in the room, any sounds coming from the body.

Cultivating the perspective of the observing self

The self is not a single thing. The self can be sensed or viewed from different perspectives including the 'narrative' self (Hood, 2012) as well as the 'observing' self. When viewing the world from the perspective of the narrative self, the person sees themselves as the same as their experienced thoughts, feelings, sensations, memories, stories and images – including such adjectives, labels and judgements as 'bad', 'unworthy', 'unlovable', 'selfish', 'stupid', 'weak' or 'lazy'. Viewing the world from this perspective can be associated with uncomfortable and painful private experiences, distress, avoidance and difficulty in taking helpful actions toward valued living.

The AC coach helps their client adopt the perspective of the observing self, sensing and experiencing the part of themselves that is ever-present, the part of them that observed all kinds of experiences in the past, and the part of them that now notices the thoughts, feelings, sensations, memories and images that flow in and out of awareness but is not changed by them. This 'observing self' can be considered a kind of viewing or observation platform where the client can go to help them 'defuse' or 'disentangle' themselves from unhelpful, unwanted or unpleasant thoughts and feelings, and increase their freedom to act in a more values consistent manner. Exercises and activities the coach might use to help clients experience and adopt the perspective of the observing self include having people notice their breathing, and then to notice that they are noticing, or to notice the sounds present in the room, and then to notice that they are noticing these sounds, and variations on these activities.

CASE STUDY

Lana (name changed) was a 41-year-old married female working as an office manager for a university in the United States. She came to see Dr Blonna for help with work-related stress.

Session one

During the initial session I conducted an intake interview to assess Lana's needs, develop a set of goals related to her stress, and obtain her consent. I explained the AC approach to stress coaching, that it was not psychotherapy, and my confidence that Lana was quite capable of learning how to get unstuck and manage her stress with this approach. Her main goals for our sessions together were:

1 To learn how to reduce the stressors within her control.

2 To learn how to accept the stressors that were beyond her ability to control.

3 To learn to reduce the stress response by using relaxation techniques.

To prepare for the next session I gave Lana material on ACT and the AC approach to coaching to read, instructions on how to perform mindful meditation and mp3 files on mindful breathing and mindful meditation to listen to, and explained that our next session would start with five minutes of practising these techniques.

Session two

We began by meditating together for five minutes.

> Coach: *'We are going to do this together. For the next five minutes notice your breathing and the sensations that you feel in your body. Notice the thoughts and feelings that your mind tells you. Don't judge them or try to change or fix them. Just notice and accept them and then get back to your breathing.'*
>
> Lana: *'Ok but I think I am going to have a hard time doing this right. I have no experience doing this kind of stuff.'*
>
> Coach: *'Lana, you can't get this wrong. Just follow your breathing and notice what is going on in your mind, your body, and the environment.'*

We then reflected on the experience, and spoke about the concept of mindfulness and how it relates to managing stress. We explored her homework assignment (understanding the components of AC coaching and ACT) and looked together (using psychoeducation and Socratic questioning) at the following topics: the four aspects of acceptance; the ACT view of commitment; how the mind processes stressful information; how past frames of reference influence current thinking and stress; and how common thinking and feeling traps contribute to getting stuck. I gave Lana information on values and a values-clarification assignment to prepare for our next session.

Session three

We practised mindful meditation for 10 minutes, and reflected on the experience. I explained that it can take several weeks of regular practice to get comfortable and that acceptance plays a big part in this.

> Lana: *'I had a hard time practising this all week because I felt I wasn't doing it right. My mind kept racing and I couldn't focus on my breath.'*
>
> Coach: *'My own mind still races on occasion when I meditate. What I've learned is to note when this happens, accept it, and shift my attention back to my breath.'*
>
> Lana: *'You mean it is OK when your mind wanders.'*
>
> Coach: *'Yes, that is what our minds do. They are 24/7 thinking and feeling machines.'*
>
> Lana: *'Ok. I will work on noticing, accepting and getting back to my breathing.'*

I then shifted the focus of the session to Lana's values and how they related to her stress – explaining that people often get stuck and stressed because of a values conflict. I asked Lana to describe what she found out about her values and how they related to her stress.

Lana: *'I found out that my core values revolve around my husband, daughter, grand-children, and my volunteer work with helping injured animals. Those are the things I value most in life.'*

Coach: *'So how are these values related to the stress you have at work?'*

Lana: *'I seem to be bringing my work problems home and dumping them on my husband, complaining a lot about work. Work has also been cutting into my free time and that has really stressed me out. I have a new boss and she is very demanding. She is constantly pressuring me to stay later and come in on weekends, and speak to groups of students about our programmes. She is young, single, and work is so much more important to her than to me.'*

Coach: *'I noticed that you did not mention work in your values summary.'*

Lana: *'I do value my work but it is just that, work. I am not very career motivated. I look to work as a source of income, nothing more.'*

Coach: *'How does the income you value connect to your husband, daughter, grandchildren and animal-rescue work?'*

Lana: *'It gives my husband and me the extra money we use for travelling and seeing the grandchildren and also contributing to the animal-rescue agency I volunteer at.'*

Coach: *'Other than your new boss, what else about your job is stressful or comes into conflict with the things you value most?'*

Lana: *'Really nothing. I like being on a college campus and wouldn't want to work anywhere else. I love being around the young people and it is really beautiful. I have a short commute from home and the people I work with are very nice.'*

Coach: *'So it doesn't seem that you want to change jobs or are looking for something better?'*

Lana: *'No.'*

I then shifted the focus to acceptance, and explained how acceptance helps when exploring values conflicts like Lana was experiencing between her work, her family and her animal work. I offered to share a technique to help her talk with her boss about working conditions using acceptance.

Coach: *'I want you to start being mindful of what your mind is telling you about your boss and your job. Rather than judge these thoughts in terms of their rightness or wrongness, goodness or badness, look at them in terms of their helpfulness.'*

Lana: *'Helpfulness?'*

Coach: *'Yes, do they help you meet the goals we set for managing your stress or do they hinder them? And do they help you meet your other goals related to the things you value; your family and your work with animals? Because if your thoughts are not helpful it's ok to simply dismiss them as unhelpful thoughts.'*

Lana: 'Ok, I get it.'

Coach: 'If this makes you feel uncomfortable it is ok. Perhaps say to yourself: "I am willing to accept my discomfort at work in the service of my husband, daughter, grandchildren, and animal service work." Try saying this right now for me a few times.'

Lana repeated this phrase a couple of times and we talked about what it was like, and she agreed to say this to herself during the week when her mind told her unhelpful things about her boss and work situation. I shared with Lana some readings on commitment training and a relaxation training CD with instructions on systematic muscle relaxation, visualization, and autogenic training which she agreed to practice, along with her meditation practice.

Session four

We explored how people often get stressed when they try to control things that can't be controlled, along with how her own efforts to avoid, control, or eliminate events and experiences were keeping her stuck and stressed. We explored how to take committed action despite being unable to control all potentially stressful events.

Coach: 'After reading the material I gave you, what's your understanding of what you can control?'

Lane: 'I can control my behaviour. When my mind tells me something to do that is not helpful I do not have to do it. I can accept what my mind is saying but not act like it wants me to.'

Coach: 'Great, can you give me an example?'

Lana: 'At work today my boss made a comment that really pissed me off. My mind told me say something hurtful but I realized that doing that would not be helpful so I accepted it and ignored the comment. It felt good to take control like that.'

Coach: 'What else did you learn about control?'

Lana: 'That I can control some parts of my environment – like keeping my office neat, and putting cheerful things around like flowers and inspirational sayings.'

Coach: 'How about what you cannot control?'

Lana: 'That I can't control what my mind says or feels, like some thoughts, images, and emotions. So rather than waste my energy trying I need to learn how to accept them.'

Coach: 'And what happens then?'

Lana: 'They start to go away because I am not buying into them and I am refocusing my attention on stuff I need to do.'

Coach: 'Great!!!'

I then shared with Lana a metaphor about the mind as an mp3 player with two buttons that control the volume – but instead of controlling the volume, the buttons influence two different strategies: control versus willingness. Using the button called control increases attempts to control, avoid or eliminate unhelpful thoughts, scripts, mental images and emotions, and reduces willingness to accept these things. Using the button called willingness increases her acceptance of these things and her willingness to take valued action despite experiencing them, while reducing her efforts at control. We explored and played around with the metaphor, and how when the desire to control thoughts, images and feelings came up Lana could visualize placing her finger on the willingness button and noticing her desire to control start to fade as her willingness level increased to 10.

Lana: 'Thanks for sharing this. It helps me understand how this control and willingness stuff works.'

I provided some reading material and an assignment on defusion for the next session.

Session five

We practised mindful meditation for 15 minutes to start the session together. Lana told me she was becoming more comfortable with the breathing and relaxation training exercises.

Coach: 'Last week I gave you some reading material on what AC coaches call the conceptualized self and how to defuse from it. What did you get from this?'

Lana: 'It was confusing but one thing I remember is not to take what my mind tells me about myself too seriously, especially the bad stuff.'

Coach: 'Why so?'

Lana: 'Because so much of it is not real. It is kind of made up from memories or fears about the future.'

Coach: 'Very good. The key stressful thing about your conceptualized self is the fusing part. Fusing means getting stuck. When you get stuck on an unhelpful or outdated part of your conceptualized it can immobilize you.'

Lana: 'Sometimes I don't want to try new things because I'm afraid they won't be fun or will be embarrassing. I connect them to things I remember my mother or father or old boyfriends telling me.'

Coach: 'Like what?'

Lana: 'Like public speaking. My boss wants me to speak to large groups of students and I freeze. My high school teacher used to embarrass me whenever I got up in front of the room to give a book report. I tell my boss I can't speak in front of groups. When she asks I see myself in front of my school class being made fun of. What a stupid thought.'

> Coach: 'Let's call it an unhelpful thought. Can I share with you an activity to help you defuse from this thought? It's called The Whiteboard.'

Using an actual whiteboard in my room I had Lana write the heading: Unhelpful Thoughts My Mind Is Telling Me About Speaking in Front of Groups, and then had her list all her thoughts, however crazy or silly she thought they were. I then has her step back a few feet from the board or pad, telling herself: 'These are merely my thoughts, they are not me. I am much more than these thoughts.' I asked her to feel the distance she had between her and her unhelpful thoughts. And then to keep moving back, a couple of steps at a time until she could feel the connection to your thoughts loosening.

> Coach: 'So how much power do these thoughts have now?
>
> Lana:　'Not as much as when I first thought them up.'
>
> Coach: 'Could you feel them losing their power as you got further removed from them?'
>
> Lana:　'Absolutely.'

We agreed that Lana could use this distancing activity in her head or using a piece of paper whenever she felt fused with unhelpful or outdated pictures of herself.

Comment

After five sessions Lana felt that she had met her goals for coaching and decided to make progress with the approach on her own, managing her stress by reducing the number of stressors within her control. She felt that most of her stressors were related to unhelpful thoughts, mental images and emotions and felt confident about using AC principles and practices to defuse many of them, reducing the number of stressors she was dealing with. She felt comfortable in her ability to accept stressors she had no control over and how to commit to valued action, and felt more relaxed as a result of her meditation practice and relaxation exercises.

When might AC coaching be most suitable?

Being an holistic, flexible, theory driven and empirically supported approach to helping people, AC coaching is likely to prove helpful in a range of different coaching situations and contexts with a wide range of clients. It should be emphasized, however, that several elements of the approach are not unique. For instance, many coaches help clients to clarify their values, to set goals in harmony with their values, to take action towards goal achievement, to develop and improve various life skills and to cultivate mindfulness, just as AC coaches do.

Perhaps the main difference between AC coaching and other forms of coaching may be its emphasis on reducing experiential avoidance and increasing psychological flexibility, on noticing, accepting and making space for unwanted, unpleasant and unhelpful thoughts and feelings, rather than trying to challenge or change them. This is in marked contrast to traditional cognitive behavioural coaching approaches that typically help clients to identify, challenge, dispute and replace their unhelpful, irrational and illogical beliefs, their rigid shoulds, musts and oughts, and their various cognitive errors or thinking traps, using a range of empirical deductive methods including behavioural experimentation.

A recent systematic review and meta-analysis of studies (Ruiz, 2012) that have empirically compared ACT versus CBT using random and mixed effects models, showed that mean effect sizes on primary outcomes significantly favoured ACT over CBT, with ACT showing a greater impact on its putative processes of change than CBT. This does not, of course, mean that AC coaching is more likely to bring about helpful change in coaching clients than traditional CB coaching. But it does suggest that coaches give serious consideration to getting trained in AC coaching or ACT.

Conclusion

AC coaching involves the application of (evidence based) acceptance and commitment therapy concepts, tools, strategies and techniques within the coaching context and with coaching clients. The aim of AC coaching is to help clients live more fulfilling, valued, meaningful and rewarding lives by increasing their psychological flexibility and reducing their experiential avoidance. Clients are encouraged, guided and supported to give up their attempts to control, avoid or suppress thoughts, feelings and experiences which they find uncomfortable, and to change their relationship with these thoughts using a range of mindfulness and acceptance skills – while all the time taking committed action towards important life goals in harmony with their values.

Developing yourself as an acceptance and commitment coach

Developing your skills

Coaches wishing to learn more about and develop their skills in AC coaching may wish to explore the following practitioner texts:

- *ACT Made Simple.* An easy to read primer on Acceptance and Commitment Therapy. Harris, R. New Harbinger. 2009
- *Getting Unstuck in ACT.* A clinician's guide to overcoming common obstacles in Acceptance and Commitment Therapy. Harris, R. New Harbinger. 2013.
- *Brief Interventions for Radical Change.* Principles and practice of focused acceptance and commitment therapy. Strosahl, K, Robinson, P and Gustavsson, T. New Harbinger. 2012.
- *Learning ACT.* An Acceptance and Commitment Therapy skills training manual for therapists. New Harbinger. 2007.
- *Maximise your Coaching Effectiveness with Acceptance and Commitment Therapy.* Blonna, R. New Harbinger. 2010.

Deepening your understanding

Coaches wishing to recommend Acceptance and Commitment based self-help books and workbooks for their clients may wish to consider the following:

- *The Happiness Trap.* Based on ACT: a revolutionary mindfulness-based programme for overcoming stress, anxiety and depression. Harris, R. Robinson. 2007.
- *The Confidence Gap: From fear to freedom.* Harris, R. Robinson. 2010.
- *The Reality Slap: How to find fulfilment when life hurts.* Harris, R. Robinson. 2011.
- *The Mindfulness and Acceptance Workbook for Anxiety: A guide to breaking free from anxiety, phobias and worry using acceptance and commitment therapy.* Forsyth, J and Eifert, G. New Harbinger. 2007.
- *Get out of Your Mind and Into Your Life: The new acceptance and commitment therapy.* Hayes, S and Smith, S. New Harbinger. 2005.

References

APA Div 12 SCP (2012) Website on research-supported psychological treatments. Retrieved from: www.div12.org/PsychologicalTreatments/treatments.html

Bandura, A (1977) Self-efficacy: toward a unifying theory of behavioral change, *Psychological Review*, **84** (2), pp 191–215

Barlow (2002) *Anxiety and its disorders: The nature and treatment of anxiety and panic* (2nd edn), Guilford Press, New York

Biglan, A and Hayes, S C (1996) Should the behavioral sciences become more pragmatic? The case for functional contextualism in research on human behavior, *Applied and Preventive Psychology: Current Scientific Perspectives*, 5, pp 47–57

Blonna, R (2010) *Maximise your coaching effectiveness with Acceptance and Commitment Therapy*, New Harbinger, Oakland, CA

Bond, F and Bunce, D (2000) Mediators of change in problem-focused and emotion-focused worksite stress management interventions, *Journal of Occupational Health Psychology*, **5** (1), 156–63

Bond, F W and Bunce, D (2003) The role of acceptance and job control in mental health, job satisfaction, and work performance, *Journal of Applied Psychology*, **88**, pp 1057–67

Borkovec, T D and Roemer, L (1994) Generalized anxiety disorder, in *Handbook of Prescriptive Treatments for Adults*, eds R T Ammerman and M Hersen, (pp 261–81), Plenum, New York

Bouton, M E, Mineka, S and Barlow, D H (2001) A modern learning theory perspective on the etiology of panic disorder, *Psychological Review*, **108**, pp 4–32

Branstetter, A D, Wilson, K G, Hildebrandt, M and Mutch, D (2004) Improving psychological adjustment among cancer patients: ACT and CBT. Paper presented at the Association for Advancement of Behavior Therapy, New Orleans

Donaldson, E and Bond, F W (2004) Psychological acceptance and emotional intelligence in relation to workplace well-being, *British Journal of Guidance and Counseling*, **32**, pp 187–203

Dykstra, T A and Follette, W C (1998) *An agoraphobia scale for assessing the clinical significance of treatment outcome*, Unpublished manuscript

Flaxman, P, Blackledge, J and Bond, F (2011) *Acceptance and Commitment Therapy*, The CBT Distinctive Features series, Routledge, London

Forman, E M, Butryn, M L, Hofmann, K L and Herbert, J D (2009) An open trial of an acceptance-based behavioural intervention for weight loss, *Cognitive and Behavioral Practice*, **16**, pp 223–35

Forsyth, J P and Eifert, G H (2007) *The Mindfulness and Acceptance Workbook for Anxiety*, New Harbinger, Oakland, CA

Forsyth, J P, Parker, J D and Finlay, C G (2003) Anxiety sensitivity, controllability, and experiential avoidance and their relation to drug of choice and addiction severity in a residential sample of substanceabusing veterans, *Addictive Behaviors*, **28**, pp 851–70

Germer, C K, Siegel, R D and Fulton, P R (2005) *Mindfulness and Psychotherapy*, Guilford Press, New York

Gifford, E V, Kohlenberg, B S, Hayes, S C, Antonuccio, D O, Piasecki, M M, Rasmussen-Hall, M L and Palm, K M (2011) Acceptance theory-based treatment for smoking cessation: an initial trial of acceptance and commitment therapy, *Behavior Therapy*

Gold, S D, Marx, B P and Lexington, J M (2007) Gay male sexual assault survivors: the relations among internalized homophobia, experiential avoidance, and psychological symptom severity, *Behaviour Research and Therapy*, **45**, pp 549–62

Gratz, K L and Roemer, L (2004) Multidimensional assessment of emotion regulation and dysregulation: development, factor structure, and initial validation of the Difficulties in Emotion Regulation Scale, *Journal of Psychopathology and Behavioral Assessment*, **36**, pp 41–54

Greco, L A, Heffner, M, Ritchie, S, Polak, M, Poe, S and Lynch, S K (2005) Maternal adjustment following preterm birth: contributions of experiential avoidance, *Behavior Therapy*, **36**, pp 177–84

Gregg, J A, Callaghan, G M, Hayes, S C and Glenn-Lawson, J L (2007) Improving diabetes self-management through acceptance, mindfulness, and values: a randomized controlled trial, *Journal of Consulting and Clinical Psychology*, 75, pp 336–43

Gutiérrez, O, Luciano, M C, Bermúdez, M P and Buela-Casal, G (2007) *Prevention of HIV among adolescents: comparing the effect of information-based protocols vs. information plus values-based protocols on risky patterns of behavior.* Paper presented at the 5th World Congress of Cognitive and Behaviour Therapies, Barcelona

Harris, R (2010) *The Confidence Gap: From fear to freedom*, Penguin, London

Hayes, S (1993) Goals and varieties of scientific contextualism, in *The Varieties of Scientific Contextualism*, eds S C Hayes, L J Hayes, H W Reese and T R Sarbin, (pp 11–27), Context Press, Reno, NV

Hayes, S (2004) Acceptance and Commitment Therapy, Relational Frame Theory, and the third wave of behavioral and cognitive therapies, *Behaviour Therapy*, 35, pp 639–65

Hayes, S C, Barnes-Holmes, D and Roche, B (eds) (2001) *Relational Frame Theory: A post-Skinnerian account of human language and cognition*, Plenum Press, New York

Hayes, S C, Bissett, R, Roget, N, Padilla, M, Kohlenberg, B S, Fisher, G, Masuda, A et al (2004) The impact of Acceptance and Commitment Therapy and multicultural training on the stigmatizing attitudes and professional burnout of substance abuse counsellors, *Behavior Therapy*, 35, pp 821–35

Hayes, S C, Follette, V M and Linehan, M M (2004) *Mindfulness and Acceptance: Expanding the cognitive behavioral tradition*, The Guilford Press, New York

Hayes, S C, Hayes, L J and Reese, H W (1988) Finding the philosophical core: a review of Stephen C Popper's world hypotheses, *Journal of Experimental Analysis of Behavior*, 50, pp 97–111

Hayes, S C, Hayes, L J, Reese, H W and Sarbin, T R (eds) (1993) *Varieties of Scientific Contextualism*, Context Press, Reno, NV

Hayes, S C, Jacobson, N S, Follette, V M and Dougher, M J (eds) (1994) *Acceptance and Change: Content and context in psychotherapy*, Context Press, Reno, NV

Hayes, S C, Masuda, A, Bissett, R, Luoma, J and Guerrero, L F (2004) DBT, FAP, and ACT: how empirically oriented are the new behavior therapy technologies? *Behavior Therapy*, 35, pp 35–54

Hayes, S and Smith, S (2005) *Get Out of Your Mind and Into Your Life: The new acceptance and commitment therapy*, New Harbinger

Hayes, S C, Strosahl, K D, Wilson, K G, Bissett, R T, Pistorello, J, Toarmino, D et al (2004) Measuring experiential avoidance: a preliminary test of a working model, *The Psychological Record*, 54, pp 553–78

Hayes, S, Wilson, K, Gifford, E, Follette, M and Strosahl, K (1996) Experiential avoidance and behavioral disorders: a functional dimensional approach to diagnosis and treatment, *Journal of Consulting and Clinical Psychology*, 64 (6), pp 1152–68

Hernández-López, M, Luciano, M C, Bricker, J B, Roales-Nieto, J G and Montesinos, F (2009) Acceptance and Commitment Therapy for smoking cessation: a preliminary study of its effectiveness in comparison with Cognitive Behavioral Therapy, *Psychology of Addictive Behaviors*, **23**, pp 723–30

Hood, B (2012) *The Self Illusion: Who do you think you are?* Constable, London

Lillis, J, Hayes, S C, Bunting, K and Masuda, A (2009) Teaching acceptance and mindfulness to improve the lives of the obese: a preliminary test of a theoretical model, *Annals of Behavioral Medicine*, **37**, pp 58–69

Linehan, M M (1993) *Cognitive-Behavioral Treatment of Borderline Personality Disorder*, The Guilford Press, New York

Lundgren, A T, Dahl, J, Melin, L and Kees, B (2006) Evaluation of acceptance and commitment therapy for drug refractory epilepsy: a randomized controlled trial in South Africa, *Epilepsya*, **47**, pp 2173–79

Lundgren, A T, Dahl, J, Yardi, N and Melin, L (2008) Acceptance and Commitment Therapy and yoga for drug-refractory epilepsy: a randomized controlled trial, *Epilepsy and Behavior*, **13**, pp 102–08

Marx, B P and Sloan, D M (2005) Experiential avoidance, peritraumatic dissociation, and post-traumatic stress disorder, *Behaviour Research and Therapy*, **43**, pp 569–83

Masuda, A, Hayes, S C, Fletcher, L B, Seignourel, P J, Bunting, K, Herbst, S A, *et al* (2007) Impact of Acceptance and Commitment Therapy versus education on stigma toward people with psychological disorders, *Behaviour Research and Therapy*, **45**, pp 2764–72

McCracken, L M, MacKichan, F and Eccleston, C (2007) Contextual cognitive-behavioral therapy for severely disabled chronic pain sufferers: effectiveness and clinically significant change, *European Journal of Pain*, **11**, pp 314–22

McCracken, L M, Vowles, K E and Eccleston, C (2004) Acceptance of chronic pain: component analysis and a revised assessment method, *Pain*, **107**, pp 159–66

Montesinos, F and Luciano, M C (2005) Treatment of relapse fear in breast cancer patients through an ACT-based protocol. Paper presented at the 9th European Congress of Psychology, Granada, España

Morton, J, Snowdon, S, Gopold, M and Guymer, E (2012) Acceptance and commitment therapy group treatment for symptoms of borderline personality disorder: a public sector pilot study, *Cognitive and Behavioral Practice*, **19**, pp 527–44

Mo'tamedi, H, Rezaiemaram, P and Tavallaie (2012) The effectiveness of a group-based acceptance and commitment additive therapy on rehabilitation of female outpatients with chronic headache: preliminary findings reducing 3 dimensions of headache impact, *Headache*, **52** (7), pp 1106–19

Oldfather, W A (1925) *Epictetus: Discourses*, Loeb Classical Library

Páez, M, Luciano, M C and Gutiérrez, O (2007) Tratamiento psicológico para el afrontamiento del cancer de mama: estudio comparativo entre estrategias de aceptación y de control cognitive, *Psicooncología*, **4**, pp 75–95

Polusny, M A, Rosenthal, M Z, Aban, I and Follette, V M (2004) Experiential avoidance as a mediator of the effects of adolescent sexual victimization on negative adult outcomes, *Violence and Victims*, **19**, pp 109–20

Quirosa-Moreno, T, Luciano, C, Navarrete-Navarrete, N, Gutiérrez-Martínez, O, Sabio-Sánchez, J M and Jiménez-Alonso, J (2009) *Acceptance and Commitment Therapy (ACT) in the treatment of psychological problems associated with systemic lupus erythematosus.* Paper presented at The Third World Conference on ACT, RFT and Contextual Behavioral Science, Enschede, The Netherlands

Reese, H W (1968) *The Perception of Stimulus Relations: Discrimination learning and transposition*, Academic Press, New York

Roche, B, Barnes, D and Smeets, P M (1997) Incongruous stimulus pairing and conditional discrimination training: effects on relational responding, *Journal of the Experimental Analysis of Behavior*, **68**, pp 143–60

Rost, A D, Wilson, K G, Buchanan, E, Hildebrandt, M J and Mutch, D (2012) Improving psychological adjustment among late-stage ovarian cancer patients: examining the role of avoidance in treatment, *Cognitive and Behavioral Practice*, **19**, pp 508–17

Ruiz, F (2012) Acceptance and commitment therapy versus traditional cognitive behavioral therapy: a systematic review and meta-analysis of current empirical evidence, *International Journal of Psychology and Psychological Therapy*, **12** (2), pp 333–57

Ruiz, F J and Luciano, C (2012) Improving international-level chess players' performance with an acceptance-based protocol: preliminary findings, *The Psychological Record*, **62**, pp 447–62

SAMHSA (Substance Abuse and Mental Health Services Administration) (2012) National Registry of Evidence based Programs and Practices (NREPP). Retrieved from http://nrepp.samhsa.gov

Sánchez, L C and Luciano, C (2005) *Acceptance and Commitment Therapy (ACT) in multiple sclerosis patients: how does it influence on psychological processes and on the neurodegenerative course of the disease?* Paper presented at the 9th European Congress of Psychology, Granada, Spain

Shawyer, F, Farhall, J, Mackinnon, A *et al* (2012) A randomised controlled trial of acceptance-based cognitive behavioural therapy for command hallucinations in psychotic disorders, *Behav Res Ther*, **50**, pp 110–21

Smout, M, Hayes, L, Atkins, P, Klausen, J and Duguid, J (2012) The empirically supported status of acceptance and commitment therapy: an update, *Clinical Psychologist*, **16**, 97–109

Smout, M F, Longo, M, Harrison, S, Minniti, R, Wickes, W and White, J M (2010) Psychosocial treatment for methamphetamine use disorders: a preliminary randomized controlled trial of cognitive behavior therapy and acceptance and commitment therapy, *Substance Abuse*, **31**, 98–107

Stotts, A L, Green, C, Masuda, A, Grabowski, J, Wilson, K, Northrup, T F and Schmitz, J M (2012) A stage I pilot study of acceptance and commitment therapy for methadone detoxification, *Drug and Alcohol Dependence*, **125**, pp 215–22

Strosahl, K D, Hayes, S C, Bergan, J and Romano, P (1998) Does field based training in behavior therapy improve clinical effectiveness? Evidence from the Acceptance and Commitment Therapy training project, *Behavior Therapy*, **29**, pp 35–64

Teasdale, J D, Moore, R G, Hayhurst, H, Pope, M, Williams, S and Segal, Z V (2002) Metacognitive awareness and prevention of relapse in depression: empirical evidence, *Journal of Consulting and Clinical Psychology*, **70**, pp 275–87

Toarmino, D, Pistorello, J and Hayes, S C (1997) *Validation of the Acceptance and Action Questionnaire*, Unpublished manuscript

Tull, M T, Gratz, K L, Salters, K and Roemer, L (2004) The role of experiential avoidance in posttraumatic stress symptoms and symptoms of depression, anxiety, and somatization, *Journal of Nervous and Mental Disease*, **192**, pp 754–61

Weineland, S, Arvidsson, Kakoulidis, T and Dahl, J (2012) ACT for bariatric surgery patients – a pilot RCT, *Obesity Research and Clinical Practice*, **6** (1)

Wells, A (1994) Attention and the control of worry, in *Worrying: Perspectives on theory, assessment and treatment*, eds G C L Davey and F Tallis, (pp 91–114), Wiley, Oxford

Westin, Z V Z, Schulin, M, Hesser, H, Karlsson, M, Noe, R Z, Olofsson, U and Andersson, G (2011) Acceptance and commitment therapy versus tinnitus retraining therapy in the treatment of tinnitus: a randomised controlled trial, *Behaviour Research and Therapy*, **49**, pp 737–47

Wetherell, J L, Afari, N, Rutledge, T, Sorrell, J T, Stoddard, J A, Petkus, A J, Solomon, B C, Lehman, D H, Liu, L, Lang, A J and Atkinson, J H (2011) A randomized, controlled trial of acceptance and commitment therapy and cognitive-behavioral therapy for chronic pain, *Pain*, **152** (9), pp 2098–107

White, R G, Gumley, A I, McTaggart, J, Rattrie, L, McConville, D, Cleare, S and Mitchell, G (2011) A feasibility study of acceptance and commitment therapy for emotional dysfunction following psychosis, *Behaviour Research and Therapy*, **49**, pp 901–07

Wicksell, R K, Melin, L, Lekander, M and Olsson, G L (2009) Evaluating the effectiveness of exposure and acceptance strategies to improve functioning and quality of life in longstanding pediatric pain – a randomized controlled trial, *Pain*, **141** (3), pp 248–45

Wilson, K G, Hayes, S C, Gregg, J and Zettle, R D (2001) Psychopathology and psychotherapy, in S C Hayes, D Barnes-Holmes and B Roche (Eds), *Relational Frame Theory: A post-Skinnerian account of human language and cognition* (pp 211–38), Kluwer Academic, New York

Wilson, K G and Murrell, A R (2004) Values work in acceptance and commitment therapy: setting a course for behavioral treatment, in S Hayes, V Follette, M Linehan (Eds), *Mindfulness and Acceptance: Expanding the cognitive-behavioral tradition* (pp 120–51), Guilford, New York

Motivational interviewing

11

JONATHAN PASSMORE

Introduction

This chapter describes the motivational interviewing (MI) approach. MI is a highly effective and efficient approach to helping people, which is supported by substantial research evidence gathered from hundreds of research studies in a wide range of settings, from health to organizations.

MI has developed over the past three decades from a health-based intervention, focusing on addictive behaviours, to one which is now used in a wide range of contexts to help clients explore their ambivalence to a situation or challenge. This includes its adaptation to use in helping managers deal with perceived poor performance and helping others manage redundancy.

The development of MI, unlike a number of approaches, is not static, as both originators, Bill Miller and Stephen Rollnick, are both still active in applying and researching the approach and continue to run training sessions for practitioners. In recent years a third edition of the core text *Motivational Interviewing* (Miller and Rollnick, 2013) has offered a revised framework for applying the model using four key phases to guide the conversation. However, both writers are keen to emphasize that what is most important is the spirit of MI as opposed to the use of specific techniques.

In this chapter I will firstly describe the model and briefly review the research evidence underpinning MI. I will then explore some of the commonly used techniques within MI, before setting out a typical case from my own experience of using MI with clients in organizational settings. Finally, I will briefly discuss when MI may be the preferred psychological approach to use in contrast to other approaches described in this book.

The evidence base for motivational interviewing

Over the past two decades MI has built a substantial evidence base. The majority of evidence in support of MI comes from the field of healthcare, where MI originated. In this section I will briefly review the theoretical heritage of MI and review the research evidence asking two key questions: first, does MI work? Second, what are the active ingredients within MI?

The theory behind MI

In the beginning, MI was 'a-theoretical'. The approach developed out of applied practice rather than as a theoretical idea which was later developed into a model for application. Over the first decade of its use from the mid-1990s to 2005, links were built with existing theory and research in behaviour change.

One key linkage is the work of cognitive dissonance (Festinger, 1957). At the core of MI is seeking to encourage the client to develop 'change talk' and thus create a plan for new behaviours themselves which is different from their current behaviour.

A second link is to self-determination theory (SDT) (Deci and Ryan, 2008). Markland *et al* (2005) proposed that SDT provides a coherent theoretical framework for understanding MI processes and efficacy. They outlined and described the parallels between the two approaches and showed how both MI and SDT are based on the assumption that humans have an 'innate tendency for personal growth towards psychological integration' and suggested that motivational interviewing 'provides the social-environmental facilitation factors suggested by SDT to promote this tendency'. Vansteenkiste and Sheldon (2006) too have highlighted the link between MI and SDT, focusing on the issues of need satisfaction and the internalization of therapeutic change. They suggested that basic need satisfaction may be one of the key mechanisms by which MI delivers its helpful effects.

Miller and Rose (2009) sought to 'look under the hood' of motivational interviewing in an attempt to understand the underlying mechanisms by which it affects behaviour change. They proposed an emergent theory of MI with two main active components: a relational component focused on empathy and the 'spirit' of MI, and a technical component involving the differential evocation and reinforcement of 'change talk'. They shared a causal chain model linking practitioner training, practitioner and client responses during sessions, and post-session outcomes.

Anstiss and Passmore (2013) further developed Miller and Rollnick's model to create a revised framework that may be more compatible with the application of MI in a coaching context (see Figure 11.1).

A final link is with the work of Prochaska and DiClemente (1984) who proposed a multi-stage model of behavioural change – the transtheoretical model of change (see Figure 11.2). The model proposed key stages; pre-contemplation, contemplation, planning, action, maintenance/managing relapse.

What is distinctive about the model is that it includes a pre-contemplation phase. For some individuals the need for change is not apparent, but most

FIGURE 11.1 MI framework

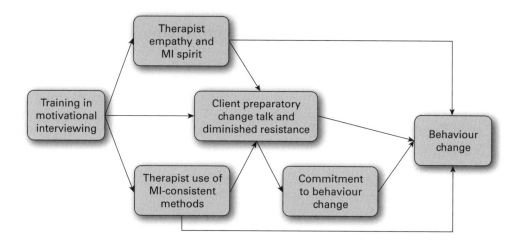

FIGURE 11.2 Transtheoretical model of change

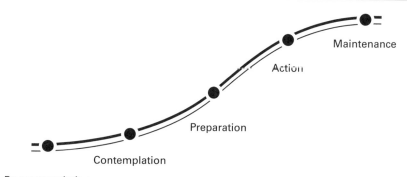

change models start by discussing the thoughts about change or the goals for change, as in the GROW coaching model. This pre-contemplation stage can be seen in the case of individuals misusing alcohol, as well as those in conflict situations in the workplace, where often the perception is that either there is not a problem or that others need to make a change to accommodate the individual.

The second element that differentiates the transtheroretical model from other behavioural change models is the recognition that behaviour change is hard and requires repeated effort. This includes an acceptance of failures, as an integral part of making a change. These failures are when we keep to the plan we have made for one reason or another, by eating the slice of cake or failing to go to the gym on a rainy night. Simply setting the goal is not enough. Instead MI seeks to support, encourage and gently challenge. It helps clients maintain the change, thus helping to sustain the longer-term behavioural change as the new habit is integrated into the person's way of doing things.

Having considered the unpinning theory, let us look at the research evidence.

Does MI work?

MI originated as an intervention to address drug and alcohol addiction within the health sector and as a result it is now one of the most researched counselling interventions with over 650 outcome studies. These studies provide conclusive evidence that MI is a highly effective intervention for facilitating behavioural change, and is more effective than other well-known models such as CBT, for specific types of problems. The details of this will be explored below.

A detailed literature review by Bricker and Tollison (2011) found over 550 peer-reviewed publications, with some 200 randomized controlled trials (RCTs), which is considered to be the gold standard research model for scientific research. In addition, MI research has been subjected to 18 meta-analyses (for example, Burke et al, 2004; Lundahl et al, 2009; Lundahl et al, 2010). If the RCT is the gold standard, a meta-analysis could be considered to be the platinum standard research methodology. In a meta-analysis the data from multiple RCTs is pooled to help researchers remove potential bias arising from individual studies and a single research team or a restricted sample population, such as older people or drug users.

While MI research has been concentrated in health-based settings, a growing number of studies are now being conducted in new settings with different groups of people experiencing different issues. There is good quality research evidence that MI is helpful in bringing about beneficial change in the following behaviours, conditions and contexts: eating disorders (see, for example, Cassin et al, 2008), domestic violence (see, for example, Kistenmacher and Weiss, 2008), smoking cessation (see, for example, Heckman, Egleston and Hofmann, 2010) and weight loss management (see, for example, Armstrong et al, 2011).

MI has also been applied in coaching, but as with much of coaching research the research has been limited and has focused on qualitative studies that have explored the translation of MI to coaching at work (see, for example, Passmore and Whybrow, 2007). Burke Arkowitz and Menchola (2003) conducted a meta-analysis on controlled clinical trials investigating what they termed 'adaptations of motivational interviewing' (AMIs) and found them equivalent to other active treatments – yielding moderate effects compared with no treatment and/or placebo for problems involving alcohol, drugs, and diet and exercise. Overall, the percentage of people who improved following MI interventions (51 per cent) was significantly greater than the percentage who improved (37 per cent) with either no treatment or treatment as usual.

Burke *et al* (2004) subsequently conducted a meta-analytic, qualitative and process review of the empirical literature for MIs and once again found them equivalent to other active treatments, yielding moderate effects compared to no-treatment/placebo for problems involving alcohol, drugs, and diet and exercise. They suggested that while MIs are equivalent in efficacy to Cognitive Behavioural Skills Training (CBST) approaches, they are commonly briefer, and thus hour for hour are more effective for specific types of presenting issues. Since MI's focus on developing readiness to change while CBST targets the change process, they suggested that MIs can be useful as preludes to CBST interventions.

Rubak *et al* (2005) conducted a systematic review of the effectiveness of motivational interviewing in a wide range of disease areas. A search of 16 databases produced 72 randomized controlled trials dating back to 1991. Rubak and colleagues conducted a quality assessment with a validated scale and a meta-analysis. The results showed a significant effect for motivational interviewing for changes in body mass index, total blood cholesterol, systolic blood pressure, blood alcohol concentration and standard ethanol content. MI had significant and clinically relevant effects in approximately three out of four studies, with equal effects on physiological and psychological conditions. Psychologists and physicians obtained an effect in approximately 80 per cent of the studies, while other healthcare providers obtained an effect in 46 per cent of the studies. Even when motivational interviewing was used in brief encounters of 15 minutes, 64 per cent of the studies showed an effect. Further encounters with the patient increased the effectiveness of motivational interviewing. They concluded that motivational interviewing in a scientific setting outperforms traditional advice giving in the treatment of a broad range of behavioural problems and diseases.

Vasilaki, Hosier and Cox (2006) examined the effectiveness of MI in reducing alcohol consumption. A literature search revealed 22 relevant studies upon which they performed their meta-analysis. They concluded that brief MI is effective and recommend that future studies of MI explore predictors of efficacy and compare different components of MI to determine which are most responsible for long-term changes in behaviour.

Lundahl and Burke (2009) highlighted the evidence from the three published meta-analyses of MI and a meta-analysis of their own. They concluded that MI is significantly more effective than no treatment and generally equal to other treatments for a wide variety of problems ranging from substance use (alcohol, marijuana, tobacco and other drugs) to reducing risky behaviours and increasing client engagement in treatment. They also found that group-delivered MI appears to be less effective than one-on-one MI, and that delivering MI with 'problem feedback' seemed to generate better outcomes for some problems than MI alone.

In the most comprehensive review of MI for smoking cessation conducted to date, Heckman, Egleston and Hofmann (2010) conducted a systematic review and meta-analysis involving 31 smoking cessation studies: eight with adolescent samples, eight with adults with chronic physical or mental illness, five with pregnant/postpartum women and 10 with other adult samples. These studies involved a total sample of almost 10,000 individual participants. They concluded that MI smoking cessation approaches can be effective for adolescents and adults alike.

A similar comprehensive review of MI has also been conducted for weight loss (Armstrong et al, 2011). This study found 3,540 citations, and of the 101 potentially relevant studies, 12 met the inclusion criteria and 11 were included for meta-analysis. Motivational interviewing was associated with a greater reduction in body mass compared to controls (SMD = –0.51 [95% CI –1.04, 0.01]). There was a significant reduction in body weight (kg) for those in the intervention group compared with those in the control group (WMD = –1.47 kg [95% CI –2.05, –0.88]). For the BMI outcome, the WMD was –0.25 kg m^{-2} (95% CI –0.50, 0.01). As a result the research team concluded that MI appeared to enhance weight loss in overweight and obese patients.

Lundahl et al (2010) investigated the unique contribution of motivational interviewing on counselling outcomes and how the approach compared with other interventions. The results from 119 studies were subject to a meta-analysis, with targeted outcomes including substance use (tobacco, alcohol, drugs, marijuana), health-related behaviours (diet, exercise, safe sex), gambling, and engagement in treatment. Across all 132 comparisons they conducted they found that MI interventions were associated with a statistically significant and durable improvement in outcomes and that the added benefits of MI showed no signs of fading up to two years or more after the intervention. Stronger effects were shown when MI was compared to doing nothing, being placed on a waiting list control group, or being handed a leaflet – when compared to another specific intervention such as cognitive-behavioural therapy MI interventions were pretty much equivalent. Studies incorporating feedback to the client on the results of assessments or screening tests were associated with significantly greater improvement, and therapists trained and instructed to follow a manual achieved less good results than those not so trained or instructed.

In conclusion a wide range of meta-studies have found that MI is a highly effective intervention for a wide range of clinical presenting issues and is as effective, at equivalent levels to cognitive behavioural therapy (CBT), and is more effective than CBT for some types of presenting issues. Further, the outcomes achieved appear to be sustained over longer periods of time, suggesting that MI is highly effective at delivering sustained behaviour change for even the most challenging of habituated behaviours.

The active ingredients within MI

The second question was to explore what makes MI so powerful. In short, what are the active ingredients that appear to differentiate MI from other approaches that lack a scientific evidence base with RCT and meta-analysis research evidence such as neuro-linguistic programming.

If MI is highly effective as an intervention, what factors are contributing to these outcomes? A second stand of research has explored this question. This strand of research has tried to identify the active ingredients from MI. Once again a brief review of the key papers is presented here.

One study (Miller, Benefield and Tonigan, 1993) found that problem drinkers randomly assigned to MI versus a direct instructional approach displayed 111 per cent more change talk (talk about making a change in behaviour) than in the instruction group. These findings were consistent with the findings of the within-subject clinical experiments of Patterson and Forgatch (1985), which also showed how clients' use of language changed during MI's application. Its seems that by using a Socratic approach with questions aimed at eliciting benefits of making a change, clients are more likely to consider and reflect on the issue than those told of the benefits.

Amrhein et al (2003) used psycholinguistic analysis to explore the relationship between the actual language clients used during MI and its relationship with drug use outcomes. They coded 84 videotapes of conversations with drug abusers for the frequency and strength of client utterances expressing commitment, desire, ability, need, readiness, and reasons to change or maintain their habit. The results showed that commitment strength predicted outcomes and was in turn predicted by strength of statements relating to desire, ability, need and reasons for change. The results suggest that commitment strength is a pathway for the influence of client language on subsequent behaviour change (Amrhein et al, 2003). The evidence supports the theoretical position of the Transpersonal Model, which suggested that contemplation (thinking and talking about making a change) was a precursor to planning and making the change (Prochaska and DiClemente, 1984).

Moyers and Martin (2006) examined 38 motivational enhancement therapy sessions from Project MATCH (Matching Alcoholism Treatments to Client Heterogeneity), using a sequential behavioural coding system to investigate the relationship between therapist behaviours and client speech. They found that MI-consistent therapist behaviours were more likely to be followed by self-motivational statements and that MI-inconsistent therapist behaviours were more likely to be followed by client resistance – lending support to the importance of therapist behaviours in shaping client speech during MI sessions. This evidence provides further support to the key role of listening and asking focused questions based on the changing patterns and intentions of the client.

In a separate paper (Moyers et al, 2007) explored the role of clinician behaviour in influencing client speech, and the extent to which client speech predicted treatment outcome in clients receiving treatment for substance abuse. Coding sessions using the Sequential Code for Process Exchanges (SCOPE) behavioural coding system and the MISC 1.0 behavioural coding system, they found client speech during early therapy sessions to be a powerful predictor of substance abuse outcome. They also found that the pattern of therapist behaviours and subsequent client language provided support for a causal chain between therapist behaviours, subsequent client speech and drinking outcomes. They suggested that aspects of client speech influence the likelihood of behaviour change and that the occurrence of such speech is influenced by the therapist.

Apodaca and Longabough (2009) attempted to summarize and evaluate the evidence for possible within-session mechanisms of change. The four aspects of therapist behaviour they looked at were: MI-Spirit; MI-Consistent behaviours; MI-Inconsistent behaviours; and therapist use of specific techniques. The five aspects of client behaviour they looked at were: change talk/intention; readiness to change; involvement/engagement; resistance; and the client's experience of discrepancy. They reviewed 152 studies and found that 19 provided data on at least one link in the causal chain model under examination. The most consistent evidence was found for client change talk/intention (related to better outcomes); client experience of discrepancy (related to better outcomes); and therapist MI-Inconsistent behaviour (related to worse outcomes).

Vader et al (2010) examined the relationship between language, personalized feedback and drinking outcomes in a sample of heavy-drinking college students. MI was delivered in a single session with or without a personalized feedback report. They found that MI-consistent counsellor language was positively associated with client change talk, that MI with feedback was associated with lower levels of sustain talk, that higher levels of change talk were associated with improved drinking outcomes at three months, and that higher levels of sustain talk were associated with poorer drinking outcomes. They highlighted the relationship between counsellor MI skill and client change talk and the important role of feedback in the change process.

Magill et al (2010) explored whether or not within-session therapist and client language predicted a client's decision to complete a written Change Plan in alcohol-focused motivational interviewing using data from an ongoing hospital-based clinical trial involving 291 subjects. Analyses showed that therapist MI-consistent behaviours and client change talk were both positive predictors, and therapist counter change talk was a negative predictor of the decision to complete a Change Plan regarding alcohol use.

In conclusion, these studies show the critical nature of six aspects of MI which contribute to the successful outcomes noted in the section above. These are the importance of actively listening to the language of the client and noting changes in language as signals of changes in attitude, using these changes in language to inform how the coach responds to stimulate further motivation for change, the value of building discrepancy in the mind of the client, the importance of consistency in the coach's behaviour/intervention and the importance of feedback as a tool in the process.

The six active ingredients of MI

1 Actively listening to the language of the client.

2 Recognizing changes in language as signals of changes in attitude.

3 Formulating questions and affirmations which echo changes in the client's language.

4 Building discrepancy in the mind of the client between the new thoughts and recent past behaviour.

5 Consistency in the coach's behaviour.

6 Using feedback as a tool.

Practice: tools and techniques

Motivational interviewing has been very well researched as I have highlighted in the section above. As well as having a good understanding of its efficacy, research has confirmed the active ingredients within MI. However, the approach places its priority on a well-defined set of principles and some core skills (sometimes called micro-skills), as opposed to placing the emphasis on specific tools or techniques. This makes MI a more complex and challenging approach to learn for the novice and thus, I believe, makes MI an approach more suited to the advanced practitioner.

The spirit of the approach

The spirit of MI is characterized by the following three adjectives:

- evocative;
- collaborative; and
- autonomy supporting.

MI is evocative in that the coach tries to draw things out from the client, rather than put things in. Things evoked from the client include concerns about the current situation, reasons for change, ideas for changing and ideas for staying changed – including thoughts about barriers and obstacles that might be encountered and ways around them. Reasons for being confident that change is possible may also be evoked. The more the client comes up with ideas, reasons and arguments, the more likely it is change will occur

– in contrast to the coach generating a list of reasons why the person should change and telling them how they should go about it.

Secondly, MI is collaborative in that it is very much an approach adopted *with* someone, not something done to them. Coach and client work together in partnership, jointly and collaboratively viewing the person's life, their goals, their strengths, their difficulties, their hopes, their concerns and their ideas for change. In this sense MI can be considered to be 'an inter-view', like two people looking together at a family album (or in this case the presenting issue). When the conversation ceases to become collaborative the practitioner may notice one or more manifestations of resistance, which is a cue for the practitioner to change what they are doing or saying, in order to get back to a collaborative process.

Thirdly, MI is autonomous. In MI the client is always the active decision maker, exploring options and deciding what they want to with their lives – including doing nothing and letting their life continue in its current direction. However, such decisions are taken by helping the client to understand the implications and consequences for the choices they make in a conscious (contemplative) way. Thus linking MI to the desire to build client self-awareness and 'choicefulness', the two key aspects highlighted by Whitmore (1992) in his pioneering work on coaching.

The principles

The principles of MI can be remembered by the acronym RULE:

- Resist the righting reflex.
- Understand and explore the client's motivation.
- Listen with empathy.
- Empower the client, encouraging optimism and hope.

The 'righting reflex' is the natural tendency in humans to want to fix things and to make them better. This usually helpful reflex commonly gets in the way of empathic, non-judgemental relationships, triggering resistance and reactance. The client feels their autonomy is being undermined by the coach's attempts at being helpful. The righting reflex may prompt practitioners to jump in with such questions as: 'Could you try this...' or 'Why don't you do such and such...' and this can result in falling into the 'yes, but...' trap, and may even prompt the client to do the opposite of what is suggested as they attempt to demonstrate their autonomy and self control.

Secondly, the MI coach understands and explores the client's motivation by asking them open questions and following these up with empathic listening statements, more questions, affirmations and the occasional summary. Questions such as: 'Why might you want to change?'; 'What are your three best reasons for doing it?' and 'What is the best that might happen?' Using empathic listening skills helps with the further exploration of these motivations, and listening for and then developing 'change talk' can help build the client's motivation for change.

Thirdly, the MI coach listens with empathy. They try to imagine what it might be like to be the other person, trying to feel 'as if' they were in the other person's shoes, communicating this attempt at understanding with reflective listening statements of varying degrees of complexity and summaries. If nothing else happens in the session, the client should go away feeling heard, listened to and understood.

Finally, the MI coach empowers their clients, encouraging optimism and hope, by working with clients to develop their sense of confidence about being able to change (their self-efficacy), as well as helping them see how change is likely to result in the desired outcomes they seek for themselves and others. Open questions such as: 'How do you think you might go about it to be successful?'; 'What do you think would be most helpful here?'; 'How confident are you that you can change and stay changed for six months?'; as well as affirmations such as: 'You're the kind of person who works hard to be successful' or 'When you set your mind to things, you get results' can be helpful in empowering people. Helping clients think through the type, volume and duration of change required for success helps build hope, as does reflection on previous positive experience where the person has successful made a change or mastered a new skill.

A second set of principles adds to RULE. These can be summarized under the acronym RID:

- Roll with resistance.
- Information sharing.
- Develop discrepancy.

MI coaches seek to minimize the manifestation of resistance in the consultation in the first place, and adapt their behaviour in the session to reduce resistance as and when it is noticed. They 'roll' with resistance, as opposed to confronting and directly challenging. This rolling may take the form of a reflection: eg 'you really don't want to be here' or 'making a major change in your diet is simply isn't a priority for you at the moment, what with the other things you have going on'; a reframing or change of focus: eg 'you're right, perhaps dieting isn't where we should be focusing, but things at home'; an apology, eg 'I'm sorry, I think I've rushed ahead a bit, can we go back a little, please forgive me'; or a re-emphasizing of client control and autonomy, eg 'you're very much the one in charge here, and you will only change this when it feels right for you'.

Secondly, the MI coaches seek to evoke or draw things out from a person. But sometimes the information just isn't there and has to be shared before the client can make an 'informed' decision. Things which it might be helpful to share with a client include: what works in managing conflict; how to become more assertive; how to prepare for an interview; what other people find helpful when seeking promotion at work; aspects of the law or company policy, etc. MI coaches commonly share this information using the

A-S-A (ask, share, ask) format of: asking what the person already knows; asking for permission to share information; sharing the information; and then asking the person what they make of the information. This approach may help the information become more easily 'digested' by the client. Compare 'Why don't you consider the following...' with: 'Can I share with you some things which other people have found helpful?' The latter question is more inviting, respectful and thus more likely to engage the client by allowing them to make a choice. All factors that will help reduce resistance and increase engagement.

Lastly, the MI coach develops discrepancy in their clients, helping their clients become more aware of the gap between how things are at the moment and how they would like things to be. This contributes to the desire to change, which the practitioner is trying to develop. Discrepancy can be developed by having the client talk about their goals, talk about their values (what is important to them), have them explore 'two possible futures', and/or having them 'look back' and 'look forwards'. But while discrepancy (or a gap or mismatch) needs to be present before change will occur (why change if everything is perfect and the person is perfectly satisfied), too much discrepancy may be de-motivating, especially if the person doesn't feel that there is any way they can close the gap in a significant and meaningful way. So hope and confidence about changing to bring about the desired future needs to be developed in parallel with raising awareness about the gap between how things are and how things might be.

The core skills (or micro-skills)

In this section I will review the core skills used by the coach when applying the principles before finally reviewing a selection of tools and techniques.

The MI coach seeks to ask skilful open questions, make skilful reflections (accurate empathy statements), make occasional, genuine and heartfelt affirmations and use occasional summaries to bring things together, review progress, or as a prelude to moving the conversation in a different direction.

Open questions encourage the client to talk more than closed questions. Rather than ask closed questions such as 'Could you...?', 'Have you thought of...?', MI coaches prefer such open questions as 'Why might you want to...?', 'What do you think would be most helpful?', 'How might you go about this?'.

MI coaches make affirmations – statements recognizing and acknowledging some aspect of client effort or character, such as: 'You're the kind of person who sticks with things once you've made your mind up'; 'You go out of your way to be kind to people, even when you don't really feel like it'; or 'I appreciate the fact that you've stuck with this, even though the results are not happening as fast as you wanted'.

MI coaches make a lot of use of reflective listening or accurate empathy statements to check out that they understand the client correctly, help the client feel understood, and perhaps even generate some insight in the client as they hear what they said (and what they think) articulated back to them, but with a slight (and hopefully helpful) change of wording.

MI coaches use summaries intermittently throughout the session to check and reflect on progress, check for correct understanding, bring several things the client has mentioned together for their benefit (especially change talk), and after one tool or strategy, before moving on in the same or a slightly different direction (Table 11.1).

TABLE 11.1   Using MI and other interventions within a model of change

Change stage	Most useful interventions
Pre-contemplation	• Create relationship through empathy and rapport • Use reflective listening • If reluctant to change, encourage gathering of evidence/feedback • If lack of belief that can change, offer belief encourage hope • If giving reasons for not changing, explore wider values, beliefs and impact of behaviour on others
Contemplation	• Explore the reasons not to change and reasons to change • Explore the 'problem' • Explore the client's most important aspects/goals of their life • Reflect back discrepancy between goals/values and current behaviour • Explore confidence to change • Explore barriers to change • Reflect back desire to change and confidence statements
Planning	• Check for congruence in change communications • Explore confidence to change • Clarify and refine goals • Review options and select chosen options • Identify allies to support client • Use visualization to build confidence

TABLE 11.1   *continued*

Change stage	Most useful interventions
Action	• Monitor and affirm small steps • Explore next steps • Explore barriers being encountered • Plan actions to overcome barriers
Maintenance	• Provide positive feedback on success • Plan for coping if slip back • Reinforce long-term goals fit with values • Encourage use of allies to continue positive progress
Managing relapse	• Empathize and normalize • Explore reasons for relapse • Plan to prevent next time • Explore successes and affirm • Reflect back positive statements of desire for change • Return to contemplation actions

Tools and techniques

Motivational interviewing is primarily a style of communication, a skilful and helpful way of interacting with another person which tries to bring about the right conditions for positive change to occur. It is not a set of tools and techniques. That being said, tools and techniques form part of the commonly used methods by MI coaches. However, they need to be used in an 'MI-consistent way', that is consistent with the spirit of MI and using the micro-skills described in Table 11.2.

As I have noted earlier in this chapter, the founders of MI have consistently highlighted the central nature of the spirit of MI over the application of any one or a combination of tools and techniques. This is because at the heart of MI is the centrality of the client and the need to work in their best interest rather than being driven by a model or framework.

I believe there is a danger for some coaches adopting tools or techniques and applying them as a recipe. From my experience in training coaches over the past 15 years working with managers and with those undertaking postgraduate studies in coaching, this is certainly the case for novice coaches. This may not be surprising that the novice wishes to stick to a recipe rather than adapt and flex to meet the client's needs within a broad framework.

TABLE 11.2 Ten common MI techniques

1. Setting the scene
2. Agreeing the agenda (agenda mapping)
3. Typical day
4. Decisional balance
5. Importance and confident rulers
6. Looking back, looking forwards
7. Two possible futures
8. The key question
9. Exploring options
10. Agreeing a plan

Having said this, setting out principles rather than practice and examples leaves the writer open to question and challenge. As a result, both Miller and Rollnick (2013), and myself in this chapter, try to offer samples of commonly used tools and techniques in the process. In the following section we offer three tools – agenda mapping, typical day and decisional balance, and two techniques – evoking change and reflective listening.

Technique 1: agenda mapping

Agenda mapping is a technique used during the early part of the process and is one that many coaches may be familiar with but in a less detailed and planned way than is employed within MI. Miller and Rollnick (2013) suggest 'agenda mapping' is like inviting the client to look at a map, seeing the places they might travel and planning a route for the next stage of their journey.

'Agenda mapping' offers an opportunity to help the client to establish for themselves the focus of the conversation and thus explain to themselves and the coach what they want to achieve from coaching. By offering a sequence of stages from generating alternative options to evaluating these choices to agreeing the focus, it offers a number of clear steps.

Where clients are unable to establish a clear agenda, after using the approach, the coach may ask themselves (and the client) whether the client is ready to engage in coaching. The approach can thus also act as a tool to help inform the decision whether coaching is a helpful and useful approach for the client and whether they are ready to engage in coaching.

'Agenda mapping' usually takes the form of a series of questions. The first is to gain agreement to move into a meta-conversation. 'Is it ok if we spend a few minutes exploring what you want to get from our meeting today?' or for those in mid-session, 'Can we stop for a few moments so we can take stock of where we are?'.

The second element is to help identify the objectives of the client. Once identified the coach can help the client to prioritize these objectives and settle on a specific focus. Finally, the coach can help the client to refine and clarify the objective. As an example I have included further possible questions that could be used in the box below.

From personal experience it is not uncommon for the client to have a number of goals that they wish to achieve during the coaching assignment. In this case 'agenda mapping' becomes a task of helping the client to prioritize which of the multiple goals they wish to focus on first. In many cases, particularly with more junior managers, long-term goals and short-term goals may be mixed up: 'I want to become a better leader of my team' alongside 'I want to get my manager's job when they move next year'. In this instance the coach might help the client to focus on immediate short-term goals, working gradually towards long-term goals as the coaching assignment continues and shorter-term goals are achieved.

Examples of useful agenda setting interventions

What change shall we talk about?

Why are we talking about x, and not y?

I wonder about z, but what about you?

Should we shift direction?

During agenda mapping it is important not to disappear into too much detail. The aim is instead to remain at a high level and move across a number of different issues before settling on the most important to the client.

So what are the outcomes that the coach should expect (seek) from 'agenda mapping'? Firstly, and most importantly, the client should set the goal themselves and thus have a strong commitment to achieving this goal. Secondly, they should have a clear goal, which is understood and agreed with the coach. Thirdly, the goal should be supported by a series of subgoals. These may be short-term or intermediate goals (milestones), which effectively enable the client to track their progress towards the longer-term goal. For each of these, both the long and intermediate goals, the client knows what success looks like at each stage. With an agreed set of goals the coach also helps the client to prioritize these goals, with one or more goal being the focus for each session.

The more clearly defined and personally held the goal, the more likely the client will be able to move forward to and achieve the goal.

Technique 2: typical day

The 'typical day' technique appears later in the process, as the coach aims to encourage the client to talk in detail about their current reality. But rather than talking specifically about the perceived problem the coach asks a more open question to take a wider view of the issue within its context. The coach may introduce the technique or exercise by saying: 'Perhaps you could help me get a better understanding how your average day goes – starting from when you get up in the morning until when you go to bed? Would that be okay? How does your day start?'

In response to this question some clients will rush ahead and focus on the issue that they wish to discuss, for example stress and work–life balance. They may say: 'well, nothing really happens until...'. My suggestion is to slow these clients down by asking them to tell you a little bit more about how the day starts. Other clients may take several minutes telling you about their thoughts even before they get out of bed. Good coaches will direct attention and manage the process through intervening, speeding up the slow clients and helping those who are racing ahead to take the day in a step by step order.

During the description of their day clients will frequently use both 'sustain talk' (eg 'I just can't stand the place, the bureaucracy drives me wild') and 'change talk' (eg 'I used to work in the private sector and had an enjoyable time working there'). These will spontaneously emerge during the exercise without coach direction. Such responses provide the opportunity to 'go with the flow' while trying to develop more change talk by asking the client to elaborate. A further useful intervention from the coach is to make affirming statements or to reflect back what is being heard.

In using the technique in a MI spirit, the coach should try to avoid too many 'assessment' questions such as: 'On a scale of 1–10, just how stressed do you feel at that point of the day?'. Such interventions may have the effect of making the person feel judged or rated and may lead to them being less open later in the session.

The overall aim is to encourage the client to start talking and continue talking from an evidence-based perspective about their day and how the issue that they wish to focus on manifests itself within their day (Anstiss and Passmore, 2013). By directing attention through questions the coach gains a deep insight into the life of the client and a good sense of their current situation. Towards the end of the exercise it will be helpful for the client if the coach summarizes the key points that have emerged.

The technique is useful in that it provides an opportunity for the coach to empathetically listen to the client and for the client to talk at length and feel heard. In this sense the technique is useful at helping build the relationship. The technique is also useful in helping the client to step back from the immediate to see their life (and the issue) in a wider context. The story also provides detailed evidence and hopefully an understanding for the coach about the situation. This can be useful for the coach when reflecting back, when using affirmation and in selecting the next appropriate intervention. Finally the technique allows the client an opportunity to tell their story and thus provides a platform on which to build through the subsequent sessions.

Technique 3: the decisional balance

The third in our set of techniques is the decisional balance. This is useful in exploring current behaviour and reflecting on planned new behaviours. The technique decisional balance helps people think through their ambivalence in an open and systematic way. It helps the client to deepen their self-understanding and reflect on their own behaviour. As a result of the exercise the person's perceived importance for changing (or confidence about changing) is likely to increase and alongside this their motivation and readiness to change may also increase.

For the coach, the technique provides another opportunity to demonstrate good quality non-judgemental listening and to work in a way that is consistent with the spirit of MI, by reflecting back to demonstrate understanding, rolling with resistance (as opposed to offering arguments for change) and to notice and elicit change talk that comes directly from the client (see, for example, Anstiss and Passmore, 2011).

I have found in an organizational setting the technique works best with a sheet of paper (I have also used a flip chart or wipe board when these have been available – but be aware of removing the results at the end of the session to prevent others from reading the notes you have left behind in the meeting room). Divide the sheet into two main columns and two sub-columns (see Table 11.3).

Using the responses from the client recorded on the balance sheet, the coach can direct the focus of the client to start talking about the current benefits of the behaviour, which they may want to change, through an open question such as 'tell me a little more about how X can be exciting'. Such behaviours are often maintained as the client derives some pleasure or positive affect from them. By starting with positives this reduces the chances of defensiveness from the client and the perception that the coach has a fixed agenda to make the client change their behaviour. In most applications of MI in coaching, I would suggest the role is not to lead the client towards selecting a specific behaviour (although MI is often used in clinical settings in this way to address offending or serious drug misuse behaviours) (Passmore, 2007), but instead to help the client to be choiceful and self-aware.

The coach may specifically target aspects to encourage the client to talk more about the positive aspects of the desired behaviour. The coach may do this through directing attention to this aspect through a further question or by asking the client to give an example. Alternatively the coach may ask the client to talk about the feelings they have when they have made progress towards this new behavioural goal or when engaging in the desired behaviour.

As the client talks about each point in turn, the coach should invite the client to summarize the point in three or four words on the decision balance

TABLE 11.3   Decision balance sheet

Benefits of activity	Costs of activity	Benefits of change	Costs of change

sheet. I have found it works best when the client writes down the points rather than the coach doing this. Table 11.3 shows a sample table.

Depending on the individual and their state, some clients jump from one point to another and start talking about 'disadvantages' when they were asked about advantages of making a change, or vice versa. This is not a reflection on the coach, but a reflection on the client giving voice to their ambivalence and is natural and common. The coach may reflect back to let them know you have heard and at the end of the point may direct attention back to the side of the equation that was the original focus of the question, by saying something like: 'Well, we're going to talk about the disadvantages in a minute. But are there any other possible benefits to you?'

As a result of these interventions change talk often emerges from the client. Clients may say something like: 'I'd really like to be home on time to put the children to bed', reflecting their desire to make a change to the time-consuming nature of their role and the desire to break the pattern of behaviour.

The exercise can be completed more quickly if time is a challenge. This can be done by just using two boxes as opposed to four columns. These two columns can be summarized under the heading: 'good things' and 'less good things' (see Table 11.4). By using a two as opposed to four-column approach repetition is avoided with items being repeated by the client in the disadvantages of one side of the balance sheet as well as the advantages of the other side. I have found, however, that on occasions, clients can miss items when two rather than four columns are used.

At the end of the exercise the client has a sheet that they have completed which they can take away. The coach might ask them to spend some further

TABLE 11.4   Two box model for decisional balance

Good things	Less good things

time reflecting on this before the next session. Rather than leaving this free form, this works best when attention is directed towards the focus of change.

While we are looking at tools and techniques, it is also worthwhile to briefly look in detail at a couple of key techniques in the process. The two examples we will consider are evoking change talk and reflective listening as these are two key skills which the coach needs to employ to successfully facilitate the client addressing the ambivalence of their current situation.

Technique 4: evoking change talk

Evoking change is at the heart of MI. In essence this is the skill by which the coach encourages the client to talk positively and actively about making the change. But how does the coach know that the client is ready to engage in talking about change as opposed to still exploring whether this is an issue (pre-contemplation), or is thinking about change but has yet to decide this is what they wish to do (contemplation)? So what are we looking for in the words and phrases used by the client to judge where the client is on the stages of change model (Transtheoretical model) of change described above? The coach is able to identify this by listening closely to the change talk being used by the client.

Miller and Rollnick (2002, 2013) have suggested that change talk is like a hill. It comes in two parts: the uphill and downhill of change. The uphill side of the equation is the preparatory change talk. This is most likely to occur during the contemplation phase. The person is thinking about change and is weighing up whether change is really for them. In many cases the person is well aware of the advantages of making the change, but balanced

FIGURE 11.3   Transpersonal model of change and change talk phases

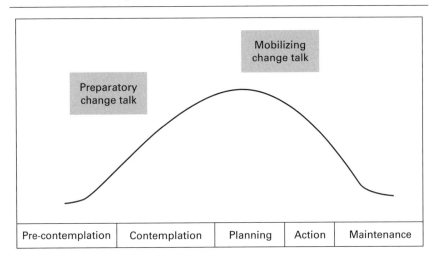

against this are a series of barriers which have blocked their path to successfully making the change. It is this aspect which has created the ambivalence to making the change in the past.

During this phase the coach needs to listen for what Miller and Rollnick (2013) have labelled DARNs. It is these statements which reveal an interest and consideration of change, but which lack a specific commitment to make the change. Such statements might express the individual's personal desires about making a change, the ability to make the change, their reasons for making the change and the need to change. Examples of these are summarized below:

Examples of DARN statements

Desire: 'I really want to do Y.'

Ability: 'I think I could do Y if I really wanted to.'

Reason: 'If they did X, then I think that would be enough and I would then do Y.'

Need: 'I really need to do Y, or ... will happen.'

In general terms the coach should look out for statements which are conditional or hypothetical. These statements express desires (need to and want to), they may express ability (I can or I could), they express reasons for making the change and they may also express the need to make the change and the consequences of failing to do so. However, while such statements reveal the client has shifted from the pre-contemplation to contemplation phase of the stages of change model (Prochaska and DiClemente, 1984) there is no expressed commitment to make the change, or a specific plan as to how the change is going to be made, particularly how barriers and hurdles which have held the individual back will be overcome.

At this stage the role of the coach is to encourage this preparatory talk and continue to explore the ambivalence to change. The coach may use techniques such as the decisional balance sheet to explore the advantages or disadvantages of different choices, they may help the client think through the skills needed to make a change or the barriers which have got in the way before.

As this happens, and the coach maintains effective listening and interventions, the client language is likely to change. In place of DARN statements, CAT statements are likely to increasingly emerge. CAT statements are phrases which reflect the client's commitment, present action or specific steps which they are taking to realize the new goal or behaviour. As CAT statements grow, a shift will also be seen from commitment to mobilization; from

'I want to' to 'I will'. The following box provides examples of the three types of CAT statements that the coach should be looking for.

Examples of CAT statements

Commitment: 'Next week I will do Y.'

Action: 'I am really keen this time to make a success of it; I have thought about what went wrong last time and it's going to be different on Tuesday.'

Taking steps: 'In advance of next Tuesday, I have already done X. This will mean that when the meeting comes on Tuesday, Y should be much easier this time.'

As this shows, commitment statements are concerned with intentions and promises. The client makes an unambiguous statement expressing their plans for the future. Key words to look for as examples are 'will', 'promise' or 'guarantee'. Action statements reflect the individual's state of being: willing, ready and prepared to act. Finally at the mobilization stage the client may express statements reflecting their preparatory actions towards the goal.

This shift from DARN to CAT is one which the coach can provoke and elicit through both reflective listening and through focused questions which encourage or evoke the client to focus their talk towards the advantages of change over the current situation.

So what is different about the reflective listening skills of the MI coach over listening when used in different coaching approaches?

Technique 5: reflective listening

In popular language 'listening' often means just keeping quiet; waiting for our turn to talk. This level one style of listening is unhelpful for even the novice coaching. Yet sadly I have too often seen the novice coach so focused on what they are planning to ask, that they fail to listen accurately to what is being said. As a result their intervention sounds mis-timed and often crass.

In the five levels of listening the competent coaches should be aiming to listen at level 3 or 4, with excellent coaches occasionally stepping in to work at an interpretive level, sharing their insights where this is helpful to their client at level 5.

Level 1: Waiting to speak – at this level we are simply waiting for our turn to talk.

Level 2: Basic listening – at this level the listener focuses on the words being said.

Level 3: Attentive listening – at this level the listener focuses on the words and tone of the communication to understand the true meaning.

Level 4: Active listening – at this level the listener listens to the words, tone and body language of the speaker and is aiming to understand what the speaker is intending to communicate.

Level 5: Interpretive listening – at this level the listener is seeking to listen beyond the intended communication. They are interpreting meaning from the whole communication, both the intended meaning and unintended communications.

At level 1 the coach might be drawn into one of the road block statements (Gordon, 1970). These statements include directing, cautioning, moralizing, agreeing, reassuring or labelling. For the client who is stuck, such behaviours are likely to increase the ambivalence towards change rather than evoke mobilization change talk.

If the coach is to avoid these road blocks, what else can the coach say? That is not to say there is not a place for open questions, challenge or affirming statements. However, reflective listening serves a different purpose for the MI coach. The coach can listen and reflect back in a number of different ways, using a simple reflection, an understated reflection or an overstated reflection. Each has a different role to play.

Simple reflection

In using a 'simple reflection' the coach tries to understand the meaning of the client and reflect this back, capturing the words, phrases and critically the meaning of the client's communication. Using a reflective statement is less likely to provoke resistance. For example, if the coach asked about the meaning of the statement, this directs the client to step back and reflect on whether they really do mean what they have said. As an example the coach could ask: 'You're feeling unsure?' This is done through an inflection in the voice, with the tone rising towards the end of the sentence. In contrast, the coach could use reflective listening to reflect back 'You're feeling unsure'.

This involves using a neutral tone throughout the sentence. The reflective statement communicates understanding and becomes a statement of fact. Such statements are more likely to encourage the client to talk more about their emotional state. As the client talks they think about this state and draw out for themself the evidence of why they are feeling as they do.

Reflective statements can be quite simple and often can involve reflecting back a single word or pair of key words from the client's story.

A more sophisticated series of options however are also available to the coach. These involve overstating or understating the reflection. The use of these and the frequency of use will vary with the coach's skills, as inappropriate use can leave the client believing their coach is not listening to them and undermine the coaching relationship.

Understated reflection

This is best used when the coach wishes the client to continue exploring an issue. The coach may select to reflect back a lower level of emotion than that communicated by the client, for example the client communicates 'anger', the coach may select to reflect back a lower intensity of 'anger', such as using the word 'irritation' or 'annoyed'. This works well with British clients where understatement is a feature of British culture. The key skill is to avoid understating to the extent that the client feels that the coach has not listened to what has been said. This takes both a high level of listening to the whole communication and a high level of skill of sophistication in selecting the right word to reflect back – highly articulate coaches thus have less trouble than those with a more limited range.

Overstated reflection

In contrast, if the coach selects to amplify the emotional content and overstate the emotion compared with the client's original communication, the likely effect is for the client to deny and minimize the emotion. Once again the dangers of the client feeling they have not been heard are present and in a British cultural context this is further magnified. As a result the coach needs to be careful and limited in their use of overstatement, to avoid danger to the coaching relationship.

By combining the range of effective listening, and listening deeply to their client's communications the coach can both demonstrate empathy and also support the client's growing motivation to change.

The five tools and techniques in this section are just a sample of the wider repertoire used by the skilled MI practitioner. However, they give an insight into how MI coaching draws on classic coaching skills and adds a level of greater sophistication which is informed by evidence-based practice. In the next section we will review a brief case study of applying MI when working with clients in an organization.

CASE STUDY

Nisha is a fund manager in a financial services firm. The firm is based in the United States but has offices in the United Kingdom, and across the world. The assignment came about when I was e-mailed by the HR director who had been referred to me by a colleague in another organization.

At the time of our first meeting she had been in post for more than 10 years and was well respected. However, in the past two or three years her performance had suffered and from being one of the team's best performers, she had slipped to being one of the worst.

Performance conversations between Nisha and the UK HR manager resulted in Nisha revealing that she lacked motivation in her role and felt de-motivated by the continual pressure to perform during what was a challenging financial market where luck seemed to have a bigger impact on success than company analysis or experience. Having been a good performer, the organization wanted to deal with the issue sensitively, and offered coaching to explore these issues.

I initiated the contract through meeting the HR manager and agreeing terms for the project. This initial meeting was followed by a tri-partite meeting between myself, Nisha and the HR manager. The coaching assignment brief was to support Nisha in reviewing her career over the next six months, address the performance issue and plan an internal or external move to another role through a series of six coaching sessions.

During the first session I focused on providing space for Nisha to share her story. This concentrated on her motivations in the early part of her career. Her motivation during this period was to make money and to outplay the market. However, having been through the global financial downturn during 2008 and 2009, things had been more difficult in recent years.

During the second and third meeting we explored her feelings of ambivalence in her current role, alongside her desire to take on a fresh challenge. Nisha was financially secure and shared her interests in photography and art, as well as in managing finances for organizations which took a long-term view, such as sterling funds, as opposed to a short-term or quarterly perspective.

I used the decision balance to explore the attractions of staying in her current role, balanced against her motivation for continuing to use her skill and market knowledge in a different role outside of the organization, possibly a sterling fund. I also encouraged Nisha to consider alternative perspectives, of those of her manager, the HR manager and capital markets director. Her conclusion was that her motivation and performance was an issue which needed to be addressed.

During these sessions Nisha moved to identify the pressure to move, which while not explicit, was about her leaving the organization. In this sense Nisha moved from pre-contemplation about the need to leave the organization to contemplation through reflecting on the recent conversations with HR, my arrival as a coach and what the organization was likely to really want to happen.

The next stage was to support Nisha in starting to plan a move. In doing this I wanted to develop her motivation to make a move rather than focus exclusively on the negative situation in her current role. This involved encouraging Nisha to spend time talking about these possible roles. As she talked more about them, her motivation grew and she started to move into planning how she could make such a change. By focusing more on the current negatives of her current position, and how things had been better when she had a team, Nisha's motivation also grew to secure a new opportunity which offered her the staff resources to do her job using such market analysis, as well as take a long-term view.

During subsequent sessions we focused on options. I encouraged Nisha to talk about her values and her dreams, checking out whether a move to a sterling fund was preferable to setting up a photography studio.

During these sessions I drew on the RULE principles of resisting the temptation to provide careers advice or wider advice on what Nisha should do in the situation. Secondly, helping her to explore her motivations: what attracted her to the role and engaged her during her early years in the role and what motivated her now. I sought to really listen to what she was saying and finally encourage and affirm her as a human being and a successful individual in what she had done in her career to date.

One specific technique I drew upon was offering the opportunity to explore two futures. In this Nisha considered her future compared to her values, as she considered photography versus a move to a different financial services company.

By the close of session four Nisha had made a clear decision to leave. She wanted to identify a specific role and we moved to discussing how she might do that with a sector through using her network built up over the past decade. By the fifth session Nisha had already secured a new role, and this session turned into a discussion focused on planning how she would manage the transition, what her priorities would be during her first 100 days and how she would communicate her departure to her boss and colleagues.

While not all assignments are suited to the application of all stages of MI, where clients are ambivalent, MI offers a route to explore these feelings and to help clients identify alternatives for themselves rather than be forced into situations which many often find negative and depressing – such as redundancy or dismissal. Further, the key skills of listening, reflecting back and focusing on affirming the attributes of the individual offer hope and reaffirm the individual, giving them confidence to move forward.

When might the MI approach be most suitable?

The efficacy of MI makes it an obvious choice for many health-based assignments. Evidence shows MI to be as effective, and in many cases a more effective intervention, than CBT for addictive behaviours including drug, alcohol, smoking cessation and weight loss coaching. Specifically, MI is more likely to achieve the desired goal, and for clients to show continued adherence to their goals after the intervention, than other methodologies.

However, the case of using MI for other areas, such as in career transition, managing redundancy or poor performance, is more controversial and lacks evidence to support a claim that MI is more efficacious than CBT or other methodologies. The truth is that for most areas of coaching we are unable to make such claims as the evidence from comparative studies is not present.

Instead we need to turn to qualitative, case study and experiential evidence. Here a case may be made that positive individual results appear to have been achieved through using MI in these types of presenting issue. From my own experience I have seen benefits for clients who have been exploring ambivalence around their work (which others perceived as poor performance), around issues of conflict at work (which others perceived as inappropriate behaviours) and around potential role and job change (redundancy and dismissal). In these cases individuals appeared to feel more motivated by the close of the coaching, they felt they retained power over their destiny and thus did not present any of the traditional emotions of sadness, depression or anger which can be associated with these types of issues when handled badly within organizations.

An amount of caution, however, is required. As this is a small sample, the evidence from these case studies should not be generalized to a wider population.

The methodology however appears to show promise for these areas, and wider and more detailed research is needed through comparative studies with other methodologies.

Conclusion

Over the past 20 years MI has come of age from a specialist drug and alcohol intervention to a methodology that can usefully be applied across a wide range of setting and presenting circumstances. MI is now recognized as a highly efficacious intervention that fits the spirit of coaching, with a forward focus and respectful open approach to clients that contrasts it with many therapeutic approaches.

In this chapter I have sought to set out briefly what MI is. In the first section I set out the links between MI and psychological theories and secondly the evidence from research, with a particular focus on RCT and meta-analysis research. In the second section I summarized the spirit of MI, drawing extensively on the work of Miller and Rollnick (2013) and the micro-skills before turning to a select set of tools and techniques. I have offered a short case study to help put MI into context as a psychological skill and finally identified briefly where MI may be more better suited than other psychological interventions as a framework to guide conversations.

Developing yourself as an MI coach

Developing your skills

Coaches wishing to learn more about and develop their skills in MI coaching may wish to explore the following practitioner texts:

- Miller, W R and Rollnick, S (2013) *Motivational Interviewing: Helping people change*, third edition, Guilford Press, New York
- Fuller, C and Taylor, P (2008) *The Toolkit of Motivational Skills: Encouraging and supporting change in individuals*, Wiley, Chichester
- Rollnick, S, Miller, W and Butler, C C (2008) *Motivational Interviewing in Health Care: Helping patients change behavior*, Guilford Press, New York

Deepening your understanding

Coaches wishing to recommend MI based self-help books and workbooks for their clients may wish to consider the following:

- Rosengren, D (2009) *Building Motivational Interviewing Skills: A practitioner's workbook*, Guilford Press, New York

Web resources

Useful websites for both coaches and clients include:

- The key site for MI resources is **www.motivationalinterview.org**
- There are a wide selection of additional resources to download for free at: **www.motivationalinterviewing.info/mi_resources.html**
- There are also a good selection of videos to watch to complement your reading. See for example:

    http://www.youtube.com/watch?v=s3MCJZ7OGRk – a basic introduction to MI

    http://www.youtube.com/watch?v=6EeCirPyq2w – another excellent video giving an explanation of the approach

- For skills videos showing the application of MI by experienced practitioners check out:
  www.youtube.com/watch?v=67l6g1l7Zao
  www.youtube.com/watch?v=dm-rJJPCuTE

References

Amrhein, P C, Miller, W R, Yahne, C E, Palmer, M and Fulcher, L (2003) Client commitment language during motivational interviewing predicts drug use outcomes, *Journal of Consulting and Clinical Psychology*, **71** (5), pp 862–78

Anstiss, T and Passmore, J (2011) Motivational interview, in M Neenan and S Palmer (ed) *Cognitive Behavioural Coaching In Practice: An evidence-based approach*, pp 33–52, Routledge, London

Anstiss, T and Passmore, J (2013) Motivational interviewing, in J Passmore, D Peterson and T Freire (eds) *The Wiley Blackwell Handbook of the Psychology of Coaching and Mentoring*, pp 339–64, Wiley, Chichester

Apodaca, T R and Longabaugh, R (2009) Mechanisms of change in motivational interviewing: a review and preliminary evaluation of the evidence, *Addiction*, **104** (5), 705–15

Armstrong, M J, Mottershead, T A, Ronksley, P E, Sigal, R J, Campbell, T S and Hemmelgarn, B R (2011) Motivational interviewing to improve weight loss in overweight and/or obese patients: a systematic review and meta-analysis of randomized controlled trials, *Obesity Reviews*, **12**

Bricker and Tollison (2011) Comparison of motivational interviewing with acceptance and commitment therapy: a conceptual and clinical review, *Behavioural and Cognitive Psychotherapy*, 22 February, pp 1–19

Burke, B L, Arkowitz, H and Menchola, M (2003) The efficacy of motivational interviewing: a meta-analysis of controlled clinical trials, *Journal of Consulting and Clinical Psychology*, **71** (5), pp 843–61

Burke, B L, Dunn, C W, Atkins, D C and Phelps, J S (2004) The emerging evidence base for motivational interviewing: a meta-analytic and qualitative inquiry, *Journal of Cognitive Psychotherapy*, **18** (4), pp 309–22

Burke, B L, Vassilev, G, Kantchelov, A and Zweben, A (2002) Motivational interviewing with couples, in W R Miller and S Rollnick (Eds), *Motivational Interviewing: Preparing people for change* (2nd edn, pp 347–61), Guilford Press, New York

Cassin, S E, von Ranson, K M, Heng, K, Brar, J and Wojtowicz, A E (2008) Adapted motivational interviewing for women with binge eating disorder: a randomized controlled trial, *Psychology of Addictive Behaviors*, **22** (3), pp 417–25

Deci, E L and Ryan, R M (2008) Self-determination theory: a macrotheory of human motivation, development and health, *Canadian Psychology*, **49** (3), pp 182–85

Farbring, C Å and Johnson, W R (2008) Motivational interviewing in the correctional system: an attempt to implement motivational interviewing in criminal justice, in *Motivational Interviewing in the Treatment of Psychological Problems*, eds Arkowitz, H, Westra, H A, Miller, W R, Rollnick, S, New York, pp 304–23

Festinger, L (1957) *A Theory of Cognitive Dissonance*, Stanford University Press, Stanford, CA

Heckman, C, Egleston, B and Hofmann, M (2010) Efficacy of motivational interviewing for smoking cessation: a systematic review and meta-analysis, *Tobacco Control*, **19**, pp 410–16

Kistenmacher, B R and Weiss, R L (2008) Motivational interviewing as a mechanism for change in men who batter: a randomized controlled trial, *Violence and Victims*, **23** (5), pp 558–70

Lundahl, B and Burke, B L (2009) The effectiveness and applicability of motivational interviewing: a practice-friendly review of four meta-analyses, *Journal of Clinical Psychology*, **65** (11), pp 1232–45

Lundahl, B W, Kunz, C, Brownell, C, Tollefson, D and Burke, B L (2010) A meta-analysis of motivational interviewing: twenty-five years of empirical studies, *Research on Social Work Practice*, **20** (2), pp 137–60

Magill, M, Apodaca, T, Barnett, N and Monti, P (2010) The route to change: within-session predictors of change plan completion in a motivational interview, *Substance Abuse Treatment*, **38** (3), pp 299–305

Markland, D, Ryan, R M, Tobin, V J and Rollnick, S (2005) Motivational interviewing and self-determination theory, *Journal of Social and Clinical Psychology*, **24** (6), pp 811–31

Miller, W R, Benefield, R G and Tonigan, J S (1993) Enhancing motivation for change in problem drinking: a controlled comparison of two therapist styles, *Journal of Consulting and Clinical Psychology*, **61** (3), pp 455–61

Miller, W R and Rollnick, S (2002) *Motivational Interviewing: Preparing people for change*, second edition, Guilford Press, New York

Miller, W R and Rollnick, S (2013) *Motivational Interviewing: Helping people change*, third edition, Guilford Press, New York

Miller, W R and Rose, G S (2009) Toward a theory of motivational interviewing, *American Psychologist*, **64** (6), pp 527–37

Moyers, T and Martin, T (2006) Therapist influence on client language during motivational interviewing sessions, *Journal of Substance Abuse Treatment*, **30** (3), pp 245–25

Moyers, T B, Martin, T, Christopher, P J, Houck, J M, Tonigan, J S and Amrhein, P C (2007) Client language as a mediator of motivational interviewing efficacy: where is the evidence? *Alcoholism: Clinical and experimental research*, **31**, Issue Supplement s3, 40s–47

Passmore, J (2007) Addressing deficit performance through coaching: using motivational interviewing for performance improvement in coaching, *International Coaching Psychology Review*, **2** (3), pp 265–79

Passmore, J and Whybrow, A (2007) Motivational interviewing: a specific approach for coaching psychologists, in *The Handbook of Coaching Psychology*, eds S Palmer and A Whybrow, pp 160–73, Brunner-Routledge, London

Patterson, G R and Forgatch, M S (1985) Therapist behavior as a determinant for client noncompliance: a paradox for the behavior modifier, *Journal of Consulting and Clinical Psychology*, **53** (6), pp 846–51

Prochaska, J O and DiClemente, C C (1984) *The Transtheoretical Approach: Towards a systematic eclectic framework*, Dow Jones Irwin, Homewood, IL

Rubak, S, Sandbaek, A, Lauritzen, T and Christensen, B (2005) Motivational interviewing: a systematic review and meta-analysis, *British Journal of General Practice*, **55** (513), pp 305–12

Vader, A M, Walters, S T, Prabhu, G C, Houck, J M and Field, C A (2010) The language of motivational interviewing and feedback: counselor language, client language, and client drinking outcomes, *Psychology of Addictive Behaviors*, **24** (2), pp 190–97

Vansteenkiste, M and Sheldon, K M (2006) There's nothing more practical than a good theory: integrating motivational interviewing and self-determination theory, *British Journal of Clinical Psychology*, **45** (1), pp 63–82

Vasilaki, E I, Hosier, S G and Cox, W M (2006) The efficacy of motivational interviewing as a brief intervention for excessive drinking: a meta-analytic review, *Alcohol and Alcoholism*, **41** (3), pp 328–335

Whitmore, J (1992) *Coaching for Performance*, Nicholas Breadley, London

Acknowledgement

The author would like to thank Tim Anstiss for his contribution to this chapter.

THE ASSOCIATION FOR COACHING

AC membership benefits

The Association for Coaching (AC) is one of the leading independent and nonprofit-making professional coaching bodies aimed at promoting best practice and raising the standards of coaching. Founded in 2002, with representation in over 50 countries, the AC has become known for its leadership within the profession and responsiveness to both market and members' needs.

Becoming a member gives you the opportunity to be involved in an established yet dynamic membership organization dedicated to excellence and coaching best practice.

Membership includes three categories:

1 Individual (aspiring/professional coaches);
2 Organizational (training/coach service providers);
3 Corporate (organizations involved in building internal coaching capability or cultures).

Areas of coaching include: Executive, Business, Personal, Speciality and Team Coaching.

Our vision

To inspire and champion coaching excellence, by being bold, collaborative and purposeful, so that we advance the coaching profession, and make a positive and lasting difference in the world.

Our core objectives

- To actively advance education and best practice in coaching.
- To develop and implement targeted marketing initiatives to encourage growth of the profession.
- To promote and support development of accountability and credibility across the industry.
- To encourage and provide opportunities for an open exchange of views, experiences and consultations.

- To build a network of strategic alliances and relationships to maximize the Association's potential.

There are many benefits coaches and organizations can access by joining the AC:

- *Journal*: receive *Coaching: An international journal of theory, research and practice*, twice a year by post, the AC's international coaching journal.
- *Gain new customers and referrals*:* through a dedicated webpage profile on the AC online membership directory.
- *Regular seminars and events*: monthly workshops and forums across the United Kingdom on current relevant topics. This allows an opportunity to network, compare notes and gain knowledge from industry experts and colleagues. Members are entitled to discounts on attendance fees.
- *Accreditation*:** eligibility to apply for AC individual coach accreditation after being approved as a full AC Member for at least three months.
- *International AC Conference*: attend the AC's annual conference at discounted rates, with international speakers drawn from top coaching experts.
- *Press/VIP contacts*: raise the profile of coaching through PR activities, through the influential honorary board and contacts across the AC.
- *Member newsletters*: increase knowledge through sharing best practice and learning in the quarterly *AC Bulletin* and *AC Update*.
- *Co-Coaching*: practise your coaching skills and learn through experience and observation at any of our many regional co-coaching forum groups.
- *AC forums*: an opportunity to participate in AC's online forums – networking and discussion groups for members to share their views and receive advice and support from others.
- *Industry/market research*: gain first-hand knowledge into the latest industry trends via the AC's market research reports.
- *Dedicated AC website*: gain access to up-to-date AC activities, members' events, reference materials and members-only section.
- *AC logo/letters*:* add value to your service offering and build credibility through use of AC logo/letters in marketing materials.
- *Ongoing professional development*: acquire CPD certificates through attendance at development forums, workshops and events.
- *Improve coaching skills*: through special invitations to professional coaching courses and participation in workshops.

- *Networking opportunities*: enjoy networking opportunities to draw on the advice and experience of leading-edge organizations that are also passionate about ethics, best practice and standards in the coaching profession.
- *Strategic partnerships*: receive member discounts, discounted training offers, and product and service deals through strategic partnerships.

*   Associate level and above only.
** Member level only.

Each approved individual member will receive a member's certificate with embossed seal.

For further information on the AC or joining, please visit the membership section of the website or e-mail **members@associationforcoaching.com**

'promoting excellence and ethics in coaching'

www.associationforcoaching.com

INDEX

NB: page numbers in *italics* indicate figures or tables.